Hot Flush Cold Truth

BEYOND THE PAUSE

WOMEN, WORK AND POLICY REFORM

Julie Dimmick

Cover and design layout by Julie Dimmick
First Edition
ISBN: 978-0-646-72671-7
Published in Australia

For permissions, inquiries, or rights, contact:
Julie Dimmick
author@juliedimmick.com

Printed in Australia.

Disclaimer

This book is a work of analysis, commentary, and personal interpretation. It presents the author's views through a combination of lived experience, research, and policy critique. While it addresses health, workplace, and systemic reform, it does not provide medical, legal, or professional advice.

References to medical treatments, pharmaceutical products, clinical practices, or workplace policies are intended for general informational purposes only. Readers should not rely on this material as a substitute for professional medical diagnosis, treatment, legal counsel, or human resources guidance. Always consult qualified professionals regarding health concerns, workplace issues, or legal obligations.

References to real organisations, government agencies, or individuals are limited to their public roles, widely documented policies, or observable practices. These references are not intended to be defamatory, accusatory, or diagnostic in nature.

The author makes no claim of expertise in medicine, psychiatry, or law, and any interpretations offered are for educational, reflective, and advocacy purposes only.

This book does not represent the views of any government, organisation, or institution with which the author is or has been affiliated. The material is provided "as is," and readers accept full responsibility for how they choose to engage with its content.

All trademarks, brands, and names remain the property of their respective owners and are used here solely for commentary, analysis, or reference under applicable fair use principles.

To every woman who has ever suffered in silence.

To those who've been dismissed, gaslit, or told
"it's just your age."

This is for you.

Acknowledgements

This book is the product of deep personal truth and collective resilience. To the thousands of women who shared their stories with me, through coaching, community, and candid moments in the quiet corners of life, thank you. Your courage shaped every word on these pages.

To my *family*, who bore witness to both my unravelling and my rebuilding, thank you for your patience, your love, and your faith when I had lost my own. To my sisters, *Evelyn* and *Elizabeth*, your presence in my life has been both grounding and uplifting, a reminder of the strength that runs through our family.

To my best friend, *Megan*, who has walked beside me through decades of life's turns, thank you for knowing my heart, holding my truths, and reminding me that joy and loyalty endure.

To the *mothers* before me, who endured their transitions without language, support, or safety, this is a bridge back to you, and forward for all of us.

To my daughter *Keneesha* and granddaughters *Amber*, *Ciara* and *Kyra*; I hope this book marks the beginning of a world where knowledge is shared freely, care is delivered with compassion, and no woman walks this path alone.

To *Dr. Rita Tajeddin*, thank you for seeing me, hearing me, and guiding me back to health when the system had all but erased me. The medical world is better because of you.

To the *doctors* who listen, the *employers* who choose empathy, and the *policy makers* who dare to lead: the change starts with you.

And to every woman navigating the hormonal wilds of midlife:

You are not broken. You are becoming.

Table of Contents

PART I:

The Personal Awakening

Chapter 1:
When It Begins But No One Tells You

It didn't start with a dramatic hot flash or a missed period. It started subtly. A slow drift into fatigue I couldn't shake. A creeping anxiety that felt foreign to my usually grounded self. Skin that felt like it didn't belong to me. A fog settling over my thoughts that made me question whether I was just burned out, or worse, broken.

But no one had told me this could be perimenopause.

There were no warning signs in my workplace. No pamphlets in the doctor's office. No conversations over wine with girlfriends where we swapped stories about what was happening to our bodies. There was silence. A suffocating, generational silence.

So I did what so many of us do: I blamed myself. I worked harder. Slept less. Drank more coffee. Pretended I was fine. I had learned, like many women, that vulnerability was a luxury we could not afford. Not at work. Not at home. Not in the world that still expected us to have it all together.

What followed were months of conflicting diagnoses, a carousel of prescriptions, and an internalised shame that something was wrong with me, because if it weren't, someone would have told me.

This chapter begins the story not just of what happened to me, but of what happens to millions of women who enter a life stage they weren't prepared for. Not because they failed to read the signs, but because no one had ever written them down.

It's time to break the silence.

It is time to name the centuries of quiet we inherited. The truth is that women have always been expected to endure in silence. Our grandmothers bled, birthed, and broke down behind closed doors. Our mothers soldiered on through hot flushes while packing lunches or presenting in school committees. They were praised for being strong, for not complaining. That strength, while admirable, was also a silencing.

In the workplace, we were taught to whisper. If we were lucky enough to be there at all, we learned quickly to contain ourselves. Not just our ambitions or our frustrations, but our symptoms. Our sweating. Our bleeding. Our aching. There was no room for discomfort. No language for transition. No policy for what came next. We were told to be grateful. And to keep going.

At home, we carried generations on our backs. We cooked dinners through bone-crushing fatigue. We parented through hormonal storms. We smiled through clenched teeth. Because we thought that was just what women do. And when we crumbled, it was behind locked bathroom doors, always apologising for the mess.

The message was clear. Be everything to everyone. But do not speak of your needs. Do not ask for help. Do not cry too loudly. Do not bleed publicly. Do not age visibly. And under no circumstances, do not speak of menopause.

That is how erasure happens. Not with bans or censorship, but with cultural silence. And in that silence, myths thrive. Women are labelled hysterical. Overdramatic. Depressed. Unstable. A hormonal problem to be medicated or managed. Not a person in transition. Not a body doing what it was biologically meant to do.
In 2025, we still live with the ghosts of that silence. But we are also the generation who can end it.

To the woman reading this in her car, in her office cubicle, in the small hours of the morning while the rest of the house sleeps, I want you to know this is not all in your head. You are not broken. You are changing. And you do not have to do it alone.

This book is your mirror. Your megaphone. Your map. And this chapter is the beginning.

Chapter 2:
Gaslit by the System

When the institutions we trust deny the symptoms we live
When I finally walked into a doctor's office to ask if something was wrong with me, I already knew I would have to fight to be believed. I just didn't realise how hard the fight would be.

I was tired, forgetful, aching, angry, and unrecognisable to myself. I explained my symptoms; the weight gain, the sleeplessness, the bone-deep anxiety, the memory lapses, the vomiting, the aching body, the migraines, the dry itchy skin, the itchy ears, the breaking hair, the brittle nails. I asked if this could be perimenopause. My doctor glanced at me and said, *"You're too young. It's probably just stress."* He offered me antidepressants and told me to come back in a few months if it didn't improve.

It did not improve.

What followed was a long journey through the medical maze. Each hallway lined with experts, none of them offering answers. Just more tests. More scripts. More suggestions that maybe I was just overreacting. Maybe I needed to slow down. Maybe I needed therapy. Maybe it was all in my head.

This is how the system gaslights us. It does not call us liars. It simply erases the truth.

It tells us that what we feel is not real. That what we know about our bodies is irrelevant. That our pain is ordinary. That our symptoms are exaggerated. That our lives, disrupted by hormone shifts and silent suffering, are somehow our fault.

But that erasure does not begin in the doctor's office. It begins in our homes. Our schools. Our workplaces. It is a legacy of silence passed from mother to daughter. Our grandmothers did not talk about it. Our mothers pushed through it quietly. We were taught to endure, not to question. To suffer, not to name.

The cultural silence around menopause has never been benign. It has shaped our biology into pathology. Our voices into weakness. Our symptoms into shame.

And then comes the night.

The sleeplessness is cruel. Not just because we are exhausted. But because at 2 a.m., when the world is quiet, the brain is not. That is when the health anxiety begins. The *"what ifs."* The endless search for answers. And when there is no doctor to call and no friend awake to listen, there is only Dr Google.

We scroll in the dark. Searching for what this ache could mean. What this heart flutter could be. What this fog, this fatigue, this forgetfulness is trying to tell us. The internet is a minefield for a tired woman in a fragile state.

We read everything. We convince ourselves we are dying. Then we feel foolish. Then we cry. Then we scroll again.

And here is the part I never thought I would write.

I lay in bed for months wondering if suicide was the only way out. I felt like I had lost myself. Not just my personality or my strength, but my reason to keep going. I was throwing up so often I thought I had food poisoning. It felt like morning sickness, but it wasn't. It was happening every hour. I was exhausted, overwhelmed, and breaking apart in private.

And when I did ask, at every Dr or Specialist appointment, every scan, every clinic room, if this could be menopause, the answer was always no.
"It sounds like stomach cancer." "Could be bowel cancer." "Possibly thyroid." "Maybe pancreatic."

What followed was a relentless parade of cancer screenings. Bloods. Scopes. Imaging. Biopsies. Each one more terrifying than the last. Each one deepening the belief that something was catastrophically wrong with me, that I was dying and no one could find the proof.

And still, no one looked at my hormones.

No one paused to ask about my cycle. No one mentioned estrogen. No one said the word *perimenopause*.

I paid for every appointment. Every scan. Every invasive test. Thousands of dollars. Dozens of hours. The only thing being treated was the medical system, to my bank account.

I was not receiving care. I was receiving debt and doubt.

Can you imagine what that year of misdiagnoses actually felt like? Living every day believing your body is shutting down. Walking into every office with hope and walking out with another theory, another referral, another list of things to test, but never the thing that mattered.

Can you imagine the terror of Googling *'symptoms of pancreatic cancer'* at 3 a.m. while your heart races and your chest aches, and still being told, *"You're too young. It's probably just stress"*?

That's not care. That's cruelty dressed in a lab coat. This is what happens when women's health is an afterthought in medicine. We get labelled, not listened to. Investigated, not supported. **Disbelieved, until we break.**

And all the while, what we needed was shockingly simple. *To be heard. To be believed. To be informed.* To have menopause considered as a possibility, not dismissed as a punchline.

Instead, the medical system gaslit me into a trauma spiral. Not because of what it found, but because of everything it refused to see.

Then, by accident, I ended up at an appointment with Dr Rita Tajeddin.

One appointment. One compassionate, educated, tuned-in appointment.

She listened. She looked at the whole picture. She ran the right tests. And she said the words no one else had: *"You are in perimenopause."* She explained what was happening in my body. She validated my symptoms. She gave me a name for the storm I had been drowning in. And in doing so, she gave me my life back.

I will never forget that moment. I will never stop being grateful that the medical profession still has people like her in it. Because if I had continued down the path I was on, I do not know if I would have survived it.

If you want to know what gaslighting looks like, it looks like a woman at 3 a.m. alone in her bed, reading about diseases she does not have, because no one told her that menopause can feel like this.

Real Stories, Real Women, Real Dismissal

Sarah, 44, Public Servant
Sarah was a high performer. She suddenly found herself blanking out mid, sentence and forgetting names she had known for years. Her GP said she was stressed and gave her sleeping tablets. When she asked about hormones, he replied, *"You're still menstruating, so no."* Six months later, after a breakdown at work, she paid for a private menopause clinic. She got answers in 20 minutes that changed everything.

Lani, 39, FIFO Worker
Mood swings. Night sweats. Skin, crawling anxiety. The nurse said, *"Probably hormones or homesickness."* There were no protocols for perimenopause in the mining industry. So Lani stayed silent. She started calling in sick. Then she stopped returning roster calls altogether.

Marita, 51, Baker
Snapping at customers. Burning bread. Crying in the fridge. Marita's GP suggested she take a holiday. But it wasn't burnout. It was menopause. HRT turned her life around in less than a month.

Anika, 46, Single Mum and Uni Student
Fatigue. Rage. Night sweats. Her doctor tested her thyroid and said, *"You're fine."* She wasn't. She thought she was going mad. A university lecturer's comment about brain fog helped her finally connect the dots.

These are not edge cases. These are everyday women. And they are being failed.

Across every touchpoint: doctors, nurses, specialists, even hairdressers and beauticians, women are met with confusion or silence.

The misdiagnosis machine is not a glitch. It is a symptom of a bigger disease: the absence of women's health as a priority in medical education, policy, and culture.

Until that changes, gaslighting will continue. But this book, this conversation, this moment is part of the undoing.

The Deeper Problem: It Was Never Just the Medicine

What happened to me did not happen in a vacuum. It happened in a world where women's health is still not seen as a priority. Not in research. Not in hospitals. Not in policy. Not in everyday clinics. Not in the scripts handed over the counter or the diagnostic pathways programmed into the system.

It happened because we still live in a world that does not treat women equally.

We are not equal in the home. We carry more of the unpaid labour, the mental load, the caregiving. We are not equal in the workplace. We make less, are promoted less, and are expected to perform regardless of our biology. And we are certainly not equal in medicine, where our symptoms are under, researched, under, treated, and under, acknowledged.

Women's health has always been seen as niche. Secondary. Optional.

There are still universities that offer more lectures on erectile dysfunction than they do on menopause. Pharmaceutical trials that exclude women because our hormones are '**too complex**.' Government funding that flows toward conditions that affect men more visibly, while women's pain is normalised or psychologised.

This isn't just an oversight.

It's systemic erasure.

Even the Women's Health Initiative report from the early 2000s, built off flawed data, still lingers on warning labels today. Despite decades of evidence showing the safety and benefits of HRT when prescribed appropriately, many doctors remain too afraid, too outdated, or too misinformed to prescribe it.

And in the vacuum left behind?

Women suffer.

They lay awake, anxious and exhausted. They question their sanity. They drown in fear, misinformation, and silence. They try to show up for work. For family. For life. But inside, they are burning out, breaking down, or disappearing altogether.

We were never supposed to carry this alone.

But we have.

And we do.

Until now.

Chapter 3:
Fear, Pharma, and the Patch

When it was finally suggested to me that I try a hormone patch, I had no idea what that even meant. Hormone Replacement Therapy was not part of my vocabulary, let alone my plan. I didn't grow up hearing about it. I didn't know anyone who talked openly about it. It wasn't something you casually Googled.

So when Dr Tajeddin wrote the prescription for the Climara Patch and explained that my body needed estrogen, I trusted her. I left her office that day feeling hopeful, maybe even a little relieved. I called my best friend from the car and told her what had just happened. That was when the first ripple of doubt arrived.

She said, gently, that I should do my research. That there were warnings. That the media had once made a lot of noise about HRT and cancer risks. Still, I was so desperate for relief, I was willing to take the risk.

But what happened next almost stopped me from ever starting.

I walked into the pharmacy with my prescription in hand. It was a female pharmacist behind the counter. She looked at the script, then looked at me, and said, "*You know this can give you breast cancer, right*?"

I blinked. "*What?*"

She went on. "*All HRTs carry that risk. It's on the box.*" Then she went to the shelf, brought out the packaging, and physically showed me the manufacturer's warning label. The words were **Bold. Stark. Frightening.**

It felt like being slapped.

I walked out of that pharmacy in tears. Shaking. The hope I had only just started to feel was gone. I ran, literally ran, back to Dr Tajeddin's office and barged in without an appointment. I was emotional, accusatory, and overwhelmed. I couldn't think straight.

And still, she met me with calm. She didn't dismiss me. She didn't defend herself. She reminded me of who I was. She said, *"You are a strong woman. You are not broken. You're simply taking a detour. Go read. Do your research. Come back in a few days. We'll talk about it again."* Words I needed to hear, a warm and loving touch, I needed to feel.

So I did.

I became a woman on a mission. I read every article I could find. I went deep into the data. I ordered books, not blogs. Academic texts, not Instagram posts. And out of all of them, there was one book that changed everything for me. **Oestrogen Matters by Dr Avrum Bluming and Carol Tavris, PhD.**

It wasn't just informative. It was liberating. It unpacked the flawed interpretation of the Women's Health Initiative. It broke down the fearmongering. It laid out the actual evidence, not the media spin. And most importantly, it framed hormone therapy not as a risk, but as a serious, **evidence, based option for women** looking to improve quality of life and health outcomes during menopause and beyond.

It was that book that gave me my nerve back.

Seventy-two hours later, I walked back into Dr Rita's office and said, *"I'm ready. But I'm doing this my way."*

I told her I was going to document everything. I was going to track every symptom, every day, and rate them. I would become my own research vessel. If no one else was willing to invest the time in understanding women's health, then I would.

Because I was one of them.

I wasn't just a patient. I was part of a much bigger story. A story of women being misinformed, misdiagnosed, and misled. A story of scientific fear eclipsing fact. A story of strength buried under cultural silence.

The Patch, the Panic, and the Shift

I placed the patch on at precisely 6pm on that Sunday.

A thin, clear square. Nothing special to look at. But everything about it felt symbolic, a line in the sand between survival and possibility.

That first night, I slept.

Not the broken, wired sleep of the anxious and hormonal, but deep, uninterrupted, **peaceful** sleep. The kind of sleep that **restores**. That says, *"You're safe now."*
And in the morning?
I didn't throw up.

My bones didn't ache like they had for months.

My mind was quiet. Clear.
And for a few fleeting moments, I wondered:

Is this what being normal feels like?

Not elevated. Not numbed. Not suppressed.

Just... **okay**?

Journal Entry: Week One, Patch Two Goes On

"So last week I decided to take the plunge and put my first patch on. I think I explained the hesitation and nervousness, but in reality, it was worse than I let on..."

It's all there in the entry, the aching bones I thought were arthritis. The shame of growing older. The comparisons to my sister who seemed untouched. The silence I carried. The vulnerability I only dared to share with strangers online.

But once the patch went on?

Sleep returned. Bone pain softened. Mental fog began to lift.

Yes, I had the expected hormonal adjustments , breast tenderness, fatigue, that weird sense of *"what now?"*, but I had movement. I had something shifting inside me. And for the first time in a long time, **I didn't feel like I was disappearing**.

But then came the hardest part, the silence from those closest to me. My best friend, the one who had first warned me off HRTs didn't celebrate this with me. She said, *"I'll wait and see how you go. You can be the tester."* **And I realised, most women I love have no language for this. No roadmap. No mother, daughter conversations. Just silence.**

So maybe I needed to go first.

Maybe I needed to become the voice I never had.
Because by the end of that first week, something else had returned, not just sleep or clarity, but **self, trust**.

I realised I could still be the strong one. The sporty one. The one who **chooses** to age in power, not in shame.

And I wasn't doing it for a movement or a message. I was doing it because I needed my life back. And I knew, *if I could find even one other woman in the fog*, I could help her find hers, too.

Taking the patch wasn't just a treatment decision. It was an act of reclamation.

I needed my life back. And I needed to understand what was happening to me with clarity, not confusion.
It is time to shift the narrative.

Hormone therapy is not a death sentence. It is not the villain in the menopause story. When used correctly, and prescribed with care, it can be a lifeline.

It was mine.

I've worked in pharmaceuticals. Reputable ones. The kind of companies built on healing, science, and ethical supply chains. I know the good that medicine can do. I know the years of research, the layers of compliance, the regulations that ensure what we take is tested and trusted. I believe in medicine. I am not anti-pharma. I am not anti-science.
But logic does not always survive the hormonal storm.

When your brain is fogged and your body is unrecognisable, when you haven't slept in days and every nerve is on edge, fear becomes a second skin. You stop thinking clearly. You stop trusting yourself. You stop knowing what's real and what's not. Hormonal shifts do that. They cloud judgment, amplify anxiety, and open the door for doubt to creep in.

In that moment at the pharmacy, standing under fluorescent lights with a woman waving a warning label at me, I was not a professional. I was not a rational adult. I was a terrified woman clinging to hope and watching it get torn away.

And here's what made it worse, those warning labels are based on outdated data. The Women's Health Initiative, launched more than 20 years ago, was a randomized controlled trial with good intentions but flawed execution. It used hormone formulations and delivery systems that are no longer standard. It tested women who were, on average, much older than the ones typically starting HRT today. And yet the conclusions, and the panic, spread like wildfire.

The media reported half, truths. The nuance was lost. Risk was exaggerated. And for decades, women have paid the price. Even now, those warnings still appear on boxes. Even now, pharmacists and practitioners quote numbers that have long been challenged or disproven.

I am not a doctor. I am not a scientist. But I am someone who is 100 percent impacted by the work they do. **I expect better. I demand better**.

Because here's the truth that doesn't fit on a label; the fear women carry into menopause is not just about the hormones. It's about what those hormones disrupt.

They disrupt our identity. Our memory. Our skin. Our sleep. Our weight. Our marriages. Our careers. They also disrupt our sense of safety in our own bodies.

Many women feel like they are dying. Every headache becomes a brain tumour. Every stomach cramp feels like cancer. Every skipped heartbeat becomes a stroke in waiting. This isn't hypochondria. This is the lived experience of thousands of women whose hormones are crashing and whose nervous systems are under siege. It is real. It is terrifying. And it is happening in bedrooms, in bathrooms, in workplaces, and on public transport every single day.

For some, it becomes too much.

Some women stop leaving the house. They cancel plans. They isolate. They shut down. Others push through but feel numb. Disconnected. Robotic.

And when they finally build the courage to see a doctor, they sit in waiting rooms flooded with panic. Because if you've been Googling your symptoms at 2 a.m. for the past six months, you're not going in to talk about menopause. You're going in to be told you have six weeks to live. That's what anxiety does. That's what happens when the fear is untreated, and the information is inaccessible.

The irony is cruel. The very symptoms that HRT can help alleviate are the ones that stop us from accessing it.

It takes courage to ask for help. It takes strength to return after being dismissed. It takes resilience to wade through the noise and find the truth.

But we shouldn't have to be warriors to get well.

We deserve to walk into a pharmacy and feel supported, not shamed. We deserve to be guided, not guilted. We deserve to trust the label and still be told the full story.

We deserve care that heals, not fear that harms.
We are not a fringe group. We are not a risk category. We are women. And we are watching.

The patch didn't just give me estrogen. It gave me clarity. It gave me calm. It gave me the strength to feel like myself again.

And for that, I will always be grateful, not just to Dr Tajeddin, not just to the authors who opened my eyes, but to the part of me that refused to give up.

Because that woman… She's coming back.

But once I felt like myself again, I started asking harder questions. How had it come to this? Why was I, an educated woman with resources, nearly scared off the one thing that helped? What chance did other women have? That's when I began to unravel the system itself.

Here's what we need to talk about next.

There is a difference between **pharmaceuticals, Big Pharma**, and **pharmacies**. But most women don't have the energy or the context to untangle those roles when they're already exhausted and in crisis.
So let's break it down.

Pharmaceuticals, at their core, are medicines. Science, backed, clinically tested Tools that exist to heal, alleviate, and restore. They are not the enemy. In fact, when used properly, they are lifesaving. I have no interest in demonising medicine. I am alive today because of it.

But medicine doesn't exist in a vacuum. It exists inside a system. And that system includes powerful players with vastly different incentives.

Big Pharma refers to the corporations, the global manufacturers, and the billion, dollar conglomerates. These companies fund research, influence medical education, lobby policymakers, and decide what gets developed, marketed, and distributed. While many of them do good work, they are not non, profits. Their business is profit. Their job is to deliver value to shareholders.

And too often, women are not seen as a priority market.

Men's health is studied earlier, funded more heavily, and taken more seriously. Even in the year 2025, most medical studies have historically excluded women or failed to account for our hormonal fluctuations. Perimenopause and menopause remain under, researched and misunderstood. Many treatments are outdated. Some were paused entirely after the Women's Health Initiative caused widespread fear, and only recently has momentum begun to shift.

That is not a science problem. That is a values problem. And it is one Big Pharma must own.

Then there are *pharmacies*. These are the chemists on every corner, the shelves of prescriptions, and the pharmacists behind the counter. These are the places where women go to collect the medication that might just save them. But too often, they leave confused, scared, or shamed.

I experienced it myself. The pharmacist who warned me about cancer didn't ask how I was feeling. She didn't inquire about my symptoms. She didn't offer information about newer studies or safer delivery mechanisms. She pointed to a box. She quoted a label. She made me feel reckless for wanting relief.

That is not care. That is fear-based compliance dressed up as safety advice.

Pharmacists are healthcare professionals. They hold immense trust. But many are not being adequately trained in the latest evidence around women's hormones. Many still operate on decades, old guidelines that were never updated to reflect newer research. This is a training gap, yes, but it is also a cultural one.

Too many women walk out of pharmacies feeling ashamed, not supported. Afraid, not informed. That must change.

Here's how we start shifting that experience, from fear to empowerment.

Your Right to Clarity: What to Ask at the Pharmacy

You are not just a customer. You are a woman navigating a major life shift. You deserve care that supports, not startles. Here are questions and rights to take with you into the pharmacy:

- *"Can you tell me what study this warning label is based on?"* (If they say "WHI," ask if they're familiar with the newer findings.)
- *"Have there been any updated guidelines from the Endocrine Society or AMS?"* (These organisations release contemporary evidence on HRT safety.)
- *"Can you explain how the risk numbers apply to someone my age?"* (Most WHI risks involved women over 60. You deserve context.)

- "Would you mind printing the consumer information leaflet and walking me through it?" (Don't just read the label, understand it.)
- "I'm not comfortable with how this was delivered. Is there another pharmacist I can speak with?" (You can ask. You should ask. And you deserve respect.)

And then there's us. The women caught in the middle.

We are told to trust the science, but we are not shown the full data. We are handed a script, but not the story behind it. We are warned of side effects, but not given hope for outcomes.
I am not anti-pharma. I am not anti-science. But I am **anti-silence**. I am **anti-stigma**. And I am against outdated labels and fearmongering that ignore decades of progress.

If I can be terrified by a pharmacist with a box and a warning label, even after seeing a specialist and doing the reading, what chance does a woman have who doesn't yet know what perimenopause even is?

So here is what needs to happen:

Big Pharma **must reinvest** in women's health. Not as a token initiative. Not as a pink-branded product line. But as a serious commitment to research, trials, and reform. They **must** stop resting on old studies and start funding new ones. They **must prioritise safety and quality of life**.

Pharmaceutical companies **must update their packaging and communication** to reflect current science. That means clear language, balanced risk framing, and removal of outdated warnings that cause unnecessary panic.

Pharmacies and pharmacists **must be trained to provide compassionate, evidence-based guidance**. Not just dispensing drugs, but dispensing calm. **Reassurance. Context**. A reminder that the woman standing across from them is not just a customer, but a human being desperate for clarity.

And most importantly, the healthcare system as a whole **must stop treating women's health as a side issue**.

Because this isn't small. This isn't niche. This is half the population navigating a massive hormonal transition that impacts mental health, physical health, relationships, productivity, and quality of life.

We deserve better from every part of the system. From the top-floor boardroom of pharmaceutical giants to the corner pharmacy checkout.

The False Promise of Wellness: When Hope Becomes a Product

If the mainstream medical system gaslights women, the unregulated wellness industry seduces us.

When you're in crisis, physically exhausted, emotionally unravelling, sleep-deprived, and afraid; you're not thinking logically. You're desperate. And the wellness industry knows that. It counts on it.

At every stage of my journey, when traditional medicine left me empty-handed, I turned to *Google*. Like so many women, I searched for relief. Not just for answers, but for something, anything, that might give me back a sense of control. That search leads many of us into a glittering world of *biochemicals*, *natural* therapies, and *premium-grade supplements*, each more expensive than the last and all promising miracles.

You've seen them.

Powders to "balance hormones." Drops to "heal the gut." Pills to "detox the liver," "support adrenals," or "calm the nervous system."

And let's not forget the celebrity-endorsed hormone reset kits, priced at hundreds of dollars and backed by nothing more than persuasive copywriting and high-end packaging.

These products market **hope, not evidence**. They speak directly to women who feel unseen by their GPs. And worst of all, they wear the mask of science without any actual proof.

Most of these supplements are *not clinically tested*, not approved by any regulatory body, and not backed by rigorous peer-reviewed research. But that doesn't stop them from taking up space in our Instagram feeds, our wellness podcasts, and our pharmacy shelves.

It's a multi-billion-dollar industry built on our *silence* and our *suffering*.

And while some women do find relief through certain herbs or micronutrients, many are spending thousands on products that do absolutely nothing. Or worse, they interfere with real treatment, interact with prescribed medications, or mask underlying issues that require genuine medical attention.

Let's be clear.

I'm not against exploring alternative therapies. I'm not against trying things that might support your body. I am, however, against an industry that **targets hormonal women in distress** with solutions that **sound scientific but are not**.

Because at the end of the day, this is not empowerment, it's exploitation.

You cannot turmeric your way out of estrogen loss. You cannot sage-burn your way through debilitating health anxiety. You cannot self-heal when your system is depleted and unsupported by real care.

What we need is not more products. What we need is *accurate education*, *accessible care*, and *evidence-based options*.

We need doctors who will listen. We need pharmacies that will guide, not shame. And we need governments and health systems that invest in *real solutions*, not just watch as women empty their wallets on snake oil dressed up in recyclable packaging.

There is a reason women are reaching for these products. It's not because they're gullible. It's because they've been abandoned.

And until the system shows up with something better, the exploitation will continue.

What They'll Tell You, You Need, And What It's Really Costing You

When you're deep in hormonal chaos, exhausted from symptoms you can't name, and desperate for answers, the internet becomes a tempting oracle. So do the women in your DMs, the well-meaning friends with *"this worked for me"* stories, and the influencers selling pastel promises with a side of supplements.

Here's a taste of what you're told you **need** to survive perimenopause:

- Celery juice before sunrise
- Seed cycling with flax, sesame, sunflower, and pumpkin-timed to your menstrual moon
- Cold plunges and infrared saunas (because temperature shock heals ovaries, apparently)

- Maca powder from Peru (only raw, organic, fair trade)
- Fasting based on lunar energy
- Custom-compounded *"bioidentical"* hormone creams made at backroom clinics
- Dry brushing to "move lymph and trauma"
- Reiki for your uterus
- Somatic therapy to "reclaim your womb space"
- Vaginal steaming (please, no)
- $280 blood tests recommended by non-medical practitioners
- Adaptogen elixirs sold at $99 per bottle
- Hormone balancing kits endorsed by celebrities and backed by... vibes

Sounds wild? It is. And it's working.

Because the global **"hormone wellness"** market is projected to hit **$50 billion+**, and women like us are the primary target.

Let's Talk Cost. The Real Cost

This isn't just about quirky trends. It's about *real harm*, in three devastating forms:

1. Your Health
Many of these unregulated supplements and DIY protocols interfere with real treatments. They *mask symptoms, confuse diagnoses, and delay proper care*. Some herbs can **interact dangerously** with medications. Others simply do nothing, while your condition worsens in silence.

You wouldn't treat diabetes with moon water. You wouldn't treat thyroid disease with breathwork. Why are we treating **hormonal collapse** with smoothies and sage?
2. Your Mental Health

Constant Googling. Self-blame. The emotional rollercoaster of hope, hype, and disappointment. Women spiral into *health anxiety*, convinced they're failing at healing because the 'natural path' isn't working. The guilt is crushing. The stress? Unrelenting. And the shame of 'not trying hard enough' becomes a second diagnosis.

You're not broken. You've just been marketed to-at your most vulnerable.

3. Your Bank Account
The average woman in perimenopause spends **$1,500-$5,000 a year** on wellness fixes. Some spend more. On powders, tinctures, elixirs, online programs, and boutique diagnostics that aren't Medicare rebated or clinically required. All while many can't even afford to see a specialist.

And here's the brutal irony:
*The **real** solution, evidence-based, medically supported hormone therapy, is often cheaper, safer, and significantly more effective than the entire shelf of unproven supplements combined.*

So, what do you **actually** need?

- A doctor who listens.
- A script, not a scam.
- Blood work guided by clinical relevance, not Instagram trends.
- Hormones dosed for your body, not your algorithm.
- Real answers. Not just 'support your adrenals and journal more.'

Because if your house was on fire, you wouldn't light a candle and hope for the best. You'd call the fire department. Perimenopause is your fire. Medicine is your hose. And those overpriced moon-charged tinctures? They're just glitter in the wind.

So yes, the wellness industry plays its part in the confusion. But it's not the only one. Because when Big Pharma fails to update the science, and pharmacists pass on outdated fear instead of informed care, women are left to wander a maze with no map.

Let's untangle that next.

Big Pharma, Pharmacies, and the Pharmaceu- twisted Maze

The moment you're prescribed hormone therapy; you don't just walk into a pharmacy. You walk into a minefield.

It's where marketing, outdated science, institutional caution, and miseducation collide. It's where pharmacists pass on information that is often driven by fear, not fact. And it's where women, already in distress, are left to untangle decades of controversy with nothing but a Google search and a credit card.

But here's the truth **Big Pharma, pharmacies,** and **pharmaceutical companies** are not interchangeable.

Big Pharma *is the multi-billion-dollar system* of production and influence. It funds trials, lobbies governments, and determines what drugs get priority. It is responsible for enormous advancements in medicine. But it is also responsible for prioritising profit, sometimes over people.

Pharmaceutical companies *manufacture and distribute* the medications. Some operate ethically, funding peer-reviewed research and disclosing risks with integrity. Others exploit vulnerable markets. And when it comes to women's health, the track record is... mixed.

Pharmacies, on the other hand, are the public face. They are meant to be places of trust, yet they often amplify public

48

fears rather than educate or comfort. Remember that pharmacist who pointed at the HRT box? She wasn't quoting science. She was quoting a label written in 2002, backed by a study whose findings have since been challenged, questioned, and re-evaluated multiple times.

The Study That Changed Everything.

The 2002 Women's Health Initiative (WHI) trial changed the way HRT was viewed across the world. It was a massive, randomised, double-blind placebo-controlled study. It was also deeply flawed. As documented in *JAMA 2002, Climacteric 2004, The Lancet, and Cochrane Reviews*, the original WHI findings exaggerated risks and applied conclusions across populations that weren't aligned with the majority of real-world menopausal women. The average participant in the WHI trial was 63. Most women begin HRT in their late 40s to mid-50s. That's not a small discrepancy. That's a different biological phase.

Over time, further studies clarified the picture. Some, like the **REMEMBER pilot study** (Menopause 2006), looked at timing and cognition. Others reviewed breast cancer risk, osteoporosis, coronary outcomes, and quality of life. Slowly, the tide of understanding began to turn.

But not fast enough. The warning label on the *Climara* box didn't change. The fear stuck. And women stopped being offered HRT as a frontline option for years, if not decades.

So where does this leave us?

It leaves us confused. It leaves us untreated. It leaves us spending **thousands of dollars** on blood tests, scans, and specialist visits as we're shuffled from thyroid to bowel to stomach cancer testing. All while our actual condition, menopause, remains unnamed, unacknowledged, and untreated.

And then, in our desperation, it leads us somewhere else entirely:
The supplement aisle.

Crisis Capitalism and the Rise of the "Natural" Fix

Women in crisis make perfect consumers.
Cue the rise of *Biocueticals*, wellness influencers, and the endless parade of capsules, tinctures, and teas that promise to *"balance hormones naturally"* or *"reset your cycle."* None of this is properly regulated. Most of it is not supported by peer-reviewed, placebo-controlled clinical trials. But it is packaged beautifully, marketed cleverly, and targeted directly at women like me, awake at 3 a.m., Googling their symptoms, convinced they are dying.

Some of these products are harmless. Some may even help. But many prey on hope, not evidence.

As shown in the *2003 and 2006* reviews by *MacLennan et al., Huntley,* and *Newton et al.*, the vast majority of alternative therapies either lack consistent efficacy or come with their own risks. Black cohosh, for example, has been linked to hepatotoxicity in several case studies. Acupuncture shows some promise but is highly variable. Gabapentin and SSRIs, tested in major trials, offer relief for some, but not all.

Meanwhile, companies like Biocueticals rake in millions.

They are not bound by the same regulatory frameworks as prescription medicine. They don't need to prove efficacy. They only need to suggest improvement. When women are desperate, that's enough. I know. I was one of them.

A Demand, Not a Plea

I am not anti-pharma. I believe in medicine, in science, and in the people who dedicate their lives to discovery.

But I am against:
- Labels and warnings that haven't kept pace with science, they terrify instead of clarify
- Pharmacies that operate on outdated scripts rather than updated protocols
- Supplement industries profiting from silence and confusion

I may not wear a white coat, but I live with the consequences of their decisions.

<u>And I expect better.</u>

Menopause Treatments and Where They Fit

Treatment Type	Examples	Category	Notes for Menopause Use
Hormone Replacement Therapy (HRT)	Estrogen patches, progesterone pills, bioidentical creams	Pharmaceutical (with some **biopharmaceutical** variants, e.g., bioidentical hormones derived from plants)	Gold-standard for addressing root hormonal depletion. Often under-prescribed due to fear, stigma, or outdated studies.
SSRIs (Selective Serotonin Reuptake Inhibitors)	Fluoxetine (Prozac), Sertraline (Zoloft), Citalopram (Celexa)	Pharmaceutical	Prescribed for depression/anxiety, but used *off-label* for hot flushes and sleep. Symptom management only, does not address hormonal cause.
Gabapentin	Neurontin, generic gabapentin	Pharmaceutical	Developed for epilepsy, repurposed for neuropathic pain and sometimes hot flushes. Side effects can be significant (dizziness, fatigue). Not hormone-specific.

Treatment Type	Examples	Category	Notes for Menopause Use
Nutraceuticals & Botanicals	Black cohosh, red clover, phytoestrogens, ashwagandha	Nutraceuticals / Supplements	Widely used due to accessibility and "natural" marketing. Evidence base is inconsistent; regulation is minimal compared to pharmaceuticals.
Biopharmaceutical Innovations (Emerging)	Selective estrogen receptor modulators (SERMs), tissue-selective estrogen complexes	Biopharmaceutical	Engineered molecules targeting estrogen receptors with fewer risks. Still under development and not mainstream for most women.

Chapter 4:
Finding My Voice.

Becoming a Menopause Coach

I placed the patch on at exactly 6pm on that first Sunday. And that night, I slept like a baby. Not just any sleep, **real** sleep. Deep. Peaceful. Healing. The kind of sleep I hadn't felt in years.

When I woke, something was... different. My body didn't ache. My bones didn't scream. I didn't throw up. My mind was clear. I could think. Properly.

For the first time in what felt like forever, I felt like I was back in the room. Present. More me.

Journal Entry: Patch 2, What Am I Doing?
"Prior to the patch, I thought I had arthritis. I hated my sister in secret for breezing through this. I hadn't told anyone the truth of what I was going through, not really. But I knew one thing: I didn't want to be ashamed anymore. I didn't want to suffer in silence. I wanted my life back."

That entry came at the end of week one. I'd tracked every symptom. The sleep. The tenderness. The aching that eased. The fatigue that flared. And the anxiety that lifted. I had expected confusion. I didn't expect clarity.

From Survivor to Storyteller

Something shifted that week. It wasn't loud. It didn't arrive with fireworks or fanfare. But it was unmistakable, a quiet uprising inside me that whispered: *You don't have to survive this in silence.*
For the first time in months, maybe years, I felt like I had enough energy, clarity, and self-worth to *look outward, instead of just holding myself together.*

I wasn't just surviving. I was starting to pay attention. And what I saw broke my heart.

If I, with all my education, support networks, and resources, had to fight tooth and nail for a patch….. what were other women up against? The single mum. The rural woman. The woman who couldn't take a week off to figure out what the hell was happening to her body.

That's when I began to speak.
First in a private Facebook group, a quiet post, typed late at night.

Then a comment on someone else's story. Then a message. Then another. And another.

What started as a trickle became a flood.

Women were **desperate** to be seen, heard, validated. They weren't looking for influencers. They were looking for *answers*. For *truth*. For someone who would say, *"Yes, me too, and here's what helped."*

They asked me about everything:

- Why was their hair falling out?
- Was it normal to feel like they wanted to scream?
- Was this tiredness something more serious?
- Which vitamins helped? Which were a waste of money?
- Why did their libido vanish, and their marriage start crumbling with it?
- Why couldn't they remember simple things anymore?
- Why did doctors keep brushing them off?

At first, I just shared what worked for me. My patch. My blood tests. My sleep hacks. My tears. My hard, won clarity.

But soon, I knew I had to do more than just talk about myself.

I started a group, mostly just to express my own journey. A space to get the thoughts out of my head and into the world.

But women started joining. Commenting. Connecting. And then, something beautiful happened.

They began sharing their own truths.

Stories poured in. **Grief. Rage. Humour. Hope**. Women who felt invisible were finally finding each other. They were no longer asking for permission, they were demanding to be seen, heard, and loved.

I realised then: I wasn't just telling my story.

I was holding the microphone for others to tell theirs.

I went back into the research. I re, read the studies. I dove into guidelines, medical journals, evidence, based resources. Not out of fear, but out of fury. Fury that women were being left to figure this out in isolation, while society politely pretended it wasn't happening.

I studied not just symptoms, but systems. The social systems that silence us. The medical systems that gaslight us. The economic systems that profit from our confusion. I couldn't not learn.

And then came the message that changed everything: "Julie, have you ever thought about coaching? Women need someone like you."

At first, I laughed. I was just trying to survive menopause, not become someone's guru.

But the message stayed with me. Because deep down, I knew something else was rising.

Not just a voice.

A vocation.

Coached, But Still Caught

Here's what's wild: I was already a certified, practicing, **damn good** coach.

I knew how to create space where people could feel seen. I could spot limiting beliefs a mile away. I knew the power of language, the importance of reframing, the value of holding discomfort without fixing it.

I'd coached executives through multi-million-dollar decisions, held space for people on the edge of reinvention, and helped others transform breakdowns into breakthroughs.

But when menopause hit?

None of that training saved me.

Because this wasn't a mindset block. It wasn't a limiting belief. It wasn't a fear I could coach myself out of.

This was *physiological*. This was *chemical*. This was *systemic*.
And I didn't have the language for it, not yet.

I didn't even realise how far I'd fallen into the trap until I was deep in it. The trap of silence. The trap of shame. The *"just push through it"* lie.

Despite everything I knew professionally... I still believed the inner voice that whispered:

- You're being dramatic.
- Other women aren't complaining, why are you?
- You're a coach, you should be able to fix this.

So instead of seeking help, I analysed. Instead of honouring my pain, I intellectualised it. Instead of holding space for myself, I white, knuckled it in private.

And let me be clear, it nearly broke me.

That's the thing they don't tell you about menopause. It doesn't care who you are. It doesn't care how accomplished you are, how much self, awareness you've cultivated, or how many self, help books you've highlighted.

Menopause levels the playing field.

I was a coach who could help **everyone**, except myself. Because I was still clinging to the same story society sold me: That strong women don't need help. That aging is something to hide. That if you're suffering, you're doing it wrong.

What I didn't realise at the time was that *even coaches need coaching*. Even leaders need someone to say: "I see you. This is real. And you don't have to go through it alone."

It wasn't a lack of knowledge. It was a lack of permission. I didn't need to be taught, I needed to be witnessed. I didn't need motivation, I needed medicine.

And most of all, I needed to forgive myself for not seeing the signs sooner.

Because once I did? Everything changed.

The Turning Point

There's always a moment. A moment when the denial cracks. When the masks slip. When the coping strategies fray at the edges. And what's been quietly unravelling inside finally breaks the surface.

For me, that moment wasn't dramatic. It was devastatingly ordinary. A forgotten word. A missed meeting. A body I no longer recognised.

I was sitting in my car, holding the steering wheel, and I couldn't remember where I was going. And in that silence, I heard it, the truth I didn't want to admit: Even I, a trained coach, was drowning.

I had Tools.
I had frameworks.
I had years of helping others navigate the storms of life.
But I had never been taught how to survive this one.
No one had.

Because no one talked about it.

Not like this.
Not with truth. Not with power. Not with solutions.

And that's when it hit me. Not like a whisper, but like a freight train. This wasn't just about me.

This was about every woman who's ever been misdiagnosed with anxiety instead of perimenopause. Every woman who thought she was *"going crazy"* because her hormones were shifting, but no-one told her what that meant. Every woman who disappeared from the boardroom, the bedroom, the conversation, and blamed herself for fading.

This was a gap.
Not just in the healthcare system.
But in language.
In policy.
In visibility.
In permission to even speak.
We had built a culture that teaches women to endure, but not to evolve.

And maybe…just maybe…

I wasn't supposed to just survive this.
Maybe I was meant to translate it.
To decode it.

To hold up a mirror and say: "This is real. You are not broken. You are becoming."

That was the seed.
That quiet question that wouldn't leave me alone:
What if everything I had been through, every symptom, every silence, every sleepless night, was never meant to be wasted?
What if my breakdown wasn't a failure, but a portal?
A portal to purpose.
A mess becoming a map.
A personal reckoning becoming a public mandate.

And from that question, a calling emerged. One I could no longer ignore.

Reclaiming the Table

I didn't start coaching in this space to build a brand or launch a business. I did it because I had to. Because I knew what it felt like to sit in front of a doctor and be dismissed. To Google your symptoms at 3am and spiral into fear. To wonder if you were losing your mind, when in truth, you were evolving. But more than that, I knew how dangerous it was to be in that spiral *without language, without leadership, and without support*.

And I knew I wasn't alone.

So I took everything I'd lived through, the years of silence, the breakdowns, the bone-deep exhaustion, the unspoken shame, and I fused it with everything I **already knew** as a trained, experienced coach and executive leader.

Coaching wasn't a new lane for me.
It was a *return*.
To clarity.
To purpose.
To power.

I didn't want to coach women because I thought I could fix them.
I wanted to stand beside them, and remind them they were never broken.

This isn't a rebrand. It's a re-emergence.
I am not starting over. I'm stepping forward.

Yes, I coach women through menopause.
But I also coach boards through transformation.
I lead organisations through culture reform.
I guide executives through the complexity of change with courage, care, and clarity.
And I help businesses design the kind of environments where women **want** to work, and **thrive** when they get there.

This is not about symptoms. This is about systems.

This is not about hormones. This is about humanity in leadership.

I'm not just here to talk about menopause. I'm here to talk about **power**.

Policy. People. And how we do better, together.

Because what happened to me in that medical chair should never happen to another woman. Because what happens to women in boardrooms, in HR meetings, in return-to-work plans, and in wellness strategies matters deeply, to your culture, your performance, and your bottom line.

So, no, this is not a sales pitch. But it **is** a call to action.

If you're a business leader, policy shaper, or executive who wants to get this right, I'm your partner. If you're building a future that includes women not just in name, but in voice, experience, and wellbeing, I'm your asset.

And if you want someone who can speak the language of both **lived experience and executive strateg**y, I'm already there.

This isn't personal branding. This is personal leadership. And I'm just getting started.

I didn't pivot, I returned. This isn't a side hustle. It's a soul shift. I didn't pivot. I expanded. I didn't rebrand. I **returned**, to my voice, my strength, my truth. This wasn't about creating something new to sell. It was about **becoming** who I had been all along, but louder, clearer, and with no apology.

For years, I'd helped others unlock transformation, guiding teams through complexity, coaching executives through crisis, and shifting behaviours at the highest levels. I held space like a pro. Because I **was** one.

But when my own body began to change, I lost that clarity. I stopped trusting myself. I forgot my own power.

And here's the part that still floors me: I **knew better**, and it still happened.

Because menopause doesn't care about your résumé. It doesn't care how many people you've coached or how many businesses you've fixed. It will still walk in the door, sit you down, and ask: *"Who are you, really, without the mask, the role, or the title?"*

And if you're lucky, you'll answer.

That's what this is. Not a career detour. A reclamation. I had the skills. I had the science. What I'd been missing was *permission. Not from others, from myself.* Permission to speak boldly. To take up space. To name what was once unspoken. And to use every inch of my training, pain, and power in service of something bigger. Because if I, a qualified, experienced, leadership-level coach, could feel that lost, that ashamed, that gaslit during this chapter… What chance did the everyday woman have?

That's when I knew: This work isn't optional. It's *necessary*. And I didn't return to this space to play small.

I came back to lead.
To lead with clarity.
To lead with conviction.
To lead women, and the businesses who care about them, into a new conversation that's overdue by decades.

This isn't reinvention. It's remembrance.

And I am not here to pivot. I'm here to *rise*.

The Questions I Wished Someone Had Asked Me

Not medical charts. Not online quizzes.
Just **human** questions, honest, clear, and kind.
Questions that could've cut through the fog.
Questions that wouldn't have made me feel small.
Questions that might've reminded me I wasn't alone.

For instance:
• *Are you overwhelmed, or just unheard?*
Because they're not the same. But they **often** go hand in hand. One screams, the other gets silenced. Both hurt.

• *Has anyone actually explained what perimenopause is?*
Not vaguely. Not dismissively. But properly. With science. With clarity. With compassion.

• *How's your sleep?*
I don't mean, "Are you tired?" I mean: "Are you waking up at 3am, wired, panicked, drenched in sweat, thinking something's wrong with you?"

• *Are your symptoms being dismissed because of your age, gender, or tone?*

Let's be honest: sometimes it's all three. And that dismissal cuts deeper than the symptoms ever could.

- *Do you feel like you're disappearing inside your own life?*
Like you're watching from the sidelines, exhausted, foggy, numb, while the world keeps spinning?

- *Have you been made to feel guilty for asking for help?*
Because that shame? That stigma? That *"just tough it out"* narrative?

It ends here.
I didn't need a diagnosis. I needed a *mirror*.
Someone to look me in the eye and say: *"You're not broken. You're becoming."*

And Then Came the Sisterhood

After I spoke up, something unexpected happened. The floodgates opened. Women began reaching out, quietly at first, then with urgency. Not because I had all the answers, but because I had dared to say out loud what they were too afraid to name.

They whispered things like:
- "I feel like I'm losing my mind."
- "Why does no one talk about this?"
- "My doctor doesn't take me seriously."
- "I don't recognise myself anymore."
- "I thought I was the only one."

And every time, I met them where they were.
Not with scripts. Not with fixes. But with space.
With truth. With science. With sisterhood.
Because this isn't a marketing funnel. This is a lifeline.

There's something sacred that happens when a woman says, *"Me too."* When she realises that what she's going through isn't weakness, it's biology. It's power in transition. It's a rite of passage we were never taught to honour.

69

Some of them wanted help sleeping.
Others wanted to understand HRT.
Some just wanted someone to listen without judgement, shame, or being told to "calm down."
And as each woman opened up, something else shifted, in them, and in me.

They didn't just need information.
They needed reflection.
They needed validation.
They needed a safe place to fall apart, and to rise again stronger.

That's what this space became.
A place where questions are welcome. Where tears are sacred. Where no symptom is too weird, no story too messy, no woman too far gone.

We're not building a community, we're building a movement.
One voice, one conversation, one brave truth at a time.
Because once you stop suffering in silence,
you realise just how powerful you really are.

Why It Matters So Much
This isn't branding. It's belonging.
This isn't self-help. It's collective healing.
This isn't a midlife crisis. It's a full-body awakening.
Because women don't need to be fixed. We were never broken.

We need to be seen for who we are becoming, not just remembered for who we were.
We need to be heard without having to raise our voices or prove our pain.
We need to be informed, so we stop blaming ourselves for what was never our fault.
And we need to be believed, because the body doesn't lie, even when society tells us to doubt it.

- We need systems that honour biology instead of overriding it.
- Workplaces that see through the exhaustion and recognise the endurance.
- Partners who lean in, not away, who ask what we need, and listen to the answer.
- We need governments, businesses, and medical boards to stop filing menopause under "*optional reading*" and start seeing it for what it is, a structural equity issue with physiological consequences.

Because this isn't just about hormones.
It's about dignity.
Autonomy.
Safety.
Trust.
Truth.
It's about the thousands of women who walk into GP clinics carrying symptoms they don't yet have names for and leave with nothing but shame, a script for antidepressants, and a quiet voice telling them to cope harder.

It's about careers that never reach their peak, not because she wasn't capable, but because no one gave her the context.

It's about marriages that fray, friendships that fade, and women who forget who they are because the world forgot them first.

It's about reclaiming midlife not as the beginning of the end,

but the beginning of *beginning* again.

Wiser.
Fuller.
Unapologetically whole.

And if I can help even one woman interrupt the spiral,
If these words find her in the middle of the night as she's Googling symptoms with tears in her eyes and a fear in her

chest she can't explain. If she reads this and whispers, *"Oh my god... that's me,"* then it was worth it.

Every late-night journal entry.
Every dismissed symptom.
Every patch panic.
Every scribble soaked in shame and sweat and survival,
It was all worth it.

Because when one woman finds language for what she's living, she opens a door for hundreds more to walk through. And each woman who steps through doesn't just heal herself, she becomes a lighthouse.

And that, That is why this work matters. Because it doesn't just change the story for one. It changes the story for all of us.

From Voice to Vision

Because this is no longer just about me. It began in a place I couldn't name. Pain that arrived without warning, without diagnosis, without language. Sleepless nights. Skin that felt foreign. Rage I couldn't explain. A fog that settled over everything I once found easy. And a shame I didn't earn, but carried anyway.

It started with pain. It moved through power. And now, it has crystallised into purpose. Not the kind of purpose you write on a vision board. The kind that wakes you up at 3 a.m. The kind that whispers, *"You have to do something about this."* Because I've seen it unfold again and again. A woman enters the conversation small. Shoulders hunched. Voice low. She's ashamed of what she's feeling, and even more ashamed for not knowing how to fix it. She thinks she's broken. Failing. Falling apart. And the world around her, with its cheery HR slogans and five-minute GP consults, tells her to breathe, do yoga, or take antidepressants.

But something shifts. She starts asking questions. She finds the words she was never given in school, in media, in medicine. She sees her story reflected back, maybe in a post, maybe in a friend's eyes, maybe in these pages. And for the first time in a long time, she exhales.

She shares her story. She reclaims her voice. She reclaims her power. She reclaims herself.

And then, something even bigger happens:

She remembers who she is. Not just who she was before the symptoms. But who she was becoming all along. That is the vision now. Not just to coach individual women through this storm. Not just to offer comfort while the system keeps hurting us. But to change the conditions that made silence feel safer than truth.

To walk into workplaces that still treat menopause as a private inconvenience, and open the doors wide to reality.

To stand in boardrooms and say: You don't have a women's leadership problem. You have a visibility and support problem.

To guide executives, HR leaders, and policymakers to stop managing symptoms, and start transforming structures.

To write policy that doesn't treat menopause like a footnote. To challenge the medical blind spots that miss hormone shifts and call it "stress."

To confront the corporate indifference that treats women in midlife like liabilities, instead of lifelines.

Because this was never about fixing women. It's about fixing the systems that were never built with us in mind.

And here's what happens when you do that

When women are informed, they make powerful, personal choices.

When women are supported, they stay, lead, and lift everyone around them.

When women are safe to be their full selves, organisations don't just retain talent, they unlock brilliance.

Stronger teams.
Smarter companies.
Healthier communities.
And daughters who grow up never doubting that their worth continues to rise, not diminish, with age.

This is where my voice stops being personal, and becomes something bigger. It becomes political. Strategic. Intentional. Impactful. It becomes a platform. A map. A movement. Because this isn't just a single journey. This is a collective reckoning. A turning point for the narratives we inherited and the systems we're still navigating. A refusal to accept invisibility as the price of wisdom. A declaration that midlife is not a decline, it's a redefinition.

So if something stirred in you while reading this…
If a piece of you whispered *"Yes. That's me"*, then you're not just a reader. You are part of this. You are the movement. And your voice?

It's not just welcome. It's needed.

Chapter 5:
Dear Body, Mind, and Self

A Menopause Memoir in Fragments

This is not a polished narrative.
This is not a scientific paper.
This is not a self-help guide.
This is a woman, me, documenting the unravelling and the reassembly.
What follows are fragments.
Moments captured in real time.
Thoughts scribbled between aching bones, between tears, between doctor's appointments. Between remembering who I am and forgetting where I put my keys.

These pages are raw. Some entries came in the middle of the night, when sleep betrayed me and anxiety filled the space. Some were written with trembling hands and a racing heart. Some were written after the patch, when the fog lifted, and I could breathe, finally.

Each one is a letter.

To my body, for the ways it changed without warning.
To my mind, for the confusion, the grief, the rage, and the resilience.
To myself, the part that endured it all, even when I didn't recognise her in the mirror.

This is the private made public. The silent made visible. The invisible made undeniable. You won't find a linear path here. Just honesty. Because this is what it means to live through the in-between, not broken, not finished, just fiercely, unapologetically becoming.

Patchwork Woman: Reclaiming Myself One Layer at a Time

What does it mean to unravel? To peel away the layers of silence, shame, and survival we've stitched around ourselves just to keep functioning in a world that never paused long enough to ask how we truly were? I didn't know the answer. Until I stuck a hormone patch on my butt at 6pm one Sunday night and unknowingly detonated the life I'd been numbly enduring.

Let me be honest with you. I didn't go gently. I didn't march into menopause with grace or wisdom or one of those breezy Instagram captions about "*embracing the change.*" I hesitated. For seven weeks I circled the patch like it was a live wire. Which in many ways, it was. A single adhesive square that threatened to shatter the silence I'd built so well.

Before the patch, my bones ached like I'd lived a thousand years. Every joint felt like it was rusting shut. My neck was so stiff, I wouldn't shoulder-check in traffic. My mind-a foggy, vibrating, exhausted mess-was too thick with shame to speak out loud: I thought my life might already be over.

And nobody knew. Not even my sister. Because we don't talk, do we?

Because we were raised in the generation of silence. Where your mum never explained why she bled, let alone why she suddenly stopped. Where your first period happened at eight, and pads were bricks, and shame was the currency of girlhood. Where your mother's hysterectomy was a footnote, not a conversation. Where ageing felt like punishment, not evolution.
So yes, I envied my sister. She seemed fine. Better than fine. While I was curled into myself like a wounded animal, she was breezing through life. Until one night, I picked up the phone and told her everything. The aches. The breakdowns. The migraines. The fear. The patch. Her response? *"Oh, I've been on the cream for five years."* And just like that, I shattered. Not because she was hiding it from me out of malice-but because she hadn't known it was something you're allowed to say out loud. And isn't that it? Isn't that exactly the root of our collective agony? We are all out here drowning, quietly, beautifully, in parallel. Because

we've been taught not to speak. Not to burden. Not to bleed out loud.

That night, I realised: I will be the one to break the cycle.

So here I am. Writing in real time. Patch 1. Reporting from the front lines of meno-aging (*yes, that's my word now*). Logging the good, the bad, and the damn near unbearable. Because someone has to. And maybe, if you're reading this in bed with bones that scream and a heart that races with no reason, this will be the soft landing you didn't know you needed.

The first week was chaos. Sleep returned-for one glorious night-and so did my breasts, swollen and angry like they'd been resurrected from 1997. The tenderness was unbearable. But then... my bones didn't hurt as much. My joints unclenched. I could turn my head again.

That may sound small to you. But to me, it was freedom.

Day 1 of the Estradiol 50 Once Weekly Patch

Ok ladies across the globe, I decided that it's time I-or for some of us, we-got real.

This phase in our lives is scary, and to be honest, hard to comprehend that we have to go through such changes as a gender in our lifetime... BUT it is what it is.

I've decided to share updates as I transform into a newer and better version of myself. You can take what you want out of it, scroll on past, or actively interact. Either way, I will keep every post real and unfiltered.

I am 50 and peri-menopause-or so they say. What does that even mean?

Of course I'm tired: long days, personal stress, grandkids. Easy to call it burnout.

The signs were there. The migraines returning, the body aching, the stiff joints, the brain fog, the anxiety... and still I dismissed it all.

Until my GP added it up.

Heart palpitations, poor sleep, itchy skin, brain fog, loss of appetite, mood swings, bloating, hair thinning.

All the symptoms I thought were just "age" or "stress" were screaming for help.

I was prescribed the patch. And I panicked. The pharmacist told me I'd get breast cancer and die. The WHI study warnings loomed.
But then I researched. I read Estrogen Matters. And I decided: no more fear. No more silence.

On Sunday at 6pm, I took the plunge.

By Patch 3, I'd cried twice in one day. Not from sadness, but from the realisation that I had abandoned myself. That I had let a world built on male-dominated research convince me that everything wrong with me was just in my head. That I was weak. That ageing was shameful. That menopause was some invisible milestone I should pass without ripple or roar.

I Can See Clearly Now

The more I learned about hormones, the more I realised how much I didn't know about my own body. My skin regained its glow. The wedge between my brows softened. I felt betrayed-not just by medicine, but by silence. I called my sister. Finally told her what I'd been going through. She said, *"Oh, I've been using the cream for five years."* I felt rage. But also release.

We don't talk about this because no one showed us how. Our mother didn't speak about periods, let alone menopause. Her hysterectomy was a whispered memory. That silence stops here. With me. For my daughter. For my daughter-in-law. For my granddaughters.

I'm not hiding anymore. This patch brought more than estrogen. It brought awakening.

I see clearly now.
But I'm roaring now.

You see, I used to be a keynote speaker. A powerful one. I transformed lives from the stage. And then, quietly, I stopped. My voice-once full of fire-was overtaken by fatigue, apathy, dread. I started hiding behind my own narrative. I forgot how to eat my own dog food. I was watching my identity fade into the background of my pain.

Until the patch became a symbol. Not of weakness. But of refusal.

Refusal to believe I had to live like this.
Refusal to shrink.
Refusal to be silent one moment longer.

It hasn't all been roses. Week 4 felt like laying on shards of glass. The nausea, the bloating, the insomnia returned with a vengeance. I woke up at 1:18am in sweat and sadness and rage. By 4am, sleep was still nowhere. But I learned something in the darkness: my health may spike and plummet with the estrogen, but my resolve doesn't.

From a Bed of Roses to Shards of Glass

This week... was hard. The fatigue came back. So did the sinus headaches and the morning sickness that haunted me for decades without explanation. I realised how often I'd been dismissed. *"Drink more water." "You're just tired."*
This was hormones. This was real.
There was a virus going through the house, so maybe it wasn't the patch. Or maybe it was both. But my sleep was broken, my body bloated, and my heart... fragile.

Still, there were small wins.

My feet softened. My grey hairs stayed hidden a little longer.

At the lake with the grandkids, I saw an 80-year-old woman jog by, and I envied her. But then I smiled. I will be that woman one day.

Just not today.

This week, the shard of glass cut deep. But I will heal. I always do.

The patch became ritual. Every Sunday night at 6pm, like communion. A private act of defiance. Data collection. Dignity reclamation. A moment where I chose to believe I am still worth fixing, even at 50.

And I am.

Because here's the truth that no one gave us:
Your relevance doesn't die with your period.

Your beauty doesn't disappear with your estrogen.

Your joy, your sex, your purpose, your curiosity, your edge—none of it expires.

If anything, this phase is the rebirth of your rawest self.

The skin that returns to glow.

The joints that soften.

The thoughts that once turned so dark you questioned continuing... now replaced with visions of adventure, energy, and running beside your grandkids in the park.

Even your grey hair seems to surrender. (Yes, I'm tracking that too.)

And what of the friends who didn't understand, the GPs who dismissed, the sisters who stayed silent? I forgive them. Because we are all recovering from a lineage of hush. But I won't stay quiet anymore.
What am I doing? I was terrified. But I did it anyway.

My bones had ached like I had arthritis everywhere, and suddenly-relief. My breasts swelled and hurt like I'd stepped back into my breastfeeding years, but I told myself: I didn't come this far to tear the patch off now.

I was fatigued. Unbearably so. But I could sleep. Actual restful sleep.

I told my best friend about the patch. Silence. Then judgment.

I realised she didn't know. No one does. Because we're not talking about it.

I decided then: I will be the one to start the conversation.
I was on Vitamin C and D, then came the magnesium and the calcium, not to mention the complex Vitamin B, plus the turmeric, and the essential greens, and lets not forget the Glucosamine Sulfate, the triple strength Fish Oil, the Spirulina, the Collegen and still I needed help.

And now, I was finally helping myself.

The body pain eased. The anxiety loosened its grip. I even started thinking of the future.

I was reclaiming parts of me I thought were lost.

If I can give you one gift from this chapter of my life, it's this:

You are not broken.
You are not alone.
You are not done.

This isn't the end. It's the shedding of an old skin. A patchwork process of becoming-again and again and again.

So here I am, patch on, heart open, tracking my Tuesday crashes and Sunday resurrections, telling the truth one raw post at a time.

The Gel of Becoming: A New Kind of Ritual

It started with a patch. It continues with a pump. When the pharmaceutical supply faltered, when the shelves echoed empty where estrogen once lived, I had a choice: freeze in fear or evolve. I chose the latter.

So I moved to the gel. It sounds simple, doesn't it? One pump to each inner forearm. Rub gently. Done. But nothing about this has been simple. Not the transition. Not the loss. Not the deep retraining of my mind, body, and soul to stop fearing the clock, the symptoms, the silence.
In the beginning, I was terrified. What if I wasn't home when it was time to apply it? What if I missed a dose? What if this wasn't enough?

That fear followed me like a shadow, whispering through dinners out, weekends away, and late-night commitments: *You need to get home. You need your dose.*

I had to learn to trust my body again. To realise that healing isn't a house of cards-one gentle breeze won't destroy it. That pushing a dose out by a few hours wouldn't undo everything I'd reclaimed. That I am not as fragile as I once believed.

Now, the ritual comes at night. There's something sacred about the moment.

Two pumps, one to each forearm, gently massaged into the skin that once sagged with exhaustion and now holds strength again. It's quiet. It's mine. Not an inconvenience, not a burden.

A gift.

A year has passed. A year since I shifted to the gel.

A year of rising.

And this is what I know now:

My asthma? **Gone.**
Migraines? **Ghosts.**
Energy? **Reclaimed.**
Joy? **Back.**
Words? **Flowing.**
Skin? **Radiant.**
Sleep? **Restful.**
Libido? **Renewed-not because I need it for anyone else, but because I feel** *alive* **again.**
Breasts? **No longer throbbing battlegrounds.**
Mood? **Levelled.**
Focus? **Sharpened.**
Confidence? **Rebuilt.**
My sense of *me*? **Reunited.**

I am not just healing.
I am reinhabiting.
From the cellular level up.
From the silence out.

And what I now know is this: what I once thought were "random" ailments... were not.
They were not isolated
Not imagined.
Not "just ageing."
They were symptoms.
Of perimenopause.
Of a body trying to whisper louder and louder until I finally listened.

I'm writing again. Not just surviving-but creating.

This book, these words, are proof. Proof that I've returned-not to the woman I used to be-but to the woman I **real**ly am.

I've stepped back into my community with full heart and open arms.
I'm present. I'm visible. I'm *me*. No longer cloaked in fatigue, no longer crushed by bone-deep aches or silenced by fear.

I speak again.
Not to please.
Not to perform.
But to be heard.
I am unfiltered. Unshy. Unapologetically loud when I need to be.

I am a woman who wears her healing on her forearms. A woman who turned hormones into hope. Who turned fear into fuel. Who turned menopause into a movement.
I no longer measure my days by symptoms, or the shadows they once cast. I measure them by sunrises, deep breaths, belly laughs, and writing sessions. By grandkids' hugs and lakeside mornings and the mirror that now reflects a woman who doesn't just look alive-but **feels** it.

This is my life now. And the best part?

I'm just getting started.

PART II:

The Unspoken Crisis

This is where we stop whispering. Because menopause isn't just personal, it's political. It's professional. It's public.

It shows up in absenteeism reports and mental health claims. In missed diagnoses and rising resignation rates. In the silent suffering behind boardroom doors and checkout counters. In the billions lost to businesses every year, not because women are broken, but because systems are.

In this part, we step beyond the patch and into the patterns, the patterns of dismissal, inequity, cultural erasure, and workplace shame.

You'll read about:

- The multi-billion-dollar cost of ignoring menopause at work,
- The medical failures that deepen our crises,
- The physical pain women carry in silence,
- The link between hormones and mental health no one's mapping,
- The rural women left out of the conversation entirely,
- The cultures whose stories have been overwritten or ignored,
- And the truth: that healthcare is still catching up.

These are not just chapters. They are warning signs, policy gaps, and a call to action.

This is the near the beginning of the book for a reason.

Because this is the part most people never reach, the part where truth demands more than tears. It demands change.

Chapter 6:
The Blind Spot. Menopause at Work

When support is absent, women walk-taking their brilliance, leadership, and legacy with them. This is where the gear shift happens.

If you are a policymaker, a legislator, a senior advisor, or an architect of the systems that shape public and private life in Australia, this chapter is for you.

Because menopause is no longer just a women's health issue. It is no longer just a workplace wellbeing matter. It is a systemic, structural, and economic blind spot, one with measurable national impact. And your name is now on the cost.

Each year, menopause costs the Australian economy an estimated $10 billion, not in vague wellness metrics, but in cold, hard, budget-line losses:

- Productivity hits
- Absenteeism
- Presenteeism
- Lost talent
- Preventable resignations
- Increased healthcare utilisation
- Underleveraged leadership capital

This is not fringe. This is foundational. And yet, the policy silence is deafening.

Menopause isn't just a personal health issue. It's a multi-billion-dollar workplace issue, and no one is talking about it loud enough.
That being said, if menopause costs Australian businesses an estimated $10 billion in lost productivity, absenteeism, presenteeism, underperformance, and premature exits from the workforce. Then this isn't just a statistic, it's a slow, quiet drain of wisdom, leadership, and institutional knowledge. It's a silent, shame-laced off-ramp for women who have spent decades building careers, only to be left unsupported at a critical physiological turning point.

"The economic cost of untreated menopause in the workplace is high. Not just in lost productivity and underperformance, but in the loss of deeply experienced women who exit the workforce entirely."
Submission 185: Julie Dimmick to the Senate Inquiry on Menopause

And yet the irony is, these women aren't leaving because they can't cope.

They're leaving because their workplace won't adapt. They're leaving because the stigma of menopause has made it easier to quietly resign than to request reasonable support.
This isn't a story of weakness. It's a story of systemic blindness. Of decades of policy, culture, and leadership failing to account for the lived experience of half the workforce.

In a professional landscape that celebrates longevity in men, where grey hair and prostate issues are signs of wisdom, not weakness, menopausal women are held to a crueller standard. A man can show up unshaven, fatigued, or subdued and still be read as competent. A woman shows up without makeup, pale from a night of hot flashes, and suddenly she's "not coping."

"There is still deep-seated cultural discomfort around women aging visibly. While men go grey and are seen as distinguished, a woman without makeup during menopause is seen as failing." Submission 185

The truth is that these women are not liabilities. They are untapped leadership capital.

"These are not broken women. These are experienced professionals who need time-limited support. With that, they can return to high performance, remain in leadership, and mentor the next generation."
Submission 185

The workplace does not need to reinvent itself overnight, but it does need to evolve.

Simple changes in culture, leave policies, environmental controls, and leadership literacy can drastically reduce attrition and reclaim performance. That's not just good for women, it's economically smart for business.

So why haven't we moved?

Because stigma is cheaper than systems change. Until now.

This chapter, and the research I presented to the Australian Senate, are designed to break that silence. To turn that $10B+ billion loss into an opportunity for reform. And to make one thing clear:

Menopause at work is not just a woman's issue.
It's a workforce issue. A leadership issue. A national economic issue. And it's time we treated it like one.

The Unspoken Line Item

Menopause isn't just happening at home. It's happening in meetings. In boardrooms. In classrooms. In courtrooms. It's showing up in policy planning sessions, in high-stakes negotiations, in operating theatres, and on the frontline of emergency services. It's profoundly economical.

It's in high-vis on construction sites.
It's in heels on parliamentary carpets.
It's in bare feet on kindergarten floors, where educators kneel to comfort children while bracing themselves against dizzy spells and rising heat.

It's in every workplace, at every level, whether we acknowledge it or not. And yet, despite this ubiquity, menopause remains **invisible** in workplace discourse, policy, and culture.

We pride ourselves on *"inclusive workplaces,"* on *"psychological safety,"* on creating environments where people can bring their whole selves to work. But the truth is: that inclusion has conditions.

You can bring your mental health struggles, if they're already de-stigmatised.
You can bring your identity, if it doesn't challenge tradition too loudly.
You can bring your burnout, if you frame it as a learning curve.

But what if you bring your menopause?
What if you bring your sweats, your rage, your memory lapses, your insomnia, your shame, your soul-deep exhaustion?
What if the self you're bringing is navigating hormonal chaos with no roadmap, no grace, and no policy support?
That self is still unwelcome.

The Great Pretend
We talk about resilience, but only if it looks like stoicism. We talk about wellbeing, but only in terms we already know how to manage. We talk about high performance, while ignoring the biological realities that shape it. In truth, we don't want the whole self. We want the edited, filtered, post-recovery version. A woman in active menopause challenges all of that.

She can't always regulate her body temperature.
She might cry in the middle of a presentation and not know why.
She might forget a key word she's used for 30 years.
She might wake up after four hours of fragmented sleep and still lead the team.
She might fight back the rising panic that comes out of nowhere, mid-email, mid-meeting, mid-conversation. And she's still expected to hit KPIs, mentor staff, and smile through performance reviews.

That woman is often at the peak of her career, and the edge of her capacity. And because the system hasn't been built to hold her, she either hides, breaks, or leaves.

The Disappearing Experts
This is the great irony:
We say we value experience.
We say we want women in leadership.
We say we care about retention, diversity, equity.
But we are quietly, consistently, systematically **pushing women out** at the exact moment they carry the most wisdom, judgment, and strength.

We're losing CEOs, surgeons, teachers, engineers, founders, public servants, and scientists, not because they're incapable, but because they're unsupported.

Some step away temporarily.
Some never return.
Some downshift their career trajectory because it feels easier to shrink than to explain.
It doesn't show up as "menopause exit" in the data.

It shows up as:
- "Retired early"
- "Seeking better work-life balance"
- "Lost confidence"
- "Left to prioritise health"

What the data doesn't show is the internal reckoning:
- "I was too embarrassed to say what was really happening."
- "I thought I was the only one."
- "I thought I was going mad."

This isn't just attrition.
It's **extraction**, of brilliance, experience, and perspective.
It's a loss we don't even have the language to count.

Corporate Cognitive Dissonance
We celebrate International Women's Day.
We send out branded emails.
We host photo ops with cupcakes and pink banners.
We applaud women's contributions, but only when they're polished, composed, and convenient.
We run unconscious bias training
We talk about empathy.
We recite values on lanyards and PowerPoint slides.
We host panel discussions on women in leadership, but we avoid the one topic affecting over half of all working women in their careers: menopause.
We commission glossy reports on gender equity.
We publish stats about board representation.
We monitor promotion rates and exit interviews.

But we don't ask how many women left because their bodies betrayed them, or rather, because the system did.
We promote flexible work.
We write policies that look good on paper.

But the moment a woman **uses** that flexibility for anything other than a sick child or school pickup, she's labelled *"difficult," "disengaged,"* or *"no longer a culture fit."*
We build leadership pipelines, in spreadsheets.
We map out succession plans and talent pools.
We invest in female leadership training, confidence programs, and empowerment workshops.

But we never ask if those same women will still be standing, still supported, when the hot flushes hit, when the memory blanks strike, when the confidence crumbles at 3am with no clear reason why.

Because when menopause walks into the office?
We look away.
We freeze.
We pretend it isn't happening.
We fail to name it, let alone plan for it.
And when the impact becomes impossible to ignore?
We pathologise the woman.

We call it stress.
We call it burnout.
We offer therapy.
We suggest mindfulness apps.
We treat her biology as a breakdown, rather than a breakthrough.
We shrink the story to fit the system.
We diagnose her instead of diagnosing the workplace.

Corporate Rhetoric vs Workplace Reality

Corporate Rhetoric	Workplace Reality
We champion inclusion.	Menopause isn't in the HR manual.
We value lived experience.	Women over 45 are quietly passed over.
We want you to bring your whole self to work.	But not if that self is sweating, anxious, or forgetful.
We care about mental health.	Until it's hormonal. Then it's "too personal."
We've got flexible work policies.	But using them triggers performance scrutiny.
We retain top talent.	Until menopause makes her disappear.

If your DEI strategy doesn't include menopause, it's not inclusive. If your leadership pipeline isn't built to hold hormonal change, it will leak. And if your workplace can't say the word 'menopause' out loud, you're not ready for real equity.

When Inclusion Has Limits

Let's be honest: inclusion is often conditional. We include women when they show up polished. We support mental health, but only when it fits neatly into a category we've already approved. We back parents, but only when parenting is visibly about children, not aging parents or invisible exhaustion. We're fine with empathy, until it costs us comfort. We're fine with flexibility, until someone asks for it without apology. We talk about the *"whole self,"* but we mean the *sanitised self*. The version of womanhood that doesn't shake, cry, forget, rage, or sweat through her blouse mid-meeting. The woman who walks into work in midlife, managing night sweats, anxiety, disrupted sleep, irregular bleeding, and a complete rewiring of her brain chemistry?

She doesn't fit our current model of professionalism.
So we shrink her.
We silence her.
We watch her fade, and call it personal choice.

The Silent Exit
What does it look like when a woman leaves because of menopause?
It rarely says so on paper.
Instead, it's coded:

- "Seeking better work-life balance."
- "Pursuing new opportunities."
- "Decided to take some time out."

What it doesn't say is:
- "I can't function on two hours of sleep and I'm terrified I'll break down in front of my team."
- "I'm embarrassed by my memory lapses and no one's helping."
- "I asked for support and was met with silence."

This isn't just attrition. It's **structural loss**, of wisdom, leadership, and continuity. And it's preventable. But only if we're willing to stop pretending menopause is a private problem. Only if we stop medicalising women and start modernising policy.

Menopause Is Not a Side Note
Menopause isn't a niche health concern. It's not a quirky footnote in a woman's professional story. It is a **biological**

certainty for every woman who remains in the workforce long enough.

And yet it remains absent from:
- Diversity and inclusion strategies
- Psychological safety frameworks
- Leadership training programs
- Retention plans
- Wellness budgets
- Organisational risk registers

Menopause is not a deviation from the path. It is part of the path.

Until we make space for it in our systems, We will continue losing women, misdiagnosing leadership potential, and misaligning our policies with the realities of our people.

The Door Doesn't Just Knock

Menopause doesn't arrive like a polite visitor. It doesn't wait for you to finish your quarterly report or wrap up that leadership course or reach a neat milestone in your five-year plan. It barges in. Sometimes slowly. Sometimes overnight. Sometimes with whispers, a little anxiety, a change in your period, a feeling you can't name. Sometimes with screams, a panic attack in the supermarket, a meltdown in the car park, a resignation letter drafted in tears. It shows up in presentations, in performance reviews, in casual Fridays, in leadership retreats. It shows up in every system that wasn't built with hormonal change in mind. And when it comes crashing through the door, we look away.

We hand out vague wellness advice.
We offer "time off" instead of understanding.
We shrink from the mess instead of meeting it.
But the mess isn't the problem. Our **refusal to see it** is.

Chapter 7:
The Cost of Silence

Most Companies Track Turnover. Few Know How to Trace It Back to Menopause.

Walk into any executive boardroom and you'll find dashboards detailing employee turnover. You'll see charts showing exits by age group, department, and tenure. But what you won't find is the truth behind a silent pattern. Because while the numbers tell us who's leaving, they rarely tell us *why*. We see women exiting at 45, 48, 52, right at the peak of their leadership potential, and we write it off as "career change," "family reasons," or "burnout." But the reality is far more complex. For many, the true cause is a biological transition so under-recognised that it doesn't even make it into HR systems: **perimenopause and menopause**.

We can no longer afford this blind spot. Not in business. Not in government. And certainly not in the lives of the women bearing its cost in silence. If we're serious about workforce retention, gender equity, and psychological safety, menopause can no longer be invisible.

Most Managers Know How to Approve Leave. Few Understand the Cause Behind the Leave Being Taken.

A mid-career woman applies for another sick day. "She's struggling with her workload," someone suggests. "Maybe she's not cut out for this level of leadership anymore," someone else says. The whispers start. Performance is questioned. Confidence is shaken. And quietly, without support or understanding, another capable woman is lost to the system.

Nowhere in the performance review does it say:
- Night sweats causing sleeplessness.
- Brain fog interfering with memory.
- Crushing fatigue that arrives without warning.

Instead, it says:
- Inconsistent.
- Disengaged.
- Needs to improve.

This is how high-performing women become exit statistics. Not because they've lost capability, but because the system hasn't evolved to accommodate the biological reality of half the population.

What if managers were trained to spot these signs with empathy? What if menopause wasn't taboo, but treated like any other occupational health consideration?
Because once we name it, we can support it.

This Isn't Just About Individual Women.   It's About Organisational Integrity and National Productivity.
When a woman walks out the door because her symptoms have gone unrecognised and unsupported, what leaves with her? Decades of expertise. Mentorship for younger colleagues. Continuity in critical projects. A trusted voice in leadership. A ripple effect through team morale. This isn't a niche health issue, this is a **workforce capability issue**.

When menopause goes unacknowledged:

- **Leadership pipelines dry up.**
- **Institutional memory is lost.**
- **Trust in management erodes.**
- **Psychological safety deteriorates.**

And that's just inside the organisation.

On a national level, the economic implications are staggering. Every unsupported resignation compounds the gender leadership gap. Every quiet suffering compounds the gender pay gap. And every premature retirement cuts short the return on decades of investment in training, development, and expertise.

Let's be crystal clear:

This is not just about women.

It's about the **system** that fails them, and all of us who pay the price.

*The Sentence That Echoed in Every Submission: "**I Didn't Know What Was Happening to Me. And No One at Work Asked.**"* In preparing my Senate submission, I read hundreds of stories, raw, brave, and often devastating. Different industries. Different locations. Different symptoms. I spoke to just as many women of all ages, all walks of life and at all stages of their journey.

But one thing was the same, hidden in all comments.

"I thought I was losing my mind."
"I thought I had early onset dementia."
"I was terrified, but too ashamed to speak up."
"My doctor didn't even mention perimenopause."
"I hid it for two years before I finally quit."

These are not fringe cases. They are the unspoken norm. Women didn't leave because they were unwilling. They left because they were unsupported. Menopause was not framed as a health transition. It was framed as a performance decline. And in that framing, careers were quietly dismantled, piece by piece, symptom by misunderstood symptom. For many, this wasn't just a hormonal shift. It was a full-blown **identity collapse** with no scaffolding to catch them.

The Training Doesn't Exist. The Policies Don't Exist. The Standards Don't Exist.

Think about your organisation. There are training modules for cyber safety, for WHS, for bullying and harassment. There are frameworks for mental health, parental leave, chronic illness, disability inclusion.

But where is menopause?

In most workplaces, it's nowhere.

- No onboarding reference.
- No manager training module.
- No formal leave code.
- No psychological risk framework.
- No work health and safety policy.

And what's worse, no conversation. Not from leadership. Not from HR. Not even whispered in the corridors. This isn't an oversight. It's an omission that reinforces stigma, even in well-meaning, progressive organisations. When we fail to name menopause, we fail to support it.

And when we fail to support it, we fail the women, and teams, who need it most.

The $10 Billion Black Hole in Our Economy

The number is now well known: **$10 billion lost every year in Australia** due to menopause-related productivity losses. But that number is conservative. It doesn't account for the ripple effects:

- High-performing women stepping back or stepping down
- Mid-level leaders opting out of promotion pathways
- Delayed project outcomes due to unmanaged executive fatigue
- Institutional knowledge drain due to premature exits

- Costly recruitment cycles to replace senior women who didn't need to leave, they needed support
- The unmeasured grief, anxiety, and identity loss carried quietly in women's bodies, alone

This isn't just a women's issue. It's a **national capability and economic resilience issue**. Governments fund workforce participation initiatives and gender equality programs, yet ignore the most biologically predictable inflection point in a woman's working life. It's time to connect the dots, and close the policy gap.

Behind Every Statistic is a Story of Loss, and Silence

She was a trusted project manager. She called in sick again. She didn't explain why. She was too ashamed. Too tired. Too unsure herself. Eventually, she stepped down. He was her director. He noticed something had shifted. But he didn't know how to ask, or even what to ask. So he said nothing. And she disappeared from the team like vapor. This is how the silence continues. And the cost is measured in far more than dollars. It's measured in lost confidence. In lost voice. In lost self-belief. In leadership gaps and vacant board seats that once had a brilliant woman sitting in them.

This Is a National Imperative, and a Cultural Reckoning

If you are a *Head of HR:* **This is your focus.**

If you are a *legislator:* **This is your focus.**

If you are a *woman wondering what the hell is happening* to you: **This is your focus.**

Because menopause is not just a personal journey.

It is a **workplace journey**, a **policy journey**, and a **societal reckoning**.

We cannot build inclusive workplaces if we exclude the hormonal and health realities of half the population. We cannot say we support women in leadership if we ignore the most common reason they leave. The silence is costing us too much. And the solution isn't complicated. It begins with listening.

Then policy.
Then training.
Then change.

Real, embedded, lived change, where menopause is no longer invisible. Where women are no longer ashamed. And where workplaces finally grow up and evolve, the way women always have.

Chapter 8:
Invisible Women, Visible Loss

A Data-Backed Warning from Australia's Own Reports

And the global silence that allows it. Australia's national conversation on menopause in the workplace is no longer emerging, it has arrived. Not because our leaders chose to elevate it, but because the data finally made ignoring it impossible. For decades, menopause has been excluded from workplace discourse. Tucked away behind euphemisms. Dismissed as "personal." Reduced to whispers. And yet the lived experience of millions of women, and the mounting cost to our economy, tells a very different story. The findings are now public. The reports are clear. The numbers are staggering. And they reveal a confronting truth:

Most public sector agencies in Australia, despite being among the most resourced, regulated, and gender-equity-mandated workplaces in the country, still have no formal policies, training, or frameworks to support employees experiencing menopause.

None.
No policy.
No risk assessment.
No structured manager training.
No HR guidance.
No leave options tailored to hormonal health.
No protections.
No pathway.
No language.
What we are witnessing is not a minor oversight.

It is a **nationwide structural blind spot**, one that reflects just how deeply menopause has been excluded from the definition of occupational health and gender inclusion.

What the Reports Tell Us
2024 Senate Inquiry into Menopause in Australia

"Menopause was not acknowledged in any formal risk assessments or workplace policy documents across the majority of public submissions."

This is not a quote from a 1994 report. This is from a Senate Committee in 2024, a sobering admission from dozens of government departments, health bodies, and educational institutions.

2021 Circle In Report: Driving the Change
Surveyed over 700 women working across corporate, public, and not-for-profit sectors.

- **83% said menopause had negatively impacted their work.**
- **60% rated their employer's support as poor or very poor.**
- Only **3% felt their workplace was truly supportive.**

The same report found women were leaving jobs, stepping down from leadership roles, or refusing promotions, **not because of lack of capability, but because of unmanaged, misunderstood, and often invisible symptoms.**

WHISE (Women's Health in the South East) Case Study:

- Conducted a deep dive into local government and community health services.
- Found that while **many agencies had wellbeing programs,** virtually **none had menopause-specific initiatives.**
- HR systems were ill-equipped, frontline leaders were untrained, and cultural awareness was nearly absent.

These reports aren't anomalies. They are mirrors. And what they reflect is a dangerous inconsistency between our stated values and operational realities. We celebrate gender equity, while ignoring the most defining hormonal event of a woman's working life. We set targets for female leadership, while building no scaffolding to retain them. We fund programs for workplace health, but leave menopause in the shadows.

The Global Silence That Made This Possible

Australia's failure to act on menopause in the workplace is not happening in isolation. It exists in the vacuum left by the **World Health Organization (WHO)**, the very body tasked with setting international health priorities. Despite its leadership on reproductive health, maternal care, and ageing, the WHO's guidance on menopause is strikingly limited.

- It defines menopause primarily as a biological event, the "permanent cessation of menstruation."
- It briefly acknowledges symptoms such as hot flushes, mood changes, and night sweats.
- It makes occasional references to quality of life.

But there is no classification of menopause as a global health priority.

No practical policy frameworks to guide governments or workplaces.
No integration of menopause into mental health strategies.
No clear acknowledgment of its implications for gender equity or economic participation.
And no meaningful update to its menopause guidance in over a decade.

This absence is not neutral, it is a form of erasure.
When the most influential health organisation on earth fails to frame menopause as a public health, workplace, and equity issue, that silence ripples outward.
National governments take their cue.
Health systems deprioritise research and training.
Workplaces remain unprepared.

And women, across every continent, are left unsupported, unseen, and under threat of avoidable career derailment.
If pregnancy or childbirth were treated with this level of indifference, it would be global news.

But menopause, despite affecting every woman who lives long enough, remains excluded from the global health agenda.
This is not just a gap in policy.
It is a failure of imagination, leadership, and basic public health ethics.

The Consequences Are No Longer Hidden

This global and national inaction is not without consequence. It is costly, economically, institutionally, and personally.

- **Economically**, we are haemorrhaging value.
  Productivity losses, absenteeism, presenteeism, early retirement, and leadership attrition add up to **an estimated $10 billion annually** in Australia. That figure does not even capture the ripple effects: missed mentoring, fractured teams, or reputation loss in gender-sensitive industries.

- **Institutionally**, we are creating risk.
  When managers are untrained and policies are absent, women are more likely to disengage, underperform, or resign. This opens the door to discrimination claims, legal risk, and cultural toxicity.

- **Personally**, we are abandoning women.
  Women who have served their organisations for years, sometimes decades, are now walking away in silence. Many feel ashamed, confused, or medically

gaslit. Others are punished for physiological changes they cannot control.

This isn't just a policy failure.
It's a human one.
And it's time the world caught up.

Snapshot: Menopause at Work in Australia

Circle In Report: "Driving the Change" (2021)
One of the most comprehensive Australian workplace menopause surveys to date, capturing the lived experience of over 700 women.

The Impact:

- **83%** said menopause negatively affected their ability to work
- **60%** rated their employer's support as poor or very poor
- **Only 3%** rated their workplace support as excellent

The Consequences:

- Nearly **1 in 2** considered leaving or actually left their job
- Many turned down promotions due to unmanaged symptoms and lack of flexible support
- Most **did not feel safe disclosing menopause** as the reason for performance changes or leave

The Cultural Void in Public Institutions

Progressive on paper. Silent in practice. While the absence of menopause policy in Australian workplaces is alarming, it is the deeper, more pervasive **cultural void** that may be doing the most harm. In many institutions, particularly within the public sector, there exists a troubling disconnect between stated values and lived experience.

An additional study by **WHISE (Women's Health in the South East)** pulled back the curtain on this silent contradiction:

"Very few public agencies had any structured menopause support. Many had wellbeing initiatives, but nothing specific to perimenopause or hormonal health, which left a policy and cultural vacuum."

WHISE Case Study on Menopause at Work, 2023
In other words: we have frameworks for wellness, resilience, flexibility, inclusion, even gender equity, but **none for the hormonal reality of half the workforce.**

The result is not just neglect.
It is a kind of **institutional gaslighting**, where women are told they are supported, but the systems themselves erase the very thing they're experiencing.

The Illusion of Progress

These agencies are not failing because they lack resources or awareness. Many are celebrated for their innovation and social responsibility. They publish strategic plans with bold equity targets. They acknowledge International Women's Day. They form diversity working groups.

But when menopause enters the room, or more accurately, when it takes hold of a woman's body and mind, the conversation **stops**.

Instead of direct, compassionate, and informed infrastructure, most institutions lean on vague placeholders:

- "We're committed to staff wellbeing."
- "Flexible work is available upon request."
- "We value inclusion."

Yet none of these slogans translate into **tangible, menopause-specific support**. This is not inclusion. It's inertia dressed in inclusive language.

What This Looks Like on the Ground

Behind the rhetoric, here's what the WHISE report, and countless firsthand accounts, tell us is actually happening inside so-called progressive institutions:

- No *HRIS (Human Resource Information System)* categories for menopause-related leave.

Women are forced to misclassify their absence under "sick leave," "mental health days," or "carer responsibilities", erasing the true reason for their withdrawal and skewing internal data.

- No *workplace adjustments* for temperature sensitivity, night sweats, migraines, or brain fog.

Standard accommodations for ergonomic seating or pregnancy exist, but nothing to assist someone managing 15 hot flushes a day under fluorescent lights or trying to stabilise anxiety between high-stakes meetings.

- No *training for managers* on how to respond to menopause disclosures, identify symptoms, or offer basic support.

In some cases, managers avoid the topic altogether for fear of saying the wrong thing, leaving women to navigate it alone.

- No *acknowledgment in DEI* (Diversity, Equity & Inclusion) portfolios.

Menopause is still not considered part of the diversity conversation in most agencies, despite its profound gendered impact on career longevity, pay equity, and leadership retention.

- No *psychologically safe pathway* for women to name what is happening.

Disclosure is often met with awkward silence, discomfort, or worse, performance management.

The Consequence of Silence

This void doesn't just create inconvenience. It **amplifies isolation**, erodes confidence, and drives capable women out of the workforce at a time when their leadership is most needed.
Let's name it for what it is:

- A woman in her 40s or 50s, struggling to remember her password for the fourth time in a day, begins to question her competence.
- A senior executive starts declining keynotes and leadership panels because she fears a visible flush or mental blank.
- A public health professional starts arriving late, not because she's careless, but because her insomnia left her awake at 3 a.m. and exhausted at 7.

And in every case, the workplace says nothing, because it doesn't know what to say. This is the cultural cost of avoidance.

When we exclude menopause from the cultural lexicon of the workplace, we don't just ignore biology, **we betray trust**.

Performative Equity vs. Lived Inclusion

In recent years, many public institutions have worked to improve gender representation.
They celebrate hiring women into executive roles.
They track promotions by gender.
They produce glossy reports on equity.

But here's the truth:

You cannot call your workplace inclusive if you have no plan for menopause. You cannot say you value women's leadership while forcing them to suffer in silence through one of the most disruptive phases of their life. You cannot achieve true equity while pretending hormonal health has no role in workplace performance or progression.

This isn't just a gap in HR practice. It's a **moral and strategic failure.** And it is time to name it.

The Consequences of Doing Nothing

These failures have cascading effects, measurable and immeasurable:

Impact Area	Consequence of Inaction

Workforce Retention	Mid-career women leave early, citing burnout or personal reasons
Leadership Pipelines	Gender parity at senior levels stalls or reverses
Productivity	Unacknowledged symptoms disrupt concentration, memory, confidence, and output
Disclosure Safety	Women fear being labelled "emotional," "unstable," or "difficult"
Cultural Trust	Women disengage from organisations that don't support their reality
Public Spend	Taxpayer-funded training and experience is lost with every resignation

The **Senate Inquiry** conservatively estimated that the **economic cost of menopause-related attrition, presenteeism, absenteeism, and early retirement exceeds $3.5 billion annually**, a figure that does not include lost superannuation, healthcare burden, or gender pay gap escalation.

What This Means for Every Employer

Let us be unequivocal: **Failing to acknowledge menopause at work is no longer a neutral act. It is a risk.**

A risk to talent. A risk to strategy. A risk to inclusion. The evidence has been tabled before Parliament. The stories have been told. The data is public.

If you are a government department, a large employer, or a leader of people, and you have no menopause strategy, you are part of the problem. And the cost is compounding.

Two Private Worlds: Menopause in the Private Sector

One workforce. Two realities. And a $10 billion blind spot.. Menopause doesn't discriminate. It enters every business, from high-rise boardrooms to suburban bakeries, quietly, powerfully, and often invisibly. And yet, across Australia's private sector, there are two completely different responses unfolding side by side. In one workplace, a woman discloses her symptoms and is met with support: flexibility, understanding, and a menopause-aware manager. Next door, another woman is silently battling night sweats, insomnia, migraines, and emotional whiplash under fluorescent lights, with no policy, no pathway, and no idea how to explain what's happening without risking her job. These two women could work on the same street. They often do.

The difference?
Not budget.
Not headcount.
Not legal obligation.

The difference is awareness, leadership, and the willingness to act.

But it shouldn't be left to leadership alone. Expecting individual businesses, especially small and medium employers, to design their own menopause response without guidance is not just unrealistic. It's unfair.

Without government policy, national standards, or legislative scaffolding, support will remain uneven, optional, and exclusionary.

That's why government has a role to play.

Not in overregulation, but in enabling reform:
- By creating clear policy frameworks
- Offering model Tool kits and training packages

- Embedding menopause into workplace health and safety codes
- And publicly recognising businesses that lead the way

Just as we legislated for parental leave, pregnancy safety, and anti-discrimination in the past, It's time to bring menopause into the modern definition of gender equity at work.

What the Data Shows, Australia's Menopause-at-Work Snapshot

The statistics are not marginal. They are monumental:
- **83%** of women said menopause negatively impacted their ability to work
- **60%** rated employer support as poor or very poor
- **Only 3%** rated their workplace support as excellent
- **1 in 2** considered leaving or actually exited their job due to unmanaged symptoms
- **55%** reduced hours or quit altogether due to lack of support
- Only **8%** of workplaces had awareness training
- Only **6%** had a menopause-specific policy

(Source: Circle In: Driving the Change Report 2021; Jean Hailes Foundation; WHISE; The Guardian)

The economic cost to businesses?

An estimated **$10 billion annually** in lost productivity, absenteeism, presenteeism, disengagement, and turnover. (Source: Office for Women's Workplace Awareness Report, 2025)

The *economic cost* to women themselves?

A staggering **$17 billion per year** in lost earnings, missed promotions, and superannuation impacts. (Source: Australian Institute of Superannuation Trustees, 2024)

Which ever report you believe the figures and impact is staggering.

Business by Business: How Menopause Is Handled (or Ignored)

Small Business (Under 20 employees)

In small enterprises, there is often no HR function, no documented health policy, and no formal process for support. Whether menopause is recognised depends entirely on the emotional maturity or personal empathy of the owner or manager.

What we see:
- No leave categories
- No training
- No disclosure pathways
- No awareness of symptoms like brain fog, fatigue, or emotional sensitivity

"I had to explain a hot flush to my 28-year-old male boss who thought I was having a panic attack. I wasn't. I was having five of those a day. I started lying instead.": Coaching Client

Medium Enterprises (20-199 employees)

With growing complexity but limited HR capacity, most medium-sized businesses fall into the trap of **generic wellness programs** and **reactive responses**. Menopause remains "not our lane," even as midlife women begin to withdraw, step down, or disappear from pipelines.

Typical patterns include:
- Menopause symptoms mislabelled as underperformance
- Leadership succession plans quietly skipping mid-career women
- Mental health programs used as a placeholder for hormonal support
- Managers unsure how to respond, or unwilling to ask

"They told me I needed to work on my 'emotional regulation.' I didn't need a coach. I needed estrogen.":
Coaching Client

Large Corporates (200+ / ASX-listed)

Big business has the structure to lead, but most are failing to do so. Menopause is rarely integrated into DEI frameworks, risk assessments, or talent strategies. Even in companies that champion *"women in leadership"* and boast gender targets, menopause is seen as private, niche, or irrelevant.

We've found:
- No menopause-specific EAP or health cover options
- No data collection on attrition linked to menopause
- No KPI alignment between inclusion and midlife health
- Optics-driven cultures where women mask symptoms to survive

"I lead a $40 million portfolio. But I nearly walked out because I couldn't sleep, couldn't think, and didn't feel safe enough to say why.": Coaching Client

Side-by-Side: Two Realities in the Private Sector

Category	Avoidant Enterprise	Responsive Enterprise
Policy	No mention of menopause	Formal menopause support policy
Manager Capability	Untrained, uncomfortable, or dismissive	Trained in symptoms, language, and support
Leave Options	Sick/personal leave misclassification	Menopause-specific categories in HRIS
Culture	Silence, shame, self-protection	Openness, inclusion, disclosure pathways
Impact on Women	Decline, burnout, disengagement, quiet exits	Retention, performance, leadership continuity

Why Some Businesses Get It Right

What sets the responsive companies apart?
Not funding.
Not external regulation.
Not even industry.
The difference is a **leadership mindset** that says:

"If women are exiting our system mid-career, we don't ask 'what's wrong with her', we ask what's wrong with the system."

And some are leading the way. As of 2024, only **four organisations** in Australia are officially accredited as menopause-friendly: **Deloitte Australia, AngloGold Ashanti, St John WA**, and **Australian Red Cross Lifeblood**.

Another **38 are working toward accreditation**, including **BHP, Melbourne Airport, and the Commonwealth Bank**. (Source: Menopause Alliance Australia, Chalice Foundation, ABC News)

Quadruple Impact: The Cost of Silence

Menopause, when ignored, has consequences across four domains:

1. *Economic*
   - $10B+ in productivity, absenteeism, and turnover losses
   - Missed ROI on female leadership investment
   - Unacknowledged cost centres in attrition and disengagement

2. Cultural
   - Psychological safety eroded
   - Women self-censor, step down, or burn out
   - DEI efforts undermined by hidden exclusions

3. Leadership
   - Midlife women disappear from promotion pipelines
   - Loss of institutional knowledge and team continuity
   - Unconscious bias reinforced through unmanaged symptoms

4. Human
   - Women question their worth, capability, and future
   - Increased stress, depression, and workplace withdrawal
   - Loss of confidence in organisations they helped build

Silence as a Strategy

Let's be honest: In many businesses, the silence isn't accidental. It's strategic. If we name menopause, we must act. If we act, we must fund, train, and restructure. And for some, it's easier to say nothing, and absorb the silent cost.

But that era is ending. Your staff are whispering about it. Your customers are starting to expect it. Your competitors will move first.

The Decision Point

Every business has a choice: Be the company where women hide their symptoms, shrink their ambition, and quietly exit. Or be the one where women stay, lead, and thrive, because they were seen, heard, and supported. This is not a question of compliance. It is a question of **values**, **vision**, and whether your workplace reflects the world as it really is.

Menopause is not a private problem. It is a business imperative, and a national opportunity. **And the organisations that get this right won't just retain talent. They will shape the future of leadership, care, and credibility.**

Chapter 9:
The Hidden Cost of Cultural Inert

Australia is not lacking in female talent. We are losing it.

Our failure to account for menopause in workplace design, policy settings, and leadership support isn't just outdated, it's economically negligent. In every other domain of workforce retention, we've developed targeted strategies: graduate pathways for youth, return-to-work programs for carers, diversity policies for underrepresented groups. But where is the framework for retaining women in their 40s, 50s, and 60s, the same women who make up the fastest growing demographic in the Australian workforce?

This demographic shift is not on the horizon. It's here.

Women aged 45–64 are now the largest cohort of full-time working women in the country. And many of them are in, or approaching, menopause. If we do not act now, the economic and social fallout will escalate.

The cultural myth that menopause is a "private" issue is not just outdated, it's dangerous. It enables neglect, justifies silence, and leaves millions of women unsupported during a major life transition. For many, menopause is not just a hormonal shift, it's a physiological, cognitive, and emotional upheaval that affects every part of their functioning: concentration, sleep, decision-making, confidence, physical stamina, and even voice.

Let's be clear: these impacts are temporary. But the loss of a woman from the workforce, from leadership, or from boardrooms, that loss is permanent.

Each time a woman quietly exits because her workplace made no room for her reality, we lose decades of experience, wisdom, and mentorship. We lose strategic insight. We lose diversity in decision-making. We lose economic value.
Menopause is not the problem. Invisibility is.

What Gets Measured Gets Managed

We need to name menopause in the data. We must include menopause-related attrition in national employment statistics, in workforce retention metrics, and in leadership pipeline reporting. We need the Australian Bureau of Statistics, the Workplace Gender Equality Agency, and state-based workforce bodies to track and report on the intersection of age, sex, and workforce exit. Until it's counted, it doesn't count.

Policy begins with recognition. Measurement enables intervention. We cannot design workplace supports, funding models, or government incentives if we are unwilling to even name the reason women are leaving. If we fail to disaggregate the data, we fail to see the pattern. And if we fail to see the pattern, we will keep pretending that menopause is a private problem, instead of what it truly is: a public, economic, and workforce challenge that demands coordinated national response. Australia has the capacity, the evidence, and the urgency. Now it needs the will.

Let this chapter be the line in the sand.

Economic Impacts, National Blindness

The estimated $10 billion annual cost to the Australian economy, through lost productivity, absenteeism, presenteeism, and premature retirement, is just the tip of the iceberg. This figure does not account for the unseen value leakage:

- High-performing women exiting mid-career
- Missed leadership pipelines
- Delayed projects due to unmanaged executive fatigue
- Reputational damage in sectors failing to modernise

"Menopause-related attrition is not just personal, it's institutional. Organisations are haemorrhaging

experience, capability, and continuity because they haven't built a system to retain it."
- Submission 185

This policy vacuum widens the gap between good intentions and actual equity. We celebrate gender targets while ignoring gendered biology. We track leadership quotas but not the cost of exit driven by a lack of hormonal health support.

The Productivity Myth
Let's be clear: menopausal women are not less productive. They are *systemically unsupported*.

Performance management systems penalise them for symptoms they cannot control. Leave entitlements don't account for fluctuating health. Workplaces expect consistency, but offer no scaffolding when that consistency becomes biologically untenable.

The result? Women underperform not because they've changed, but because the system refuses to.

"These are not broken women. These are experienced professionals temporarily navigating transition. If we met them with policy and support, not silence, they would remain in place, and in power."
- Submission 185

Equity ≠ Equality
This policy gap also sharpens the line between *equality and equity*. Treating everyone the same ignores biological difference. True equity demands that we recognise the hormonal load women carry invisibly, and build policy that accounts for it.

Without such measures, we risk replicating historic patterns:

- Gender pay gaps widened by menopausal exits
- Superannuation disparities exacerbated by mid-career income drops
- Workplace diversity losses as experienced women vanish before the C-suite

A Health System Under Pressure
The cost isn't borne by workplaces alone. **Hospitals, GPs, and mental health services** absorb the overflow of unsupported workplace menopause. Misdiagnoses abound. Women are prescribed antidepressants or anxiety meds rather than being offered HRT, education, or referral to specialists.

This is not only **clinically inefficient,** it's economically irresponsible.

The *healthcare system* pays for what the workforce refuses to accommodate.

Family and Community Fallout
And still, the ripple spreads. Untreated menopause at work doesn't stay at work. It shows up in strained relationships, in reduced community participation, and in the intergenerational transmission of silence. Children watch their mothers burn out. Partners navigate confusion. Friendships shrink under the weight of fatigue and shame.

"When I left my role, I didn't just lose my salary. I lost identity, agency, and connection. The cost to my family was immeasurable."
- Submission 185

Policy Design That Reflects Reality

We can fix this. But only if we shift from *ad hoc* adjustments **to** structural reform. We need:

- *National guidelines* for menopause-inclusive workplace policy
- *Federal support* for reproductive health leave standards
- *Integration* of menopause into workplace health and safety frameworks
- *Reimbursement and protection* mechanisms for flexible or phased return-to-work arrangements

And above all, we need to stop treating menopause as a whisper issue.

The Opportunity Before Us

This is not a burden to be managed. It's a *policy opportunity* waiting to be seized. Done right, menopause support can:

- Extend women's working lives
- Stabilise leadership pipelines
- Reduce health system strain
- Close equity gaps
- Support Australia's economic and social resilience

But it won't happen by accident. It requires bold leadership, legislative courage, and a reframing of menopause not as a personal matter, but as a **public policy imperative**.

The cost of inaction is measurable.

But the cost of change? That's an investment in human capital, in gender equity, and in national prosperity.

A Policy Vacuum That Costs Us All

Despite decades of gender equity discourse, Australia still lacks a coordinated policy framework that recognises the real, measurable impacts of menopause on work, health, and national productivity. There are no national standards, no mandated supports, and no centralised guidance for employers, public or private, on how to respond. This is not a niche issue. It is a policy vacuum with systemic consequences.

For decades, our workplace systems have been shaped around a male biological norm. As I stated in my Senate Inquiry submission:

Our systems, both public and private, are not designed for hormonal transition. They were built by and for a male biological norm.

This default lens has left little room for biological change across the female lifespan. Menopause, a universal, predictable phase of life, has been treated as a private inconvenience rather than a public workforce reality.

It's not that policymakers don't care. It's that the systems we inherited weren't built to see this. The problem isn't empathy, it's architecture. We have policies that weren't designed to hold women's full biological experience, and a leadership class that often lacks the data, the lived experience, or the literacy to change that.

If this were any other health condition with a $10 billion impact on productivity, it would have triggered interdepartmental task forces, roundtable hearings, and national action plans. But menopause is caught in the crossfire of outdated gender norms, institutional discomfort, and medical bias. And so, it falls through the cracks.

The result? Women leave. Not because they're incapable, but because they're invisible in the eyes of policy. They fall out of career trajectories they've worked decades to build. Their experience, often their peak leadership years, is lost to silence, shame, and attrition.

This is not sustainable.

We need to move beyond acknowledging the problem. We need structural correction.

We need regulatory guidance and workplace standards, not just Tool kits and webinars.

We need data collection, reporting mandates, and integration into workforce planning.

We need training for leaders, frameworks for accommodation, and language that validates experience.

Menopause must move from the margins of health policy into the mainstream of workforce, economic, and leadership policy.

The system is not broken because individuals failed. The system is broken because we never built it to hold this reality in the first place. That is no longer an acceptable excuse.

Chapter 10:
Misdiagnosed and Dismissed.
The Medical System Fails Us.

The Long Road to the Right Diagnosis
Exploring the years of symptoms, tests, and misdirection's that leave women unheard and untreated.

Stories Behind the Stats

Behind every statistic is a woman who didn't get what she needed. Not because she lacked strength. Not because she lacked resilience. But because the very system she served, and sometimes even worked within, failed to see her.

She might have spent her life supporting others:
In medicine.
In education.
In the public sector.
At home.

She followed the rules. She paid her taxes. She showed up. She leaned in. She carried the weight.
She was told that if she just worked hard enough, stayed strong enough, gave enough, she'd be supported when it mattered.

But when the hormones shifted, the ground did too.

And suddenly the system that she helped build became silent, deaf to her symptoms, blind to her suffering, and structurally ill-equipped to respond.

In my work, across executive coaching, regulatory reform, and strategic leadership, I've listened to the stories that never make it to HR forms or medical records. Not because these women are unwilling to share. But because there is no space for them to be heard.
The silence isn't accidental. It's architectural.

It's the result of a system built with gaps where women are supposed to fit.

This silence has shape and history. It's decades of clinical trials that excluded women because our hormones were deemed *"too complex."* It's the fact that most drug dosing was tested on male physiology, and still is. It's a medical curriculum where menopause is an elective, not a core competency.

It's the implicit bias that reads a woman's distress as emotional instability, not endocrine imbalance. It's the policy omission that forgets midlife women exist. This isn't just bad luck. It's bad design.

And so the stories, of sleeplessness, palpitations, rage, tears, aching joints, dissolving confidence, vanishing memory, stay hidden: In whispered phone calls to trusted friends. In coaching sessions that feel more like crisis triage. In quiet exits filed under "burnout," "family responsibilities," or the all-encompassing "personal reasons." In prescriptions for antidepressants that were never about depression. In tears shed alone in car parks after a GP appointment that ended with "come back if it gets worse."

These stories are not hypothetical. They are raw, vivid, and urgent. And they are far more common than we are willing to admit. They belong to women who were told they were too young for menopause.

To women who begged for hormone testing and were dismissed.
To women misdiagnosed with anxiety, bipolar disorder, fibromyalgia, anything but menopause.

To women prescribed sleeping pills when what they needed was progesterone.

To women labelled as unfit for leadership because their symptoms made them unpredictable.

138

To women referred to psychologists when they needed a gynaecologist.

To women who walked out of the system, or were pushed, because it simply didn't know what to do with them.

These women are not fragile.

They are formidable.

They are the ones who led departments, raised children, managed crises, built companies, saved lives, and held families together, they are everyone, everywhere, across the globe.

And yet, in the face of perimenopause and menopause, they were left to piece together their own treatment plans from podcasts, Facebook groups, and late-night Google searches, while trying to stay afloat in a world that never pressed pause to ask how they were really doing. Let's be clear: when systems are not built to hear us, the problem isn't with the volume of our voices. It's with the architecture of the listening.

When a woman walks into a doctor's office and her symptoms are minimised, when her pain is questioned, when her bloodwork is declared "normal" despite her lived experience screaming otherwise, that is not clinical neutrality.

That is clinical gaslighting. And the longer we ignore this, the more women we lose, not just from jobs, but from their sense of self.

We lose their presence in leadership.
We lose their voice in policy rooms.
We lose their energy in innovation.
We lose their wisdom in community.
We lose their stories from our collective memory.

And the data doesn't even come close to telling us the cost.

Because data only counts what we bother to measure.
And we haven't measured this properly. Not yet.

But the stories are there They live in journal margins. In private emails to friends. In coaching notes. In diaries. In departure lounges. In bedrooms. In bathrooms. And now, they are being written down. Because this is no longer just a personal reckoning.

It is a public failure. And it's time we turn our attention, and our action, to every woman who was misdiagnosed, dismissed, and disappeared from the record.

The Women I've Coached

I've worked with women who rewrote the rules of resilience every single day, not because they wanted to be heroic, but because they had no other choice.
Women who:

- **Scheduled high-stakes meetings around hot flushes**, memorising the trajectory of sunlight in the boardroom to avoid the shame of sweat dripping down their spine mid-presentation.
- **Carried spare underwear, deodorant, wipes, and tissues in their handbags,** not for convenience, but because their bodies betrayed them on buses, in airports, at conferences, in classrooms.
- **Sat through senior leadership meetings with ice packs tucked discreetly into their bras,** smiling politely while every cell in their body screamed for relief.
- **Said they had "a migraine," "back pain," or "just a rough day",** because "my hormones are in collapse" wasn't seen as valid, professional, or legitimate.
- **Turned down promotions or overseas secondments,** not from lack of ambition, but because they were

terrified of losing control, of their bodies, their memory, their temper, or their tears.

- **Resigned from positions they worked decades to attain**, not because they lacked competence, but because they couldn't keep performing under a system that refused to acknowledge what they were enduring.
- **Sat in doctors' offices and were told it was stress, aging, or "just one of those things"**, sent home with an SSRI instead of a conversation about oestrogen, lifestyle support, or options.

These women are **not fringe cases**.
They are **not the unlucky few**.
They are **everyone**.

They are:

- **The CEO** whose boardroom presence shrunk with every night of sleeplessness and rising anxiety.
- **The police officer** working shift rotations while silently battling memory loss, dizzy spells, and rage she can't explain.
- **The single mother** managing three jobs, caring for aging parents, and wondering why her body feels like it's on fire every night at 2am.
- **The Muslim nurse** who prays five times a day and whose deep commitment to caring for others has not spared her the sense of drowning in her own body.
- **The Catholic school principal** who has led with conviction for twenty years and now wonders why the walls feel like they're closing in.
- **The truck driver** hauling freight across states while managing vaginal dryness and insomnia in roadhouse bathrooms.
- **The florist** who can no longer hold scissors for too long because her joints ache like they've aged two decades overnight.
- **The executive assistant** who colour-codes a minister's diary to perfection, even while forgetting her own home address some days.

- **The cleaner** who wakes at 4am to mop university floors, her back aching, her sleep disturbed, and no sick leave to fall back on.
- **The hospitality worker** who jokes with customers through the flushes, brushing off her sweat as "the hot kitchen" while wondering if she's going mad.

I've coached **start-up founders, paramedics, authors, teachers, disability support workers, call centre supervisors, public sector directors, tech engineers, police detectives, flight attendants, and surgeons**. And they all said some version of the same thing:

"I thought it was just me.
"I didn't want to be dramatic."
"No one told me this could happen."
"I felt invisible."
"I was terrified to speak up."
"I used to be so sharp. Now I feel broken."

Let me share one of their stories with you.

A woman in her early fifties. Director level. Fiercely competent. The kind of leader who never missed a deadline and knew everyone's kids' names. One morning, in the middle of facilitating a strategic planning workshop, she forgot the word strategy. It just left her. Her brain blanked. Her mouth hung open. Her colleagues smiled, assuming it was a joke. She laughed too, made a flippant comment about needing coffee, but inside, she shattered. That night, she cried in the carpark. Not because she forgot a word. But because she forgot herself.

She didn't know what was happening to her. And neither did her GP.
Instead of answers, she was offered:

- A stress leave form
- A sleeping pill
- A recommendation to "cut back on work for a bit"

No one thought to check her hormones.
No one asked about her cycle.
No one used the word *perimenopause* let alone *menopause*.

And so she began to question her entire identity.
Her sharpness. Her leadership. Her worth.
She's not alone.

I've worked with women who:

- **Locked themselves in bathroom stalls between client meetings**, holding back tears and pressing cold water-soaked tissues to their chest.
- **Snapped at their children**, then sobbed into a pillow, ashamed and exhausted.
- **Woke at 3am every night for weeks**, heart racing, drenched in sweat, convinced they were dying, only to be told it was "anxiety."
- **Were prescribed antidepressants they didn't want**, and when they said it wasn't working, were told to double the dose.
- **Asked their manager if they could move to flexible hours** and were met with, "This isn't really the time to ask for special treatment."

These women didn't lack discipline.

They lacked **recognition**.

They lacked **language**.

They lacked **clinical validation**.

They lacked **policies**, **support systems**, **open conversations**, and **safe pathways** to say, "This is happening to me. I need help."

They are:

- The **Muslim woman** who feels guilty for feeling rage when her faith has taught her patience.
- The **Christian pastor's wife** who hides her insomnia and suicidal thoughts behind prayer circles.
- The **atheist scientist** who trusted evidence-based medicine until it failed to see her.
- The **woman in a wheelchair** who thought her existing disability had prepared her for discomfort, but nothing prepared her for this.

Menopause is indiscriminate.

It doesn't ask about your religion, your rank, your postcode, or your marital status.

It arrives when it chooses, and when it does, **every woman, every kind, is made to carry it differently, but alone.**

There are women right now:

- **Working double shifts in healthcare**, feeling dizzy from hormone fluctuations, smiling through the fog.
- **Running multinational corporations**, only to find themselves unable to remember what they said five minutes ago.
- **Living in rural communities**, where there is no gynaecologist, no support group, and often, no one who will even say the word "menopause."
- **Driving trains, climbing ladders, serving tables, studying PhDs**, while trying to hide the tremors in their hands or the spirals in their minds.

They are the silent millions.

And when one of them walks away, from the job, the relationship, the ambition, or the life she spent decades building, it's not weakness.

It's because she was left to carry a system's ignorance on top of her own biology.

And one day, the weight became too much.

"I wasn't leaving because I couldn't do the job. I was leaving because I couldn't keep pretending to be okay."
- Submission 185, Senate Inquiry into Menopause

These are the women I've coached.

These are the stories that shaped this book.

They are more than anecdotes.

They are **evidence of a national blind spot**.

They are **case studies in courage, gaslighting, resilience, and reform**.

And they all have one thing in common:

They should never have had to go through this alone.

Beyond the Boardroom: This Is Systemic

This isn't just about gender equity in the boardroom.

This is not about a wellness initiative.

This is not about a KPI on a dashboard.

This is about the **woman saving your life, teaching your child, writing your prescription, protecting your community, driving your bus, fixing your teeth, managing your accounts, growing your food, delivering your parcels, or preparing your coffee,** all while her hormones wreak havoc and the system looks the other way.

This is systemic.

This is structural.

This is a **human rights issue dressed up as a policy oversight**.

She might be:

- **The General Practitioner** who breaks into tears between patients and hides in the staff bathroom, because her body is screaming, but there's no protocol, no leave type, no mentorship that recognises what's happening.
- **The Emergency Nurse** working the graveyard shift, drenched in sweat and nauseous by 2am, too ashamed to ask for time off in a workforce already stretched thin.
- **The Police Officer** called to a domestic violence scene, trying to regulate her breathing while her uniform sticks to her skin from a flush she can't control.
- **The Surgeon** midway through a delicate procedure, experiencing double vision and heart palpitations no ophthalmologist can explain.
- **The Midwife** helping bring life into the world while privately mourning the loss of her own vitality and self-assurance.
- **The Dentist** who keeps forgetting patient histories, not because she's inattentive, but because her brain fog has blurred everything.
- **The Optometrist** who tests others' vision while her own inner clarity has disappeared.
- **The Psychologist** gently guiding others through their crises while quietly wondering why her own mood swings are spiralling.
- **The Pharmacist** explaining contraindications, while silently begging her own body to give her one good night's sleep.

- **The Specialist** who has mastered fertility, PCOS, and pregnancy complications, but was never trained to recognise or treat the 10-15 year hormonal journey that follows.

And it doesn't stop at the clinical frontline.

It includes:

- **The Pathologist** examining blood under a microscope, but whose own hormonal markers were never checked.
- **The Radiographer** who scans for osteoporosis but doesn't realise her own career is cracking from the inside out.
- **The Dietitian** recommending protein and iron while her own metabolism rebels against every food group.
- **The Physiotherapist** supporting post-natal recovery, while enduring hot flushes and chronic joint pain that make lifting clients near unbearable.
- **The Speech Pathologist** helping stroke patients find their voice again, while struggling to articulate her own fatigue and anxiety.
- **The Allied Health Team**, composed of more than **90% women**, delivering care across aged care, disability, and rehab sectors, while receiving none of the system's care in return.
- **The Aged Care Worker** lifting your mother gently from her bed while her own spine throbs and her joints ignite.
- **The Receptionist** answering the phones in your doctor's office, trying to suppress the feeling that her heart is skipping beats.

These are women trained to care, to serve, to keep society functioning.

And yet, **they, too, are being medically and occupationally abandoned**.

They are part of the workforce. They are part of the economy. They are part of our families.

And yet their bodies are treated like inconvenient side effects of employment.

The Business Case Has Been Missed, and the Human Cost is Mounting
Let's talk numbers, because sometimes, that's the only language systems listen to.

According to the **Australian Bureau of Statistics** (2023):

- **47.9%** of the employed workforce in Australia are women.
- Of the total female population aged 45-64, the core perimenopausal and menopausal age group, over **2.8 million women** are employed.

And here's the real headline:

At any given moment, **over 6 million women in Australia** are estimated to be in some stage of perimenopause or menopause.

That's nearly **one in four Australians**, a demographic so large, **you cannot touch a single industry, service, or sector without being impacted by it**.

Now zoom out:

Globally, **100% of the population is affected by menopause**,

Because every person alive has been:

- Cared for by a woman,
- Taught by a woman,
- Served by a woman,

- Hired by a woman,
- Loved by a woman,
- Created by a woman

who either has gone through, is going through, or will go through menopause.

- Every coffee you drink.
- Every policy you review.
- Every spreadsheet you approve.
- Every seat you sit on in a plane, classroom, or office.
- Every product you buy, every call you make, every bill you pay,

Has been touched by a woman in some stage of life's hormonal transition.

Yet the system dares to call this issue niche.
Yet boards still ask if menopause is "really a priority."
Yet executive teams still defer the policy review to next quarter.
Yet public servants are still asking for permission to speak the word in meetings.

This Isn't About a KPI
Put plainly, this is not about a checkbox on a diversity dashboard. This is not about measuring "engagement" during Hormone Health Month. This is about whether we treat people as humans or as productivity units.

It is about whether the dignity of a woman's body, in all its complexity, is **worthy of policy, accommodation, protection, and respect.**

- Menopause support is not a nice-to-have.
- It is a workplace right.
- It is an occupational health matter.
- It is a gender equity imperative.
- It is a signal of institutional maturity.

And it is one of the clearest markers of whether we are designing workplaces for real people, or for imaginary employees who never bleed, cry, sweat, forget, or age.

Workplaces that fail to support women during menopause are not just risking burnout, attrition, absenteeism, and reputational damage.

They are **violating the basic principle that every worker has the right to feel safe, supported, and seen.**

If women are expected to give 40 years of service, we should not be discarded or dismissed at the 30-year mark because the system couldn't accommodate the final ten. This isn't a chapter in a diversity report. This is the **heartbeat of half the workforce.** And ignoring it isn't just negligence. It's systemic discrimination.

And When She Finally Asks for Help.... For all the stories we've just explored, of women in boardrooms, back rooms, break rooms, and behind-the-scenes, one thing is tragically consistent:

They asked for help. These women, strong, smart, resourceful, didn't just sit in silence. They went to their doctors. They asked their managers. They Googled symptoms, tracked their cycles, brought spreadsheets of data to their GPs. They showed up with courage, clarity, and a desperate need to be heard.

And still, they were dismissed. Not because their stories weren't clear. But because the system wasn't trained to see them.

And this is where the heartbreak becomes something even more dangerous:

The Diagnostic Abyss
Many of these women **did** seek help. They sat in GP offices, sometimes for the fifth or tenth time. They filled out forms

with trembling hands, listing symptoms that sounded unrelated but were all part of the same internal unravelling. They asked the right questions, after researching for hours in the middle of the night, hoping to be taken seriously this time. They brought symptom trackers, articles, books, spreadsheets of temperatures, moods, and sleep patterns. They came prepared, determined, hopeful, and sometimes desperate.

And were met with responses like:
"You're probably just stressed."
"Maybe try some yoga."
"Let's cut back on caffeine."
"You're too young for menopause."
"That's just what happens when you get older."
"You're still getting your period, so it can't be that."
"This is just part of being a woman."
"Have you thought about going on antidepressants?"
"It's probably work or family pressure."
"Come back if it gets worse."

Spoiler: it did.

It got worse.

In boardrooms, where sharp minds hesitated mid-sentence, forgetting words they used daily.

In classrooms, where once-confident educators doubted their ability to connect.

In kitchens, where dinner plans were abandoned mid-prep as anxiety surged.

In marriages, where disconnection grew because no one could articulate what was happening.

In public bathrooms, where women crouched in stalls, drenched in sweat or tears, trying to pull themselves together.

In emergency rooms, where heart palpitations and shortness of breath were attributed to panic attacks, not hormonal fluctuation.

At conferences, where brilliant women questioned if they belonged anymore.

On morning commutes, where hot flushes and nausea struck without warning.

In early retirements, filed quietly, long before their time.

And in 3am panics, where Google became the last hope, and forums became lifelines.

And in the quiet resignation of women who gave up on ever getting answers.

Who stopped trying. Who internalised the system's neglect. Who learned to perform wellness while silently falling apart.

And this is not personal failure.

This is professional negligence.

This is clinical omission.

This is **institutional betrayal** of half the population.

The magnitude of this failure cannot be overstated. This isn't a handful of unfortunate cases or a statistical blip in clinical data. This is a **nationwide pattern**. A **global epidemic** of dismissal. A **medical negligence** so widespread, so chronic, that it has become normalised. Generations of women, our mothers, our grandmothers, ourselves, have been treated as if our suffering is expected, our confusion exaggerated, our decline inevitable.

When the healthcare system fails to acknowledge, diagnose, or support the hormonal transitions that affect over 50% of the population, it is not an oversight. It is a **cultural design flaw**. One that has cost women their health, their careers, their relationships, and in too many cases, their lives.

Women in perimenopause and menopause are being misdiagnosed at scale. Sent home with psychiatric drugs for endocrine symptoms. Prescribed pills for problems that originate in their ovaries. Told they are depressed when they are depleted. Told they are anxious when they are inflamed. Told they are overreacting when they are unravelling.

They are turned away, not because their symptoms aren't real, but because medicine has never been trained to see them. Hormonal health has been treated as secondary. Menopause as elective. Women's pain as unreliable. Their experiences as emotional rather than biological.

What does it mean to live in a society where the most universal experience of female biology is systematically ignored?

It means women don't trust their doctors. It means women don't trust themselves. It means women spend years in diagnostic limbo, trying to solve a puzzle their clinicians never learned to recognise.

This is not just about missed appointments. It is about missed decades of research. Missed opportunities. Missed diagnoses. Missed lives.

There are women who have undergone unnecessary hysterectomies because their doctors could not identify perimenopausal symptoms. Women who have been told they were bipolar. Women institutionalised. Women medicated into silence. Women who took their own lives because they thought they were losing their minds.

This is not sensationalism. This is documented reality.

Women in their forties and fifties make up the fastest-growing demographic for antidepressant use in Australia. They are also among the most likely to be misdiagnosed. Many are prescribed medication without even being asked about their cycle, their hormones, or their stage of life.

The diagnostic abyss isn't a gap, it's a void. And we are losing women to it every day.

We are losing their leadership. Their laughter. Their light. Their labour. Their legacy.

We are losing everything they were building because we refused to build a system that could hold them while they transitioned.

The next generation is watching. Our daughters are watching. Our sons are watching. They are watching a culture that glorifies youth but punishes aging, especially when that aging is female. They are watching workplaces that reward consistency but offer no accommodation for a biology in flux. They are watching a medical system that hands women painkillers instead of answers.

This chapter, this abyss, is not where the story ends. It is where the reckoning begins.

Because there is nothing more dangerous than millions of dismissed women who finally realise the problem was never them.

It was the system.

And now, they are ready to rewrite it.

The Illusion of Help
Women did what society told them to do. They followed the instructions to be proactive about their health. They made the calls. They booked the appointments weeks or months

in advance. They navigated waitlists, time off work, traffic, childcare, and the mental load of explaining symptoms they could barely name. They arrived prepared. They were articulate. Composed. Thoughtful. Researched. They brought symptom logs, printed medical histories, and calendars of erratic periods. They came armed with the language clinicians respect, *"anhedonia," "dyspnea," "neuroinflammation," "autonomic instability."* They came ready to self-advocate, because by now, most had learned no one else would.

And still, they were dismissed.
They showed up again and again, believing in the system, believing that the next visit would be the one where someone finally connected the dots. But instead of clarity, they received confusion.

Instead of a diagnostic pathway, they were offered lifestyle advice.

Instead of a medical investigation, they were handed wellness brochures.

Instead of a treatment plan, they were told to try magnesium, yoga, or herbal tea.

Instead of curiosity, they received condescension.

Instead of belief, they received blank stares and premature scripts.

Let's be clear: these women were not hysterical.

They were not overreacting.

They were not under-informed.

They were **desperate for relief** and **willing to work for it**.

Yet time after time, they were told:
- "You're probably just tired."

- "Let's wait and see."
- "Menopause is natural, everyone goes through it."
- "You're a bit young, maybe next decade."
- "Try not to worry too much."
- "This sounds like anxiety."
- "Here's something to help you sleep."
- "Let's start with an antidepressant and see how you go."

It wasn't just what they heard. It was **what they didn't hear**:

No one said:
- "Tell me more."
- "I believe you."
- "Let's look into hormone levels."
- "You're not imagining this."
- "I've seen this before, and you're not alone."

Instead, the silence, and the redirection, sent a louder message: **"What you're experiencing isn't important enough to treat."**

One woman, a high-ranking public sector leader, told me she cried silently in the bathroom between meetings for nearly a year before she could put a name to what was happening.

She'd been to three GPs. Each had ruled out thyroid dysfunction, confirmed she wasn't pregnant, and handed her a script for Sertraline.

Another woman, a single mother and social worker, was told to consider *"cutting back on work"* when she reported debilitating fatigue, brain fog, joint pain, and panic attacks that came out of nowhere. When she asked about perimenopause, the GP laughed and said, *"Well, it's a bit early for that, but sure, try black cohosh."*

No blood work. No follow-up. No consideration of her cycle.

A third was a teacher, 52 years old, who had been bleeding heavily for months, had zero libido, joint pain so bad she could hardly grip her steering wheel, and heart palpitations that woke her at night.

She was told: "This is just part of the aging process. Try to embrace it." She didn't feel embraced. She felt invisible.

Antidepressants were nearly always the first response. Not after careful evaluation. Not after endocrine testing. Not after eliminating physical causes.

First. Reflexively. Without context. Without question. Without warning.

This isn't an isolated clinical preference. It's a system-wide pattern, driven by undertraining, underfunding, and unconscious bias. Doctors are doing what they were taught.

And what they were taught? **Did not include us.**

Medical school curricula around the world have, for decades, treated menopause as an elective, something to be covered after the "real" conditions are taught. It's not required learning.
It's not integrated.
It's not prioritised.
And the result is a health system full of practitioners who don't recognise the most common symptoms of a life-altering biological stage.

Women were told their weight gain was their fault.
That their sleep disturbance was due to stress.
That their irritability was poor emotional regulation.
That their pain was somatic.
That their sadness was depression.
That their brain fog was early dementia or just "being busy."
That their crushing fatigue was lifestyle.
That their migraines were tension.
That their heart palpitations were anxiety.
That their breathlessness was panic.

That their reduced productivity was laziness.

They were told to meditate the hormones away.

But you can't deep-breathe your way out of oestrogen collapse. You can't gratitude-journal your way through neurochemical imbalance. You can't fix cortisol surges with a weighted blanket and hope. What you need is a system that recognises you. A doctor who knows this terrain. A society that doesn't expect you to suffer in silence. A framework of care that doesn't start with sedation. A healthcare culture that doesn't pathologise your transition as a mental breakdown.

The illusion of help, that's what hurts the most. Because it's **performative care**. It **looks** like support. It **sounds** like concern It **feels** like progress, until you realise nothing is changing. Until you realise the burden is still on you. To research. To prove. To advocate. To endure. It is a dangerous mirage. And it is everywhere.

Behind closed doors in GP rooms. In online forms. In over-the-counter consultations. In HR meetings. In therapy rooms not trained in hormonal health. In women's clinics where menopause is still considered "optional."

This isn't just a medical oversight.
It's a moral failing.
It's the system pretending to care, while maintaining the exact conditions that caused the crisis in the first place.

Women aren't asking for special treatment. They are asking for **accurate treatment**. They are not asking to be prioritised over others. They are asking to be **seen** with the same urgency, depth, and diagnostic rigour that any other complex condition demands.

The illusion of help is not neutral. It delays diagnosis. It erodes trust. It undermines mental health. It robs women of years. It allows preventable suffering to become normalised. And while the system reassures itself that women are being "*supported*," what's really happening is a slow, quiet devastation. A mass mismanagement of health. A silent abandonment of responsibility. A generation of women left to cope, adjust, disappear, and pretend they're fine. They're not fine. They're done pretending.

Let this be where the illusion ends.
Let this be where the curtain is pulled back.
Let this be the moment we call it what it is:

Neglect.   Minimisation.   Institutional gaslighting. Gendered harm.

And from here, let this be the beginning of real help.
With real names.
Real language.
Real answers.
And real change.

Left Behind Twice: Regional Women and First Nations Women in the Menopause Void

If menopause is under-recognised in mainstream healthcare, it is barely a whisper in rural clinics and remote communities.

In these places, the silence is not only louder, it is deadly. Women outside the major cities are often navigating not just the absence of care, but the absence of acknowledgment. There is no local menopause clinic, no hormone-literate GP, no trauma-informed nurse with experience in women's health across the life cycle. The services simply do not exist, or exist in such limited capacity that the journey to find help becomes its own exhausting burden.

Women in regional and remote Australia are often forced into an impossible decision: stay silent and endure it, or try to self-diagnose and self-manage with information scraped from the internet. Many must travel hundreds of kilometres for a single consult, only to find that the health professional they finally reach is unfamiliar with perimenopause or dismissive of its impact. Even worse, they are frequently told to wait it out, to calm down, or to "try natural remedies" without being offered a single diagnostic test.

The barriers aren't just geographic. They are financial. Emotional. Cultural. Structural. Private telehealth might exist on paper, but access to reliable internet, privacy, and a culturally safe practitioner? That's a lottery most rural women don't win. Public waitlists are stretched to breaking point. Pharmacies don't stock a full range of HRT. And community awareness campaigns rarely make it past city borders.

And if they are First Nations women, they are not just battling systemic neglect, they are carrying generations of systemic harm. These women face racism, historical and present-day trauma, language and cultural barriers, and a deeply ingrained distrust of medical institutions that have too often failed them, or punished them, for seeking help. The health system has not only ignored menopause in their communities, it has erased the language for it. For many First Nations women, there are no words for menopause in their local tongue, because no one ever spoke of it. Not their mothers. Not their aunties. Not the doctors. Not the schools. Not the media.

So when it hits, and it hits hard, they carry the symptoms alone. They are left questioning whether what they are experiencing is real or personal or just their burden to bear.

This is not about gaps in care.

This is about **the total absence of infrastructure** to support these women through a fundamental biological transition.

These women are not "falling through the cracks." That phrase suggests there was once a solid floor beneath them, that the system simply missed a step. But the truth is harsher. There were never bridges built for them to begin with. No culturally appropriate pathways. No menopause-specific health education. No government mandates to train rural clinicians. No proactive outreach. They were not forgotten. They were never included.

And yet, they survive. They persist. They share stories in hushed tones across generations. They try to help each other with what little they have, often becoming the educators, advocates, and carers they never had themselves.

But survival should not be the benchmark.

It is not enough for women to just "get through it" while their bodies unravel and their health is dismissed. If we are serious about equity, then menopause support for regional and First Nations women must become a national priority, not a policy footnote. Because until the bridges are built, millions will remain stranded, in silence, in suffering, and in a system that was never designed to serve them.

The Regional Divide
For women in regional Australia, menopause support isn't just inadequate, it's often inaccessible altogether.

Access to a GP, let alone a menopause-literate one, can take weeks or months. Clinics often rely on rotating locums, meaning there's no continuity of care. You can't build trust with a doctor when you never see the same one twice. Specialist services may be hundreds of kilometres away, and referrals to endocrinologists or gynaecologists are a luxury few can realistically pursue. There is no funded travel for basic endocrine consults, no public menopause clinics outside metropolitan hubs, and barely any HRT-literate pharmacists in remote areas.

Telehealth, the so-called equaliser, fails them too. Internet access is patchy at best. In many towns, it's not stable enough to sustain a confidential or reliable consultation. Women often drive four hours for a ten-minute appointment. They take time off work, arrange childcare, spend money they can't spare, and still leave with nothing but a pamphlet and Panadol.

Even then, they're told it's *"just the heat,"* *"a tough season,"* or worse, *"probably all in your head."* The physical geography of rural life is mirrored by an emotional one, vast, isolating, and often without visible pathways forward. There is no menopause support group in their town.

No trusted midlife health educator at their local community centre.

No workplace awareness training, because no one talks about it, and everyone's just expected to push through.
They may not have reliable internet, but when they can get online, often late at night, after the kids are in bed and the house is quiet, they seek out Facebook forums and menopause groups, desperate for validation, answers, or even just someone to say, "me too."

This is not rural resilience.
This is rural abandonment, dressed up as stoicism, and ignored in policy. These women are not being failed *once*, they are being failed at every point of the system: by infrastructure, by funding models, by cultural neglect, and by the persistent myth that "toughing it out" is a badge of honour.

They are not invisible because they are quiet.
They are invisible because the system never thought to look.

The Deep Cultural Silence: First Nations Women
For many First Nations women, the silence around menopause is not merely an oversight. It is the echo of colonisation. It is the consequence of intergenerational trauma. It is the inherited weight of centuries of being

unseen, unheard, and uninvited to their own healing. Menopause, for these women, is not simply a biological transition. It is a culturally significant moment that is made invisible, not by accident, but by design. It is a passage long honoured in traditional knowledge, yet buried under generations of colonial erasure. It is a conversation stolen, silenced by systems that never asked, never listened, and never cared to learn. In many communities, menopause is still referred to as *"women's business."* A sacred, private, spiritual experience, not meant to be clinicalised, pathologised, or explained away in western terms.

But colonisation never made space for women's business. It disrupted and dismantled the systems of knowledge that had supported Aboriginal and Torres Strait Islander women for millennia. It replaced ceremony with shame, wisdom with whispers, and healing with silence. The same institutions that stole children, sterilised women without consent, removed babies from arms and Elders from their land, now expect trust. They expect First Nations women to show up to a GP appointment and disclose their pain to a stranger trained only in white medicine, speaking white language, under white policy mandates. They expect compliance to models of care that were never designed with culture in mind, let alone consultation.

And when First Nations women don't fit the mould, they are labelled.
Non-compliant.
Drug-seeking.
Too angry.
Too quiet.
Too poor.
Too difficult.
Too complex.

There is no cultural safety in most menopause care pathways.
There is no recognition that "symptoms" might look different when layered with trauma. There is no room for ceremony, for story, for spirit.

163

Instead, we offer cookie-cutter prescriptions and clinical brochures. We force biomedical frameworks into communities that have never been given the power to co-design their own health responses. We flood communities with mandates, but not with consultation.

This is what colonised healthcare still looks like.
It is protocol without partnership.
It is policy without people.
It is the white coat version of control, dressed up as care.
Many First Nations women have never heard the word "*perimenopause*" in a clinic.
Not because they are uneducated, but because the system is uninterested in educating.
Their hot flushes are misdiagnosed as anxiety.
Their mood changes as "mental illness."
Their pain as a sign of addiction or abuse.
Their silence as consent.
Their questions as resistance.

One woman described feeling "like I was being punished for not knowing how to speak their language, and for not being believed even when I tried."

Another was told her symptoms were likely "*menopausal depression*", with no discussion of hormones, no explanation of what was happening in her body, and no follow-up. Just antidepressants and a warning to "come back if it gets worse."

We do not collect national menopause data on Aboriginal and Torres Strait Islander women.
We do not train clinicians to understand the way historical trauma shapes present-day health outcomes.

We do not fund culturally led menopause education.
We do not offer free, community-based hormone testing.
We do not create culturally safe clinics.
We do not prioritise listening.
And then we wonder why women don't return.

The truth is, many never came to begin with.
Because there was no place to come to.
Because the system was never built for them.
When we exclude First Nations women from the narrative of menopause, we are not just failing to care, we are continuing a long line of colonial silencing.

This isn't historical pain.
It is current policy.
It is structural violence.
It is national neglect.
Because despite all this, First Nations women show up for each other.

They gather in backyards, on Country, in kitchens, in whispers and in strength.
They trade stories and share healing.
They listen to Elders.
They pass on knowledge in the absence of formal education.
They carry each other, as they always have.
But they shouldn't have to carry the full weight of systemic failure.
They shouldn't have to survive the health system.
They shouldn't have to translate their pain into a language that ignores culture.
They shouldn't have to choose between silence and stereotyping.
They shouldn't have to bury their biological changes inside a racist framework that has never recognised their womanhood as whole.

We must do more than apologise for the past.
We must dismantle the present.
We must design new systems with First Nations women leading them, not as participants, but as architects.
We must embed menopause education in culturally relevant formats, on Country, with Elders, with truth.
We must fund healing spaces, not just clinics.
We must measure what matters, not just what is easy.
Until we do that, the silence will remain.

And it will not be broken by a pamphlet.
It will only be broken by justice.

When Place and Race Become Risk Factors
When you are a woman…

And you live outside a capital city…

And you are Aboriginal or Torres Strait Islander…
And you're in your 40s or 50s…

The odds of receiving appropriate menopause care collapse.

You are more likely to:

- Be misdiagnosed
- Be prescribed medication without explanation
- Be offered antidepressants instead of HRT
- Be referred to services that don't exist in your region
- Be judged rather than supported
- Be blamed for your symptoms
- Be passed from practitioner to practitioner with no follow-up
- Be told "it's just life"
- Be left to figure it out on your own

These are not rare events. These are normalised experiences.
And in these stories, the damage isn't just medical, it's existential.

A First Nations woman experiencing hot flushes, insomnia, panic attacks, joint pain, and memory lapses may never hear the word *"perimenopause."* Her symptoms may be chalked up to *"grief," "burnout,"* or worse, *misread as signs of alcohol abuse or non-compliance.* She might be handed a script for antidepressants, a flyer for domestic violence support, or a lecture on lifestyle choices, but not once asked when her last period was.

This isn't incidental. It's embedded.

The healthcare system, built around a white, urban, male-centric model, has never been redesigned with First Nations women in mind. It pathologises trauma but ignores the trauma it has inflicted. It demands compliance to a model that never consulted the communities it claims to serve. And in menopause care, this becomes dangerously quiet.

This is not just about poor service delivery. It is the structural inheritance of colonisation, a system still echoing the same principles that once removed children, dismissed elders, silenced women, and erased ways of knowing. The modern medical model demands data, while refusing to fund research that reflects Indigenous lives. It touts best-practice guidelines that weren't written in consultation with First Nations women. And it applies one-size-fits-all protocols to bodies shaped by vastly different histories, burdens, environments, and beliefs.

Every time we enforce a white medical mandate without consultation, we reinforce colonisation. Every time we ignore traditional knowledge systems, we repeat the theft of voice and agency.

Every time a First Nations woman is given a treatment without explanation, or offered nothing at all, we are not simply failing to support her health. We are re-traumatising her biology.

There is no mainstream protocol that accounts for the compounding weight of intergenerational trauma, systemic racism, chronic stress, housing insecurity, environmental hardship, or grief, all of which have direct and measurable impacts on hormonal regulation, immune function, and menopausal severity. And yet, when a woman presents with fatigue or pain, these factors are rarely even asked about, let alone meaningfully addressed.

When place and race become risk factors, a woman's postcode becomes a proxy for her access. Her cultural identity becomes a liability instead of a lens of care. And menopause, which should be a time of honouring wisdom, transition, and community, becomes instead a season of confusion, misdiagnosis, and abandonment.

Even where local Aboriginal Medical Services do exist, they are chronically underfunded. Many lack specialists or consistent pharmaceutical supply. Some do not have the staff or resourcing to offer midlife women's health checks, let alone tailored menopause care. Clinicians doing their best are stretched beyond capacity, and often have no clinical pathway to escalate unresolved symptoms, because there's no gynaecologist, no menopause educator, and no culturally-safe telehealth service at the other end.

And yet, women persist.

They ask questions.

They seek each other out.

They build informal networks of care, aunties, cousins, nurses, community workers, whispering to one another the truths the system won't say aloud.

In some communities, menopause is quietly referred to as "lady business."

Not because it is shameful, but because it is sacred.

But sacred should not mean unsupported.

Sacred should mean protected.

Held.
Resourced.

Seen.

In traditional knowledge systems, women in midlife are not disposable.

They are essential.
They are the holders of lineage, language, and legacy.
They are caretakers, educators, mediators, and memory-keepers.

But Western systems do not recognise this value. They see a woman in distress and prescribe sedation.
They do not ask what she knows.
They do not listen for what she remembers.
They do not consult her community before prescribing her fate.

Every policy that fails to account for the lived experience of First Nations women reinforces a silent message:

You do not matter here.
And that message, spoken or unspoken, continues the work of erasure that began with colonisation.

It tells women their pain is inconvenient.
Their biology is abnormal.
Their presence is peripheral.
Their culture is incompatible with care.

But the truth is:
It is not their biology that is broken.
It is the system.

If we are serious about reconciliation, truly serious, then menopause cannot remain outside the scope of cultural safety, health equity, or gendered justice.
We must stop pretending this is fringe.

We must **centre** First Nations voices in the design of midlife health care, not as a gesture, but as a foundation.
We must **fund research** that reflects Indigenous lives.

We must **train practitioners** in trauma-informed, culturally competent care.

And we must **rebuild trust**, not just with good intentions, but with outcomes that matter. Until then, place and race will remain dangerous determinants of wellbeing. And every woman who falls through the cracks will be forced to carry the cost of our silence. Let us no longer ask these women to adapt to our system. Let us remake the system, so it finally serves them.

Their Stories Must Be Central, Not Token

A menopause movement that does not centre the stories of regional and First Nations women is not a movement. It is a marketing campaign. A brand wrapped in bias, claiming progress while leaving the most vulnerable behind.

If we elevate only the voices of urban, middle-class, privately insured women, we are not liberating women from silence, we are reinforcing a hierarchy within it. **We must do better.**

We must not simply **acknowledge** the added layers of marginalisation, we must **centre** them.

Their experiences are not side notes. They are the frontline. They show us not just how the system cracks, but where it breaks wide open.

A First Nations woman navigating menopause in a regional town without a local GP, without reliable internet, without safe community spaces, **she** holds the blueprint for reform. A nurse whispering truths to women between shifts because no formal education exists, **she** reveals where the system has failed. A woman who drives hours to get HRT only to find the pharmacy out of stock, **she** is not a problem to be solved. She is the reality we must design for.

We do not need more panels of experts who have never walked that road. We need to listen to those who have. We must **redesign** the system, not just decorate its edges.

That means health services that do not ask First Nations women to fit into colonial frameworks, but instead, reshape those frameworks with **cultural safety, trauma awareness, and lived wisdom** at the centre.

That means practitioners trained not just in oestrogen and progesterone, but in **history.**

In **truth-telling.**

In **Country, culture, language, and loss.**
In what it means to sit beside someone without needing to fix them, but to hear them.

What We Need Now:

- **Funded menopause outreach** in rural and remote areas, staffed by practitioners who don't leave after six months.
- **Culturally safe perimenopause education** embedded in First Nations health clinics, developed with women, not just for them.
- **Community-led menopause support circles and yarning groups**, where women can speak in their own way, in their own time.
- **Hormone-aware trauma care**, because unmanaged menopause symptoms can mirror trauma responses, and trauma can worsen menopause.
- **Locally embedded peer educators**, aunties, elders, midlife women who are known and trusted in their community.
- **Access to subsidised HRT and telehealth**, that doesn't drop out, glitch, or put women on hold for months.

- **Research that doesn't exclude them,** no more studies where First Nations women are an asterisk or a footnote.
- **Policy recognition that menopause is a health equity issue,** not a lifestyle concern, not a first-world problem, and not a luxury of the educated class.

They are not *"hard to reach."*
They are *easy to find.*
They are *already speaking.*

But we have built no system that listens with respect. So let's stop blaming the woman for not fitting the clinic hours. Let's stop using the excuse of geography to justify systemic neglect. Let's stop branding menopause as empowerment, while ignoring the women most disempowered by the system we refuse to change.

Let us instead **lift their stories** out of the shadows and into the centre of the national agenda. Let us **make space,** in every funding application, every training package, every medical curriculum, and every legislative reform, for the voices that carry generations of resilience.

Because **true menopause reform will not happen without them.**

And it should not happen without **their leadership.**

We've just walked through one of the most visible cracks in the system, where place, race, and identity compound to create deep disparities in care. But even when you remove those factors, even when the postcode is privileged, the language is shared, and the provider is well-intentioned, the outcomes for women are still falling short. Because the problem isn't just in who gets seen. It's in what the system sees, or more often, fails to.

At its core, the menopause care crisis is not simply one of geography or culture. It's a failure of education. A failure of curriculum. A failure of institutional priority.

And that failure begins long before the appointment. It begins in the classroom.

The Training Gap

As we return from the stories of women in remote and First Nations communities, we confront the uncomfortable truth at the heart of this failure: **the system isn't broken, it was never built for us**. And nowhere is that more obvious than in the training of the very people we are told to trust.

In Australia today, there are **no national, mandatory training standards** for menopause education in general practice programs. No embedded clinical pathways for midlife women's health. No compulsory CPD (Continuing Professional Development) hours in menopause management.

That means a woman in her 30s, 40s or 50s could walk into her GP's clinic, exhausted, anxious, bleeding for weeks, unable to sleep, forgetting words mid-sentence, and her doctor may have received **no formal training** in how to recognise the most common cause of her symptoms: **perimenopause**.

In most Australian medical schools, menopause is not a core unit. It's not a practical rotation. It's not a specialty. It's an elective. A footnote. A one-hour lecture delivered somewhere in the shadows of the curriculum, long after contraception, pregnancy, fertility, and cancer treatment have had their say.

Medical training teaches future doctors how to bring babies into the world. How to prevent pregnancy. How to treat endometriosis, insert IUDs, screen for cervical cancer. How to remove reproductive organs entirely. But the hormonal chaos that begins, not ends, in midlife? The complex, overlapping effects of oestrogen and progesterone withdrawal on the brain, heart, bones, gut, skin, and immune system?

That's barely covered, if at all.

There is **no national framework** to help doctors identify, diagnose, and support perimenopausal patients in primary care. There is **no requirement** to understand how hormonal changes affect:

- Mood regulation
- Thermoregulation
- Memory and cognitive processing
- Libido
- Bone density
- Cardiovascular function
- Metabolism and weight
- Eye health
- Hearing
- Skin
- Hair
- Gut health
- Dental health

These are not niche issues. They are central to a woman's physical, mental, emotional, and social wellbeing. Yet the average GP may not be trained to recognise them as part of a hormonal transition at all.

Instead, women are misdiagnosed with anxiety. Prescribed antidepressants. Dismissed with "*it's just life.*" Told they're stressed. Sent away with iron supplements, sleep hygiene tips, or a referral to a psychologist, while the root cause remains unspoken, untreated, and misunderstood.

The lack of training isn't just a curriculum oversight. It's a systemic blind spot, one that reveals how deeply gendered medicine remains.

Menopause is a fundamental biological transition experienced by half the population, but it remains one of the **least taught, least resourced, and least understood** aspects of women's health. There is no continuity of care pathway. No nationally recognised screening or midlife health check. No incentive structure in general practice to diagnose and treat the hormonal shifts of perimenopause. And in rural, remote, or underfunded areas, the gaps become even more dangerous.

So, women do what women have always done:
They figure it out themselves.
They join online forums.
They talk in whispers to one another.
They build their own vocabularies.
They become experts in the very thing their doctors were never taught.
But this is not empowerment.
It's abandonment dressed up as resilience.

Until we fund and embed menopause education across medical training, not as an afterthought, but as essential knowledge, we will continue to misdiagnose, mistreat, and misunderstand the millions of women entering midlife each year.

This isn't just a knowledge gap. It's a justice issue.

Because a system that fails to train its doctors to recognise and treat the most common hormonal transition in adult women is not just outdated,

it is dangerous.

When Systems Don't Speak Hormone

The reality is this:

- **There is no mandatory menopause education** in Australian medical schools.
- **There is no standardised diagnostic Tool** for perimenopause.
- **There are no consistent clinical pathways** in general practice.
- **There is no requirement** that any doctor, in any specialty, understands the systemic impact of hormone depletion across a woman's lifespan.

And while this vacuum exists, the consequences are far-reaching, not just in general practice, but across every arm of the health system.

- **Endocrinologists,** the very specialists trained in hormone function, remain underutilised or out of reach, especially for public patients or those in regional areas.
- **Gynaecologists** often remain focused on fertility, reproductive surgery, or cancer screening, leaving perimenopause and menopause as medical orphans.
- **Psychiatrists** diagnose hormonal shifts as anxiety or depression, prescribing SSRIs for what is often a biochemical deficiency.
- **Cardiologists** treat heart palpitations and rising blood pressure without testing oestrogen or progesterone levels.
- **Neurologists** see women for dizziness, brain fog, migraines, or forgetfulness, without a single question about menstrual cycles or hormonal history.
- **Dietitians** write up calorie-controlled plans, unaware that declining oestrogen radically alters insulin sensitivity, fat storage, and metabolic resilience.
- **Physiotherapists** treat joint pain, frozen shoulder, or pelvic floor weakness without considering hormonal causality.

Each clinician is doing their job, but not the **whole** job.

Not when it comes to women in midlife.

And so, in this fragmented system, women are:

- **Questioning their minds.**
- **Blaming their personalities.**
- **Assuming they've failed at life.**

Not because they've failed.

But because no one gave their symptoms a name.

This is what happens when systems don't speak hormone.

The ripple effect is devastating, and invisible.

A woman in perimenopause may have 4-6 different specialists across 2-3 years, none of whom link her escalating symptoms back to a common hormonal thread. Instead, she's handed a grab-bag of explanations: anxiety, stress, IBS, burnout, adult ADHD, migraines, early onset dementia, reflux, arthritis, fibromyalgia. One by one, parts of her body are treated, but the system never treats her as a whole.

Meanwhile, she internalises the breakdown.

She thinks she's losing her edge.

She feels ashamed of her emotions.

She stops trusting her memory, her instincts, her voice.

This isn't just inefficient medicine.

It's negligent design.

A health system that fails to embed hormonal literacy across its clinical fabric will continue to misdiagnose women, not because it doesn't care, but because it doesn't see. And what it does not see, it cannot heal.

This is why menopause is not a niche issue.

It is a systems issue.

It is a structural literacy issue.

And until we weave hormonal education into **every discipline**, women will continue to fall through gaps, not because they're hard to treat, but because the system refuses to look at them fully.

When the Diagnosis Is Invisible

Medical systems pride themselves on precision. On the scientific method. On the noble pursuit of evidence-based care.

Diagnosis is considered the cornerstone of good medicine, the moment where uncertainty gives way to clarity, where the right label leads to the right treatment, and where patients feel seen. But how precise can a system claim to be if it doesn't even have a **category** for what's happening to half the population in midlife? How can it boast clinical excellence when it routinely fails to recognise one of the most common, predictable, and biologically inevitable transitions in a woman's life?

The truth is: **there is no standardised diagnostic framework for perimenopause in Australia.**

No national Tool. No universal checklist. No formalised diagnostic code that triggers tailored care pathways. No guidance embedded into Medicare billing. No clinical prompts coded into GP software.

We are living in an era of extraordinary medical advancement.

We can sequence the human genome in hours.

We can image microscopic structures of the brain.

We can map the gut microbiome and analyse hormonal markers with the tap of a screen.

And yet, **we cannot reliably diagnose perimenopause**?

This is not a technological failure.
This is not a scientific limitation.
This is a systemic omission.

This is a blind spot forged by gendered bias, medical history, and policy inertia.

Let's call it what it is: **women are being gaslit by data**.

They are being failed not by ignorance, but by omission.

They are walking into clinics with textbook symptoms, sleep disturbances, menstrual changes, anxiety spikes, night sweats, palpitations, cognitive fuzziness, skin dryness, weight gain, fatigue, and are told it's "just stress," "just life," or worse, "just you."

This is what it looks like when the diagnostic lens doesn't account for hormonal transition.

It renders the real, invisible.
It treats the expected, as abnormal.
It interprets biology, as pathology.
And it leaves women not only undiagnosed, but **self-doubting**.

When your body changes and no one gives you the language for it, you don't just lose medical clarity, you lose your sense of self.

You start to wonder if you're imagining things.
You start to question your memory, your mood, your energy, your worth.
You start to apologise for being tired, for being irritable, for being slower, for needing space.
This is not compassionate medicine.
This is clinical neglect, wrapped in polite indifference.

And the cost is profound. Because **without a diagnosis**, there is:

- No access to subsidised care.
- No standard treatment pathway.
- No appropriate Medicare item number.
- No follow-up or care plan.
- No language to bring to your workplace.
- No support group referral.
- No sense of closure or control.

Instead, women are handed painkillers, pamphlets, or Prozac, all while their hormones fluctuate wildly in the background, unacknowledged and unmanaged.

It doesn't have to be this way.
We don't need new inventions, we need new intention.

The diagnostic frameworks exist. The symptom patterns are well-known. The evidence is vast. What we lack is **the will to systemise it**.

Until we embed perimenopause into mainstream diagnostic thinking, not as a vague concept, but as a recognised **stage of life with distinct clinical criteria**, women will continue to be mislabelled, mistreated, and missed entirely.

This isn't about asking the system to do more.
It's about asking it to do better.
To see what is already in front of it.
To name what women have been naming for decades.

And to finally build a diagnostic bridge for the invisible decade that changes everything.

What Needs to Change

We've heard the stories. We've seen the gaps. We've felt the cost, in late diagnoses, lost productivity, mental health spirals, shattered confidence, and silent suffering. Now it's time to be clear about what must change.

We need systemic correction, not just individual compassion.

- **Mandatory menopause education** across all medical and allied health training programs, not as a footnote, but as a foundational unit of human biology.
- **Public health campaigns** to normalise hormonal literacy, so women and clinicians alike understand what's happening, when, and why.
- **Workplace policies and resources** that acknowledge hormonal health as an occupational factor, with flexibility, support, and open conversation.
- **Reforms to psychiatric diagnostic frameworks** to include the hormonal transitions of midlife, so that women are not labelled with mood disorders when they are experiencing biological shifts.
- **Incentivised continuing education** for general practitioners in menopause and midlife care, so no woman is left to educate her doctor.
- **Inclusion of hormonal assessment and staging** in chronic disease and mental health management,

because unmeasured hormones are unmanaged health.

- **Integrated care models** that connect endocrinology, cardiology, neurology, psychiatry, and allied health, bringing menopause out of the silo and into the centre.

This is not a niche issue.
This is not a women's issue.
This is a health system issue.
This is a national performance issue.
This is a **mainstream correction**.

It is time for a medical reckoning, one that names menopause not as an afterthought, but as a core component of women's health across the lifespan.

Because the truth is:

We've measured everything else.
Blood pressure. Glucose. BMI. Steps. Sleep.
But we have failed to measure the cost of **not knowing**.
The result isn't just a gap in care,
It's a canyon.
A canyon women fall into every day.
Quietly. Invisibly. Devastatingly.

And too often, they are blamed for the fall.
Told they're too emotional.
Too tired.
Too old.
Too difficult.
Too much.
But it was never their failure.
It was the system's failure to build the bridge.

Because a diagnosis is not just about data,
It's about dignity.
It's about language.
It's about saying: "I see you, and what you're experiencing is real."

Hot Flush, Cold Truth

And the longer we pretend the silence is harmless, the more women we lose.
Not because they're broken,
But because the system is.

Let's rebuild it.
From the bloodwork to the boardroom.
From the clinic to the classroom.
From the regions to the research grants.
Let's make menopause visible, not someday, but now.
Not just for ourselves, but for every woman who comes after us.

Chapter 11:
Pain in Private.
The Physical Cost of Silence

She didn't tell her manager why she stopped coming to meetings. She didn't tell her partner why she cried after school pickup. She didn't tell her doctor the full story; not because she didn't want to, but because she didn't have the words. Instead, she said she was tired. Stressed. Busy. She said what women have always said to keep the world comfortable while their bodies fell apart behind closed doors.

This is the quiet architecture of menopause in Australia:
Pain behind professionalism.
Bleeding behind boardrooms.
Dizziness behind the wheel.
Rage behind a smile.

Women are showing up in pain, every day, everywhere, and doing it silently. Not because they want to, but because they're expected to. Because the systems around them have made no room for their biology, their mess, their humanity.

And so they grit their teeth, self-manage, downplay, apologise, and disappear.

This chapter is about the toll that silence takes.
On their bodies.
On their lives.
On all of us.

When Resilience Is Just Silence in Disguise

Women are taught to be grateful for inclusion, even when that inclusion requires self-erasure. We reward them for not complaining. We praise their *"resilience"* while ignoring the structural violence of silence. But what we call *"resilience"* is often just compliance with systems that refuse to evolve. What's framed as **personal choice** is so often *structural inevitability*. Because when your body is crashing and your workplace has no name for it, let alone support for it, the only thing left to do is leave. And when they leave, they take with them more than just headcount. They take with them decades of knowledge. They take networks. They take wisdom. They take the future we were counting on.

These are not just human losses.
They are economic leaks.
They are leadership vacuums.
They are cultural failures.
And they are entirely preventable.
We cannot afford to lose one more woman to silence.
Not in healthcare.
Not in government.
Not in education.
Not in remote communities already underserved by the system.
Not in industries still run by legacy norms that pretend biology is neutral.

This isn't just a women's health issue.
It's a national capability issue.
A workforce retention issue.
A leadership pipeline issue.
A public safety issue.
An economic prosperity issue.
And if we don't act now, we will continue dismantling the very future we claim to champion.

It's time to replace shame with systems.
To swap whispered survival for structural reform.
To build workplaces that don't punish biology, but evolve with it.
Because the next woman walking out the door?
Might be the one you were relying on most.

The Business Case for Reform

When we support women through menopause, we don't just do the right thing, we do the smart thing.

Workplaces that acknowledge and accommodate the physiological realities of menopause aren't offering charity or bending the rules. They are future-proofing their workforce, fortifying leadership pipelines, and insulating their organisations against preventable financial loss.

Because when women feel safe, seen, and supported, they don't just stay.

They rise.
They lead.
They deliver more, influence more, and uplift those around them.
Yet too many employers are still blind to the cost of inaction, or worse, complicit in the quiet erosion of capability from their own ranks.

The $10 Billion Blind Spot

Let's set aside emotion for a moment, and speak the language of ledgers and logic. Each year, **menopause costs Australian businesses an estimated $10 billion** in lost productivity, increased absenteeism, presenteeism, and premature exits from the workforce. This figure is not hypothetical. It is the product of real-world modelling, workforce participation data, and the voices of women who leave not because they are underperforming, but because they are **under-supported**.

Every woman who walks quietly out the door takes with her:

• Decades of institutional knowledge

- High-trust client relationships
- Leadership continuity
- Diversity of thought
- And irreplaceable mentoring capital

In hard numbers, each early departure results in:

- Project delays
- Loss of IP
- Team destabilisation
- Recruitment costs
- Training and onboarding expenditure
- And reduced morale across teams

These are not soft losses.

They are bottom-line hits.

And let's not forget **presenteeism**, when women show up but cannot fully function due to unmanaged symptoms like insomnia, hot flushes, anxiety, and brain fog. This silent drain on performance metrics goes unreported in exit interviews, but shows up in missed KPIs, poor engagement scores, and spiralling turnover.

A 2023 UK study found that **one in ten women had left** their jobs due to menopause-related challenges, and *over 40% had seriously considered* it.

Apply those figures to your executive team, your STEM pipeline, your healthcare frontline, and the impact is not just financial.

It is systemic.

Retention Is Cheaper Than Replacement
The cost of replacing a senior woman can exceed *200%* of her annual salary. That includes advertising, recruitment, transition planning, productivity gaps, onboarding, and the risk to culture and continuity.

Now compare that to the cost of offering:

- Access to a menopause-literate doctor
- A flexible work arrangement during flare-ups
- Simple equipment like desk fans or breathable uniforms
- A supportive policy framework
- Education for managers to reduce stigma

We are not talking about gold-plated benefits.

We are talking about **practical, cost-effective, scalable strategies** that reduce attrition and maximise return on experience.

This isn't charity.

It's cost avoidance.

It's risk management.

It's workforce stability in action.

Midlife Is Not the Exit Point, It's the Leverage Point
Women in their 40s, 50s, and 60s often sit at the intersection of wisdom and influence. They've done the years. Built the skills. Navigated complex systems. They are not beginners, they are builders.

These are the women:

- Chairing your risk committees
- Leading your hospital wards
- Running entire departments
- Mentoring emerging leaders
- Carrying the load in households and communities
- Managing multiple generations at home and work

Yet they are often the first to disappear from senior roles, not due to a lack of capability, but due to workplaces that force them to choose between health and professionalism.

And here's what every boardroom needs to understand:

Support doesn't need to be complex.

Sometimes, it's as simple as:

- Flexible scheduling during symptom flare-ups
- Normalising conversations about hormone therapy
- Removing the side-eye in the staff bathroom for HRT patches
- Giving women agency in how, when, and where they work

None of these require dramatic overhaul. But the impact is exponential, not just for the woman, but for every team she leads, mentors, or inspires.

Health-Positive Cultures Drive High-Performance Results
When organisations take menopause seriously, they send a message that echoes far beyond the women experiencing it: *"Your full humanity is welcome here."* This message builds trust. And trust builds performance.

In today's labour market, where workers are seeking values alignment as much as salary, menopause-inclusive workplaces become:

- Talent magnets
- Brand builders
- Culture protectors
- Market leaders

They are seen as **progressive, human-centred, and modern**, not just in values, but in operations.

And as investors, stakeholders, and consumers grow more conscious of social impact, the organisations who act now will carry the **reputational capital** of having done the right thing before it became mandatory.

The Workforce Is Aging, and Evolving

Demographic trends don't lie. Women aged 45 to 64 are now one of the fastest-growing segments of the global workforce. They are also the most likely to occupy caregiving roles, professionally and personally, meaning they often represent the backbone of both our economy and our community fabric.

Ignore them, and you weaken your institution.

Support them, and you tap into a wellspring of:

- Capability
- Commitment
- Institutional continuity
- Strategic thinking
- And intergenerational mentoring

This is not about "retention at all costs."

It is about **retaining what matters most,** the people who already know how to make your business, agency, or institution work.

The Time to Act Is Now

The cost of inaction is no longer abstract.
It is written in resignation letters.
It is whispered in HR corridors.
It is felt in lost leadership potential and eroded team confidence.

We are at an inflection point.
Where once menopause was a private matter, now it is a public imperative.

This isn't just a health issue.

This is a leadership issue.
A productivity issue.
A legislative issue.
A *nation-building* issue.
If we do not act, we are knowingly presiding over a preventable erosion of capability in every sector of the economy.
And if we do?

We don't just support women.
We support families, teams, communities, and the national future they hold up.
This is not a *'nice to have.'*
This is a non-negotiable.

What Reform Looks Like

In my submission, I provided a blueprint. Not vague suggestions, **tangible reforms** for both government and the private sector, including:

- Dedicated reproductive health leave
- Menopause-aware workplace policies
- Inclusion of hormone health in Occupational Health and Safety frameworks
- Training for leaders, HR teams, and peer supports
- Flexible work arrangements during symptom escalation
- Access to evidence-based clinical care without stigma or delay

This is not revolutionary. It's overdue.

When Government Leads, Industry Follows

That's why I want to acknowledge the bold action of the Queensland Government under Premier Steven Miles, which has legislated reproductive health leave for all public servants, and crucially, made it inclusive of all genders.

From mammograms to menopause. From prostate checks to fertility screening.

This is health equity in action. This is what leadership looks like. When government policy reflects lived experience, the ripple effect is immense.

Now we need every jurisdiction, and every employer, to follow.

A Call to Leaders

If you are a CEO, a policymaker, a head of HR: This is your moment. You don't need to wait for legislation. You can make your workplace hormone-literate today. You can retain your women leaders by acknowledging their biological realities, and meeting them with support, not silence.

This chapter began with a number: $10 billion.

But it ends with a question: What is the true cost of not acting, and who pays the price?

Chapter 12:
Mind Fog, Mood Swings, and Mental Health

The Silent Collapse

It starts subtly. You forget a colleague's name mid-sentence. You reread the same paragraph three times before the words make sense. A sharpness you once relied on has softened, and you wonder if this is what burnout feels like. Or worse, the early signs of dementia.

At the same time, your emotions no longer feel predictable. A sudden wave of rage rises in a meeting over something trivial. A moment later, tears sting your eyes over an email you know isn't personal. To the outside world, it looks like instability. To you, it feels like losing yourself.

This is not coincidence. This is menopause in the brain.

The Brain on Estrogen

For decades, research has focused on estrogen as a reproductive hormone. Yet neuroscience is clear: estrogen directly affects neurotransmitters like serotonin, dopamine, and acetylcholine. These systems govern mood regulation, memory, and focus.

When estrogen levels fluctuate, and later decline, the brain's circuitry is disrupted. The result?

- Cognitive fog: Difficulty concentrating, memory lapses, slower processing.
- Mood instability: Anxiety, irritability, sudden depressive episodes.
- Sleep disturbance: Which compounds both cognitive and emotional symptoms.

What women describe as *"losing their edge"* is often a measurable neurological shift. Yet medicine rarely frames it this way. Instead, women are told they're stressed, overreacting, or "just aging."

Misdiagnosis: Depression or Depletion?

Primary care providers frequently reach for psychiatric explanations. Women present with anxiety, low mood, and fatigue, and leave with a prescription for antidepressants or sedatives.

The problem is not that these women are depressed. It's that their hormones are in transition. Antidepressants may blunt the symptoms, but they do not treat the cause. Worse, the woman begins to wonder if she is "mentally ill." The language of pathology compounds the stigma.

A study from the UK revealed that **one in four women in midlife are prescribed antidepressants**, often without a conversation about perimenopause. These prescriptions can mask the real issue and delay appropriate treatment such as hormone therapy

Antidepressant Prescriptions in Midlife Women

Country	% of Women 45–60 Prescribed Antidepressants	Notes
United Kingdom	25%	One in four women in midlife are on antidepressants, often without menopause being discussed.
Australia	22%	PBS data shows prescriptions peak for women aged 45–54.
United States	24%	CDC reports antidepressant use doubles in women over 40 compared to men.
Canada	20%	Similar patterns noted in Ontario health data.

Antidepressants are the frontline treatment for menopausal mental health symptoms, despite limited evidence that they address underlying hormonal causes.

Case Study 1: *"I thought it was early dementia"*
At 52, Anna* was a respected project manager leading a major IT rollout across three states. She had always been known for her memory, colleagues joked she was a walking filing cabinet. Then, almost overnight, she began to falter.

She forgot a colleague's name in the middle of a client presentation. She mislaid critical documents she had personally compiled. Words that had once flowed easily began to stall in her throat. At home, she wrote notes to herself on scraps of paper and hid them around the house, terrified she might forget the simplest of tasks.

Her first thought wasn't menopause. It was dementia. She didn't tell her team. She didn't tell her family. Quietly, she began researching nursing homes, fearing she might need one within a decade.

When she finally found the courage to speak to her GP, the response was swift: "You sound depressed. Let's start you on an antidepressant." She left with a prescription and a new identity, a woman with "mental illness."

Months later, still declining, she was referred to a menopause clinic. Within fifteen minutes, a specialist explained what was happening: her brain was starved of estrogen. With the right treatment, Anna's sharpness returned. Within weeks, she was back at work, astonished by the clarity that resurfaced.

"I lost almost two years of my life to fear," she said. "And it wasn't depression. It was menopause."
*Name changed for anonymity

At Work: The Performance Penalty

In workplaces built on constant cognitive output, fog and mood swings are unforgiving. Deadlines don't wait for hormones. A few patterns emerge:

- Women decline promotions, fearing they cannot handle the pressure.
- Memory lapses are misinterpreted as incompetence.
- Emotional shifts are read as "unprofessional."

One executive told me: *"I walked into a board meeting and couldn't remember the name of the company we were negotiating with. I had led the project for six months, and suddenly, it was gone. I felt humiliated. I left the room and handed my resignation in three weeks later."*

The talent pipeline shrinks not because these women lack ability, but because they lack recognition and support.

Case Study 2: *The teacher in the supply cupboard.*
Maria* loved teaching. For 25 years, she thrived in the classroom, improvising lessons, mentoring new teachers, and connecting with students others struggled to reach. But during perimenopause, her classroom became a battlefield she felt she was losing.

Her brain fog arrived suddenly. She would find herself mid-sentence, unable to remember the question she had asked only moments before. Her heart raced when a student raised their hand, not because she doubted their ability, but because she doubted her own.

During breaks, she hid in the supply cupboard. She leaned her back against the cool wall, trying to slow her breathing and clear the fog before the bell rang again.

"I was afraid a student would notice," she admitted. "I was terrified a parent would complain. I didn't want my colleagues to think I'd lost it."

No formal support was available. Her school had no menopause policy, no training for leaders, no space for disclosure. Maria resigned three years earlier than planned. The education system lost a devoted teacher, mentor, and role model, not because she couldn't teach, but because she couldn't hide her symptoms anymore.
*Name changed

Workplace Productivity Loss: Menopause and Mental Health

Factor	Estimated Impact	Source/Notes
Presenteeism (reduced focus, brain fog)	16-20 days per woman per year	UK Fawcett Society survey, 2023
Absenteeism (mental health leave, stress-related sick days)	3-5 days per woman per year	Australian Menopause Centre survey

Factor	Estimated Impact	Source/Notes
Early retirement due to unmanaged symptoms	10% of women leave workforce early	Chartered Institute of Personnel and Development (CIPD), UK
Talent leakage (women stepping back from promotions)	Up to 25% report declining opportunities	Deloitte Women @ Work Report, 2022

Takeaway: Productivity loss is not just physical symptoms, mental health dimensions amplify the economic impact.

Case Study 3: Union submission, 2023
In 2023, a major Australian union submitted evidence to a parliamentary inquiry on workplace barriers for women. Of the thousands of survey responses collected, menopause surfaced as an unexpected but consistent theme.

More than 20% of women surveyed said they had considered leaving their jobs because of unmanaged menopausal symptoms. The submission outlined:
- HR dismissing requests for flexible hours as "special treatment."
- Line managers minimising concerns: "Everyone gets moody sometimes."
- Colleagues attributing mistakes to incompetence rather than symptoms.

The union warned Parliament that without policy reform, industries risked losing a generation of senior female talent. "This is not just a women's issue," the submission argued. "It is a workforce sustainability issue."

Their recommendation was clear: legislate for menopause-friendly workplaces, just as has been done for pregnancy, disability, and mental health.

The Cost of Silence

The cultural framing of menopause as *"private"* adds another layer. Women are reluctant to disclose their struggles for fear of being seen as weak or unstable. The stigma of mental illness doubles the silence.

This has economic consequences. Mental health-related absenteeism and presenteeism cost billions annually. Layer menopause on top, and the numbers climb, yet few organisations account for this intersection.

Stories Behind the Stats
- A teacher who hides in the supply cupboard when brain fog overwhelms her in front of students.
- A nurse who begins to doubt her clinical judgment and quietly scales back her shifts.
- A manager who starts avoiding client pitches because she can no longer trust her recall.

These are not isolated failures of willpower. They are systemic failures to recognise the neurological impact of menopause.

What Needs to Change

1. **Clinical training**: GPs and psychiatrists must be taught to differentiate between depression and hormone-driven depletion.
2. **Workplace policies**: Mental health programs must include menopause as a legitimate factor.
3. **Research investment**: Fund studies into the cognitive and emotional dimensions of menopause, not just hot flushes and fertility.

4. **Narrative shift**: Stop telling women they're "unstable." Start recognising the neurological reality.

The Mandate for Mental Health

When women say, *"I feel like I'm losing my mind,"* they are not being dramatic. They are describing a physiological reality that medicine, workplaces, and culture have refused to see.

Menopause does not make women weak. What weakens them is silence, misdiagnosis, and the shame of being told their mental health is failing when in truth their biology is shifting.

Case Study 4: **The manager who walked away**
Clare* had been in finance her whole career. By 48, she was the only woman on her executive team and was proud to have broken barriers in a male-dominated sector.
Then came the board meeting she never forgot. She had led a six-month project evaluating a merger. As she presented the findings, a colleague asked for the name of the partner company. Her mind went blank.

It wasn't a slip. It was a blackout. She couldn't recall a single detail. Her vision blurred, her chest tightened, and she excused herself mid-meeting.

She never went back. Within three weeks, she handed in her resignation.

"I could have stayed if someone had told me what was happening," Clare reflected later. "I wasn't incompetent. I wasn't unprepared. I was in menopause. But no one said those words."

*Name change

The Hidden Economic Cost

Category	Annual Cost Estimate (Australia)	Details
Lost productivity (absenteeism + presenteeism)	$10 billion	Based on Treasury + workplace data
Mental health treatment misallocated (antidepressants, misdiagnosis)	$1-2 billion	Conservative PBS/MBS estimate
Loss of leadership pipeline (women exiting early)	Immeasurable	Decades of skill, mentorship, and institutional knowledge loss

Until we acknowledge the mind–menopause connection, we will continue to lose brilliant, capable women, not to illness, but to neglect.

Case Study 5: **Submission 185. Not broken women**
During Australia's Senate Inquiry into Menopause and Perimenopause, submissions poured in from across the nation. Among them was **Submission 185**, a striking reminder that behind every number is a human story.

"These are not broken women," the submission read. "These are experienced professionals who need time-limited support. With that, they can return to high performance, remain in leadership, and mentor the next generation."

Placed in the official record, Submission 185 gave policymakers what too many women had been denied: recognition.

Chapter 13: Stigma in the Staffroom. The Cost of Shame at Work

In 2009, I often commuted to work by bus into Melbourne's CBD. Each morning I stood at the bus stop with colleagues, chatting casually as we waited. One of them, Anne, had always been vibrant, warm, and friendly. Then, one day, she stopped talking to me.

At first, I thought I had done something wrong. She began standing off to the side, in quiet isolation. I was in my mid-thirties at the time. Menopause was not even on my radar, and it certainly was not something spoken about openly.

Over time I noticed that Anne carried a small cabin-sized suitcase to work each day. I could not understand why. Almost a year passed before I finally found the courage to ask her why she kept her distance and why she always travelled with luggage.

Her answer has stayed with me ever since. Anne told me, with sadness in her eyes, that she had to use the bike room showers three to four times a day because of uncontrollable sweating. Her suitcase carried multiple changes of clothes. She would buy the same outfits in bulk so that no one would notice she was changing.

Anne confessed she had kept her distance from me and others because she was terrified her sweat made her smell offensive. She told me it was the loneliest year of her life. She withdrew from social circles, avoided conversations, and carried her struggle alone.

That was my first real encounter with menopause. And all I learned at the time was this: menopause meant sweat, smell, and shame. I was failed by my lack of knowledge. Anne was failed by a world that gave her no safe space, no language, and no dignity to speak about what she was going through.

The Culture of Shame

Anne's story is far from unique. Across workplaces, menopause is cloaked in silence and shame. Symptoms that should be recognised as part of a natural transition are

209

instead treated as character flaws. Hot flushes become the subject of office jokes. Mood swings are dismissed as being "hormonal" or "unstable." When memory falters, it is not understood as brain fog but labelled as incompetence or carelessness. The normal physiology of midlife is transformed into a stigma, and women pay the price.

This stigma does not appear overnight. It is created by cultures where difference is mocked, where health is only acknowledged when it is visible, and where silence is safer than disclosure. In many workplaces, menopause is still a taboo subject. Colleagues are uncomfortable mentioning it, managers are untrained to respond to it, and women absorb the message that their symptoms must be hidden at all costs.

When this kind of culture takes hold, women withdraw. Like Anne, they step away from conversations, not because they have nothing to say, but because they fear their bodies will betray them. A hot flush during a presentation, a lapse in memory at a meeting, or a wave of irritability in a busy office can become moments of humiliation rather than opportunities for support. The safest response is silence.

But silence is not neutral. Silence compounds the impact of symptoms. A woman who hides her struggles also hides her strengths. She loses confidence, stops speaking up in meetings, and avoids leadership opportunities. She withdraws from the informal networks where decisions are shaped, the staffroom chat, the after-work drinks, the quick exchange in the hallway. The workplace loses her presence long before it loses her employment.

Research confirms what many women already know. In surveys across Australia, the UK, and the US, more than half of working women say they feel unable to discuss menopause symptoms with their employer. The stigma is so entrenched that many would rather leave quietly than risk being seen as "difficult" or "past it." The cost is not just personal but organisational. Companies lose experienced staff, valuable mentors, and future leaders because shame drives women into early exits.

The tragedy is that these losses are entirely preventable. What makes a woman step back is not the symptom itself but the fear of how others will interpret it. A hot flush does not end a career. The ridicule attached to it can. Brain fog does not erase decades of skill. But if it is treated as incompetence, the result is the same.

The culture of shame teaches women to internalise blame for a process that is universal. It tells them to manage their symptoms in secret, to buy extra uniforms, to shower three times a day, to sit alone in their cars at lunch. It strips them of dignity at the very moment they most need compassion and understanding.

Until this culture shifts, no amount of policy change will be enough. Women do not just need access to leave entitlements or workplace adjustments. They need environments where they can exist without fear of being mocked, marginalised, or misunderstood. Breaking the culture of shame requires more than words on paper. It requires leaders, colleagues, and workplaces willing to replace silence with conversation and stigma with dignity.

The Silence Effect

Silence is one of the most common survival strategies women adopt when faced with menopause at work. It is not silence chosen freely but silence imposed by culture. When jokes, dismissive comments, or outright ignorance surround menopause, women quickly learn that disclosure is risky. They weigh the cost of being open against the fear of being judged, and in most workplaces the calculation falls on the side of secrecy.

This silence can take many forms. Some women conceal their symptoms entirely, pushing through as though nothing is happening. Others find ways to mask them: keeping fans hidden in their desk drawers, sneaking away to change clothes, or using medical leave days without explanation. A few attempt to speak up but retreat after a dismissive response from a colleague or manager. The message is reinforced, "don't talk about it."

The problem with silence is that it does not make symptoms disappear. It only makes the woman disappear. She stops contributing in the same way, becomes less visible in meetings, and avoids situations where her symptoms might betray her. She may no longer volunteer for high-stakes projects or speaking roles. In effect, silence diminishes her professional presence, shrinking her career opportunities alongside her confidence.

This loss of voice has ripple effects. The staffroom, once a place of camaraderie, becomes a space of quiet withdrawal. Women choose to eat lunch alone rather than risk sweating in front of colleagues. They skip networking events because they fear hot flushes in crowded rooms. They avoid car-pooling to conferences in case they need space to recover from a sudden wave of anxiety. The workplace loses not only their labour but their social presence, their mentoring capacity, and their informal leadership.

The silence also isolates women emotionally. Without trusted colleagues to confide in, symptoms feel heavier, shame deepens, and resilience wanes. Many describe menopause as one of the loneliest times of their lives, not because they lacked medical options, but because they lacked anyone to talk to about what was happening. As one woman in a union submission put it: *"I wasn't afraid of the symptoms. I was afraid of the jokes."*

This pattern of withdrawal is confirmed by research. Surveys show that more than 60 per cent of women experiencing menopause do not feel comfortable discussing it with their employer. Nearly half say they fear it would harm their career. Silence becomes a protective shield, but it is one that cuts women off from the very supports that might help them remain in work.

The economic consequences are profound. When women remain silent, organisations fail to see the problem and therefore fail to act. Absenteeism is misattributed to other causes. Turnover is chalked up to "personal reasons." Promotions go unfilled because talented candidates never put themselves forward. The silence disguises a systemic issue as individual failure, and businesses absorb the cost without ever understanding its cause.

Perhaps most damaging is the way silence reinforces stigma. Each time a woman hides her symptoms, the myth persists that menopause is rare, irrelevant, or unworthy of attention. Colleagues and leaders remain unaware of its prevalence, and the cycle of ignorance continues. Silence protects the individual in the short term but perpetuates the cultural neglect in the long term.

Breaking the silence requires both individual courage and institutional change. Women must feel safe enough to speak, and workplaces must provide environments where that speech is met with respect. This is not about forcing disclosure but about creating conditions where it is possible. Managers need training to recognise menopause as a legitimate workplace issue. Policies should explicitly include menopause in wellbeing and diversity frameworks. Most importantly, leaders must model openness, sending a clear signal that silence is no longer the only option.

The silence effect is not inevitable. It is the result of choices made by organisations and cultures that prefer discomfort to dialogue. Changing those choices can transform silence into conversation, isolation into community, and shame into dignity. Until that happens, women will continue to carry the burden alone, retreating into quiet survival at the very moment they should be thriving.

Case Study 6: **The Teacher Who Stopped Eating Lunch**
For more than twenty years, Helen* loved her job as a high school teacher in regional Queensland. She thrived in the classroom, guiding students through literature and history,

mentoring younger teachers, and being part of a staffroom community that had always felt like a second family.

But as she entered her late forties, Helen's relationship with the staffroom changed. Hot flushes began to arrive without warning. Sweat would soak through her blouse within minutes. On humid days, she felt like she was burning from the inside out. The embarrassment became unbearable.

At first, Helen tried to laugh it off. She kept a small desk fan in her classroom and opened windows whenever possible. But the staffroom was harder. Surrounded by colleagues, she became convinced they noticed her flushed face, damp clothes, and constant trips to the bathroom.

One afternoon, after overhearing a passing comment, *"She's always fanning herself"*, Helen decided she could not face the staffroom anymore. She stopped joining her colleagues for lunch. Instead, she walked to the school car park, climbed into her car, and ate alone with the air conditioning blasting.

"It wasn't the symptoms that hurt me most," she said. "It was the shame of thinking everyone was laughing at me."

Days turned into months. While her colleagues chatted over sandwiches and shared stories about students, Helen sat in her car, isolated. She missed the jokes, the camaraderie, and the informal networks where so much of school life was shaped. More than once she wondered if her absence was costing her opportunities, committee roles, leadership chances, the subtle endorsements that come from being visible.

By the time she eventually opened up to another teacher she trusted, nearly a year had passed. "I thought I was the only one," she admitted. Her colleague, ten years older, smiled sadly. She too had spent time hiding her symptoms, though she had never confessed it to anyone before.

Helen's story shows how stigma pushes women out of the heart of their workplaces, even if they never leave their jobs. Menopause did not make her less of a teacher. Shame made her less visible. The cost was not just hers but the school's, which lost the benefit of her leadership in those invisible spaces where culture is shaped.

The Systemic Blind Spot

Stigma and silence do not exist in isolation. They are reinforced by structures that have, for decades, failed to recognise menopause as a legitimate workplace or health issue. The absence of clear policy, training, and leadership leaves women to navigate this transition alone. This is the systemic blind spot: not seeing menopause as part of the working life course, and therefore failing to design workplaces, health systems, and social policies that acknowledge its impact.

Policies That Pretend Menopause Does Not Exist

Most workplaces have well-developed frameworks for maternity leave, parental support, disability accommodations, and mental health. These are now considered standard inclusions in human resources manuals and diversity policies. Yet menopause, a stage that affects half the population and intersects with decades of working life, is absent in many of these documents.

This omission is not neutral. By leaving menopause out of the official language of policy, organisations send a message that it is not a valid category of need. Women are left to piece together accommodations informally, often negotiating in private with sympathetic managers or using unrelated leave categories. Some disguise sick leave as "flu" or "stress." Others draw on disability provisions not designed for hormonal transition. The result is patchwork support, dependent on individual goodwill rather than structural recognition.

Diversity Dashboards and Invisible Data

The oversight is also visible in the data organisations collect. Diversity dashboards proudly track gender, ethnicity, age, and sometimes disability. Yet menopause is invisible in most of these systems. When metrics are missing, so too is accountability.

Without measurement, leaders can claim there is no problem. If exit interviews do not ask about menopause, women who resign due to unmanaged symptoms are recorded as leaving for "personal reasons." If absenteeism data does not include menopause categories, organisations misinterpret patterns of sick leave. The silence becomes institutionalised.

This blind spot perpetuates a dangerous myth: that menopause is a private matter with no bearing on organisational performance. In reality, the hidden data tells another story, one of lost productivity, early retirements, and diminished leadership pipelines. But without systemic recognition, these losses are never attributed to their real cause.

Union Evidence and Public Submissions

The gap is not just anecdotal. Unions and professional bodies have begun highlighting the issue in formal submissions to government inquiries. In the Australian Senate Inquiry into Menopause and Perimenopause, multiple unions reported that members felt unprotected by workplace policies. Nurses described working long shifts in uniforms that offered no flexibility, with no provisions for additional breaks. Retail workers reported that hot flushes and brain fog were treated as incompetence rather than health challenges. Public servants admitted they had avoided applying for promotions because they feared their symptoms would be seen as weakness.

These submissions are powerful because they move the issue from the private to the public domain. They make clear that the problem is not simply individual sensitivity but systemic neglect. When an entire profession reports stigma, the issue is cultural and structural.

Healthcare as a Parallel Blind Spot

The workplace is not the only site of omission. The health system itself demonstrates the same blind spot, and in many ways it is the root of the problem. When medicine fails to take menopause seriously, that neglect filters directly into workplaces, shaping how women are treated and whether they are believed.

Medical Education: Six Hours for Half a Lifetime
Medical education devotes shockingly limited time to menopause. A general practitioner in Australia may graduate with less than six hours of formal training on the topic, despite the fact that more than 50 per cent of their patient base will experience menopause. In some programs, menopause is bundled into a single lecture under "women's health," squeezed between obstetrics and contraception. The message is implicit: menopause is not an urgent or complex area of medicine, but a side note.

The consequence is that women in midlife walk into consulting rooms and are met by doctors who have not been taught to recognise, diagnose, or treat their symptoms. Hot flushes are misattributed to stress. Insomnia is explained away as lifestyle imbalance. Anxiety and low mood are categorised as depression. The absence of training becomes the absence of care.

Psychiatric Frameworks and the DSM Gap
This blind spot is codified in psychiatric frameworks. The DSM, psychiatry's diagnostic bible, includes conditions like premenstrual dysphoric disorder (PMDD), recognising that hormones can play a significant role in mood and mental

health. Yet menopause-related mental health conditions are excluded. This sends a powerful message: perimenopausal anxiety or depression is not a "real" category, not deserving of formal recognition or research.

Women experiencing panic attacks, intrusive thoughts, or cognitive fog during menopause often find themselves treated as psychiatric patients rather than as individuals undergoing a biological transition. Antidepressants and sedatives are prescribed as the first line of response. For some women, these medications may offer short-term relief, but they do not address the underlying hormonal shifts. Worse, they can create a false narrative that the woman is mentally ill, rather than hormonally depleted.

Pharmaceutical Priorities
Pharmaceutical research tells the same story. Investment in medications for erectile dysfunction has been vast, generating billions in profits and innovation. By contrast, hormone therapy for women has been underfunded, politicised, and neglected. The Women's Health Initiative study of 2002, later criticised for flawed methodology and overstated risks, created decades of fear around hormone replacement therapy. Even now, many doctors remain hesitant to prescribe HRT, and pharmaceutical companies are cautious about investing in new options.
The result is a treatment landscape shaped by avoidance rather than innovation. Women are left with fewer choices, outdated therapies, and ongoing uncertainty about safety and efficacy. Meanwhile, men's midlife sexual health is treated as an urgent priority worthy of global research funding.

How Medical Neglect Flows Back into Workplaces
This medical neglect does not stay within clinic walls. It has direct consequences in workplaces. When women seek medical certificates to explain their symptoms, doctors often provide vague notes citing "stress" or "fatigue" rather than naming menopause. This absence of medical legitimacy

undermines women's ability to request workplace accommodations. Employers may dismiss requests for flexibility or adjustments because there is no formal medical documentation to support them.

Equally, when antidepressants are prescribed instead of hormonal care, women may struggle with side effects that compound rather than alleviate their difficulties. Drowsiness, emotional flatness, and reduced cognitive sharpness are hardly compatible with the demands of modern work. In this way, the health system's failure becomes a workplace failure, trapping women between inadequate treatment and inadequate support.

The Personal Toll
Consider the story of one public servant who described visiting three different doctors before anyone mentioned menopause. In the meantime, she was prescribed sleeping tablets for her insomnia, antidepressants for her anxiety, and iron supplements for her fatigue. None worked. She continued to struggle at work, missing deadlines and avoiding meetings. Only after finally finding a menopause specialist did she receive hormone therapy, which transformed her quality of life within weeks. "I lost two years of my career," she said. "Not because of menopause, but because no one named it."

Her story is echoed across industries. Nurses who cannot concentrate on long shifts. Teachers who are too exhausted to prepare lessons. Executives who decline promotions because they fear their memory lapses will be misinterpreted. These are not failures of will or competence. They are failures of systems that refuse to provide timely, accurate, and compassionate care.

The Mandate for Medical Reform
If workplaces are to change, healthcare must change first. Doctors need comprehensive training in menopause management. Psychiatric frameworks must include

menopause-related conditions. Pharmaceutical research must prioritise safe, innovative treatments that reflect the scale of the issue.

Without these reforms, women will remain caught in the gap, misdiagnosed, mistreated, and misunderstood. They will continue to be told they are depressed when they are depleted, anxious when they are hormonally destabilised, and incompetent when they are simply unsupported.
The health system's blind spot is not a clinical inconvenience. It is a structural failure that ripples outward, shaping workplace cultures and perpetuating stigma. Until it is corrected, women will continue to pay the price with their health, their careers, and their dignity.

Why the Blind Spot Persists

Despite decades of progress in gender equity, menopause has remained in the shadows. It is not absent by accident. It has been systematically excluded from medicine, workplaces, and culture for reasons that are historical, cultural, economic, and institutional. Understanding why the blind spot persists is critical to dismantling it.

Historical Exclusion: Medicine Designed for Men
The first reason menopause has remained invisible is the long-standing exclusion of women's health from mainstream medical research. For much of the twentieth century, clinical trials deliberately excluded women of childbearing age, citing "hormonal fluctuations" as a confounding factor. While this may have simplified study design, it created a devastating gap in knowledge.

Men's bodies became the baseline for medical understanding. Women's bodies were treated as deviations, complex, unpredictable, and secondary. Reproductive health was studied in the context of fertility and childbirth, but the midlife transition of menopause was ignored. This exclusion has had ripple effects that continue today.

When doctors are trained on male-centric data, they enter practice unprepared to recognise and treat menopause. Research funding priorities mirror the bias: heart disease in men receives billions in investment, while menopause receives a fraction. The result is predictable, when women present with symptoms, they are misdiagnosed, dismissed, or treated with Tools designed for conditions that are not their own.

This historical exclusion is not confined to healthcare. Workplaces, too, were designed by and for male bodies. Air conditioning systems, office temperatures, protective equipment, and uniforms have traditionally been calibrated for the average male worker. Policies were written with maternity in mind, but rarely with menopause. The legacy of this design persists, embedding a structural blind spot that women are still paying for.

Cultural Taboos: Aging, Reproduction, and the Female Body
The second reason for the blind spot is cultural. Menopause sits at the intersection of three enduring taboos: aging, reproduction, and the female body.

Western culture idolises youth. Women are praised for looking younger than their age and pressured to conceal the signs of growing older. Wrinkles, grey hair, and hormonal change are framed as decline. To admit menopause is to admit aging, and in societies that value women for fertility and beauty, aging is too often equated with loss of worth.

Reproduction carries its own silence. For centuries, topics related to menstruation, pregnancy, miscarriage, and menopause have been spoken of in hushed tones, if at all. Language itself reflects stigma: "the change," "the time of life," "getting older." Few cultures name menopause plainly, and in some languages there is no direct word for it. Silence perpetuates itself.

The female body remains a site of discomfort. Menstrual blood, vaginal dryness, hot flushes, sweating, these are natural processes, yet they evoke shame in professional settings. A man sweating in a suit is under pressure; a woman sweating at a meeting is "embarrassing." A man forgetting a detail is "busy"; a woman forgetting a detail is "losing it." Taboos magnify the stigma of symptoms, pushing them out of sight.

These cultural silences mean that menopause rarely enters public discourse. Media representations are sparse and often comic. Health campaigns spotlight breast cancer and pregnancy but not menopause. Even women themselves may struggle to share openly, having absorbed the belief that their symptoms are shameful. The culture makes the silence feel natural, when in fact it is constructed.

Economic Convenience: The Cost of Recognition
The third reason the blind spot persists is economic convenience. Recognising menopause would require investment, in training, in flexible policies, in workplace accommodations, in medical research. For organisations and governments managing tight budgets, ignoring menopause is cheaper.

To acknowledge menopause as a workplace issue would mean introducing menopause leave, providing training for managers, adjusting uniforms, and embedding menopause in diversity frameworks. These measures cost money. Leaders, especially in industries with thin margins, may prefer to look away rather than commit resources.

In healthcare, recognising menopause requires funding specialist clinics, revising medical curricula, and supporting hormone therapy access. Pharmaceutical companies would need to invest in research and development of new treatments. Compared to blockbuster drugs like statins or erectile dysfunction pills, the financial incentive to innovate in menopause care has been limited.

This economic neglect is short-sighted. The cost of doing nothing is higher in the long run: billions lost in productivity, healthcare misallocation, and premature retirements. Yet because these costs are diffuse and hidden, they rarely appear in balance sheets. Silence remains the cheaper option, at least on paper.

Institutional Inertia: The Path of Least Resistance
Perhaps the most insidious reason the blind spot persists is inertia. Change requires energy, leadership, and the willingness to disrupt established norms. In the absence of visible pressure, most institutions default to the path of least resistance: doing nothing.

Workplaces argue that because menopause has never been part of their frameworks, there is no precedent for including it now. Medical schools claim there is no time in already crowded curricula to expand training. Pharmaceutical companies point to outdated studies as justification for avoiding risk. The circular logic is familiar: we don't act because we've never acted, and because we've never acted, we don't need to act.

Inertia is reinforced by a lack of visible advocacy. Until recently, few women spoke openly about menopause in public forums. Without organised voices, the issue remained fragmented, private struggles rather than collective demands. Organisations respond to pressure; in the absence of pressure, inertia wins.

The Gendered Double Standard
Overlaying all of these reasons is a striking double standard. Male midlife conditions, from erectile dysfunction to testosterone decline, are treated with urgency. Campaigns normalise treatment, pharmaceutical investment surges, and men are encouraged to seek help.

By contrast, women's midlife transition is trivialised or pathologised. Instead of being met with evidence-based support, women are handed antidepressants or told to "manage stress." This double standard is not accidental. It reflects deeper biases about whose health matters, whose productivity is valued, and whose bodies are considered worthy of investment.

The Price of Blindness

The persistence of this blind spot has profound consequences. Women lose confidence, withdraw from workplaces, and leave careers prematurely. Organisations lose talent, leadership, and institutional memory. Health systems waste billions on misdiagnoses and inappropriate treatments. Families absorb the hidden labour of supporting women who are left without care.

Most importantly, women lose dignity. To suffer in silence is not just a professional cost; it is a human cost. Every time a woman hides her symptoms, she is carrying the weight of a system that refuses to acknowledge her.

Towards Breaking the Cycle

If the blind spot has persisted for historical, cultural, economic, and institutional reasons, then dismantling it requires action on all four fronts. Medical research must include women at every stage of life. Cultural campaigns must normalise menopause as a shared human experience. Economic frameworks must calculate the real cost of neglect, not just the upfront cost of reform. Institutions must overcome inertia by embedding menopause into policies, curricula, and strategies.

This is not just about fairness. It is about building systems that reflect reality. Half the population will experience menopause. To continue excluding it is neither rational nor sustainable.

The blind spot persists because it has been convenient, comfortable, and culturally reinforced. But convenience is no longer an excuse. In a world demanding equity and inclusion, the ongoing neglect of menopause is indefensible.

Towards Systemic Recognition

The blind spot is not inevitable. It has been constructed over decades through choices: to omit, to overlook, to trivialise, and to remain silent. What has been excluded can be included. What has been ignored can be seen. Recognition is a matter of deliberate action.

To dismantle the systemic neglect of menopause, reform must be pursued across multiple domains: **workplaces, healthcare, education, unions, research, and cultural discourse**. Each area reinforces the others. Workplaces cannot fully address menopause without medical legitimacy. Healthcare cannot treat it seriously without policy support. Policy cannot change without collective voices demanding reform. Systemic recognition means aligning all these domains so women are no longer left to carry the burden alone.

1. Workplaces: From Silence to Structure
HR Policies and Explicit Inclusion
At present, menopause is often absent from HR policies. Where it appears, it is buried under "wellbeing" or "general health" clauses. True systemic recognition requires explicit acknowledgement. Just as maternity leave is named and codified, menopause must be named. Naming creates visibility, and visibility creates legitimacy.

Policies should outline:
- **Flexible working arrangements** for those experiencing severe symptoms.

- **Access to leave** that is menopause-specific, not forced into the categories of "stress" or "sick leave."
- **Adjustments to uniforms and workplace environments**, such as breathable fabrics, temperature control, and rest spaces.
- **Manager training requirements** to ensure empathy and informed support.

Diversity Dashboards: Measuring What Matters

Organisations often boast of diversity dashboards that track gender, race, and disability. But menopause rarely appears. Without data, leaders claim there is no problem. Including menopause-related metrics would make its impact visible.

For example:
- Exit interviews should ask directly whether menopause influenced resignation.
- Employee surveys should include questions about comfort in discussing symptoms.
- Absenteeism reporting should allow menopause to be recorded as a legitimate cause.

When measured, patterns emerge. Leaders see where they are losing talent. Patterns create accountability.

Workplace Culture and Leadership

Policies alone are not enough. Culture determines whether those policies work. Leaders must normalise menopause conversations by modelling openness and dignity. This does not mean managers should pry, but that they should create environments where disclosure is safe.

For instance, when a CEO or senior leader references menopause during a diversity address, it signals that the issue is legitimate. When HR includes menopause in induction materials, it sets the tone from day one. Recognition begins with leadership demonstrating that menopause is not a private burden but a shared organisational concern.

Case Example: UK Menopause Policies

In the UK, several companies have introduced menopause-specific policies. The banking sector, retail chains, and even law firms have embedded training for managers and created leave entitlements. Early research shows improved retention, higher employee satisfaction, and reduced stigma. Australia and other nations can learn from these initiatives and adapt them to local contexts.

Unions and Collective Bargaining

Individual goodwill is never enough. Systemic recognition requires collective protections. Unions play a critical role in embedding menopause into workplace agreements.

In Australia, union submissions to the Senate inquiry highlighted the need for:
- Menopause leave clauses in enterprise bargaining agreements.
- Workplace adjustments for uniforms, breaks, and hours.
- Inclusion of menopause in occupational health and safety standards.

When protections are collectively bargained, they cannot be withdrawn at the whim of a manager. They become enforceable rights. This transforms menopause support from a discretionary benefit into a structural guarantee.

Healthcare Reform: Closing the Clinical Gap

Workplaces cannot succeed without healthcare reform. If doctors dismiss menopause, workplaces lack the medical legitimacy to act. Systemic recognition requires healthcare to catch up.

Expanding Medical Education

Medical curricula must include comprehensive menopause training. Not as a footnote, but as a core competency. General practitioners should graduate with the ability to:

- Diagnose perimenopause and menopause accurately.
- Distinguish between hormonal symptoms and psychiatric conditions.
- Prescribe evidence-based treatments, including HRT, safely and confidently.

Specialists, psychiatrists, cardiologists, endocrinologists, must understand the systemic impact of estrogen decline. Training should not end at graduation; continuing education programs must include menopause as standard.

Psychiatric Frameworks: Naming What Exists

The DSM and ICD must include menopause-related mental health conditions. Without diagnostic categories, women's suffering is pathologised incorrectly. Recognition in psychiatric frameworks would legitimise research funding, clinical pathways, and insurance coverage.

Pharmaceutical Investment

Pharmaceutical research must prioritise menopause with the same urgency granted to erectile dysfunction or fertility. New hormone therapies, non-hormonal alternatives, and personalised treatments are needed. Regulatory agencies must balance caution with innovation, avoiding another decades-long freeze like that caused by the flawed Women's Health Initiative study.

The Workplace-Healthcare Feedback Loop

Healthcare reform would directly strengthen workplaces. Doctors could provide medical certificates naming menopause, enabling accommodations. Accurate treatment would reduce absenteeism and presenteeism. Legitimate diagnostic categories would give HR teams evidence to justify support programs. Healthcare and workplace recognition reinforce each other in a cycle of visibility.

Research and Data: Funding What Matters

Recognition requires evidence, and evidence requires funding. Currently, menopause research is underfunded relative to its prevalence. Governments must allocate research grants to study:

- Cognitive and mental health impacts of menopause.
- Effective workplace accommodations.
- Long-term economic costs of unmanaged symptoms.
- Best-practice treatments across diverse populations.

Without research, policy is anecdotal. With research, reform becomes inevitable. Numbers, when made visible, cannot be ignored.

Cultural and Public Recognition

Systemic recognition also requires a cultural shift. Public health campaigns have normalised breast cancer screening, safe sex, and mental health awareness. Menopause deserves the same. Campaigns should:

- Use plain language to describe symptoms.
- Share stories of women across professions and cultures.
- Challenge stereotypes that frame menopause as decline.
- Position menopause as a shared issue that affects families, workplaces, and economies.

Media representation must expand beyond jokes or stereotypes. Education campaigns in schools should teach adolescents about menopause, just as they learn about puberty. Recognition must begin early, so silence does not pass from one generation to the next.

Global Lessons

Recognition is uneven worldwide. In Japan, cultural attitudes emphasise endurance, leading to silence. In the UK, workplace reform is advancing faster than in Australia. In some Indigenous cultures, menopause is framed as a transition into wisdom and authority, offering alternative models that honour rather than diminish women.

Australia can draw from these global lessons:
- Learn from the UK's policy innovations.
- Challenge Western taboos by amplifying Indigenous and multicultural perspectives.
- Position menopause not as decline, but as transformation.

Overcoming Inertia

Finally, systemic recognition requires confronting inertia. The path of least resistance has always been silence. To break it, we must create visible pressure. Advocacy groups, professional organisations, and women themselves must demand reform. Policymakers must be held accountable. Employers must be challenged by unions, regulators, and public opinion.

Change is always resisted until it becomes unavoidable. The goal is to make menopause recognition unavoidable.

From Blind Spot to Blueprint

The blind spot is not natural. It is manufactured through omission and neglect. To dismantle it, we need a blueprint for recognition.

- **Workplaces** must revise HR policies, collect data, and lead cultural change.
- **Unions** must secure enforceable protections.
- **Healthcare** must expand training, revise frameworks, and invest in treatment.
- **Research** must fund menopause at the scale of its impact.

- **Culture** must normalise conversation and reject stigma.
- **Global comparisons** must inspire adaptation and reform.
- **Advocacy** must keep pressure constant to overcome inertia.

Systemic recognition is possible. It requires choice. The choice to see what has been invisible. The choice to name what has been silenced. The choice to design workplaces, health systems, and cultures that reflect reality: half the population will experience menopause. Ignoring it is no longer an option.

The task ahead is not merely to include menopause in policies and frameworks but to reframe it as a central element of human experience. Recognition is not a gift to women. It is the fulfilment of a long-denied obligation. It is the difference between silence and dignity, between loss and leadership, between a system that erases and a system that sustains.

Until we choose systemic recognition, women will continue to carry the cost of neglect. When we do choose it, we will not only transform workplaces and healthcare, we will transform culture itself.

Seeing What Has Been Ignored
The systemic blind spot has persisted for so long that many assume it is natural. But it is not natural, it is constructed. By failing to see menopause as part of the working life course, organisations and health systems have built structures that push women into silence, resignation, and loss.

To correct this, we must name what has been ignored. We must bring menopause out of the shadows of policy and into the centre of organisational and medical design. Until then, stigma will remain, silence will deepen, and women will continue to bear the burden of a system that chooses not to see them.

The Cost of Shame

Stigma is not harmless. It carries a price that is paid in silence, in lost opportunities, and in wasted human potential. When shame becomes the filter through which women experience menopause at work, the cost ripples outward, not just to the individual, but to families, organisations, and society as a whole.

1. The Economic Cost
Economists have begun to put numbers to what women have always known intuitively: stigma affects performance. Presenteeism is one of the clearest indicators. Women show up to work but hide their symptoms, reducing focus and productivity. Tasks take longer, memory falters, energy wanes. Instead of being open about what they are experiencing, women spend cognitive energy concealing it. That concealment itself drains performance.

Turnover is another economic consequence. Women resign earlier than planned to escape hostile environments. Many leave at the peak of their careers, when decades of expertise are finally ripening. The exit costs are high: recruitment, retraining, and lost continuity.

Leadership leakage is the third pillar. Talented women decline promotions to avoid the spotlight. Nearly one in four women, according to Deloitte's Women @ Work report, have turned down opportunities due to unmanaged symptoms. This loss is harder to measure in balance sheets but devastating in impact. Every leadership role declined is a mentorship lost, an innovation missed, a decision shaped without the full diversity of perspective.

But economics is only one layer. The cost of shame cannot be tallied in dollars alone.

2. The Emotional Cost

Shame is corrosive. It eats away at confidence, distorts identity, and narrows self-belief. Women who once thrived in their roles begin to second-guess themselves. They wonder if they are becoming incompetent, when in fact they are simply unsupported.

This emotional toll manifests in anxiety before presentations, dread of team meetings, and fear of being "found out." Women describe sitting in meetings rehearsing what they will say in their heads, terrified that brain fog will strike. They go home exhausted not only from the day's work but from the effort of hiding.

The emotional cost also spreads into personal life. Partners and families may see irritability or withdrawal without understanding its cause. Friendships can fracture under the weight of silence. Shame is isolating, and isolation is emotionally depleting.

3. The Health Cost

The link between stigma and health is profound. Women who feel ashamed are less likely to seek medical help. They delay appointments, downplay symptoms, or accept inadequate treatment because they fear judgment. The result is untreated or undertreated health conditions: insomnia, depression, cardiovascular risk, osteoporosis.
In the workplace, shame can prevent women from requesting accommodations that would improve their wellbeing. A woman who hides her symptoms rather than asking for flexibility may push herself to exhaustion. Over time, this accelerates burnout and contributes to long-term disability.

There is also a mental health toll. Shame is strongly correlated with depression and anxiety. When women internalise the idea that they are failing or inadequate, their risk of clinical mental health conditions rises.

4. The Relational Cost

Shame changes relationships. In the staffroom, women may withdraw, skipping lunches and social conversations. In leadership circles, they may stop networking, missing the informal interactions that shape careers. At home, relationships with partners, children, and friends can be strained by mood swings, fatigue, or withdrawal that go unexplained.

Colleagues misinterpret this withdrawal. They may see aloofness, disinterest, or lack of team spirit, when in fact it is self-protection. The relational cost is trust lost, bonds frayed, and connections severed. Over time, this erodes team cohesion and workplace culture.

5. The Cultural Cost
When workplaces allow menopause stigma to persist, they perpetuate a culture that tells women their bodies are a liability. This culture teaches younger women to fear aging and teaches men to dismiss their colleagues' experiences.

The cultural cost is a workplace where inclusion is shallow. Diversity statements ring hollow when half the workforce is invisible at midlife. Cultures of silence replicate themselves: younger women watch how their older colleagues are treated and learn to keep quiet about their own health struggles.

In broader society, the cultural cost is the reinforcement of taboos. Media coverage remains sparse. Policy reform stalls. Without cultural change, systemic recognition cannot take hold.

6. The Generational Cost
Shame not only affects those currently experiencing menopause, it shapes the expectations of the next generation. Daughters watch mothers suffer in silence and absorb the lesson that their own transitions will be private struggles. Sons grow up unaware of the realities of menopause and carry that ignorance into adulthood, workplaces, and leadership roles.

When knowledge is not passed down, each generation starts from scratch. This generational amnesia ensures the cycle of silence continues. The cost is a future where stigma persists unless it is consciously broken.

7. The Organisational Cost
From an organisational perspective, stigma undermines everything diversity initiatives are meant to achieve. Retention strategies fail when women exit mid-career. Leadership programs lose participants when women decline opportunities. Innovation stalls when experienced voices are absent.

Reputation is also at stake. Organisations that fail to address menopause risk being seen as out of touch. Younger employees, increasingly values-driven, may choose to work elsewhere. In a competitive labour market, being known as a workplace that shames women is not just morally questionable, it is strategically foolish.

8. The National Cost
At the national level, the cumulative effect is staggering. When women leave work early, GDP is reduced. When untreated health issues escalate, public health systems carry the burden. When leadership pipelines leak, representation in politics, business, and science suffers. Nations lose not only economic productivity but cultural progress.

A report in the UK estimated that unmanaged menopause costs billions annually in productivity loss alone. In Australia, the figure is likely similar, though under-researched. The true national cost is higher when we consider the impact on families, communities, and social capital.

9. The Personal Cost: Dignity
Perhaps the deepest cost is dignity. Shame tells women they are broken when they are not. It tells them to hide when they should be seen. It convinces them to carry burdens alone rather than demanding support.

Every time a woman eats lunch alone in her car, every time she resigns quietly from a job she loved, every time she swallows an antidepressant for a hormonal symptom, the cost of shame is paid in dignity. And dignity, once eroded, is not easily restored.

Shame as a Systemic Debt
The cost of shame is not a line item. It is a debt carried by individuals, workplaces, and societies. It is paid in lost productivity, yes, but also in lost health, lost trust, lost relationships, and lost futures.

Addressing it requires more than economic calculation. It requires cultural honesty. It requires workplaces willing to create dignity-first policies, healthcare systems willing to name and treat menopause, and societies willing to value women at every stage of life. Shame is not free. It is the most expensive silence of all.

Breaking the Silence

Policies alone are not enough. Policies sit in handbooks and on websites. They may provide technical compliance, but they rarely change hearts or culture. What truly dismantles stigma is not the creation of rules, but the breaking of silence.

Silence has been the thread holding stigma in place for generations. To break it requires courage at every level, from women who decide to share their stories, to leaders who choose to acknowledge what has long been denied, to organisations that move menopause from the margins of wellbeing programs into the core of workplace equity.

Leadership as the Turning Point
Culture shifts when leaders set the tone. If menopause remains a punchline in boardrooms, it will remain a source

of shame in staffrooms. If leaders speak with dignity, the silence cracks.

This does not mean every manager needs to be an expert in hormone therapy. It means they must be willing to say: "This matters. We see it. We will support it." Leadership is about legitimacy, and legitimacy comes from naming what has long been ignored.

Imagine a CEO opening an annual diversity report and speaking not only about gender pay gaps and parental leave, but also about menopause. Imagine a headteacher at a staff development day saying: "Menopause is part of our community. If you need support, you have it." These are not small gestures. They are cultural detonations. They break the illusion that menopause is a private shame.

Practical Steps That Transform Culture
Breaking the silence is not an abstract principle. It is enacted through practical, everyday steps that signal dignity.

- **Training managers**: Equip them to respond with empathy and accuracy. A manager who can say, "I understand this is menopause, let's talk about adjustments," dismantles years of shame in a single sentence.
- **Normalising conversations**: This can be as simple as including menopause in wellbeing newsletters, lunch-and-learn sessions, or health campaigns. Every mention chips away at taboo.
- **Providing dignity-first accommodations**: Flexible breaks, breathable uniforms, access to quiet rooms. These adjustments are often minor in cost but major in impact.
- **Creating safe spaces**: Employee networks or peer groups where women can share experiences without fear of ridicule. Support begins in community.

When these steps are embedded, silence gives way to visibility. Visibility births legitimacy. Legitimacy ends stigma.

Stories as Catalysts
Breaking the silence also means amplifying stories. Statistics make leaders think, but stories make them feel. When a teacher describes eating lunch alone in her car out of fear of ridicule, or when a manager recounts resigning after a humiliating memory lapse, stigma becomes visible in human form. Stories cut through policy jargon and reveal the cost of silence in ways no spreadsheet can.

This is why parliamentary inquiries, union submissions, and public testimonies matter. They transform private pain into public evidence. They move the narrative from individual weakness to collective failure, and from collective failure to collective responsibility.

Global Movements, Local Change
Breaking the silence is already happening globally. In the UK, the Menopause Workplace Pledge has been signed by over 2,000 organisations, from universities to supermarkets. In the US, grassroots advocacy is forcing employers to recognise menopause as a healthcare and equity issue. In Australia, the Senate Inquiry brought menopause into federal debate for the first time in history.

These movements show what is possible when silence is broken. They prove that cultural taboos are not immutable. What seems unspeakable in one generation can become commonplace in the next. But only if voices rise and institutions listen.

From Shame to Strength

Breaking the silence is not only about ending shame. It is about reframing menopause as strength. A workforce that acknowledges menopause is a workforce that acknowledges resilience, adaptation, and experience.

Consider this: women who navigate menopause while balancing careers, families, and community roles are demonstrating adaptability on a scale few leadership courses can teach. These are not liabilities. They are assets. But as long as shame dictates the narrative, that strength is hidden.

When silence is broken, women can own their stories. They can move from whispering apologies to demanding recognition. They can transform stigma into solidarity, and solidarity into change.

The Cost of Staying Silent vs. The Power of Speaking Up

Silence costs billions in productivity and millions in lost potential. But the cost cannot only be measured economically. Silence costs dignity. It costs relationships. It costs leadership pipelines and intergenerational knowledge.

Speaking up, on the other hand, generates power. It creates cultures of trust where employees feel valued. It builds reputational capital for organisations that lead. It inspires policy reform and shifts public narratives. Breaking the silence is not charity. It is strategy. It is survival. It is leadership in its truest form.

A Mandate for Every Level

Breaking the silence is not the responsibility of women alone. The burden cannot fall solely on those already carrying symptoms.

- **For colleagues**: breaking the silence means refusing to laugh at the joke, and instead offering empathy.

- **For managers**: it means choosing openness over avoidance, listening over dismissal.
- **For executives**: it means naming menopause in the same breath as other equity issues.
- **For policymakers**: it means embedding menopause in laws, frameworks, and funding priorities.
- **For media and culture**: it means representing menopause without caricature, without shame, without invisibility.

Every level has a role. Every action chips away at the silence.

Closing the Circle

For centuries, women have been told to keep quiet about menopause. That quiet has cost too much. Breaking the silence is not just a step forward; it is a circle closing. It honours those who carried shame alone, and it clears the way for those yet to come.

Every time a woman speaks openly, every time a leader acknowledges menopause, every time a workplace embeds support, the silence fractures. Eventually, it will break altogether. And when it does, we will see what was always there: women not as problems to be managed, but as leaders to be valued.

Stigma costs more than symptoms. It isolates women, erodes trust, and drives them out of workplaces long before their time. It robs them of dignity, and it robs organisations of wisdom. But the story does not have to end there.

This chapter has traced the journey of stigma, from Anne at the bus stop with her suitcase of shame, to the teacher eating alone in her car, to the countless women who have withdrawn silently from conversations, careers, and communities. These are not isolated incidents. They are the visible edges of a much larger system that teaches women to hide and convinces workplaces to look away.

Yet within these stories lies another truth: silence has always been fragile. It endures only as long as no one dares to break it. And silence is already breaking.

The Invisible Made Visible

For generations, menopause has been kept invisible. But invisibility is not the same as absence. Women have always been there, sweating in meetings, persevering through fog, carrying the weight of sleepless nights into nine a.m. presentations. They were present, but unseen.

Now, the invisible is becoming visible. Inquiry submissions, workplace pledges, and grassroots advocacy are pulling menopause out of the shadows. Employees are beginning to speak, managers are beginning to listen, and policymakers are beginning to respond. What was once treated as private shame is being reframed as public responsibility.

This is not a small shift. It is seismic. It challenges centuries of cultural conditioning that told women to keep quiet and carry on.

Wisdom on the Line

When women leave the workforce early, we do not just lose headcount. We lose institutional wisdom. We lose mentors who know how to navigate crises, who carry the history of organisations, who teach by example. We lose leaders who could have modelled resilience for the next generation.

Every staffroom conversation that silences a woman is a missed opportunity. Every boardroom that ignores menopause is a poorer boardroom for it. The cost of stigma is not only personal and economic, it is cultural. It shapes the DNA of workplaces, determining who stays, who leads, and who feels they belong.

Imagine if menopause were treated not as decline but as transition. Imagine if organisations viewed this stage of life as one where women bring a depth of perspective forged through years of balancing roles, responsibilities, and resilience. Recognition could unlock a reservoir of leadership the world desperately needs.

Dignity as a Measure of Success

Inclusion is not measured only by numbers on a diversity dashboard. True inclusion is measured by dignity. Do people feel safe to be themselves? Do they feel respected when they bring their whole selves to work?

If a workplace cannot make room for menopause, it has not yet achieved inclusion. If a society cannot value women in midlife, it has not yet achieved equity.

Dignity is not an optional extra. It is the foundation. When women are forced to hide their symptoms, they are stripped of dignity. When workplaces acknowledge menopause openly, dignity is restored. And when dignity is present, loyalty, innovation, and leadership follow.

A Collective Responsibility

It is tempting to see menopause as an individual issue, one woman's symptoms, one manager's response, one HR policy. But the reality is collective. When shame forces one woman to eat alone in her car, her colleagues lose her laughter, her students lose her mentorship, her workplace loses her presence. When stigma drives one woman to resign early, her organisation loses her skill and her sector loses her leadership.

Breaking the silence, therefore, is not an act of charity for women. It is an act of collective responsibility for all. Menopause is not a women's issue. It is a human issue. It affects families, communities, economies, and nations.

Hope on the Horizon

The silence has endured for centuries, but cracks are appearing. Leaders are beginning to name menopause. Organisations are starting to embed policies. Doctors are demanding better training. Campaigns are shifting culture. Women are sharing their stories more loudly and more bravely than ever before.

Change is possible because change has already begun. And once silence is broken, it cannot be fully restored.

The task now is to accelerate. To ensure that Anne's suitcase, Helen's car lunches, and countless other stories are not repeated by the next generation. To replace shame with solidarity, silence with conversation, stigma with dignity.

A Mandate for the Future

Stigma costs more than symptoms, but support does more than protect jobs. It preserves wisdom. It strengthens leadership pipelines. It builds cultures of trust. It transforms workplaces into communities where people thrive.

Every workplace that chooses dignity over silence is not just supporting women. It is future-proofing itself. Every policy that names menopause explicitly is not just protecting employees. It is building equity. Every conversation that interrupts a joke or challenges a dismissal is not just defending a colleague. It is dismantling a centuries-old taboo.

The mandate is clear: break the silence, dismantle the shame, recognise menopause as part of the working life course.

Support does not just keep women in jobs. It keeps cultures alive with wisdom. It ensures leadership is passed on, not lost. It ensures that humanity, not shame, defines our workplaces.

Every staffroom conversation that silences a woman is a loss. Every workplace that opens the door to dignity is a gain. And every society that recognises menopause as part of life, not a source of shame, steps closer to justice.

Stigma has taken too much for too long. The time for silence is over. The future belongs to those who listen, who speak, and who act.

Chapter 14:
Remote, Rural, and Left Behind.
Health Gaps in the Bush

It was still dark when Jenny* left her home on the edge of western Queensland. By the time she reached the hospital in Toowoomba, she had driven more than five hours. She had organised childcare, taken a day of unpaid leave, and filled her car with fuel she could barely afford. She sat in the waiting room rehearsing how to explain her symptoms, night sweats, brain fog, exhaustion, to a doctor she had never met before.

When she finally entered the consulting room, she was told, "It sounds like stress. Try exercising more and getting better sleep." There was no mention of perimenopause.   No referral to a specialist. No prescription that would help.

Jenny cried the entire drive home. The trip had cost her $200 and a day of wages. What it bought her was dismissal. She swore she wouldn't try again.

Jenny's story is not unique. It is echoed across regional and rural Australia, where women experiencing menopause are too often left behind, by distance, by culture, by systemic neglect.

The Geography of Disadvantage

Living outside a city magnifies every barrier to healthcare. The scarcity of general practitioners in rural Australia is well documented, and even when women can secure an appointment, there is no guarantee their GP has adequate training in menopause. Many rural doctors are under immense pressure, covering vast catchment areas with minimal resources.
Specialists are even scarcer.   Endocrinologists, gynaecologists, psychiatrists, the professionals who could support complex menopause cases, are concentrated in metropolitan centres. Rural women face hours of travel, long waiting lists, and significant costs for accommodation and transport.

Pharmacies in smaller towns often do not stock a full range of hormone replacement therapies. Women report waiting weeks for orders to arrive, or being told certain treatments are simply unavailable. For those in remote communities, this means either going without or making repeated trips to larger centres.

Geography also compounds financial barriers. Women must take days off work, often unpaid, to attend appointments. Travel costs can exceed the cost of treatment itself. For women in casual or shift-based work, agriculture, retail, health services, time away is not easily absorbed.

The result is predictable: many women simply do not seek care. They endure symptoms in silence, normalising suffering as the price of rural life.

The Culture of Stoicism
Geography is only part of the story. Culture plays a powerful role in shaping how rural women experience menopause. The ethos of "bush stoicism", the expectation that people should endure hardship without complaint, is deeply embedded.

In small towns, privacy is scarce. The local GP might also be a neighbour or acquaintance. Women often avoid seeking care for fear of gossip or judgement. In workplaces where everyone knows each other, disclosure feels riskier. A hot flush in the classroom or a mood swing on the ward is more likely to be remembered, repeated, or ridiculed.

This culture reinforces silence. Women convince themselves to push through, to endure, to not make a fuss. They downplay their struggles, even as symptoms erode their quality of life. In communities where resilience is celebrated, vulnerability can feel like failure.

Indigenous and Multicultural Perspectives

For First Nations women, the challenge is even greater. Indigenous Australians already experience significant health inequities: higher rates of chronic illness, shorter life expectancy, and systemic racism within healthcare. Menopause is rarely discussed in culturally safe ways. Many Indigenous women report that their symptoms are either ignored or misunderstood by non-Indigenous clinicians.

Community-controlled health organisations provide better outcomes, but coverage is patchy. For many, the nearest culturally safe clinic is hundreds of kilometres away.

Migrant women in rural and regional areas face additional barriers. Language differences, limited access to interpreters, and a lack of culturally competent providers create layers of exclusion. For those who come from cultures where menopause is even more taboo than in mainstream Australia, silence deepens.

Intersectionality magnifies disadvantage: a rural Indigenous woman, or a migrant woman in a remote town, is far more likely to be left without care.

Case Studies

Case Study 7: **The Nurse in the Mining Town**

Sophie* worked twelve-hour shifts in a mining town hospital. As her perimenopause symptoms worsened, she found it harder to concentrate during night shifts. Hot flushes in her thick uniform left her drenched. Her GP, one of only two in town, prescribed antidepressants. When she asked about HRT, she was told it was "too risky." Sophie eventually reduced her hours, then resigned. The hospital lost an experienced nurse.

Case Study 8: **The Indigenous Woman Avoiding Care**

Marlene*, a First Nations woman from northern Queensland, travelled six hours for an appointment after months of heavy bleeding and exhaustion. She sat in a waiting room where no staff member spoke her language, and no interpreter was offered. When she finally saw the doctor, she was rushed through, her concerns dismissed. "I felt invisible," she said. "Like I was wasting their time." She never returned.

Case Study 9: *The Rural Teacher Retiring Early*
Helen*, a teacher in western NSW, loved her job but found her symptoms overwhelming. With no local doctor knowledgeable about menopause, she relied on online forums for advice. The nearest specialist was in Sydney, an eight-hour trip. After missing multiple days for travel, she concluded it was unsustainable. She retired five years earlier than planned. Her school lost a mentor and her students lost a passionate educator.

Case Study 10: *The Farmer's Wife*
Margaret*, who ran a sheep farm with her husband, often endured symptoms alone. Her days started at 4am and ended long after dark. She described waking drenched in sweat and then working through exhaustion because livestock could not wait. When she sought help, the nearest GP dismissed her concerns: "You're just tired. Farming will do that." For Margaret, menopause was not just about health, it was about survival.

Policy and Systemic Failures
The neglect of rural menopause care reflects broader rural health inequities. Funding models fail to account for distance. Medicare rebates cover consultations but not the travel or accommodation required to access them. Telehealth has improved access but remains limited by patchy internet and a lack of menopause-trained providers.

Pharmaceutical access is inequitable. Rural pharmacies carry less stock, and supply chains can be unreliable. Women report being told to "try another pharmacy" hundreds of kilometres away.

Workplace policies are also metropolitan-centric. National menopause policies assume access to supportive healthcare, but in rural areas, that assumption collapses. Without medical validation, women cannot secure workplace accommodations, leaving them further exposed to stigma and shame.

International Comparisons
This rural neglect is not unique to Australia. In Canada, women in remote First Nations communities face similar barriers, with limited access to gynaecological care and mistrust of colonial healthcare systems. In New Zealand, Maori women report both cultural stigma and geographic isolation. In the UK, rural women face long wait times for specialist care despite national menopause strategies.

These parallels show that rurality itself magnifies inequities, especially when combined with cultural marginalisation. But they also offer lessons: Canada's investment in mobile clinics, New Zealand's integration of Maori health perspectives, and the UK's public campaigns all provide models Australia could adapt.

What Works / Models of Hope
There are models of success that show what is possible:
- **Mobile Women's Health Clinics**: Outreach vans providing gynaecological and menopause services in remote towns.
- **Telehealth Specialist Networks**: Pairing rural GPs with urban specialists for joint consultations.
- **Indigenous-Led Clinics**: Community-controlled health organisations that integrate cultural knowledge and provide culturally safe menopause care.
- **Workplace Innovations**: Mining companies and agricultural employers experimenting with menopause-friendly uniforms, flexible rostering, and health education.

These examples prove that the barriers are not insurmountable. They simply require will, funding, and recognition.

Menopause in the bush is not just a private struggle. It is a structural inequity. Geography, culture, and systemic neglect combine to create double silence: the silence of stigma and the silence of distance.

Every time a rural woman drives for hours only to be dismissed, the system fails. Every time a teacher retires early, a nurse resigns, or an Indigenous woman avoids care, communities lose. Rural Australia cannot afford to keep losing its women to neglect.
Recognition requires targeted funding, culturally safe services, and policies that see menopause not as a private inconvenience but as a public responsibility.

A postcode should not determine whether a woman suffers in silence or finds support. Yet today, it does. Breaking this inequity is not just a matter of fairness. It is a matter of justice.

Chapter 15:
Culture, Language, and the Forgotten Stories

Half the world will live it, yet few have words for it. Without language, there is silence. Without stories, there is erasure.

When Mai* arrived in Australia as a newly married woman from Vietnam, she was twenty-two. She had little English, a new baby on her hip, and a husband working long hours in construction. Over the decades, she built a life in suburban New South Wales. She worked in a local factory, raised three children, and learned enough English to manage shopping, bills, and conversations with her neighbours.

By her late forties, her body began to change. Her periods became irregular. Nights were restless. She woke drenched in sweat. At work, she lost her train of thought during safety briefings. She grew anxious about forgetting tasks on the production line.

But Mai had no word for what was happening. In Vietnamese, there is no single term that captures "menopause" the way English does. It is often described indirectly, "time stopping," "blood no longer coming." To Mai, it felt unspeakable, almost shameful.

When she gathered the courage to see a doctor, she struggled to explain. Without an interpreter, she mimed fanning herself, pointed to her head, and repeated the word "tired." The GP wrote a prescription for sleeping tablets and told her to rest. She left confused and embarrassed.

For years, Mai suffered in silence. She thought she was weak, perhaps even mentally unwell. She stopped attending church groups, afraid people would notice her flushed face. At home, she avoided telling her children, unsure how to explain something for which she had no words.

It was only when her eldest daughter, now a nurse, came across an article about menopause and showed it to her mother that Mai finally understood. The relief was immediate: this was not her fault, not madness, not weakness. But the knowledge had come late, and the cost had been years of shame and withdrawal.

Mai's story is not unusual. Across cultures, menopause is shaped, and often silenced, by language, tradition, and history. Where there are no words, there is no voice. Where there are no stories, there is no recognition. This chapter explores how culture and language create forgotten spaces in the story of menopause, and why reclaiming these voices is essential for justice.

Mai's silence is echoed by millions of women around the world.

Language as Power

Language is not decoration; it is definition. It is how humans make sense of their lives, and it is how societies decide what is real, what is worthy, and what can be ignored. Words are not neutral. They carry values, histories, and cultural weight.

Menopause is one of those words that has never sat comfortably in language. In English, "menopause" exists as a clinical import from 19th-century French medicine, accurate, perhaps, but bloodless. It literally means *"pause of the monthlies."* It is a word written for textbooks, not for kitchens or staffrooms. It does not carry the softness of story or the clarity of recognition.

So English did what cultures often do when discomfort arises: it reached for euphemism. "The change of life." "The midlife transition." "That time." These softened phrases made the topic easier to mention without embarrassment. But euphemisms blur truth. "The change" could mean anything. "Transition" could mean a move, a divorce, a career break. In avoiding bluntness, they also avoided clarity.

This matters. When women say "the change," daughters do not learn about night sweats or brain fog. When workers tell managers they are "going through something," no policy or support framework can respond. Euphemism hides in plain sight.

Anne and the Suitcase
In 2009, I commuted to Melbourne each morning on the same bus. At the stop, I often spoke with Anne, a colleague known for her warmth and humour. One day she stopped engaging. She began standing apart, silent. Over time I noticed she carried a small cabin-sized suitcase with her. Months passed before I gathered the courage to ask.

With sadness in her eyes, Anne told me she used the bike-room showers at work three or four times a day. Her suitcase carried clean clothes. She bought multiples of each outfit so no one would notice the changes. She stood away at the bus stop because she feared the smell of sweat. It was, she said, the loneliest year of her life.

This is the lived cost of euphemism. Because "the change" has no detail, Anne had no words to explain what she was enduring. She carried her silence in a suitcase, her dignity in a wardrobe of duplicated clothes. For me, then in my thirties, it was the first time I realised that menopause was more than a vague "change." It was embodied, relentless, and hidden in plain sight.

Generational Silence
Language not only defines experience, it transmits it. Mothers who never had words for menopause cannot pass knowledge to their daughters. Where euphemism reigns, preparation dies.

Many women recall only a whispered, "one day your period will stop." Others heard nothing at all. Some recall mothers changing abruptly, moods shifting, or health declining, but never explaining why. In such households, menopause is inherited as mystery.

This generational silence compounds shame. A daughter blindsided by symptoms assumes she is weak, unstable, or sick. Without context, hot flushes feel like panic attacks; brain fog feels like cognitive decline; mood swings feel like failure. And because her mother had no words, the daughter has no map.

The Global Language of Softening
English is not unique. Around the world, languages soften menopause with phrases that erase its specificity.
- In German, the colloquial term is *Wechseljahre*, "years of change." Like "the change" in English, it gestures vaguely to transition but avoids naming.
- In Japanese, *konenki* historically meant "renewal years," linking the body to seasonal cycles. In modern usage, however, it has been increasingly medicalised, losing its neutral poetry.
- In Russian, the common word *klimaks* is derived from "climacteric," but colloquially it has become a pejorative, shorthand for irritability, decline, or instability.
- In French, *ménopause* is clinical and widely understood, but everyday conversation often defaults to euphemisms like *"l'âge critique"*, "the critical age."

Across cultures, the instinct is the same: cloak the reality, soften the edges, obscure the specifics. But in doing so, these languages deprive women of clarity, agency, and legitimacy.

Euphemism in the Workplace
The absence of precise words has consequences far beyond the kitchen table. In workplaces, euphemism blocks reform.

If a woman tells her manager she is "going through a change," what is the HR department meant to do? Without a named category, "menopause", there is no trigger for leave policies, ergonomic adjustments, or health programs. Diversity dashboards do not measure "the change." Enterprise bargaining agreements cannot mandate support for "something."

This is why language matters. Policy does not run on euphemism. Reform requires clarity. "Menopause" must be named to be recognised, measured, and addressed. Until it is, millions of women will continue carrying Anne's suitcase, silently accommodating their own suffering.

Policy Implications of Silence
Euphemism is not harmless. It is structural. The absence of specific language has delayed medical research, workplace reform, and public health education.

For decades, Western medical curricula devoted fewer than six hours to menopause across years of study. Why? Because if menopause is merely "the change," it can be dismissed as a vague life stage, not a medical or psychological issue. If women are simply "transitioning," why study the specifics?

In workplaces, euphemism enables avoidance. Employers are not required to address what is not named. Governments are not pressured to legislate for what is not measured. Silence becomes cost-saving, at women's expense.

Words as Inheritance
Language is not just about communication; it is inheritance. Every euphemism carries forward silence. Every silence leaves daughters without maps.

Anne's suitcase is not hers alone. It belongs to generations of women who carried silence into workplaces, boardrooms, and kitchens. It belongs to daughters who learned nothing from their mothers, and so entered their own "change" bewildered and ashamed.

Words shape what we can see, name, and demand. Without the word "menopause," women cannot ask for medical care, cannot push for workplace accommodations, cannot tell their own stories. Words are power. And the words we have been given for menopause, or denied, have written women into invisibility.

When Words Are Missing

In some cultures, menopause is not softened by euphemism, it is simply absent.

Silence in First Nations Canada

Among First Nations women in northwestern Ontario, a landmark 2010 study revealed that there is **no single word for menopause in Ojibway or Oji-Cree.** Instead, women described it as *"that time when periods stop."*

The research team interviewed 18 women across several communities using interpreters. They discovered that symptoms like hot flushes, sweats, and mood swings were rarely conceptually linked to menopause. Women might complain of "heat" or "tiredness," but they did not connect these to the cessation of menstruation.

One participant explained: "It was hidden, hush-hush, especially with older women. Some of them will not talk about that kind of thing."

Yet silence did not mean disinterest. Many expressed curiosity, even hunger, for information. They wanted to know what to expect, how long symptoms would last, and whether their experiences were normal. But without a word, there was no frame to hold these questions.

The absence of language limited medical care. Without the ability to name menopause, conversations with health providers faltered. Women could not ask for support; doctors could not diagnose effectively. Silence was not neutral, it was harmful.

The Australian Gap
In Australia, the silence is even more striking. A 2012 review (Jones et al.) found that across decades of research, only **two studies** had examined the menopause experiences of Aboriginal and Torres Strait Islander women.

What little we know is sobering: in far north Queensland, women described menopause not as a single word but with phrases like *"bleeding no more"* or *"no more women's sickness."* These terms capture cessation but not transition.

Even more startling: **58.9% of Indigenous participants in one study had never heard the word "menopause."** Many did not know menstruation would eventually cease until it happened to them. This was not ignorance, it was systemic neglect. The silence was both cultural and structural, compounded by limited health education, low access to culturally safe services, and the deeply private framing of "women's business."

Indigenous women in these studies often interpreted symptoms in isolation. Sweating was seen as unrelated to memory lapses, which in turn were disconnected from irregular cycles. Without a unifying word, the fragments never cohered into a whole. And without the whole, recognition never came.

Symptom by Symptom
This symptom-by-symptom framing is common across cultures. In parts of Africa, menopause is described only as "the heat" or "the stopping of blood." In Pacific Island communities, women speak of "tiredness" or simply of becoming "elder." In Māori communities in New Zealand, research suggests menopause is viewed neutrally, folded into the natural continuum of aging. Often the language used is not about decline, but nor is it about transition. It is about fragments.

When language is fragmented, care becomes fragmented. A woman who says only "I feel hot" is tested for fever. A woman who says "I forget" may be diagnosed with depression. Without a term that gathers these symptoms under a single umbrella, misdiagnosis thrives.

A Cross-Cultural Lexicon

To understand how language, or its absence, shapes menopause globally, it helps to map the words themselves.

Language / Culture	Common Term(s)	Literal / Direct Meaning	Cultural Frame / Notes
English	Menopause; "the change"; "transition"	Pause of menses; vague euphemisms	Clinical word exists but softened in daily life.
French	Ménopause; l'âge critique	Pause of monthlies; "critical age"	Medicalised, sometimes pathologising.
German	Menopause; Wechseljahre	"Years of change"	Colloquial term is softer but imprecise.
Russian	Klimaks	"Climacteric"	Colloquial use pejorative, mocks moods.
Arabic	سن اليأس (sinn al-yaas)	"Age of despair"	Frames stage as hopeless
Hindi/ Urdu	Raja band ho gaya	"The king (period) has stopped"	Loss of authority/status implied.
Mandarin Chinese	绝经 (juéjīng); 更年期 (gēngniánqī)	"End of menstruation"; "change of years"	Neutral but clinical; workplace stigma remains.
Japanese	更年期 (konenki)	"Renewal years/seasonal change"	Historically positive; now medicalised.
First Nations Canada (Ojibway/ Oji-Cree)	"That time when periods stop"	Descriptive phrase, no single word	Silence limits recognition; symptoms not linked.

Language / Culture	Common Term(s)	Literal / Direct Meaning	Cultural Frame / Notes
Indigenous Australia	"Bleeding no more"; "no more women's sickness"	Descriptive phrases	No single word; 58.9% unaware of menopause.
Mayan (Mexico)	(no single word)	–	Menopause framed as freedom from restrictions.
Pacific Islands	(varies, often "elder")	Linked to aging/elder status	Framed as stage of respect, not pathology.
Māori (NZ)	(often English loanwords)	–	Neutral; part of natural life course.
Swahili	Kukoma hedhi	"To cease menstruation"	Functional, clinical, non-holistic.

The table reveals patterns: some cultures soften menopause, others stigmatise it, and many simply lack a single word. Where there are no words, there can be no collective story. Where there is no story, there can be no recognition.

The Cost of Silence

The consequences of missing words ripple outward.

- **In families**: mothers cannot prepare daughters; daughters inherit confusion.
- **In healthcare**: symptoms scatter into unrelated categories; misdiagnosis thrives.
- **In workplaces**: without a named category, there can be no policy.
- **In research**: what is not named is not studied. The fact that only two Australian studies exist on Indigenous menopause is itself a symptom of systemic silence.

Words are not decoration. They are scaffolding. Without them, women build their lives without blueprints, navigating a critical life stage in the dark.

When Words Are Negative

Sometimes the problem is not the absence of language, but the presence of words that wound. Across cultures, terms for menopause often embed decline, shame, or despair into their very syllables. Naming becomes a form of injury.

The Age of Despair

In Arabic, the most common phrase for menopause is سن اليأس (sinn al-yaas), literally, *"the age of despair."* An entire life stage is framed as hopelessness. A woman who uses the term is forced to speak of herself as entering decline.

One Lebanese woman, interviewed in community health research, described it like this: "When you say 'sinn al-yaas,' it is as if you are already finished. It is as if your life is past usefulness. Even if you feel strong, the word tells you not to be."

Language here functions as prophecy. A woman might otherwise see menopause as a relief, no more menstrual pain, no risk of pregnancy. But when the only available phrase is despair, the expectation of decline seeps into identity.

The King Has Stopped

In Hindi and Urdu, a common euphemism is *raja band ho gaya, "the king (period) has stopped."* Menstruation is framed as sovereignty, a monthly sign of fertility and womanhood. Its end is described as dethronement, the loss of status.

For women steeped in this metaphor, the cessation of menstruation is not just physical; it is social. A woman is no longer a queen in her household, no longer central to lineage, no longer in power. The metaphor robs dignity before biology does.

A Punjabi woman put it bluntly in an interview: "When the raja is gone, you are old. You are no longer useful."

English: Failure, Decline, Loss
Even in English, with its supposedly clinical vocabulary, the dominant metaphors are negative. Medical discourse routinely describes menopause as:

- "ovarian failure"
- "reproductive decline"
- "loss of function"

Each of these frames menopause as pathology. Women are told they are failing, declining, losing. None of these words capture resilience, adaptation, or continuity. None recognise that menopause is a normal, universal stage of life.

These words matter. A woman told she is "failing" is less likely to see herself as healthy. A woman told she is "declining" may withdraw from work, relationships, and leadership. A woman told she is "losing" may internalise grief rather than agency.

Klimaks as a Joke
In Russian, the colloquial word for menopause is *klimaks*. It comes from the Greek "climacteric," meaning a critical turning point. But in everyday use, *klimaks* has become a punchline. To say someone is "having klimaks" is to mock their moodiness, irritability, or emotional expression.

Russian women report being dismissed with phrases like: *"Oh, that's just klimaks."* The word functions not as description but as delegitimisation. A legitimate medical and social transition is reduced to a joke about irrationality.

Words as Prophecy

These metaphors, despair, dethronement, failure, decline, do more than describe. They prescribe. They teach women what to expect, and in doing so, they shape what women actually feel.

- If you are told you are entering "the age of despair," you may interpret natural mood shifts as despair itself.
- If you are told "the king has stopped," you may feel dethroned, even if you remain vibrant in life and work.
- If you are told you are in "ovarian failure," you may internalise the idea of being broken.

This is the prophecy effect of language: expectations shape experience.

A Story of Stigma

Consider Laila, a 52-year-old Egyptian woman who sought help for insomnia, sweating, and joint pain. Her GP reassured her that she was only entering *sinn al-yaas*. Laila later told her daughter: *"The doctor said I am in despair. What should I do if even he thinks this is despair?"* She withdrew from her social group, assuming she had nothing left to offer.

Or consider Rani, a 48-year-old in India, who stopped attending village meetings after relatives whispered raja band ho gaya. She explained: "It is a way of saying you are finished. Even if I have ideas, who will listen to me? I am already called the woman whose king has stopped."

These are not isolated moments. They are the daily consequences of naming.

The Double Bind

Negative words not only harm women directly; they also give others license to dismiss them. Husbands, employers, and doctors hear "despair," "decline," or "failure" and treat women accordingly. A workplace manager who believes menopause equals instability may sideline an otherwise capable employee. A doctor who assumes menopause is decline may fail to investigate treatable symptoms like thyroid disorders or sleep apnea.

Language becomes not just prophecy but policy.

The Weight of Internalisation
Psychologists studying menopause have found that women's expectations strongly shape symptom severity. Those who anticipate difficulty tend to report more intense symptoms. This does not mean their suffering is imagined; it means language and culture modulate experience. Where metaphors are negative, suffering compounds. Where metaphors are neutral or positive, women adapt more readily.

This is why some Mayan women report no significant symptoms at all, while Western women report severe distress. It is not simply biology. It is story. It is word.

From Joke to Justice
When language mocks, minimises, or pathologises, justice demands correction. The words we use are not trivial. They decide whether menopause is lived as despair, dethronement, failure, or as wisdom, renewal, and freedom.

Silence isolates. Negative language degrades. Together, they form the double bind that has trapped women for generations. Breaking that bind requires not only new words, but a new willingness to confront the poison in old ones.

Towards a New Lexicon

If silence wounds and stigma poisons, then reclamation is the cure. Menopause does not need fewer words; it needs better ones. A new lexicon can give women recognition, dignity, and authority.

Renewal Years: Japan's Konenki

In Japan, the word 更年期 *(konenki)* historically translated to *"renewal years"* or *"seasonal change."* Unlike the English "ovarian failure," *konenki* positioned menopause alongside the rhythms of nature, spring to summer, autumn to winter.

For generations, this framing allowed Japanese women to see menopause as a natural transition, not a personal decline. While modern medicine has medicalised the term, the original metaphor remains a powerful example of how language can ease rather than wound. Menopause is not an end; it is a season.

Freedom: The Mayan Frame

In rural Mayan communities in Mexico, there is no single word for menopause. Yet women describe it not as loss, but as liberation.

Because high parity and long breastfeeding mean estrogen levels are low across much of life, menopause passes with few symptoms. What women mark is not discomfort but the **end of restrictions**: no more menstrual taboos, no more fear of pregnancy, no more obligations tied to fertility.

One woman explained simply: *"It is when I am free."*
This is menopause without pathology, not a medical event, but a social opening.

Elderhood: Indigenous Respect

Among Indigenous Australian women, elderhood is culturally significant. Older women are respected as knowledge holders, teachers, and custodians of land and story. While menopause itself may not be ceremonially marked, the entry into elderhood carries dignity.

In First Nations communities in Canada, women at this stage are often described as sacred, no longer bound by childbearing, now free to serve as wisdom keepers for the young. One elder explained: *"When you are past bleeding, you are respected because you have given life, and now you give knowledge."*

Contrast this with Western biomedical language, "failure," "decline", and the poverty of our lexicon becomes clear. Where Indigenous traditions speak of wisdom, Western medicine speaks of loss.

Reclaiming What Was Lost

The work before us is not only to create new words but to **recover old ones**. Across cultures, metaphors of renewal, wisdom, and authority exist, buried beneath colonisation, medicalisation, and euphemism.

The task is to bring them back into everyday use:
- To speak of menopause not as *failure*, but as *freedom*.
- Not as *decline*, but as *renewal*.
- Not as *loss*, but as *authority*.

Policy Must Follow Language
Language is not just symbolic; it drives systems. To reclaim menopause linguistically is also to reclaim it politically.

Healthcare
- Train interpreters in reproductive vocabulary, so migrant women are not left gesturing "tired" or "hot."

- Require medical schools to teach menopause in all its cultural framings, not just biomedical decline.
- Develop multilingual resources that use empowering terms rather than euphemisms or pathologies.

Workplaces
- Diversity dashboards should explicitly include menopause-related data, not bury it under "wellbeing."
- Enterprise agreements must name menopause as a category of support, unlocking flexibility, uniform adjustments, and dignity-first accommodations.
- Public campaigns should normalise "menopause" as a word, in English and beyond.

Education
- Menopause must sit alongside puberty in school curricula. Girls should not learn only about the start of menstruation but also its end.
- Mothers and daughters need intergenerational resources that restore stories long silenced.

Stories as Lexicon

Reclamation is not only about policy, it is about stories. When Anne wheels her suitcase of shame, when Mai mimes her symptoms, when Laila hears "despair," their experiences reveal the poverty of our words. But when Mayan women speak of freedom, when Indigenous elders are revered as wisdom keepers, when Japanese culture frames menopause as renewal, those are the stories that must be amplified.

Every story told, every word reclaimed, is part of a new lexicon.

A Global Mandate

The world does not need one universal word for menopause. What it needs is a chorus of words that restore dignity across cultures. Words that reflect reality without erasure, words that empower rather than diminish.

In this new lexicon, menopause is not a hidden suitcase. It is not despair. It is not failure. It is not decline. It is renewal, wisdom, freedom, authority.

Language is not neutral. It is a mirror and a map. For too long, the words for menopause have been absent, euphemised, or poisoned with stigma. The result has been silence: in families, in workplaces, in policy, in medicine. Silence has left women unprepared, unsupported, unseen.

Half the world will live through menopause. Yet few have words for it. Without language, there is silence. Without stories, there is erasure. And in that erasure, women suffer.

The mandate is clear: we must break the silence. We must name menopause clearly, culturally, compassionately. We must build a lexicon that does not reduce women to loss but recognises them in transition, in wisdom, in power.

Language is not decoration. Language is life. Until women everywhere have the words, the silence will continue to kill.

Chapter 16:
Why Healthcare Doesn't Care (Yet)

She was 47 when the panic attacks began. At least, that's what her doctor called them. They came without warning: her heart pounding in the middle of the night, a sheen of sweat coating her skin, her body flushed with heat so sudden it felt like fire. She could barely sleep. At work, she lost track of conversations mid-sentence. She cried at her desk and had no idea why.

Her GP prescribed antidepressants. When they didn't help, he tried anti-anxiety medication. When that failed, he suggested she "cut back on stress" and take time off work. For two years she cycled through pills, side effects, and shame. No one mentioned menopause. No one suggested hormones. No one told her that everything she was experiencing had a name, a pattern, and a treatment.

It was only when a friend, not a doctor, handed her an article on perimenopause that she understood what was happening. Her relief was instant, but so was her rage: how could her doctors miss this? How could a system supposedly dedicated to women's health fail so completely to see women?

Her story is not rare. It is ordinary. That ordinariness is the scandal.

Healthcare's blind spot around menopause is not an accident. It is the product of centuries of omission, dismissal, and design. Medicine has long treated women's bodies as problems to be managed, not lives to be understood. Menopause sits at the sharpest edge of this neglect: too universal to ignore, yet too inconvenient to dignify.

Why? Because healthcare systems are built on choices: about what counts as illness, what is worth studying, what deserves funding. Those choices have systematically left menopause in the shadows.

A Pattern of Omission

Consider the numbers. In most Western medical schools, fewer than six hours of formal teaching is devoted to menopause across the entirety of training. Many GPs graduate without ever being required to study hormone therapy, brain fog, or vasomotor symptoms in detail.

The result is predictable: women arrive at clinics with hot flushes, insomnia, joint pain, and memory lapses. Instead of receiving evidence-based hormonal care, they are offered sleeping tablets, antidepressants, or told to "ride it out." This is not simply inadequate care. It is a systemic refusal to recognise menopause as a legitimate health issue.

The Long Shadow of History

This refusal is not new. For centuries, women's bodies have been sites of dismissal and distortion. Ancient Greek medicine spoke of the "wandering womb," a rogue organ said to cause hysteria. In the nineteenth century, women were institutionalised for "nerves", their pain and mood disorders reduced to psychological weakness.

Even in the twentieth century, research prioritised diseases and drugs that served men. Women were routinely excluded from clinical trials until the 1990s on the assumption that hormonal cycles made them "too complicated." The consequences were catastrophic: drugs like thalidomide and DES harmed women and their babies because female bodies were treated as afterthoughts.

When it comes to menopause, the blind spot is even more stark. Pharmaceutical innovation has poured billions into erectile dysfunction, testosterone replacement, and fertility medicine. Meanwhile, funding for hormone replacement therapy remains patchy, stigmatised, and vulnerable to panic every time a new study misinterprets data.

This is the landscape women inherit when they walk into a GP's office: a history of being ignored.

Economic Framing: The Hidden Cost of Misdiagnosis

When menopause is misdiagnosed, as depression, anxiety, insomnia, or chronic fatigue, the consequences ripple not only through women's lives but also through the healthcare system's budget:

- **Unnecessary scans and tests**: Women frequently undergo MRIs, CT scans, thyroid panels, and cardiac monitoring before anyone asks about hormones. A single MRI costs anywhere from **$500-$1,000**, while cardiac workups can exceed **$2,000 per patient**. Multiply that by the thousands of women sent down the wrong diagnostic path each year, and the costs climb into the **hundreds of millions**.

- **Prescription overload**: Antidepressants, sleeping pills, anti-anxiety medication, and even opioids are often prescribed in place of HRT. In Australia alone, women in midlife are among the **highest users of SSRIs**, a cost borne by both the PBS and patients. These scripts add billions to pharmaceutical expenditure while leaving the underlying issue unresolved.

- **Repeat GP visits**: Instead of one clear diagnosis and treatment plan, women cycle through **years of appointments**, each adding to Medicare costs. Some studies suggest menopausal women average **five to six different doctors** before receiving appropriate support.

- **Absenteeism and presenteeism**: Misdiagnosis extends the time women are unwell, feeding directly into the **$10 billion workplace productivity loss** already identified. The healthcare system's failure cascades into the economy at large.

In short: **every misdiagnosis is double-paid**, once by the health system and again by workplaces. Correcting this is not just a moral imperative, but a financial one.

The Euphemism of Care

Even when medicine does acknowledge menopause, it often does so obliquely. Women are told they are experiencing "the change," or offered vague reassurance that "this stage will pass." But reassurance without recognition is abandonment.

One Aboriginal woman interviewed in far north Queensland described how her GP dismissed her joint pain as "just getting old." She did not know the word "menopause." She left believing she had arthritis. The silence of language and the silence of medicine collided to leave her untreated and unsupported.

Another woman in Sydney recounted being told her night sweats were "probably stress." She was prescribed sedatives, which left her groggy and unable to function at work. Years later, when she finally started HRT, she felt like her life had been "given back."

These are not failures of individual doctors. They are failures of the system that trained them.

The Structural Silence
Why does healthcare not care? Not because menopause is rare or trivial, but because it is universal. **Universality makes it invisible**. Systems built on crisis, cure, and profit are designed to respond to acute illness, not to support predictable transitions.

Menopause does not kill in a dramatic way. It does not demand emergency surgery or hospitalisation. It unfolds slowly, across years, in symptoms that can be mistaken for stress, aging, or mood disorder. In a system wired to treat diseases rather than people, menopause slips between the cracks.

This structural silence is reinforced by economics. Pharmaceutical companies profit more from long-term dependency drugs; antidepressants, anxiolytics, sleep medications, than from short-course HRT. Health systems fund fertility treatments, pregnancy programs, and neonatal care, but not menopause clinics. Politicians cut ribbons at maternity wards, not at hormone health centres.

The message is clear: reproduction matters; the end of reproduction does not.

The History of Neglect

The neglect of menopause in modern healthcare is not an oversight. It is the culmination of a long, consistent pattern of excluding, minimising, and pathologising women's bodies. To understand why doctors today prescribe antidepressants instead of hormones, or why medical schools devote less time to menopause than to acne, we must first look backwards.

From Wandering Wombs to Hysteria

The story begins in ancient Greece. Physicians believed the womb was a restless organ that could "wander" through a woman's body, causing disease and madness. Women's symptoms, fainting, pain, melancholy, convulsions, were attributed not to complex physiology, but to an unstable uterus.

Centuries later, this idea hardened into the diagnosis of "hysteria." Derived from the Greek *hystera* (womb), hysteria became the junk-drawer of medicine. If a woman reported unexplained symptoms, fatigue, anxiety, hot flushes, even sexual desire, she was labelled hysterical. Treatments ranged from bed rest to clitoral surgery to institutionalisation.

Menopause was swept into this framework. Women entering midlife were seen as unstable, irrational, or dangerous. Their changing bodies were not understood as natural transitions but as evidence of decline. The absence of reproductive function was treated as absence of value.

The Silence of Research

Fast forward to the twentieth century. As modern biomedicine advanced, women were still left behind. For decades, women were systematically excluded from clinical research. The reasoning? Their hormonal cycles made them "too complicated" and might "confuse results."

This exclusion was not benign. It meant that medications were developed, tested, and dosed on male bodies, then prescribed to women. The consequences were devastating:

- **Thalidomide (1950s-60s):** Given to pregnant women for morning sickness, it caused severe birth defects.
- **DES (Diethylstilbestrol, 1940s-70s):** Prescribed to prevent miscarriage, it led to cancers and infertility in daughters.

These disasters revealed the fatal flaw of ignoring women in research. Yet even after women were formally included in trials in the 1990s, menopause remained a low priority. Conditions affecting reproduction, fertility, or male sexual function drew funding. Menopause did not.

When Men's Health Is Urgent, Women's Is Optional

The disparity is stark. Since the 1990s, pharmaceutical companies have poured billions into drugs like Viagra and Cialis, treatments for erectile dysfunction, a condition affecting a minority of men. Within years of Viagra's launch, it became a cultural icon and a political priority.

Compare this to hormone replacement therapy (HRT). Despite menopause affecting half the population, HRT research has been underfunded and unstable. The 2002 Women's Health Initiative study, which reported risks of HRT without adequate context, triggered widespread panic. Millions of women were taken off treatment overnight. Only years later did re-analyses clarify that risks were overstated and benefits overlooked. By then, damage was done. Research dollars shrank. Doctors became wary. Women were left untreated.

The message was clear: men's sexual health deserved urgent, well-funded solutions. Women's midlife health could wait.

The DSM Blind Spot (A Light Touch)

This bias is visible even in psychiatry's diagnostic bible, the DSM. The manual includes **Premenstrual Dysphoric Disorder (PMDD)**, acknowledging mood disturbances tied to menstruation. Yet it omits menopause-related depression or anxiety entirely.

The implication is telling: mood changes linked to the start of reproduction are real enough to classify. Mood changes linked to the end of reproduction are not. Menopause remains invisible in the very frameworks that guide treatment.

We will return to this omission later in the book. For now, it serves as another signpost in the long road of neglect.

Case Study 11: "Just Stress"

Mara, a 47 year old office manager, visited her GP with fatigue, hot flushes, and difficulty sleeping. She was told it was "probably stress." When she mentioned that her periods had become irregular, the doctor nodded and said: *"That's normal for your age."*

Over the next two years, Mara was prescribed sedatives, sleeping pills, and antidepressants. None helped. It was only when she saw a menopause specialist, by chance, after hearing a radio interview, that she was started on HRT. Within months, her symptoms eased.

"I felt like myself again," she said. "But I was so angry. Angry at the years lost. Angry that nobody thought to connect the dots. Angry that I had to stumble on the answer by accident."

Mara's story is not about one inattentive GP. It is about a system trained to miss menopause.

A Timeline of Neglect

Era	Dominant View of Women's Health	Consequences
Ancient Greece	Wandering womb, hysteria	Women's symptoms dismissed as uterine instability
19th century	Hysteria as catch-all diagnosis	Institutionalisation, surgical interventions, silencing
Mid-20th century	Exclusion from clinical trials	Drugs unsafe/untested for women (e.g., thalidomide, DES)
Late 20th century	Token inclusion in trials; focus on fertility/sexual health	Menopause remains under-researched
2000s	Panic after WHI study on HRT	Millions of women denied treatment; stigma reinforced
Today	Minimal medical education on menopause	Misdiagnosis, under-treatment, systemic neglect

This is not history. It is continuity. The thread of neglect runs unbroken from wandering wombs to underfunded HRT.

Why History Matters

Some might argue that the past is past, that modern medicine is more enlightened. But history is not backdrop; it is infrastructure. The decisions of yesterday shape the knowledge of today.

When medical schools allocate less than six hours to menopause, they are reproducing centuries of minimisation. When GPs reach first for antidepressants instead of hormones, they are echoing the dismissal of women's pain as "hysteria." When governments pour money into Viagra but not menopause clinics, they are repeating the same calculus: men's bodies are urgent, women's bodies are optional.

This history is not abstract. It lives in the daily frustration of women who cannot get answers, who carry symptoms in silence, who lose jobs, marriages, and confidence while healthcare shrugs.

The neglect of menopause is not a gap in knowledge. It is a legacy of choices: to exclude women from research, to trivialise their symptoms, to prioritise men's health, to retreat from funding at the first sign of controversy.

This is the inheritance every menopausal woman carries into the doctor's office. It explains why the system fails them. It shows that neglect is not accidental, it is historical, systemic, and entrenched.

And it is the ground we must stand on before we move to the next part of the story: the frontline, where women meet undertrained GPs and the cycle of neglect continues.

The Frontline of Menopause

If menopause were a medical emergency, it would be triaged in the waiting room. If it were a rare disease, it would have specialist clinics in every hospital. If it were a pharmaceutical goldmine, it would have a research budget to rival cancer. Instead, it is treated as background noise, a natural inevitability that somehow requires no system, no training, and no urgency.

Yet the first place most women turn when symptoms begin to overwhelm them is not a therapist, not a specialist, and not a support group. It is the local GP. In Australia, in the UK, and across much of the Western world, general practitioners are the front line of menopause. They are the gatekeepers of diagnosis, the scribes of medical certificates, the prescribers of medication, and the navigators of referrals.

For many women, the GP is the only medical contact point they will ever have for menopause. And for too many, that contact fails.

The Gatekeeper Role

GPs are the most trusted entry point into the healthcare system. They hold the authority to prescribe, to reassure, to diagnose, and to decide whether a woman is referred onward to specialist care. This makes them powerful, and dangerous. A GP who recognises menopausal symptoms can unlock relief, resources, and reassurance. A GP who dismisses them can condemn a woman to years of confusion and unnecessary suffering.

Statistics make the scale of this role undeniable. In surveys across Australia and the UK, upwards of 80% of women report first raising menopausal symptoms with their GP. This reliance reflects how healthcare is structured: specialists are expensive, waitlists are long, and alternative practitioners are often inaccessible. The GP becomes not only the first port of call but the only one.

And yet, surveys of GPs themselves tell a parallel story: a majority admit they do not feel confident in diagnosing or treating menopause. Many confess that they received little or no formal training in it during medical school. Others rely on outdated knowledge shaped by the panic around hormone replacement therapy (HRT) in the early 2000s. Women arrive at the frontline expecting guidance. Instead, they are met with uncertainty, minimisation, or misdirection.

*Case Study 12: **"When Stress Isn't Stress"***
Kylie was 46 when she began waking drenched in sweat. She felt anxious during meetings, her mind went blank mid-sentence, and she struggled to keep up with her teenage children's schedules. She booked an appointment with her GP.

The doctor listened, nodded, and then leaned back. "It sounds like stress. You're at a busy stage of life." He recommended yoga, prescribed a low-dose antidepressant, and sent her home.

Months passed. The symptoms worsened. Kylie returned, this time with joint pain and insomnia so severe she felt like a shell of herself. The GP added sleeping tablets to her prescription list. At no point did he mention menopause.

It was only after Kylie joined a local women's walking group and heard others describe almost identical experiences that she realised what was happening. She changed GPs, asked about HRT, and found immediate relief. But she lost two years to unnecessary medication and an erosion of her confidence at work.

Her story is not unusual. It is the frontline failure repeated daily in waiting rooms across the country.

The Power of First Impressions
What happens at the first GP appointment often sets the course for the rest of a woman's menopausal journey. If the

GP names menopause early, a woman can begin to understand, plan, and seek appropriate treatment. If the GP avoids the word, minimises the symptoms, or steers toward unrelated diagnoses, the woman can be diverted for years.

This first impression carries disproportionate weight because of the trust invested in doctors. Most women assume that if menopause were relevant, their GP would mention it. Silence is interpreted as irrelevance. Women blame themselves, believing they are weak, lazy, or mentally unstable. They lose confidence not only in their bodies but in their judgment.

One British survey revealed that nearly one in four women considered leaving the workforce due to unmanaged menopause symptoms. Many had seen their GP but had left without answers. The frontline encounter did not just fail their health; it reshaped their working lives.

The GP as Arbiter of Legitimacy

The role of the GP is not simply diagnostic. It is symbolic. Doctors decide what is considered a "real" medical issue, what is worth treating, what deserves a prescription, and what requires a certificate for workplace accommodations.

When a woman describes brain fog and is told to "make lists," the system signals that her symptoms are trivial. When a woman asks for time off due to night sweats and receives no medical certificate, the system deems her suffering invisible. This arbiting power means that the GP is not only the gatekeeper to treatment but to recognition itself.

The email accidentally landed in your inbox about UK employers mandating workplace menopause support makes this point sharply: in countries where menopause is taken seriously, policy follows recognition. But in Australia, without GPs naming and validating symptoms, workplaces have no language or legitimacy to act. Silence at the clinic becomes silence at the office.

When the Frontline Collapses

The tragedy of the GP bottleneck is that it creates a cascade of failures. At the frontline, neglect is intimate and immediate: a woman leaves the consultation confused, dismissed, or medicated for the wrong condition. But the ripple effects extend far beyond the clinic:

- **At home**, women withdraw from family life, ashamed of their changing bodies.
- **At work**, they resign, downgrade, or silently underperform.
- **In healthcare**, they become chronic patients of insomnia, anxiety, or arthritis, treated for fragments rather than the whole.

Every missed opportunity at the frontline compounds into systemic cost.

Why the Frontline Matters

If we are to reform menopause care, we must begin where women begin: with the GP. No policy on workplace accommodations, no specialist clinic, no awareness campaign can substitute for the reality that the first point of contact determines the trajectory of care.

The GP is not just a doctor in this story. The GP is the scriptwriter of a woman's health journey. If they write "stress," the story unfolds one way. If they write "menopause," it unfolds another. That single word can mean the difference between years of confusion and months of relief.

The frontline of menopause is fragile because it is underprepared. Women bring their symptoms to the people they trust most, only to find those people unequipped. The betrayal is quiet but profound. It teaches women that their suffering is invisible and their needs negotiable.

This is why the GP bottleneck is not a side issue but the central failure of menopause care. The frontline is not working. And until it does, no woman can feel confident that her story will be recognised when she opens the clinic door.

Training Gaps, Training Failures

When a GP tells a woman that her brain fog is "just stress," or that her night sweats are "probably thyroid," it is tempting to see this as a personal failing, one doctor's ignorance. But zoom out, and a different story emerges. The problem is not individual doctors. The problem is how we train them.

How the Pipeline Shapes the Practice

In Australia, medical students can graduate after six years of training having spent fewer than six hours on menopause. Six hours, to cover a life stage that half the population will experience, often for a decade or more.

Compare this to the hundreds of hours dedicated to cardiovascular disease, diabetes, or pregnancy. Even acne receives more structured attention in some curricula than menopause. The result is obvious: GPs enter practice fluent in diseases that affect everyone, but barely literate in a transition that affects every woman.

A UK survey in 2019 revealed that 41% of medical schools had no mandatory teaching on menopause at all. In the US, similar audits have found that menopause education is scattered, inconsistent, and often delivered as a side-note in reproductive health, not as a distinct, significant stage of life.

The message is clear: menopause is not worth teaching.

A Legacy of Minimisation

Why does this gap exist? Partly, it is inertia. Medical curricula have long been shaped by acute disease, surgery, and crisis management. Predictable, universal transitions like menopause are treated as background processes, "natural," and therefore not requiring intervention.

But "natural" does not mean benign. Childbirth is natural, yet obstetrics is a cornerstone of medicine. Aging is natural, yet gerontology is a recognised specialty. Menopause, by contrast, is left in the margins, as though its symptoms were inconveniences rather than drivers of lost productivity, mental health crises, and preventable suffering.

This minimisation is also historical. For centuries, medicine framed women's reproductive life as binary: fertile or barren. Anything after fertility was collapse. That framing still shadows medical education today. If fertility is medicine's focus, then menopause is simply the afterthought.

Outdated and Dangerous Knowledge

Where menopause is taught, it is often taught badly. The panic around the Women's Health Initiative (WHI) study in 2002 still dominates GP education. That study, widely reported as proving that hormone replacement therapy increased breast cancer and cardiovascular risk, led to mass withdrawal of women from HRT. Only later did re-analyses reveal that the risks were overstated, context missing, and benefits under-reported.

But by then, the damage was done. Medical schools continued to teach caution. Doctors continued to hear that HRT was "risky." Even today, some GPs refuse to prescribe it, citing outdated data. Women pay the price.

In interviews, many doctors admit their only real knowledge of HRT comes from the WHI headlines of two decades ago. Others confess they have learned more from pharmaceutical reps or from patients themselves than from formal education. This is not training. It is abdication.

Case Study 13: **Learning from Patients**

Dr. Anita, a GP in regional Queensland, recalls her first decade in practice. "I wasn't taught menopause at uni. We might have had a two-hour lecture that lumped it in with general aging. I remember more about erectile dysfunction than I do about hot flushes.

"So when women came in, I had no framework. I would treat the symptom: insomnia with sleeping pills, depression with SSRIs, joint pain with anti-inflammatories. It was only when I hit menopause myself that I started reading. My patients taught me. They would bring in articles, sometimes even books, and say, 'Could this be me?' That's when I realised I had been failing them."

Dr. Anita retrained as a menopause specialist. But she is the exception, not the rule. Most GPs never get that second education.

The Global Picture

Training gaps are not unique to Australia. They are global.
- **UK:** A 2019 Freedom of Information request revealed that almost half of medical schools had no compulsory menopause education. Those that did often bundled it with puberty or fertility. The result: doctors enter practice without the Tools to manage half their patient population's midlife transition.
- **US:** A 2017 survey found that only 20% of medical schools included menopause in required curricula. Many graduates reported feeling "not at all prepared" to manage menopause.
- **Canada:** Studies mirror the same pattern. Menopause is addressed sporadically, with no national standards.
- **Europe:** Variations exist, but few countries require comprehensive menopause training across all institutions.

The pattern is consistent: menopause is treated as optional knowledge.

Comparative Training Hours

Country	Average Hours of Menopause Education	Notes
Australia	< 6 hours	Often embedded in reproductive or geriatric modules
UK	0-10 hours	41% of schools have no compulsory teaching
USA	~4 hours	Scattered across different courses
Canada	Variable	No standardised requirement
Germany	~8 hours	Mostly in gynecology blocks
Japan	Minimal	Culturally embedded but medically under-taught

This table tells its own story. Conditions with lower prevalence and less impact receive more dedicated hours. Menopause remains the silent module.

Consequences of Poor Training

The outcome of these failures is not theoretical. It plays out daily in clinics. Poor training produces three cascading consequences:

1. **Misdiagnosis:** Without a framework, doctors label symptoms as stress, aging, or psychiatric illness.
2. **Over-prescription of non-target drugs:** Antidepressants, sedatives, and painkillers become default solutions.
3. **Patient mistrust:** Women leave feeling dismissed, sometimes never returning.

These consequences are not small. They shape lives. Careers are lost. Relationships fracture. Women spend years in unnecessary suffering, all because their GP was never taught to recognise the obvious.

The Hidden Curriculum

It is not only the formal curriculum that shapes doctors, but the informal one. In the "hidden curriculum" of medicine, menopause is often mocked or minimised. Senior doctors model dismissive attitudes, treating hot flushes as jokes or rolling their eyes at "moody midlife women."

Students absorb this culture. By the time they graduate, they have internalised that menopause is not serious, not urgent, and not worth their attention. Training is not just absent, it is actively discouraging.

Towards Reform

If the GP bottleneck is to change, training must change first. That means:

- **Mandatory modules:** At least 30 hours on menopause in medical school, spanning physiology, psychiatry, and treatment.
- **Updated frameworks:** Curricula must integrate current evidence, not outdated WHI panic.
- **Cultural competence:** Training must include how menopause is understood in Indigenous, migrant, and multicultural communities.
- **Continued professional development:** Existing GPs need structured, accessible retraining, not optional webinars but accredited requirements.

Until medical education takes menopause seriously, every GP appointment will be a lottery. Some women will find doctors who self-educated. Most will not.

Doctors are not failing women because they do not care. They are failing because they were not taught to care. They were trained in a system that treated menopause as invisible. And so they reproduce that invisibility in every consultation.

Training gaps become treatment failures. Failures become lived suffering. The bottleneck tightens.
This is not inevitable. It is curriculum. And curricula can change.

The Misdiagnosis Machine

If you want to understand the true cost of poor training, you don't need statistics, you need to sit in the clinic with a woman describing her symptoms. One after another, they sound like a carousel of common ailments: tiredness, low mood, headaches, poor sleep, aching joints, forgetfulness, palpitations. To an undertrained GP, these are not menopause. They are stress, depression, aging, thyroid problems, arthritis, early dementia. And so begins the cycle of misdiagnosis.

This machine does not operate maliciously. It operates predictably. Inputs are women in midlife with overlapping symptoms. Outputs are prescriptions, referrals, and dismissals that miss the mark. Each misdiagnosis reinforces the next. Each wrong treatment delays the right one.

A System Built to Miss
Menopause is a multisystem transition. It affects the brain, the bones, the cardiovascular system, the skin, and the

psyche. It can present as hot flushes, night sweats, insomnia, anxiety, low libido, weight changes, or cognitive fog. No single symptom is definitive, and no two women are alike.

For a doctor without a menopause framework, the symptoms scatter like marbles. Each one rolls into another diagnostic bucket: insomnia into psychiatry, joint pain into rheumatology, brain fog into neurology, palpitations into cardiology. Instead of a unifying explanation, women receive piecemeal treatment, and rarely relief.

The Most Common Misroutes
1.   Insomnia → Anxiety or Depression
A woman reports broken sleep. The GP prescribes antidepressants or benzodiazepines. She leaves medicated, but still wakes drenched in sweat. The root cause, vasomotor instability, remains unaddressed.

2.   Brain Fog → Early Dementia or Depression
Cognitive lapses are frightening. Women describe walking into a room and forgetting why, losing words mid-sentence, or struggling to recall names. Too often, these are pathologised as early dementia or dismissed as "just aging." Antidepressants are prescribed, or women are referred for neurological tests. Meanwhile, estrogen depletion, the real driver, goes untreated.

3.   Joint Pain → Arthritis or Aging
Musculoskeletal pain is common in menopause due to hormonal changes in collagen and bone density. Yet many women are told it's "arthritis" or "wear and tear." They are prescribed anti-inflammatories, physiotherapy, or simply told to live with it.

4.   Palpitations → Cardiac Anxiety
Estrogen fluctuations can cause heart palpitations, yet many women are referred to cardiologists or told it's panic disorder. Expensive tests are ordered. Few are told that menopause can directly affect cardiac rhythm.

5.   Hot Flushes → Stress or Thyroid

The most iconic symptom of menopause is often missed. Women describe "heat waves," and GPs suspect thyroid dysfunction, stress, or infection. Blood tests are ordered. When results are normal, women are told "it's nothing."

Case Study 14: **Six Years on the Wrong Pills**

Maria, 52, from Melbourne, went to her GP at 46 complaining of fatigue, low mood, and insomnia. She was prescribed antidepressants. When those didn't work, the dosage was increased. Over the next six years, Maria cycled through three different antidepressants, two sleeping pills, and counselling.

Nothing changed. Her marriage suffered, her work declined, and she began to believe she was "broken."

It was only after a workplace seminar on menopause that she recognised herself in the description. She asked her GP about HRT. The doctor admitted he had never prescribed it before but agreed to try. Within weeks, her symptoms lifted. Maria wept, with relief, but also with rage. Six years of her life had been stolen by misdiagnosis.

The Antidepressant Reflex

Antidepressants are among the most over-prescribed drugs for women in midlife. While they can help with mood disorders, they are not a first-line treatment for menopause. Yet for GPs who lack confidence in HRT, SSRIs and SNRIs become the default.

This reflex is reinforced by time pressure. It is faster to write a script than to unpack a woman's full symptom profile. It is safer, legally, to prescribe a known drug than to navigate HRT guidelines. The result: women are medicated for depression they do not have, while their actual hormonal transition remains untreated.

The Cost of Scattergun Referrals

Misdiagnosis also drives a cascade of unnecessary referrals. Women are sent to neurologists, cardiologists, rheumatologists, and endocrinologists, each testing a single symptom in isolation. These appointments cost money, time, and energy. Meanwhile, the unifying explanation of menopause remains invisible.

One UK study found that women often see five different doctors before menopause is mentioned. By then, years may have passed.

Menopausal Medical Misdiagnosis

Symptoms Reported → *GP Interpretation* → Outcome

- **Hot flushes** → *Stress* → Antidepressants prescribed
- **Night sweats** → *Thyroid issue* → Blood tests, no answers
- **Brain fog** → *Dementia* → Neurology referral, anxiety
- **Joint pain** → *Arthritis* → Anti-inflammatories, no relief
- **Palpitations** → *Panic disorder* → Benzodiazepines, stigma

At no point does the arrow land on "Menopause."

Cultural Variations in Misdiagnosis
The misdiagnosis machine is amplified for women from culturally and linguistically diverse backgrounds. Without the right words, symptoms are described as fragments: "heat," "forgetting," "tired." Doctors misinterpret these fragments

as infections, mood disorders, or aging.

For Indigenous women, where silence around "women's business" is strong, symptoms often go unspoken until they are severe. By then, GPs default to the same scattergun approach: tests, pills, dismissals.

Why Misdiagnosis Matters

Some may argue that even if doctors miss menopause, women still receive some form of care. But care without accuracy is harm. Misdiagnosis carries costs:

- **Health costs:** Unnecessary drugs with side effects.
- **Psychological costs:** Women internalise that they are mentally ill or prematurely aging.
- **Economic costs:** Time and money wasted on irrelevant specialists.
- **Social costs:** Years of avoidable suffering at home and at work.

Misdiagnosis is not benign. It is a thief of time, dignity, and trust.

The GP bottleneck does not just silence menopause. It redirects it, into false categories that fracture women's stories and prolong their suffering. This is the misdiagnosis machine: predictable, preventable, and profoundly damaging.

Until doctors are trained to see menopause as the unifying framework it is, women will continue to be misrouted through the system, medicated for illnesses they do not have, and denied the relief they deserve.

Cultural Barriers at the GP Door

When women walk into a GP clinic, they do not leave their culture at the door. They bring their language, their upbringing, their taboos, and their expectations. For migrant women, Indigenous women, and those from culturally and linguistically diverse communities, these factors shape every stage of the consultation: how they describe symptoms, what they believe is happening, how the GP interprets them, and what happens next.

Too often, the consultation collapses under this cultural weight. Words do not align. Concepts do not translate. Silence is mistaken for absence. And once again, menopause disappears from view.

The Language Gap

Language is the first barrier. In English, "menopause" itself is a clinical import. In many other languages, there is no direct equivalent. Migrant women describe symptoms in fragments: "hot," "tired," "forgetting." Without a shared vocabulary, GPs misinterpret these fragments as infections, depression, or aging.

Take Mai's story. A Vietnamese migrant to Australia, she experienced night sweats, brain fog, and anxiety in her late forties. But in Vietnamese, there is no single term for menopause. She told her GP she was "hot" and "tired." The doctor prescribed sleeping pills. Years later, when her daughter trained as a nurse, she finally discovered the word "menopause" and understood what had been happening all along.

Mai's story is not an outlier. It is the lived reality of thousands of migrant women who cannot ask for help because they lack the words to do so.

Even with interpreters, the problem persists. Most medical interpreters are trained in general vocabulary, not reproductive health. A woman who describes hot flushes may be translated as having a fever. A woman describing memory lapses may be reported as depressed. The GP hears symptoms divorced from context.

The silence is not the woman's. It is systemic.

Indigenous Women: "Women's Business"
For Aboriginal and Torres Strait Islander women, cultural silence around "women's business" creates a different barrier. Many Indigenous languages have no single word for menopause. Phrases such as "bleeding no more" or "no more women's sickness" describe cessation but not transition.

Research in far north Queensland revealed that nearly 60% of Indigenous women surveyed had never heard the word "menopause" before participating in the study. Many did not know menstruation would eventually stop. This is not ignorance, it is the result of colonisation, health neglect, and cultural privacy around reproductive matters.

In some communities, menopause is framed positively, as entry into elderhood and increased respect. But this dignity is undermined by the healthcare gap. Indigenous women face higher rates of comorbidities such as diabetes, heart disease, and obesity. These conditions amplify menopausal symptoms. Yet when women seek help, doctors often dismiss their concerns or focus only on the comorbidities. The transition itself is rarely addressed.

One woman told researchers: "I was sweating, moody, sore all the time. I thought it was just my diabetes." Without culturally safe care, menopause becomes invisible within a broader landscape of health disadvantage.

Migrant Communities: Silence by Tradition
In many migrant communities, menopause is not openly discussed. Among South Asian women, for example, menstruation itself is treated as taboo. Its cessation is

marked not by ritual but by silence. Women enter menopause unprepared, unsure of whether their symptoms are normal or dangerous.

A Hindi phrase for menopause, **raja band ho gaya**, "the king has stopped", captures the cultural loss embedded in the transition. Menstruation is tied to fertility and status. Its cessation is described as dethronement. Women internalise this as shame. When they present to GPs, they minimise their symptoms. Doctors, already under-trained, minimise them further.

For Middle Eastern women, the Arabic phrase **sinn al-yaas,** "the age of despair", casts menopause as decline. Women told from girlhood that this stage signals worthlessness are unlikely to seek care. When they do, the consultation is heavy with stigma.

These cultural metaphors travel with women when they migrate. In Australian clinics, doctors hear hesitation, vagueness, and shame. Without cultural competence, they miss the meaning beneath the words.

Case Study 15: **The Interpreter Who Had No Words**
Amira, a 50 year old refugee from Syria, sought help for relentless sweating and dizziness. She brought her teenage son as an informal interpreter. When she described her symptoms, he looked embarrassed and translated briefly: *"She is sick. Always tired."*

The GP ordered blood tests. Results were normal. Amira was sent home. She returned twice more, each time with her son. Each time the translation faltered. Only months later, when she confided in a community health worker, did the word "menopause" surface.

Amira's story shows how language is not just a barrier but a filter. Without proper interpreters trained in reproductive health, women's voices are silenced before they even reach the GP.

Double Disadvantage: Gender and Race

The GP bottleneck is bad enough for white, English-speaking women. For women of colour, migrant women, and Indigenous women, the bottleneck tightens further.

Bias plays a role. Studies show that women of colour are less likely to have their pain taken seriously. When combined with the cultural taboos around menopause, this creates a double disadvantage. GPs not only fail to recognise symptoms but assume these women are less articulate, less accurate, or less in need of help.

In one Canadian study, First Nations women reported that menopause was "hidden, hush-hush." Yet they also expressed a strong desire for more information. Silence did not equal disinterest. It meant lack of opportunity. But too often, healthcare providers interpreted the silence as choice, assuming women "didn't want to talk about it."

The Role of Trust

Trust in the medical system is another barrier. For Indigenous communities, trust has been eroded by centuries of medical neglect, forced interventions, and systemic racism. Many women avoid GPs altogether, seeking advice only when symptoms are unbearable.

For migrant women, trust can be fragile. Doctors who dismiss symptoms reinforce the belief that seeking help is pointless. Women retreat further into isolation.

Without trust, women endure alone. And the cycle of silence continues.

Policy Failure: No Cultural Lens

Despite Australia's diversity, GP training rarely includes menopause through a cultural lens. Cultural competence is treated as a general skill, not a reproductive necessity. There are no national guidelines for how to discuss menopause with women from CALD (culturally and linguistically diverse) backgrounds. There are no interpreters trained specifically in menopause vocabulary.

This is a systemic blind spot. It leaves doctors unprepared and women unsupported.

Towards Culturally Safe Menopause Care
Breaking the cultural barriers requires structural change:
- **Language resources:** Multilingual fact sheets, videos, and interpreters trained in reproductive health.
- **Cultural training:** Mandatory GP education on how menopause is understood in different communities.
- **Community partnerships:** Working with elders, migrant organisations, and women's groups to create safe spaces for discussion.
- **Respect for cultural frames:** Recognising when menopause is viewed positively (as elderhood or freedom) and building on that strength, rather than imposing Western pathology.

The GP bottleneck is not just medical. It is cultural. It silences women twice: once through under-training, and again through misunderstanding. Migrant women, Indigenous women, and women from diverse communities carry the heaviest burden. They arrive at the clinic with symptoms but no words, with shame instead of stories, with trust already fragile.

The tragedy is not only that they leave without answers. It is that their silence is interpreted as absence, absence of need, absence of suffering, absence of menopause.

But the silence is not absence. It is evidence. Evidence of a healthcare system that has failed to make space for their language, their culture, their stories.
Until that changes, the GP door will remain closed for too many.

The Gender Bias in Listening

When women speak, medicine does not always listen. This is not an abstract critique; it is a daily experience repeated in consulting rooms across the country. The dismissal of women's voices is so routine that many have learned to anticipate it before they even walk through the clinic door.

The GP bottleneck is not just about missing training or misdiagnosis. It is also about bias, about who gets believed, who gets brushed aside, and whose suffering is measured against cultural stereotypes of "female fragility." For women in midlife, the listening gap is sharpened by age. Sexism and ageism converge to tell women that their bodies are untrustworthy, their emotions are excessive, and their symptoms are an inevitable part of "getting older."

Menopause, with its diffuse and variable symptoms, becomes the perfect storm: easy to dismiss, easy to belittle, easy to silence.

The Script of Dismissal

In countless consultations, the same script plays out:
- "It's just stress."
- "Everyone feels tired at your age."
- "Maybe you should lose a little weight."
- "You're too young for menopause."
- "You're too old to expect much to change."

These phrases are not neutral. They are dismissals wrapped in authority. A woman describing brain fog or joint pain is told she is exaggerating. A woman reporting night sweats is told she is anxious. A woman asking about HRT is warned she is "taking risks" without context.

Every phrase reinforces the same message: *your voice does not count.*

Ageism at the Consultation Table

Midlife women occupy a precarious place in medicine. Too young to be seen as "elderly," too old to be seen as "fertile," they fall into what researchers call a **care vacuum**. The healthcare system is designed around reproduction at one end and chronic disease at the other. Menopause, sitting in between, is treated as an interruption rather than a stage.

GPs unconsciously absorb these attitudes. A woman in her late 40s reporting exhaustion is told, "That's what happens at your age." A woman in her early 50s asking for help with libido is told, "Sex isn't important at this stage of life." These are not medical judgments; they are cultural ones. They reflect assumptions about what aging women should want, tolerate, or expect.

The result is a **normalisation of suffering**. What would be treated as pathology in younger patients is dismissed as "normal aging" in older women.

Sexism in Listening

Bias is not only about age. It is also about gender. Studies show that women's reports of pain are consistently taken less seriously than men's. Women are more likely to be given sedatives rather than pain relief. They are more likely to be told their symptoms are psychological rather than physiological.

In menopause, this pattern is amplified. Symptoms like anxiety, palpitations, and insomnia are framed as "emotional." Cognitive lapses are reframed as "stress." Even when women describe physical experiences, sweating, burning, joint stiffness, doctors often minimise them.

The effect is cumulative. A woman who feels dismissed once may persist. A woman dismissed three times may stop seeking help altogether. Listening bias becomes a self-fulfilling prophecy: women retreat, confirming the false belief that their suffering is minor.

Case Study 16: *"You're Overreacting"*

Helena, a 49 year old lawyer, described sudden waves of heat, panic attacks, and memory lapses so severe she feared early-onset dementia. When she raised these with her GP, he laughed lightly and said, "You're overreacting. Everyone forgets things in their forties. Maybe you're just stressed at work."

She left feeling embarrassed. For months, she doubted her own perceptions. Only later, after seeing a female GP, did she learn that her symptoms were textbook perimenopause. "What hurt most," she said, "was not the symptoms. It was being made to feel foolish for noticing them."

Helena's story shows how dismissal is not passive. It actively erodes women's confidence in their own bodies.

The Tone Problem

Listening bias is not only about words. It is also about tone. Women report being spoken to in patronising voices, interrupted mid-sentence, or rushed through consultations. The tone communicates what the words may not: *you are not important enough to deserve time.*

In short consultations, often less than ten minutes in bulk-billing clinics, women describing complex menopausal symptoms are pressured to simplify. When they cannot, doctors cut them off. The tone communicates impatience. The result is another layer of silencing.

When Bias Meets Culture

For migrant and Indigenous women, bias is compounded. Not only are their symptoms minimised as "female" or "age-related," but their cultural framing is dismissed as irrelevant. A woman using traditional metaphors to describe her body is told she is "unclear." An Indigenous woman hesitant to discuss reproductive matters is seen as "noncompliant."

In these encounters, listening bias becomes cultural erasure.

Structural Listening Gaps

Bias is not simply an individual failing. It is structural.

- **Time pressure:** Ten-minute consults discourage listening.
- **Payment models:** GPs are reimbursed for volume, not depth.
- **Training:** Without menopause education, doctors lack the framework to hear symptoms accurately.
- **Cultural scripts:** Society teaches that menopausal women are moody, irrational, or irrelevant, scripts that echo in the clinic.

Together, these forces create a system where women are not only unheard but systematically misheard.

Listening Study Snapshot

- Women's pain is underestimated by doctors **twice as often** as men's.
- Women wait an average of **65 minutes longer** than men in emergency rooms before receiving pain relief.
- In menopause consultations, women are **three times more likely** to be prescribed antidepressants than HRT.

The numbers confirm what women already know: the listening gap is real.

The Emotional Cost of Not Being Heard

The consequences of bias are not only medical but psychological. Women describe leaving consultations feeling ashamed, humiliated, and angry. Some stop seeking help altogether. Others turn to online forums and self-diagnosis.

The emotional toll is heavy. When a woman is told repeatedly that her symptoms are "in her head," she begins to question her sanity. When she is mocked for her forgetfulness, she withdraws from professional opportunities. When her pain is minimised, she stops trusting her own voice.

Listening bias is not just poor bedside manner. It is a form of harm.

Reversing the Bias

Addressing gender bias in listening requires both cultural and structural reform:

- **Training in active listening:** Teaching GPs to validate symptoms even when uncertain.
- **Bias awareness modules:** Explicit education on how sexism and ageism shape consultation.
- **Longer consults:** Funding models that allow time for complex discussions.
- **Diverse role models:** More female GPs and specialists to shift the culture of listening.

Above all, it requires humility. Doctors must be willing to say, "I don't know, but I believe you."

The GP bottleneck is not only about what doctors know, but about what they choose to hear. For too long, women in midlife have spoken into a void, their voices refracted through bias until they vanish.
Menopause is not invisible. It is spoken, daily, by millions of women. The tragedy is that medicine has not listened.

Until we confront the gender bias in listening, until doctors hear not only with their ears but with respect, the bottleneck will remain.

Listening is treatment. Listening is recognition. And right now, women are still waiting to be heard.

The Cost of Failure

Every bottleneck has a price. For menopause, the cost is not just measured in dollars but in dignity, trust, and human potential. When GPs fail to recognise, diagnose, or support menopause, the effects ripple outward: from the individual woman to her family, her workplace, her community, and the nation.

This is not theoretical. It is visible in the resignations of talented leaders, in the long-term prescriptions of unnecessary antidepressants, in the economic modelling of lost productivity, and in the silent suffering of women who withdraw from their own lives.
The GP bottleneck is not only a medical failure. It is a social and economic one.

The Personal Cost: Lives Shrunk by Silence
The first cost is personal. Women describe years, sometimes decades, of avoidable suffering because their symptoms were dismissed.

- **Physical toll:** Hot flushes, joint pain, insomnia, migraines. Without recognition, women live with untreated symptoms that erode daily functioning.
- **Psychological toll:** Being told "it's just stress" or "you're too young" leads to self-doubt and shame. Women begin to believe they are weak, irrational, or broken.
- **Identity toll:** Brain fog and memory lapses erode confidence. Women who once led teams or managed households begin to withdraw, fearful of being exposed.

One woman described it as "living half a life", present, but diminished.

The Family Cost: Invisible Labour

Families absorb what medicine ignores. Partners, children, and relatives become de facto caregivers when women cannot sleep, function, or cope.

- Partners take on more household responsibilities.
- Children learn to tiptoe around mood swings or exhaustion.
- Family dynamics strain under silence, because the word "menopause" is rarely spoken aloud.

In many families, women are traditionally the emotional anchors. When menopause is unsupported, that anchor is destabilised. The cost is measured in arguments, misunderstandings, and fractured relationships.

The Workplace Cost: A Leaky Pipeline

The workplace is where the GP bottleneck reveals its most measurable consequences. If women leave a GP without answers, they go to work unprepared and unsupported.

- **Presenteeism:** Women show up physically but cannot perform at full capacity due to untreated symptoms.
- **Absenteeism:** Sleepless nights and unmanaged health lead to sick days.
- **Turnover:** Many resign entirely. Surveys in the UK show that 1 in 10 women have left the workforce due to unmanaged menopause.
- **Leadership leakage:** High-performing women decline promotions or step down from roles, unwilling to expose their struggles to the spotlight.

Deloitte research estimates the economic cost of menopause-related productivity loss in Australia at **$10 billion annually.** That number captures only part of the story: the projects delayed, the mentorship lost, the innovation untapped.

The Healthcare Cost: Misdiagnosis Multiplied

Misdiagnosis is not cheap. Each incorrect referral, each unnecessary test, each prescription of inappropriate medication carries a price tag.

- Antidepressants, sleeping pills, and painkillers prescribed unnecessarily drain pharmaceutical budgets.
- Referrals to neurologists, cardiologists, or rheumatologists trigger costly diagnostic cascades.
- Repeated GP visits for unresolved symptoms clog the system.

When the wrong treatments pile up, the system spends more, while women continue to suffer.

The National Cost: Policy Gaps

At a national level, the GP bottleneck translates into lost productivity, increased welfare dependency, and higher healthcare expenditure. It also undermines gender equality goals.

Governments invest heavily in women's workforce participation, yet ignore the menopausal exodus happening in midlife. They champion STEM pathways and leadership programs, yet fail to address the health barrier pushing women out just as they reach peak career stages.

The bottleneck is not just a health gap. It is a gender equity gap.

Case Study 17: The CEO Who Walked Away

Joanne, 52, was the CEO of a mid-sized company. She began experiencing severe insomnia, anxiety, and cognitive lapses. Her GP prescribed antidepressants and advised stress leave.

Ashamed and unsupported, Joanne stepped down from her role. "I thought I was losing my mind," she recalled. Only later did she discover that her symptoms were menopausal.

Her departure was not just a personal loss. It was a corporate loss of leadership, continuity, and institutional knowledge. The board scrambled to replace her. Shareholder confidence dipped. The cost of failure cascaded beyond Joanne into the entire organisation.

A Compounding Cycle

The true danger of the GP bottleneck is its compounding nature. Each individual failure multiplies into systemic cost:

- A woman untreated at the GP → leaves her job → contributes to workforce gaps → reduces GDP.
- A woman misdiagnosed → prescribed antidepressants → develops side effects → increases healthcare costs.
- A woman dismissed → loses trust → avoids healthcare altogether → presents later with preventable chronic conditions.

The bottleneck is not a single missed opportunity. It is a machine for manufacturing cost.

What Cannot Be Measured

Some costs defy calculation. How do you measure the loss of a woman's confidence in her own mind? How do you quantify the wisdom absent from boardrooms, classrooms, or communities when women withdraw?

The unmeasured cost is cultural: the silence that erases stories, the absence of role models, the inheritance of ignorance passed from mothers to daughters.

The GP bottleneck is not just a door that fails to open. It is a tollgate. Women pay with their health, their careers, their relationships, and their futures. Families pay with strained dynamics. Workplaces pay with lost talent. Nations pay with billions in productivity losses.

The cost of failure is staggering. But it is also unnecessary. Every dollar, every resignation, every lost year could be prevented with basic recognition, adequate training, and systemic reform.

Failure is expensive. Silence is unaffordable.

What Better Looks Like

The GP bottleneck is not inevitable. It is designed. Which means it can be redesigned. Better is possible, if we are willing to confront bias, reform training, and embed menopause into the very DNA of healthcare.

The women who walk into GP clinics deserve more than shrugs, sedatives, and silence. They deserve recognition, expertise, and dignity. Better care is not utopia. It is practical, measurable, and overdue.

1. Training that Matches Reality
The first reform is obvious: make menopause education mandatory, modern, and meaningful.

- **Medical school curricula** must include at least 30 hours on menopause, covering physiology, mental health, treatment options, and cultural contexts.
- **GP registrar programs** should require demonstrated competence in menopause care before qualification.
- **Continuing professional development** should mandate regular updates as guidelines evolve.

Just as no doctor would graduate without understanding pregnancy or diabetes, no doctor should graduate without fluency in menopause.

2. Clinical Guidelines that Empower, Not Deter
Doctors need clear, evidence-based guidelines, not relics of outdated panic. Current GP guidelines often echo the fear that followed the 2002 Women's Health Initiative study, overemphasising risks of HRT while downplaying its benefits.

"Better" means guidelines that:
- Present balanced risk/benefit profiles for HRT.
- Offer clear decision trees for non-hormonal options.
- Address symptom clusters holistically (e.g., brain fog plus insomnia plus anxiety).
- Include culturally responsive advice for diverse populations.

Guidelines should not scare doctors into inaction. They should empower doctors into confident, informed care.

3. Time to Listen
Short consultations are the enemy of menopause care. Ten minutes is not enough to unpack a decade of symptoms.

A better model would:
- Fund **long consultations** specifically for menopause and midlife health.
- Encourage **structured check-ins** for women in their forties, just as antenatal visits are routine in pregnancy.
- Use **screening Tools** to help women articulate symptoms before the appointment, so doctors have a roadmap.

Listening takes time. System design must make that time available.

4. Language and Cultural Competence
Better care recognises that words are not neutral. GPs must be trained in how menopause is described across cultures.

Clinics should provide:

- **Multilingual materials** (fact sheets, videos, symptom diaries).
- Interpreters trained in reproductive vocabulary.
- **Cultural awareness training** so GPs understand the frames women bring with them.

A woman who says "the heat" should not be sent for a fever screen. A woman who says "bleeding no more" should be recognised as describing menopause.

5. Digital and Community Support
GPs cannot do this alone. A modern system would integrate community and digital Tools:

- **Digital symptom trackers** linked to medical records, allowing women to monitor changes and share with doctors.
- **Community education programs** delivered through workplaces, unions, churches, and women's groups.
- **Peer navigators**, trained women with lived experience who can support others through the transition.

Menopause is too big for the consulting room alone. It requires a community response.

6. Shifting the Culture of Listening
Policies and programs mean little if the culture of medicine remains dismissive. Better looks like doctors trained not only in facts but in **humility**.

- Active listening must be taught as a clinical skill, not a soft add-on.
- Bias awareness modules must challenge stereotypes of "hysterical" or "moody" women.
- Clinics should measure patient satisfaction specifically on feeling heard and respected.

A woman who feels believed leaves with more than treatment. She leaves with dignity intact.

7. Economic Recognition

Workplace and national policy must reflect the economic cost of the GP bottleneck. Better looks like:

- **Medicare rebates** for menopause-specific consults.
- **Employer incentives** for workplace education and flexible support.
- **Government modelling** that integrates menopause into gender equity and productivity planning.

Recognising menopause as an economic issue shifts it from private suffering to public priority.

Case Study 18: ***The Menopause Specialist Clinic***
In 2022, a pilot menopause clinic in the UK offered extended consultations, multidisciplinary teams (GPs, nurses, psychologists, physiotherapists), and culturally responsive care. Waitlists grew immediately, not because of inefficiency but because of unmet demand.

Patients reported feeling heard, respected, and treated as whole people. Many described it as the first time menopause was taken seriously.

The lesson is simple: when you design care with menopause in mind, women respond.

What Better Looks Like

Problem	Current Reality	Better Future
Training	<6 hours in medical school	30+ hours, mandatory competency
Guidelines	Outdated, fear-based	Balanced, empowering, updated
Consults	10 minutes, rushed	Funded long consults, structured check-ins

Language	Lost in translation	Multilingual, culturally competent
Listening	Dismissive, biased	Active, humble, accountable
Economy	Ignored in modelling	Integrated into productivity frameworks

Better care for menopause is not a luxury. It is not radical. It is the bare minimum of what women deserve.

The GP bottleneck is not inevitable. It is built on silence, bias, and neglect. Better is built on recognition, respect, and reform.
When future generations look back, they should be shocked that we ever accepted less.

The Bottleneck We Built

The GP bottleneck is not an accident.
It is the predictable outcome of a health system that never made menopause a priority.

Doctors were not trained.
Guidelines were not updated.
Listening was not valued.
Cultural difference was ignored.

And so women walked in with clear voices and left with silence.

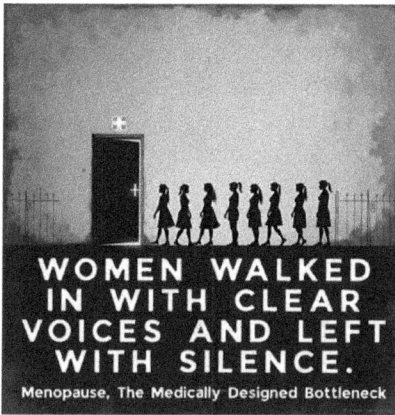

WOMEN WALKED IN WITH CLEAR VOICES AND LEFT WITH SILENCE.

Menopause, The Medically Designed Bottleneck

The costs are written everywhere:

- In lives shrunk by insomnia, anxiety, and shame.
- In careers abandoned and leadership lost.
- In families carrying invisible burdens.
- In national economies bleeding billions from preventable exits.

This is not failure by chance. It is failure by design.

But what we build, we can rebuild. The bottleneck can be dismantled, by training that tells the truth, by guidelines that empower, by consultations that give women time, by language that carries dignity instead of despair.

The GP door should not be the end of the story. It should be the place where recognition begins.

Signs of Change: The "Yet"

While the failures are stark, there are cracks of progress beginning to show:
- **Medical education pilots**: Universities in the UK and US have begun integrating dedicated menopause modules into GP and specialist training. In Australia, lobbying from women's health groups has pushed several medical schools to review their curricula for the first time in decades.
- **Parliamentary inquiries**: The UK's *Menopause in the Workplace Inquiry* has set a global benchmark, calling for national menopause strategies and

specialised clinics. Similar motions have been tabled in the Australian Senate and state parliaments, signalling political momentum.

- **NHS Menopause Clinics**: In England, the establishment of over **40 specialist menopause clinics** demonstrates what is possible when policy prioritises midlife women's health. These clinics are already reducing misdiagnosis, cutting waiting times, and normalising menopause care as standard medicine.
- **Professional guidelines**: The International Menopause Society and Royal Colleges have released updated guidelines encouraging earlier diagnosis, personalised treatment, and proactive use of HRT where safe.
- **Cultural visibility**: From Davina McCall's documentaries in the UK to Australia's *Menopause Friendly Workplace* initiatives, menopause is entering mainstream conversation. Awareness campaigns are reframing this stage of life as medical, social, and political, not just personal.

These green shoots prove the system can shift. The **"yet"** is not rhetorical, it is a space of possibility. With coordinated reform, the silence can be replaced by structured care, the waste replaced by wisdom, and neglect replaced by knowledge.

From Silence to Reform

Part II has traced the silence, in workplaces that push women out, in medical systems that misdiagnose them, in cultures that cloak menopause in shame. We have seen the cost counted not just in billions of dollars, but in lost potential, broken trust, and women diminished at the very point in life when their wisdom should be most valued.

The truth is clear: menopause is not a private weakness. It is a public health reality, an economic reality, and a social reality. And when institutions refuse to respond, the burden is not erased, it is shifted onto women themselves, who pay with their health, careers, and futures.
Yet silence does not last forever. The cracks are widening. Women are speaking up. Workplaces are beginning to listen. Medical schools are reconsidering what they teach. Parliaments are debating what was once unspeakable. The old structures may be slow, but they are not immovable.

This is the turning point. If Part II has shown us the crisis, Part III offers the response. Here we move from dismissal to design, from misdiagnosis to mandate. Here we reclaim resilience and demand reform.

PART III:

Reform, Resilience, and Reclamation

Part III marks the pivot of this book. What has been endured in silence is now placed into public view, and public responsibility. This section traces three essential arcs of change. **Reform** shows how policy, law, and workplace design must be rewritten to correct decades of neglect. **Resilience** honours the extraordinary endurance of women who carried the costs of silence, but it also exposes the limits of survival when systems refuse to evolve. **Reclamation** insists that menopause be named not as decline but as power, a stage of life to be claimed as authority, voice, and justice. Together, these chapters take the reader from structural change, to lived reality, to collective movement. The journey is not linear; it is a spiral, each stage necessary, each building on the other, until the silence is not only broken but replaced with a mandate for systemic, cultural, and personal transformation.

Every movement has a turning point, the moment when private suffering becomes public demand.

The first half of this book has mapped silence: the secrecy of symptoms, the failures of healthcare, the shame in workplaces, and the cultural erasure that has left generations unprepared. These are not accidents of biology. They are outcomes of neglect, taboos, and systems that chose not to listen.

But silence is not the end of the story. It is the beginning of resistance.

Part III exists as its own stand-alone section because this is where the arc bends. Here, menopause is no longer framed as personal struggle or institutional failure. It becomes political. It becomes collective. It becomes a movement that insists on recognition, reform, and reclamation.

Reform: Because health, law, and workplace systems will not change unless pushed. Policies must be rewritten, medical training rebuilt, workplaces redesigned.

Resilience: Because women have carried the weight of silence for decades, and yet continue to build networks, share stories, and refuse erasure. That strength is a resource in itself.

Reclamation: Because menopause must be seized back from stigma. It must be renamed not as decline but as transformation, a life stage rich with authority, wisdom, and power.

This part of the book stands alone for a reason. It is not simply about coping; it is about changing. It is not a quiet diary; it is a public declaration.

The chapters that follow take us from the whisper of individual stories to the roar of collective action, unions at the bargaining table, comedians on stage, legislators in parliament, women across cultures demanding recognition. They show what the world is already doing right, what Australia must do next, and why menopause is not a private inconvenience but a public mandate.

This is the pivot: from silence to system change, from shame to movement.

Welcome to the fight for reform, resilience, and reclamation.

Chapter 17:
Reform, Policy, Structure, and Systems

Why Menopause Must Be a Policy Priority

Menopause is a universal transition that has been systematically overlooked in health policy. Unlike maternity care, mental health, or chronic disease management, menopause has no comprehensive national framework. The consequences are significant:

Health System Burden: Women presenting with menopause symptoms are often misdiagnosed with depression, anxiety, or cognitive decline, leading to inappropriate prescriptions and repeat consultations.

Economic Loss: Women aged 45-60 are leaving the workforce early due to unmanaged symptoms, reducing labour force participation and tax revenue.

Equity Gap: Without recognition in legislation, menopause remains invisible in workplace rights, anti-discrimination protections, and gender equity reporting.

This neglect is not benign. It is a structural inequity that requires systemic correction.

The Policy Case

Health
Menopause affects 100% of women who live beyond their mid-40s.
Symptoms affect physical, mental, and cognitive health.
Misdiagnosis and under-treatment inflate health costs.

Economic
Productivity losses from absenteeism and attrition run into billions annually.
Retaining senior women strengthens leadership pipelines, innovation, and GDP.

Equity
Without recognition, women face systemic disadvantage. Menopause must be integrated into gender equity strategies alongside pay equity and parental leave.

Risks of Inaction
If governments fail to act:
- Women will continue to be over-medicated with antidepressants rather than receiving appropriate care.
- Economies will lose skilled female leaders at the peak of their careers.
- Legal systems will face rising claims as women seek justice through discrimination frameworks.
- Public trust will erode as women see their lived experiences dismissed.

The Power of Policy to Shape Health and Work
Reform is the first pillar of change. It recognises that menopause is not simply a private matter for women to manage on their own, but a structural issue shaped by government policy, legislation, and public investment. Without reform, workplaces lack clear standards, businesses improvise with inconsistent responses, and the health system continues to underserve half the population. With reform, however, governments at both state and federal levels can create frameworks that ripple outward into workplaces, communities, and homes.

Federal Reform: Setting the National Frame
At the federal level, policy determines the ground rules of healthcare access, workplace rights, and research funding.

Legislation
- The Fair Work Act (Cth) governs minimum workplace conditions. Today, it recognises carer's leave, family leave, and even compassionate leave, but it has no explicit category for menopause-related accommodations.

- The Workplace Gender Equality Act requires large employers to report gender equity metrics. Adding menopause data would give visibility to its workplace impact.

Funding & Programs
- Federal budgets dictate Medicare rebates, PBS subsidies, and public health campaigns. If menopause is not explicitly prioritised, services remain fragmented.
- Earmarked federal research grants could address the severe underfunding of menopause-related studies.

National Strategies
- The National Women's Health Strategy 2020–2030 acknowledges menopause briefly. Reform means upgrading it from a footnote to a headline priority, complete with measurable targets.

State and Territory Reform: Where Policy Meets People
While Canberra sets the national frame, it is the states and territories that run hospitals, employ health staff, and regulate many workplace practices.

Public Health Systems
- States fund and operate hospitals, community clinics, and health services. They decide how much GP and nurse training on menopause is included in public-sector programs.
- Pilot programs in Victoria demonstrate that state-backed menopause clinics can provide accessible, specialist care.

Workplace Regulation (Public Sector)
- State governments are among the largest employers (teachers, nurses, police, public service). Introducing menopause leave and policy across

state workforces would create a template for the private sector to follow.

- Victoria and NSW have already begun experimenting with reproductive health leave policies, signalling momentum.

The Impact on Business

Reform is not anti-business. In fact, it provides certainty and protects productivity.

Compliance vs Productivity

- Employers often fear "red tape." Yet Deloitte (2020) estimated that unmanaged menopause costs billions in absenteeism, presenteeism, and turnover.
- Clear reform reduces confusion and gives businesses ready-made templates for accommodation.

Insurance and Liability

- Misdiagnosed or unsupported menopause often manifests as stress claims or mental health leave. Reform redirects these from expensive litigation to proactive support.
- Employers gain by reducing long-term costs of churn, recruitment, and lost expertise.

The Impact on Health

Reform is not only about workplaces. It is also about health equity.

Access

- Longer Medicare rebates for menopause consults.
- Telehealth appointments that are funded. (at time of writing, changes to the Medicare system were being rolled out. Medicare Telehealth will only be

available IF you have physically seen a dr in the 12 month period. This makes health hard for those remote or with reduced mobility)

- Investment in rural and regional clinics so geography is not destiny.

Equity

- Federal standards for interpreter services in reproductive health, critical for migrant and Indigenous women.

Training for culturally safe menopause care in public hospitals.

Research

- Currently, cardiovascular disease and oncology receive magnitudes more funding than menopause. Reform means directed NHMRC/ARC grants to close this gap.

Why Reform Must Come First

Reform creates the floor everyone can stand on. Without it, businesses hesitate, health systems minimise, and women are left to improvise survival. With it, competence becomes the norm and dignity becomes predictable.

Reform is the structural foundation.

- Without it, businesses will hesitate, unsure of costs or obligations.
- Without it, health systems will continue to treat menopause as an afterthought.
- Without it, women will be forced to rely on resilience, shouldering systemic failure on their own.

Reform reframes menopause from a private struggle to a public mandate. It demands that governments use the Tools they already wield, law, funding, strategy, and leadership, to create systems that finally see women in midlife.

Policy That Protects

Policy is the point where principles become guarantees. Everything that has been set out in this chapter only becomes real when it is embedded in rules, budgets, and public expectations. Without policy, healthcare that listens is a matter of individual luck. Without policy, workplaces that support are dependent on a sympathetic manager. Without policy, communities that recognise are left to volunteer efforts and passing trends. Policy is the spine that allows a society to stand upright. It is the architecture that protects women who should never have to carry their dignity alone.

For most of modern health planning, menopause has existed outside the frame. Governments built strategies for children, for pregnant women, and for the elderly. They built disease strategies for cancer and cardiac illness. They wrote laws for disability, parental leave, and occupational safety. Yet they rarely wrote menopause into the plans that shape health, work, or education. This omission was not the absence of a problem. It was the absence of language, measurement, and priority. When a life stage is not counted, it is not funded. When it is not funded, it is not delivered. The silence of policy mirrors the silence of culture and medicine, and that silence has consequences.

The consequences can be traced through the themes of this chapter. When healthcare does not listen, the cause is often upstream. Medical schools have no firm mandate to teach menopause. Health departments have not built dedicated clinics or statewide referral pathways. Pharmaceutical regulators and public subsidy systems have not designed clear access routes for evidence based hormonal therapies, or for non hormonal options where they are safer or preferred. Mental health frameworks have not been revised to recognise perimenopausal mood disorders as a distinct category. Each of these gaps can be seen as a failure of individual practice. In truth, they are failures of policy design.

When workplaces do not support, the cause is again upstream. Industrial relations systems have not set a floor of obligations that recognise menopause. Equality frameworks have not required organisations to measure retention and progression of women in midlife. Public service commissions have not modelled best practice as large employers. Regulators have not written guidance that would normalise reasonable adjustments for temperature, rest, uniforms, scheduling, and appointment time. Without a baseline, support remains an act of goodwill. Goodwill is fragile. Policy is durable.

When communities do not recognise, the cause is still upstream. Curricula in schools have not been updated to include menopause alongside puberty. National health literacy programs have not created plain language resources that are translated into the languages women actually speak. There has been little investment in interpreter training that covers reproductive health vocabulary, or in community organisations that could carry accurate information into faith groups, sporting clubs, and neighbourhood networks. Policy is not only about funding clinics. It is about funding knowledge, language, and belonging so that women are not left alone to guess their way through a changing body.

Health system levers
- Mandate menopause competence in undergraduate training and continuing professional development.
- Establish specialist clinics as referral and training hubs, with telehealth pathways for remote communities.
- Fund time. Complex consults require longer appointments and rebates that make listening possible.
- Integrate mental health frameworks so perimenopausal mood disturbance is screened, treated, and referred appropriately.

The work of policy begins with naming. A national government that names menopause in its health strategy changes the signal sent to systems. Naming says this matters. Naming allows targets to be set, and targets allow budgets to be assigned. A national strategy that includes menopause can define what basic access should look like. It can state that every general practitioner must be trained to diagnose and manage common presentations. It can state that every region should have access to specialist care within a reasonable time. It can state that cultural safety is a requirement, not a courtesy, and that services must be accessible to Indigenous women and to women who speak languages other than English. A strategy is not a poem. It is a map.

Workplace levers
- Clarify reasonable adjustments in law and guidance. Examples include flexible scheduling, breathable uniforms, cool spaces, privacy for recovery, and protected time for appointments.
- Require public sector leadership and publish guidance that private employers can adopt.

Mapping begins with the health system. A policy that protects women in midlife would require medical education providers to include rigorous menopause training in both undergraduate curricula and continuing professional development. This is not an invitation. It is a condition of accreditation. Doctors who graduate should have a vocabulary that includes vasomotor symptoms, sleep disturbance, cognitive change, urogenital symptoms, bone health, cardiovascular risk, and mental health impacts. They should be able to distinguish between primary mood disorders and hormonally driven mood changes. They should know when to consider hormone therapy, when to consider non hormonal options, when to refer, and how to explain risks and benefits in plain language. Training should be assessed, not optional. Assessment turns vague awareness into clinical competence.

Policy must then translate knowledge into access. Health departments can establish specialist menopause clinics at state and territory level, integrated with primary care rather than siloed from it. These clinics would serve as referral centres for complex cases and as training hubs for local clinicians. They would offer multidisciplinary care where appropriate, with gynaecology, endocrinology, mental health, and allied health available for integrated management. They would also provide telehealth for rural and remote women, ensuring that geography does not decide dignity. A clinic is more than a building. It is a statement that women's midlife health is not an afterthought.

Access is also a function of affordability. Policy makers control the levers that determine whether treatments are covered, what consults are reimbursed, and which therapies are subsidised. A protective policy would ensure that evidence-based hormone therapies are affordable across the country. It would also support the evaluation and regulation of complementary therapies, so that women are not left to choose between high-cost products and unregulated promises. Affordability includes the price of time. Longer consultations are often required to take full histories and to discuss options without rushing. Rebate structures can be designed to allow longer appointments without punishing either the doctor or the patient. When time is funded, listening becomes possible.

Mental health policy must also evolve. If psychiatrists and psychologists are trained without a lens on perimenopausal mental health, misdiagnosis will continue. National mental health frameworks can recognise perimenopausal mood disturbance as a clinical reality that requires specific assessment and care pathways. This does not mean that every midlife depression should be attributed to hormones. It means that the possibility should be considered and that interdisciplinary care between psychiatry, general practice, and menopause specialists should be encouraged rather than left to chance. It also means investment in non pharmacological supports such as sleep programs, counselling, and stress reduction that can reduce suffering while medical treatment is optimised.

Measurement is the ally of policy. When a society begins to count, it begins to care. A national policy that protects would commission regular data collection on menopause related health outcomes, on time to diagnosis, on treatment access, and on patient satisfaction. It would measure absenteeism and presenteeism linked to unmanaged symptoms, and it would track the retention of women in midlife across sectors. Data would be disaggregated to reveal inequities faced by Indigenous women, migrant women, and women in rural and remote regions. Transparency would drive accountability. Reports would be tabled publicly so that progress is visible and neglect cannot hide behind ignorance.

The workplace dimension of policy is equally important. If work is where women spend much of their waking lives, then workplace law is where protection must be anchored. Legislators can create a clear expectation that employers will make reasonable adjustments for workers experiencing significant menopausal symptoms. This is not a special privilege. It sits comfortably alongside existing obligations to accommodate disability and pregnancy. Reasonable adjustments might include flexible scheduling, access to cooler spaces, uniforms made from breathable fabrics, opportunities to pause and recover, and protected time to attend medical appointments. The details will vary by role and sector. The principle is constant. Work should not worsen health. Health should not end work.

Law alone is not culture. A protective policy would also require public bodies to lead by example. Government departments can be instructed to implement comprehensive menopause policies that are visible, practical, and enforced. Public service commissions can publish guidance for managers and staff. Procurement policies can give preference to suppliers who demonstrate best practice. National awards programs can recognise employers who lift the standard. When the public sector models support, it creates a norm that spreads beyond government into the private and community sectors.

Education policy is the foundation of cultural change. School curricula can be updated to teach menopause alongside puberty in age appropriate ways. Health education can explain that menstruation begins and that it also ends, and that the stage in between is significant. Students can learn the basics of symptoms, the fact that experience varies, and the idea that support and empathy are normal. Teacher training can include information about supporting colleagues and about navigating their own health. Universities and vocational education providers can integrate menopause into health and human resources courses so that the next generation of managers and clinicians arrives in the workforce with language and understanding.

Community and education levers
- Update curricula so students learn that menstruation begins and ends, and that the stage in between deserves respect and support.
- Fund interpreter training and culturally specific resources.
- Partner with Indigenous health services and migrant organisations to carry credible information into communities.

Policy should speak in many languages, because the nation speaks in many languages. A protective approach would fund interpreter training that includes reproductive health terms. It would support the creation of culturally appropriate resources that describe menopause in ways that reflect different traditions and metaphors. It would invest in partnerships with Indigenous health services and migrant community organisations to deliver education that is credible because it is local. Culture is not an obstacle to policy. It is the context that makes policy meaningful.

Rural and remote access must be addressed openly. Women outside major cities face longer travel times, fewer clinicians, and higher costs. Policy can fund mobile clinics, telehealth consultations, and outreach programs that take care to where women live. Pharmacy systems can be simplified so that necessary therapies are available without impractical delays. Outreach can be coordinated with local councils and community organisations so that knowledge arrives alongside care. No woman should have to choose between staying close to family and receiving competent menopause treatment.

Rural and remote levers
- Mobile clinics, telehealth, and simplified pharmacy access.
- Outreach coordinated with local councils and community groups.

Research policy is the engine that keeps progress moving. Governments decide what questions are asked at scale. Dedicated funding calls for menopause research can stimulate studies on the intersection between reproductive aging and mental health, on the long term effects of different therapies, on the specific experiences of Indigenous and migrant women, and on the economics of workplace interventions. Policy can require that clinical trials include women in midlife as a default rather than as an afterthought. It can support research translation so that findings do not sit in journals but reach clinics, workplaces, and communities in the form of usable Tools.

Research and governance levers
- Ring-fenced research funding across neuroendocrinology, mental health, therapeutics, and workplace economics.
- Default inclusion of midlife women in trials.
- Cross-portfolio taskforce with annual public plans, timeframes, and responsibilities.

To ensure that policy survives the electoral cycle, governance structures matter. A cross portfolio taskforce can bring together health, women, employment, education, Indigenous affairs, and multicultural affairs. That taskforce can publish an annual plan with clear actions, timeframes, and responsibilities. It can consult widely with unions, employer groups, medical colleges, community organisations, and women with lived experience. It can hold systems to account by naming what has been done and what remains undone. Governance is the practice of turning promises into habits.

Funding is the mirror of belief. Budgets express what a society values. A protective policy would allocate funds to specialist clinics, to training programs, to interpreter services, to community education, and to workplace guidance. It would create small grants for local organisations to innovate and share models. It would offer incentives for employers who adopt best practice and demonstrate measurable improvements in retention and wellbeing. Money directed with clarity does not vanish. It builds scaffolds that keep women supported long after speeches fade.

Funding
- Budgets express belief. Allocate funds to clinics, training, interpreter services, community education, workplace guidance, and innovation grants. Incentivise employers who deliver measurable retention and wellbeing gains.

None of this is revolutionary. It is precise, practical, and proven in pieces across different places. The task is to gather the pieces into a whole. The international landscape shows that change is possible. The United Kingdom has demonstrated that parliamentary attention catalyses policy, that national broadcasters can normalise conversation, and that specialised clinics can be established within public health systems. Canada has shown that partnerships with Indigenous communities can produce research and care models that are culturally safe. Japan has shown that non Western frames can sit alongside biomedical care. Australia has the capacity to lead if it chooses to meet women's lives with honest policy.

Symbols and signals
- When law names menopause, culture follows. Public recognition normalises conversation, reduces stigma, and sets the weather for respect.

It is important to remember what is at stake. Behind every policy line is a person. Behind every budget item is a life that can tilt toward stability rather than spiral into confusion. A national referral pathway means a teacher can find help before she considers resigning. A funded interpreter program means a newly arrived migrant can explain her symptoms without shame. A mandated training module means a young doctor can recognise perimenopause in a forty-seven-year-old patient and offer treatment that changes the course of her year. A workplace standard means a nurse can adjust her roster while she finds a therapy that works. Policy reaches into rooms we will never see and changes choices we will never hear spoken aloud. That is its power.

Policy also has symbolic work to do. When a nation writes menopause into law, it says to women that their bodies are part of the civic story. It says that midlife is not exile. It says that elderhood is not loss of status but a change in how status is held. Symbols are not trivial. They change the weather of culture. They make it easier for women to speak and for others to listen. They make it harder for jokes to pass and for cruelty to hide. A law can open a door that culture then learns to keep open.

There will be objections. Some will say that menopause is private and therefore not the business of the state. Yet pregnancy was once called private. Domestic violence was once called private. Mental health was once called private. Policy has always moved the boundary between private suffering and public responsibility. It has done so when the scale of harm makes solitude unjust. Menopause belongs in public policy because its neglect costs too much in wasted talent, unnecessary illness, and preventable shame.

Addressing objections
- Privacy is not a defence. Pregnancy, domestic violence, and mental health were once deemed private. They became public responsibilities when the cost of neglect was undeniable.
- Scarcity is not neutral. Prevention pays for itself in participation, reduced misdiagnosis, and lower churn.

Others will say that the budget cannot stretch. Budgets always claim scarcity. The real question is priority. A policy that prevents early exit from the workforce pays for itself in increased participation and reduced rehiring costs. A policy that reduces misdiagnosis saves mental health budgets from overprescribing and inappropriate referrals. A policy that funds education lowers the hidden costs of trial and error at the individual level. Investment here is not sentimental. It is rational.

To tie the threads of this chapter together, think of policy as the instrument that makes each earlier promise durable. Healthcare that listens requires mandates for training, for clinics, for access and affordability, and for mental health integration. Workplaces that support require standards, guidance, and enforcement, as well as public sector leadership that demonstrates what good looks like. Communities that recognise require curricula, interpreters, and partnerships that take knowledge out of institutions and carry it into the places where women live. Without policy, these three domains rely on the energy of individuals. With policy, they become the common sense of a nation.

The language of this chapter has been deliberate. We have said that every woman deserves healthcare that listens. We have said that every woman deserves workplaces that support. We have said that every woman deserves communities that recognise. Policy completes the sentence. Every woman deserves policy that protects.

Protection does not mean paternalism. It means minimal guarantees that no woman can be denied. It means building a floor beneath which no one falls. It means drawing a circle of belonging wide enough to hold the real lives of women at midlife, in cities and towns, across cultures and classes.

An honest policy would end with an invitation. Governments should invite women to help design the systems they will use. Unions and employer groups should invite workers to shape the adjustments they need. Medical colleges should invite patients to speak into curriculum design. Community organisations should invite elders, interpreters, and young people to craft language that feels like home. The movement that began as a whisper and has grown into a roar must be heard in the rooms where decisions are made. Policy is not only written by ministers. It is authored by the lives it serves.

There will come a day when it seems strange that menopause was ever ignored. Children will learn about it in school health classes. Doctors will treat it without hesitation. Managers will understand it as part of the life course of their teams. Communities will weave it into story and ritual without embarrassment. Newsrooms will cover it without reaching for cliché. That day will not arrive by accident. It will arrive because policy was written, funded, implemented, and renewed.

Until then, the task is clear. Name menopause as a public priority. Train the people who will meet women at the front door of the health system. Build clinics that make specialised care accessible. Fund interpreters so that words can find their way from body to explanation. Write workplace standards that allow women to remain and to lead. Teach the next generation so that knowledge becomes inheritance rather than improvisation. Count what we have ignored so that improvement can be seen in numbers as well as in stories. Allocate budgets that match the scale of reality. Create governance that outlasts the news cycle. Listen to the women who have carried this in silence for far too long and let their experience become the shape of reform.

Policy that protects is the bridge between promise and practice. It is the way we take the insights of this chapter and carry them into every clinic, every office, every classroom, every community hall. It is the way we turn dignity from a private hope into a public norm. It is the way we ensure that the next generation of women will not depend on luck to be heard. When a nation writes such policy, it writes a different future. It tells women that they are seen. It tells managers that support is expected. It tells clinicians that listening is not optional. It tells communities that recognition is part of who we are. In that future, menopause is not a silence to endure. It is a stage of life to be met with competence, compassion, and collective care.

The circle closes as it should. A movement becomes a mandate. A mandate becomes a framework. A framework becomes a lived reality. And the women who once carried suitcases of spare clothes to work, who once ate lunch in cars to hide their fear of smell, who once lay awake wondering if they were losing their minds, find instead a society that holds them steady. That is not charity. That is public duty. That is policy that protects.

From Awareness to Accountability

This chapter has made a simple case. Dignity is not a courtesy. It is a standard. If half the workforce will traverse menopause, then half the workforce must be able to do so without penalty to health, income, leadership, or pride. Awareness has opened the door. Accountability must now walk through it. This is a manifesto written in the language of implementation. It is not a plea and it is not a slogan. It is a framework that any responsible employer, health system leader, or policymaker can adopt, measure, and improve over time.

The first principle is clarity. We name menopause as a predictable stage in the working life course. We recognise perimenopause as a multi-year transition that can present with physical, cognitive, and psychological symptoms of varying intensity. We state openly that unmanaged symptoms can affect performance, attendance, and confidence, and that these impacts are organisational issues, not personal failings. Once named, the matter moves from discretion to design.

The second principle is equity. What has long been left to individual endurance must be redistributed into systems that share the burden fairly. Menopause support belongs where other equity provisions live. It belongs in induction, in manager training, in health benefits, in facilities standards, in leave frameworks, and in performance practice. It belongs in our data, in our risk registers, and in our board reporting. Equity is achieved when a woman can seek support without trading away reputation, when a manager can provide adjustments without improvisation, and when an organisation can demonstrate outcomes without relying on anecdote.

The third principle is cultural safety. Language, identity, and history shape how women experience and describe symptoms, how they seek care, and whether they feel safe to disclose. A credible response recognises Indigenous women as knowledge holders and designs support with them, not for them. It recognises migrant women who may not have a single word for menopause in their first language and ensures that interpreters and materials make meaning in the right words, not just in English words. It recognises that privacy is not secrecy and that trust is earned through respectful options, not forced disclosure.

The fourth principle is measurement. Strategy without measurement is theatre. We will define what success looks like and we will count toward it. We will know whether training reaches managers and whether confidence to disclose has risen. We will know whether adjustments are being granted promptly and fairly. We will know whether women are staying, progressing, and leading. We will know whether complaints are resolved, whether health access is timely, and whether the culture is changing in practice rather than on paper. Measurement will be specific enough to guide action and humane enough to respect privacy.

The path from principle to practice begins at the point of contact. In healthcare, the point of contact is the clinician. In work, it is the line manager. Both must be equipped to listen, to recognise, and to respond. For managers, this means structured guidance, scenario based training, and a clear escalation pathway. It means understanding that performance management and health support are not the same process. It means knowing how to offer adjustments without challenging credibility or demanding unnecessary detail. It means scheduling with empathy, recording with accuracy, and following up with consistency. For clinicians, it means training that treats menopause as standard competence, referral networks that do not end at the clinic door, and consultation times that allow the full story to be heard.

Principles
Principle 1: Clarity Name menopause and perimenopause as predictable life stages with potential impacts on performance, attendance, and confidence. Move from discretion to design.
Principle 2: Equity Embed menopause support where equity provisions live: induction, manager training, health benefits, facilities, leave, performance practice, data, risk, and board reporting.
Principle 3: Cultural safety Design with, not for. Partner with Indigenous women and migrant communities. Fund interpreters and materials that use the right words in the right languages. Respect privacy and choice of terminology.
Principle 4: Measurement Define success and count toward it without surveillance. Track training reach, speed and fairness of adjustments, retention and progression of midlife women, time to diagnosis, and satisfaction with care.

Facilities are part of the response. Temperature control is not a luxury. Access to cool spaces, breathable uniforms where uniforms are required, and private areas for recovery are basic enablers of dignity. Technology can help with flexible rostering and remote work during worst-symptom windows, and it can hinder when presenteeism is rewarded over productivity. We will choose technology and design choices that favour health and outcomes rather than optics.

Benefits need to align with the evidence. Health plans should provide affordable access to evidence based hormonal and non hormonal therapies. Employee assistance programs should include practitioners who understand perimenopausal mental health and who can triage without pathologising hormonal transitions. Where we preventively invest in sleep, stress management, and nutrition support, we will measure whether those services are being used by the women who need them and whether they are making a difference.

Policy is the charter that protects when people change roles and when leaders change priorities. A credible policy names who is covered, what adjustments may be considered, who can approve, how requests are recorded, and how privacy is protected. It explains the difference between a short term flare and a sustained need. It clarifies the connection between adjustments and performance expectations so that support does not become a stigma. It sets review points so that adjustments evolve with symptoms. It makes complaint pathways safe and timely. Above all, it makes the organisation predictable in the best sense of the word.

Culture is the air policy breathes. We will set tone from the top without forcing disclosure from the front line. Senior leaders can speak to the principle and model respectful language. Human resources can run campaigns that normalise support options without centring women's pain as their defining identity. Team rituals can be adjusted to remove casual mockery that has long passed as humour. Every message will point to the same destination. We assume good faith. We build clear paths. We make it easy to ask. We respond with competence.

Accountability must travel all the way to governance. Boards and executive teams should see regular reporting on retention, progression, and usage of adjustments among employees in midlife, with care taken to protect individual privacy. They should understand the financial case as well as the ethical one. The cost of unmanaged symptoms expresses itself in recruitment, backfill, overtime, workers compensation claims, and lost leadership. The return on investment expresses itself in stability, loyalty, risk reduction, and reputation. When an employer gets this right, it signals to every talented woman that her contribution is expected to continue and that her health will be respected as she leads.

Partnerships extend the impact beyond any single employer. Unions can codify adjustments in enterprise agreements so that equity does not depend on individual managers. Insurers can create incentives for evidence-based programs and reduce premiums as claims fall. Industry bodies can publish shared benchmarks and case studies so that progress generalises across sectors. Governments can recognise leaders through procurement preferences and public service exemplars. Universities and colleges can embed menopause competence in management and health curricula. When partners act together, solutions become common practice rather than isolated projects.

Inclusion requires proximity to lived experience. We will convene advisory groups that include women who are currently navigating menopause at work and women who have navigated it already. We will include Indigenous women, women of colour, women with disability, and women from migrant and refugee backgrounds in design and review. We will ask what works, what does not, and what dignity feels like in practice. We will not assume one story stands for all. We will prioritise what women say they need over what is easiest to administer. Proximity will keep us honest.

Risk management has a place here too. The risks of inaction are legal, financial, and cultural. They include discrimination claims, psychological injury claims, avoidable absenteeism, and accelerated turnover among senior women. They include reputational harm when poor practice is surfaced publicly. They include the quiet erosion of culture when talented women decide that stepping back is safer than stepping forward. A mature organisation recognises these risks and treats menopause as a material people risk with controls, owners, and reviews.

Language will remain the lever that moves behaviour. We will speak precisely. We will avoid metaphors that belittle or pathologies that frighten. We will translate materials into the languages our people use at home. We will fund interpreters who can talk about reproductive health with

346

clarity. We will respect that not all women will wish to use the term menopause in describing what they are experiencing. We will make room for descriptions that feel truer in different cultures. The goal is not a single vocabulary. The goal is shared understanding.

Education will start early and recur often. We will include content on menopause in school programs alongside puberty so that the next generation views this stage as normal and manageable. We will educate managers annually, not once. We will update guidance as evidence evolves. We will expect that men learn this content as well as women, not as spectators but as colleagues, partners, and leaders who shape culture every day. Education will be framed as a normal part of capability, not as a remedial exercise.

Data will guide improvement, not drive surveillance. We will track outcomes at the right altitude. We will look for patterns across teams, functions, and locations. We will be alert to unintended consequences such as clustering of adjustments in a single team without manager support, or a spike in performance exits among women aged forty-five to fifty-five. We will use the insights to direct training, to unblock processes, and to remove friction. We will communicate transparently about what we are tracking and why, and we will secure data tightly so that trust is not traded away.

Time horizons matter. Some changes will be visible within a quarter. Adjustments will be granted. Managers will complete training. Facilities tweaks will be made. Other changes will take longer. Retention will stabilise. Promotion rates will even out. Leadership pools will rebalance. We will set a cadence for review that allows both speed and patience. We will celebrate progress without declaring victory too soon. We will keep the door open to revision when women tell us we have missed the mark.

The national frame cannot be ignored. Sector leaders can lobby for the policy reforms described earlier in this chapter.

Professional colleges can strengthen clinical curricula. Regulators can issue guidance that makes reasonable adjustments clear and consistent. Governments can add menopause to health and gender equality strategies and fund specialist clinics and community education. When the public architecture shifts, organisational practice becomes easier to implement and easier to sustain.

Everything written here rests on a straightforward belief. Work should be a place where health can be managed without fear. Menopause should be visible enough to plan for and ordinary enough to support well. The standard we set is the standard we become known for. If we build a system that listens, supports, recognises, and protects, women will stay, perform, and lead. If we do not, we will keep paying the hidden tax of silence.

This is the point at which a movement becomes a management system and a management system becomes a promise. We commit to name the reality, to educate with care, to design practical adjustments, to align benefits with evidence, to train managers to respond, to make policy that protects, to measure what matters, to include those whose voices have been least heard, and to report with candour. We commit to improve each year and to hold ourselves to the same professionalism we expect in every other area of risk and performance. We commit to make dignity predictable.

Every woman deserves to be met by a health system that listens, by a workplace that supports, by a community that recognises, and by policy that protects. As a leader, as an employer, and as a citizen, I accept responsibility for my part in making that true. The business case is strong, the legal case is growing, and the moral case is complete. We will build the systems now so that the next generation inherits competence where we inherited silence. That is how this chapter will be judged. Not by what we have said, but by what women can rely on when they need it most.

Reform can redraw the map of law, health, and workplace standards. But reform rarely arrives fast, and in its absence, women have been left to improvise survival. Until policy delivers, women continue to pay the price in their bodies, careers, and relationships. This is where the story turns: from the promise of reform to the lived reality of resilience.

Resilience will show how, despite these systemic failures, women themselves have carried the burden of adaptation. Then, Reclamation will show how women are reclaiming their voices, not just for themselves, but for the generations that follow.

90-180-365 Reform Roadmap
Action 1: Build a Roadmap
First 90 days
- Name menopause in organisational policy.
- Train managers and HR on recognition and adjustments.
- Stand up a clinician directory and referral cheat sheet.
- Quick wins on facilities: cooling, uniforms, private spaces.

By 180 days
- Update benefits to cover evidence-based therapies.
- Launch interpreter and translation supports.
- Start data collection on adjustments, retention, and time to care.
- Establish a cross-functional working group with lived experience advisors.

By 365 days
- Publish an annual menopause report to the board and staff.

- Embed menopause in onboarding, leadership programs, and risk registers.
- Partner with external bodies for benchmarking and recognition.
- Contribute to sector or state advocacy for legislative clarity.

Action 2: Policy Clauses You Can Lift

- **Scope:** All employees and contractors experiencing menopausal or perimenopausal symptoms.
- **Adjustments:** Examples include flexible hours, cooler workstations, uniform alternatives, task planning, private recovery spaces, and medical appointment time.
- **Process:** Confidential request to manager or HR. Decision within five business days. Review after eight weeks.
- **Privacy:** Health details are not required beyond functional impact and needed adjustment. Records stored securely and separately from performance files.
- **Appeals:** Clear internal pathway and external escalation options.

Action 3: Government Checklist, Policy Makers

- Add menopause targets to national and state health strategies.
- Mandate menopause training in medical and nursing accreditation standards.
- Fund specialist clinics and telehealth hubs.
- Amend workplace law and guidance to clarify reasonable adjustments.
- Require public sector policies and publish templates.
- Ring-fence research funding and require inclusion of midlife women in trials.
- Fund interpreter training and culturally specific resources.

- Table an annual parliamentary report on progress and gaps.

Action 4: KPIs That Matter
- Time to first competent consult after initial presentation.
- Percentage of managers trained and employee awareness.
- Percentage and timeliness of adjustments granted.
- Retention and progression rates for women 45-55.
- Self-reported confidence and satisfaction with support.
- Reduction in stress claims associated with unmanaged symptoms.

From Reform to Resilience and Reclamation
Reform redraws the map of law, health, and work. While policy takes root, women continue to carry the cost. The next chapters turn to Resilience and Reclamation. First, how women have adapted in the absence of systems. Then, how they are reclaiming voice and redesigning the future so that competence replaces silence and dignity becomes standard.

Chapter 18:
Resilience, Survival in the Silence

What Women Endure When Systems Fail

Reform sets the structure, but resilience describes what happens when those structures are absent. For generations, women have lived inside gaps, gaps in health systems, in workplace policies, in cultural narratives, and in public recognition. They have carried menopause not as a supported life stage but as a private burden. They have done so largely in silence, surviving without the Tools, protections, or legitimacy that should have been theirs by right.

This enforced resilience has shaped not only personal lives but also social expectations. Women are praised for their ability to "push through," to keep families functioning, to show up for work, to carry others even as their own health falters. Survival has become normalised. Strength has become mandatory. And the cost of this compulsory resilience has rarely been counted.

Resilience is a word easily celebrated. It appears in HR handbooks, motivational posters, leadership speeches, and social media soundbites. It is framed as a virtue, the capacity to adapt, to withstand difficulty, to bend without breaking. But in the context of women's health, and menopause in particular, resilience often signals something else: endurance in the face of systemic neglect. It is not resilience as choice, but resilience as demand.

Consider the medical realm. Health systems have chronically under-invested in research on menopause, leaving generations of doctors ill-prepared to recognise its impact. When women present with symptoms, they are too often misdiagnosed, medicated incorrectly, or told that what they experience is "just stress" or "just aging." Here, resilience means living with unanswered questions, finding remedies alone, piecing together care from fragmented information and communities.

Consider the workplace. For decades, employment law and workplace design have been structured around a male norm. Menopause was invisible in contracts, policies, and benefits. Women experiencing brain fog, night sweats, or overwhelming fatigue were expected to cope silently or step aside. To survive, they relied on resilience: finding personal coping strategies, rearranging responsibilities, sacrificing career progression.

Consider government policy. While reforms in maternal health, childcare, and even fertility have slowly taken shape, menopause has been largely absent from the legislative agenda. The failure to legislate protections left women dependent on goodwill rather than rights. Resilience here meant navigating bureaucracy alone, often at the expense of economic security.

And consider culture itself. In many families and communities, menopause is shrouded in silence. Without shared language, without intergenerational dialogue, women entered this stage unprepared. They improvised, endured, and adapted. Their resilience became the cultural inheritance, passed from mother to daughter not through words of guidance but through silence.

Resilience, then, is both testimony and trap. It demonstrates extraordinary strength, but it also hides systemic failure. Celebrating resilience risks romanticising hardship, turning women's survival into an excuse for inaction. Applauding women for coping allows institutions to avoid accountability for failing to provide support.

This chapter will interrogate resilience not as an abstract virtue but as lived reality. It will examine how women have been forced to endure medical dismissal, workplace indifference, governmental inaction, and cultural silence. It will explore what this endurance has cost, in health, in careers, in relationships, in dignity. And it will ask whether resilience, in this context, is truly strength or simply the demand that women carry the failures of systems never designed for them.

The Silent Resilience of Health

When women cannot access specialist care, they rely on self-education, trial and error, and informal networks.

- Self-diagnosis

Many women learn about menopause not from doctors but from online forums, podcasts, or friends whispering in private. Knowledge is pieced together like a patchwork quilt.

- Enduring symptoms

Without timely treatment, women normalise suffering. Night sweats, migraines, joint pain, and depression-like symptoms are endured as if they are simply part of being a woman.

- Emotional resilience

Women learn to reframe their suffering as personal weakness or stress, rather than systemic neglect. This mislabelling compounds shame.

Resilience here is survival, but at immense personal cost: delayed diagnoses, misused medications, and years of unnecessary suffering.

The Workplace: Carrying on Regardless

Workplaces often treat resilience as an unqualified virtue. Women are praised for "pushing through," but the cost is hidden attrition, burnout, and exit.

- Masking

Women hide symptoms to maintain professionalism. Spare clothes are kept in lockers. Meetings are endured while silently battling hot flushes.

- Overcompensation

Fearful of being perceived as weak, women work harder, take fewer sick days, and decline promotions to avoid scrutiny.

- Exiting quietly

For some, resilience means leaving, resigning before symptoms expose them, stepping down from leadership, or retiring early.

The language of resilience in workplaces can be double-edged: it applauds individual grit while excusing organisational neglect.

Resilience in Relationships
Resilience is not only professional, it is deeply personal.

Marriages and partnerships
Menopause symptoms often strain intimacy. Women resiliently suppress their needs to preserve relationships, enduring pain or disconnection without discussion.

- Parenting

Many women navigate menopause while still raising teenagers or caring for elderly parents. Their resilience becomes invisible labour, absorbed into the myth of the endlessly adaptable mother.

- Friendships

Where workplaces and families fail, friendships often become the safety net. Yet even here, stigma silences conversations. Resilience can mean carrying burdens alone.

The Cost of Resilience
Resilience is admirable, but it is not free.

- **Health costs:** unmanaged symptoms leading to long-term illness (osteoporosis, cardiovascular disease, mental health decline).
- **Economic costs:** women leaving the workforce early, losing superannuation, and reducing lifetime earnings.
- **Social costs:** diminished leadership representation, as midlife women drop out of pipelines to senior roles.

- **Psychological costs:** internalising shame, loneliness, and the belief that suffering is a personal flaw.

The story of resilience is not one of triumph. It is one of women carrying a burden that should never have been theirs alone.

From Resilience to Resistance

Resilience is necessary, but it cannot be the endpoint. The danger is that resilience becomes weaponised, a way for governments, businesses, and health systems to avoid reform. If women can survive, why change anything?

But resilience has a breaking point. Across the world, women are beginning to resist, not just endure. They are telling their stories, forming networks, lobbying governments, and pushing workplaces to respond. Resilience is transforming into resistance, and resistance is the seed of reclamation.

Resilience has carried women further than any system ever designed for them. Yet survival cannot be the destination. To stop at resilience is to accept endurance as justice. The next chapter asks a different question: what happens when women refuse to carry silence any longer, and instead reclaim menopause as a source of dignity, authority, and collective power?

Reclamation, how women are reclaiming voice, policy, and power, turning resilience into a movement for lasting change.

Chapter 19:
Reclamation, Voice, Justice, and Movement

Reclamation, The Blueprint of Justice

What does justice look like when the silence is broken? Reclamation begins by redefining menopause as a public mandate, not a private misfortune. Here, dignity is declared as non-negotiable, and "deserve" is reframed not as charity but as equity. The blueprint of justice rests on four foundations: healthcare that listens, workplaces that support, communities that recognise, and policy that protects. Each foundation is illustrated not as an ideal but as a practical demand. To reclaim menopause is to claim what was always ours: the right to health, respect, and participation without penalty.

Reclamation: The Movement

What does justice look like when the silence is finally broken?

That is the question at the heart of this chapter. Movements are not only about resisting what is wrong; they are about imagining what is right. Menopause activism cannot stop at dismantling stigma or demanding recognition. It must also paint the picture of the world that women deserve, a world where dignity is built into the fabric of medicine, workplaces, communities, and policy.

For centuries, women were told to cope in private. To sweat quietly. To cry quietly. To forget quietly. The unspoken contract was simple: you endure, and the world will look away. That contract was never consent. It was silence disguised as inevitability.

Now the silence has been broken. The roar has begun. And with it comes a responsibility: to declare what every woman deserves when she reaches this stage of life.

From Whisper to Roar

- **Kitchen-table whispers** became hashtags like #MenopauseMatters and #HotFlashChronicles.
- **Staffroom jokes** gave way to stand-up comedy and television documentaries.
- **Individual shame** turned into union bargaining tables and parliamentary debates.

This is how movements are born: not in a single eruption, but in a million small stories that accumulate until they cannot be ignored.

Global Groundswell
- **UK:** unions and parliament have pushed menopause into national debate, with NHS clinics and workplace policies following.
- **Canada**: Indigenous wisdom reframes elderhood as sacred, weaving cultural respect with modern care.
- **Japan:** menopause described as "renewal years," a reminder that language itself can liberate.
- **Australia**: unions and grassroots groups are stirring, but government lags behind.

The whisper is no longer private. The roar is global.

Why Menopause Is Next
If women's rights won the vote, maternal health, contraception, and workplace equity, then menopause is the next frontier. Because if a society only values women when they are young and fertile, it has never valued women at all.

This is our moment. This is our movement. And it begins here.

Why This Chapter Matters

This chapter is not about statistics alone. It is not about proving again the scale of loss, the billions in productivity, the thousands of resignations, the immeasurable erosion of self-esteem. Those numbers have already been made clear.

Here, we ask a different question.

- What would it mean if the system actually worked?
- What would it mean if every GP was trained to recognise menopause on the first visit?
- What would it mean if every workplace manager understood menopause as a legitimate reason for adjustments, not as a punchline?
- What would it mean if every daughter grew up hearing honest stories about what to expect, instead of inheriting silence?
- What would it mean if every government budget included menopause in its health priorities?

The answers are not theoretical. They are practical. They are possible. And they begin by declaring what women deserve.

Menopause as a Movement, From Whisper to Roar

Reclamation becomes powerful when it spills beyond the individual into the collective. What began as whispers in kitchens and staffrooms has become a global roar across parliaments, unions, social media, comedy stages, and public campaigns. This chapter situates menopause activism alongside historic health and justice movements, breast cancer, HIV/AIDS, maternal health, drawing lessons about visibility, outrage, and measurement. It shows the global groundswell from the UK to Canada, from Japan to

Indigenous communities, and it anchors Australia at a crossroads. Finally, it crescendos into The Closing Manifesto, where menopause is not an afterthought but a movement that insists on rewriting systems, culture, and futures.

Menopause is a Movement

Menopause is not an individual failure. It is a collective reality. Half the population will experience it if they live long enough. Every workplace will feel its impact. Every health system will be shaped by it. Every family will encounter it. And yet, for centuries, we have been told that menopause is a private matter, whispered about, hidden away, treated as decline, dismissed as complaint.
This lie has cost us too much.

When silence becomes unbearable, movements are born. Menopause is now at that threshold.

The Anatomy of Silence

Movements never arise out of comfort. They emerge from fractures, from the deep, unrelenting weight of being ignored. For too long, menopause has been placed at the margins: too ordinary to warrant research, too uncomfortable to talk about, too "feminine" to be respected.

Women have carried the symptoms in secret. Hot flushes laughed off as comedy. Brain fog mistaken for incompetence. Night sweats hidden with extra clothes in handbags. Depression and anxiety treated as isolated illnesses instead of linked to hormonal change.
Each woman thought she was alone.
Each daughter inherited the same silence.
And each system benefitted from our quiet.

When Private Pain Becomes Public Speech

History tells us what happens when silence shatters.

#MeToo began as whispers in offices and dressing rooms, stories carried with shame. When women finally spoke together, industries collapsed, laws changed, power shifted.

Maternal health reforms came after generations of women died in childbirth, their stories dismissed as fate. Activism transformed obstetric care into a modern discipline, saving millions of lives.

HIV/AIDS activism was born when gay men, women, and allies refused to accept silence. They marched, they lay down in streets, they demanded treatment. Activists turned stigma into global mobilisation, forcing governments and pharmaceutical giants to act.

In every case, private suffering was transformed into collective power.
Menopause stands on the same precipice.

The Collective Reality
Every statistic is staggering. Over 1 billion women will be post-menopausal by 2025. The average woman will spend more than one-third of her life in the post-menopausal stage. The economic cost of untreated symptoms is estimated at $10 billion annually in Australia alone.

But numbers only tell part of the story. What makes this a movement is not just scale, but silence.
- Women silenced in GP clinics, prescribed antidepressants instead of treatment.
- Women silenced in workplaces, mocked for flushes, overlooked for promotion.
- Women silenced in families, told to "cope quietly" and not embarrass anyone.

Silence is not neutral. It is violence.
And violence demands resistance.

For decades, women's rights movements have taken on frontiers once thought impossible. The right to vote. The right to contraception. The right to maternity leave. The right to name sexual harassment and demand its end.
Each victory opened space for the next.

Menopause is the next frontier. It has been left until last because it comes late in life, after fertility, after youth, after the years society deems women most "useful." But it is precisely for that reason that it matters.

If a society only values women when they are young and fertile, it has not valued women at all.

Menopause activism forces us to confront the final frontier of gender bias: the refusal to see women's aging as worthy of dignity, support, and power.

A Movement Already Stirring
Across the world, the silence is breaking.

Women are writing memoirs, recording podcasts, producing documentaries. Trade unions are negotiating menopause policies into workplace agreements. Legislators are debating menopause leave. Comedians are taking menopause on stage, women and men alike, turning embarrassment into shared laughter. Social media hashtags spread solidarity across borders in seconds.

What once was whispered in kitchens is now shouted in parliaments.

This is what happens when the unbearable tips into the unignorable.

A Call to Arms
This chapter is not a gentle reflection. It is a rally. Menopause is not simply a health stage to be endured. It is a social justice issue. A workplace issue. A policy issue. A human rights issue.

The bottleneck of GPs, the failures of training, the silence of language, all of it has built the crisis. But movements are not about what has been done to us. They are about what we do next.

We do not need permission.
We need power.
And power begins when we see menopause for what it is: not decline, but mandate.

History will not remember menopause as a private inconvenience.
It will remember whether we made it a movement.
Just as #MeToo redefined the boundaries of what women will accept, just as HIV activism transformed stigma into systemic change, menopause activism will decide whether the next generation suffers in silence, or lives with dignity.
This is our moment.
This is our movement.
And it begins here.

From Whisper to Roar

For most of history, menopause has been a whisper. A muttered comment at a kitchen table. A half-explanation from a mother to a daughter: *"one day your periods will stop."* A dismissive joke in the staffroom. A euphemism wrapped in secrecy, "the change," "that time."

Silence was survival. Speaking openly about menopause invited mockery, minimisation, or dismissal. Women learned to hide sweat-soaked shirts, to laugh off forgetfulness, to carry suitcases of spare clothes to the office without ever explaining why. What could not be named could not be claimed.

But silence cannot hold forever.

The Grandmother's Silence

Ask most women what they remember their mothers or grandmothers telling them about menopause, and the answer is usually: *"nothing."* For many, there was no story, no map, no preparation. Symptoms arrived unannounced and unexplained.

One woman recalled: "I thought I was dying. My periods stopped, I couldn't sleep, my heart raced. I went to the doctor and he told me it was anxiety. My mother never spoke of it. I had no idea it was menopause."
This inherited silence shaped generations. Each daughter entered menopause as a stranger to her own body. Each family carried the unspoken weight.

But silence is never neutral. It protects stigma, not women.

The Social Media Breakthrough

The tide began to turn when women started telling their stories in public, not in whispers but in hashtags.

Platforms like **Instagram, Twitter (X), TikTok,** and **Facebook** groups gave women new Tools to connect across borders. What was once a lonely struggle became collective recognition.

- Hashtags like #MenopauseMatters, #MenopauseMovement, #HotFlashChronicles amplified everyday stories.
- Women posted videos of themselves mid-hot flush, drenched in sweat, narrating their reality with humour and honesty.
- Support groups exploded: "**Menopause Chicks**" in Canada, "**Menopause Support**" in the UK, "**Peri-to-Post Menopause**" in Australia and New Zealand, thousands of Facebook communities where women compared symptoms, shared resources, and refused shame.

These digital communities functioned as counter-clinics, spaces where women could receive validation, advice, and solidarity when healthcare failed them.

The shift is seismic: what had been hidden in bedrooms and bathrooms is now global, public, and visible.

Comedy as Catalyst
One of the most surprising and effective Tools of the movement has been comedy.

For decades, menopause was the butt of tired jokes: nagging wives, cranky mothers, sweaty "old ladies." The humour came at women's expense, reinforcing stereotypes of hysteria and decline.

But in recent years, comedians women and men alike *have flipped the script.*
- UK comedian *Jenny Éclair* created stand-up routines about hot flushes, sleepless nights, and the absurdity of being dismissed by doctors.
- US actress's *Oprah Whinfrey* and *Whoopi Goldberg* openly discussed menopause on talk shows, mixing honesty with humour.
- Even male comedians have started acknowledging it, sometimes clumsily, sometimes brilliantly, as partners and sons navigating it second-hand.

Laughter has power. It transforms taboo into talk. It allows people to breathe through discomfort and recognise shared humanity. Comedy has helped menopause move from shame into the mainstream, making it something audiences can clap for instead of cringe at.

Memoirs, Podcasts, Documentaries
The roar has also been amplified through cultural production.

- Memoirs like "**Flash Count Diary**" by *Darcey Steinke* reframed menopause as a feminist and spiritual awakening, not just a medical condition.
- Podcasts such as "**The Midlife Mix**" and "**The Hot Flash Inc.**" brought intimate conversations into earbuds worldwide.
- Documentaries, from the BBC's "***Davina McCall: Sex, Myths and the Menopause***" to grassroots YouTube series, exploded myths and showed real women's stories.

These platforms did more than inform. They normalised. They created visibility where invisibility had reigned.

When women saw their own struggles reflected back at them, shame loosened its grip.

Unions and Workplace Bargaining
The roar is not just cultural; it is political.

Unions across the UK, Australia, and beyond have begun to negotiate menopause policies into enterprise agreements. For the first time, workplace menopause leave, flexible hours, uniform adjustments, and access to quiet rooms are on the table.

- In 2019, the UK's *Trades Union Congress* declared menopause a workplace issue, calling for systemic reforms.
- In Australia, unions representing teachers, nurses, and public servants have started pressing for menopause clauses in agreements.
- Even corporate giants like *Channel 4 (UK)* launched menopause policies, setting precedents for the private sector.

This is the roar made material: when whispers become bargaining power.

The Shift in Media

Mainstream media once avoided menopause altogether, or reduced it to clichés. Today, front-page stories, talk shows, and glossy magazine spreads are dedicating space to it.

- The *Guardian* runs op-eds on menopause equity.
- *Time magazine* features it as a public health crisis.
- Lifestyle outlets like *Vogue* publish features on fashion for hot flushes and brain fog.

Media coverage validates what women already know: menopause is not niche. It is central.

The arc is unmistakable.
- From kitchen-table silence to Instagram hashtags.
- From staffroom jokes to Netflix comedy specials.
- From unspoken shame to union bargaining tables.
- From invisibility to front-page headlines.

This is how movements are born: not in a single eruption, but in a million small stories that accumulate until they cannot be ignored.

The whisper was survival.
The roar is revolution.

The Global Groundswell

Movements rarely belong to one nation. They ripple outward, finding resonance wherever silence has been enforced. Menopause activism is no different. While women in every society experience this transition, how it is named, recognised, and supported varies enormously. Yet in the last decade, a global pattern has emerged: the whisper breaking into roar is not confined to one country but sweeping across continents.

Some nations have taken bold first steps. Others are only just waking up. But everywhere, the ground is shifting.

The UK: Leading the Charge

If there is a recognised epicentre of the menopause movement, it is the United Kingdom.

The UK has become the global testing ground for systemic change:

- **Workplace policies**: Channel 4 became the first major broadcaster to launch a menopause workplace policy, offering flexible working, paid leave, and awareness training. Dozens of employers followed suit, from HSBC to the civil service.
- **Parliamentary debates**: In 2021, the House of Commons held a landmark debate on menopause, framing it as both a health and workplace issue.
- **NHS clinics**: Specialised menopause clinics were launched to give women direct access to tailored care, bypassing GP bottlenecks.
- **Media figures**: Broadcaster Davina McCall's documentaries sparked national conversations, reframing menopause as mainstream.

This combination, policy, healthcare reform, and cultural visibility, has given the UK a reputation as a global leader. But it did not happen spontaneously. It was the result of years of lobbying, grassroots activism, and women refusing to accept silence.

Europe: Recognition Rising
Across Europe, menopause has begun to enter legislative and corporate conversations.

- Spain has debated whether menopause leave should be included alongside menstrual leave.
- Italy's research communities are producing comparative studies on symptom variation across cultures.
- France has seen feminist medical associations push for greater recognition in GP training.

At the EU level, discussions of gender equity increasingly mention menopause as a barrier to women's full workforce participation. While implementation remains patchy, the inclusion of menopause in EU gender frameworks is a sign that the issue has entered the policy bloodstream.

Canada: Advocacy with Indigenous Wisdom
Canada's menopause conversation has been shaped by both Western advocacy and Indigenous perspectives.

- Mainstream advocacy has focused on workplace equity, echoing UK debates.
- Indigenous communities, however, offer a different lens. A landmark study among First Nations women in northwestern Ontario revealed there is no single word for menopause in Oji-Cree or Ojibway. Women described it as "that time when periods stop." Without a unifying word, symptoms were often not conceptually linked to menopause, reinforcing silence.

Yet within many First Nations cultures, elder women are respected as knowledge holders. The cultural framing of elderhood as sacred offers a counter-narrative to Western stigma. Canadian advocacy has begun to weave these perspectives together, showing that menopause can be both a medical and cultural conversation.

The United States: Fragmented and Politicised
In the United States, the menopause conversation has been slower, fragmented, and often overshadowed by the politicisation of women's health.

- While the US has a massive healthcare market, menopause remains underfunded in research. Pharmaceutical investment prioritises erectile dysfunction over hormone therapy.

- Advocacy is splintered, often led by private organisations, celebrity voices, or wellness influencers rather than unified policy movements.
- Cultural taboos remain entrenched, menopause is frequently medicalised but rarely normalised.

That said, momentum is growing. High-profile figures are beginning to speak out, and social media has created networks of women demanding recognition. But compared to the UK or Canada, the US remains behind.

Japan: Renewal Years
Japan offers a fascinating example of cultural reframing.

The Japanese term 更年期 (konenki) historically meant "renewal years" or "seasonal change." This framing connected menopause to natural cycles, like spring or autumn, rather than decline.

Modern medicine in Japan has shifted the meaning closer to pathology, but the cultural residue remains: menopause as part of renewal, not despair. This contrasts sharply with Arabic "age of despair" or English metaphors of "decline."

Japan also highlights how diet and lifestyle intersect. Research suggests lower prevalence of vasomotor symptoms, possibly linked to soy-rich diets and cultural attitudes that emphasise acceptance. The cultural language of renewal offers a powerful model for reframing menopause globally.

Mayan Communities: Freedom, Not Loss
Among Mayan women in Mexico, menopause is not framed as crisis. Instead, it is described as freedom.

Because of high parity and long durations of breastfeeding, many women live much of their lives with lower estrogen levels. Menopause itself is less disruptive, and its social meaning is liberating: freedom from pregnancy risk, from menstrual taboos, from restrictions placed on younger women.

In these communities, menopause is not silence or stigma but a release. This cultural framing disrupts the Western medicalised narrative and offers a glimpse of what reclamation might look like.

Maori Women: Respect Amid Disparity

In New Zealand, Maori women face similar health disparities to Indigenous Australians, yet menopause is often framed with respect. The mean age of menopause is slightly younger than for non-Maori women, but post-menopausal women are seen as "women of wisdom."

The paradox is stark: even within cultures that value elder women, systemic neglect in healthcare means the transition is still under-supported. Respect exists culturally, but not institutionally.

Indigenous Australian Women: Silence and Strength

In Australia, research on Indigenous women and menopause is limited, a silence within a silence. What little evidence exists shows:

- Many Indigenous women had never heard the word "menopause."
- Phrases like "bleeding no more" or "no more women's sickness" are used instead.
- Knowledge is highly private, often not shared even within families.
- Elderhood is respected, but menopause itself is not ritually marked.

This gap is more than linguistic. It reflects systemic neglect: limited health access, cultural barriers in GP consultations, and generational silences. Indigenous perspectives must be centred in reform, not as an afterthought but as a starting point.

Case Studies of Collective Action

Across the globe, case studies illustrate what collective action can achieve:

- *UK unions* bargaining menopause policies into workplace agreements.
- *Spanish activists* linking menopause to gender equity in labour laws.
- *Canadian researchers* partnering with Indigenous women to co-design culturally safe care.
- *Grassroots Facebook groups* with hundreds of thousands of members turning private symptoms into collective solidarity.

Each case proves the same truth: when women gather, silence fractures.

The Shape of a Global Movement

The groundswell is uneven, but unmistakable. Some nations legislate. Some cultures reframe. Some communities resist silence through story, humour, or online solidarity.

What binds them all is the recognition that menopause is not niche. It is universal, and it demands systemic support.

The whisper has become a roar not just in one country, but across the world. The movement is global, and it is only gaining force.

When Movements Change Systems

Movements matter because they prove what once seemed impossible. They show that silence can be shattered, stigma dismantled, and whole systems re-engineered. Menopause is not the first frontier where women have been told to endure in silence. Nor will it be the last. But history gives us a roadmap.

Breast Cancer: From Shame to Pink Ribbons

There was a time when breast cancer was whispered like a curse. Women were told not to say the words aloud, doctors avoided frank conversations, and sufferers endured alone. In the mid-20th century, mastectomy scars were hidden, obituaries often omitted the cause of death, and the disease was wrapped in secrecy.

The change came not from institutions, but from women themselves. Survivors began to speak publicly. Advocacy groups mobilised. Campaigns like the pink ribbon movement reframed breast cancer from a private tragedy to a collective cause.

- *Visibility*: Pink ribbons, marathons, and celebrity endorsements turned the invisible visible.
- *Funding*: Billions were poured into research, early detection programs, and treatment development.
- *Policy*: Screening programs became standard. Healthcare systems began to prioritise oncology infrastructure.

The lesson for menopause is clear: once a "**shameful**" condition becomes a public movement, resources follow. If breast cancer could go from whispered to mainstream in a generation, so too can menopause.

HIV/AIDS: Activism That Changed Medicine

In the 1980s, HIV/AIDS was a death sentence, and a stigma. Governments were slow to respond, pharmaceutical

companies slower to act. The marginalised communities most affected were told to accept their fate.
They refused.

Activists formed groups like **ACT UP** (*AIDS Coalition to Unleash Power*), staging die-ins in the streets, storming pharmaceutical boardrooms, and demanding change. They reframed HIV from moral judgement to public health emergency.

Their tactics were radical, but effective:
- *Policy acceleration*: Drug approvals were fast-tracked. Entire regulatory systems were restructured.
- *Cultural reframing*: HIV was no longer seen as a *"gay disease"* but as a global health crisis.
- *Research funding*: Billions poured into treatment and prevention, transforming HIV into a manageable chronic condition.

The HIV movement shows that anger can be strategic. Outrage, when organised, bends systems. Menopause does not require the same radical urgency of a viral epidemic, but it can borrow the lesson: stigma must be confronted head-on, not sidestepped.

Maternal Health: Counting What Was Hidden
For much of history, maternal death in childbirth was treated as fate. "Women die in childbirth" was seen as natural, inevitable. Deaths were not systematically recorded, nor made a policy priority.

The **maternal health movement** changed that. Global campaigns reframed maternal mortality as a preventable tragedy. Activists demanded that deaths be counted, monitored, and reduced. Development agencies, governments, and NGOs responded with targeted funding, education for midwives, and new global benchmarks.

- *Visibility through measurement*: "What gets measured gets managed." Once maternal deaths were counted, systems were forced to respond.
- *Global accountability*: Maternal mortality reduction became a UN Millennium Development Goal, placing pressure on governments.
- *Local empowerment*: Community health programs gave women knowledge and authority to demand safer care.

For menopause, the lesson is this: **data is power**. Counting symptoms, economic costs, and misdiagnoses gives the issue weight. Without measurement, neglect continues unchecked.

What Menopause Can Learn
From these movements, three lessons stand out:
1. **Visibility drives legitimacy.** When pink ribbons turned breast cancer into a public cause, the money followed. Menopause needs its own powerful visibility markers, symbols, campaigns, shared language.
2. **Outrage can be organised**. HIV activists proved that stigma only crumbles under pressure. Menopause advocacy cannot rely on polite requests alone. It must be bold, disruptive, insistent.
3. **Measurement creates accountability**. Maternal mortality only became a global priority when deaths were tracked. Menopause needs data: lost workdays, misdiagnosis rates, prescription patterns, economic losses. Numbers force systems to act.

Imagining the Menopause Movement
What would it look like if menopause adopted these lessons?
- *Pink ribbon equivalent*: A global symbol, visible, wearable, instantly recognisable, that signals solidarity. (Not trivialisation, but empowerment.)

- *Public campaigns*: Annual awareness weeks, public art, comedy tours, government-backed advertising.
- *Policy levers*: Mandated GP training, funded clinics, workplace obligations, pharmaceutical investment.
- *Global measurement*: Annual reporting on menopause-related health outcomes, absenteeism, workforce participation.

Movements reshape the possible. Where once menopause was an invisible inevitability, it can become a visible mandate.

A Story to Tell

Every movement begins with story. The HIV crisis broke open when stories of men dying young filled newspapers. Breast cancer shifted when survivors spoke on television. Maternal mortality became urgent when activists told the stories of mothers lost in childbirth.

The menopause movement already has its stories. Anne with her suitcase of clothes. Mai miming symptoms to her GP. Teachers eating alone in cars. Executives stepping down without explanation.

These are not private failures. They are systemic betrayals. And like all movements before, menopause activism must insist on turning stories into systems change.

The Australian Context

Australia has never been immune to global shifts in women's health advocacy. From reproductive rights to workplace equality, change here has often lagged behind international movements but eventually gained force through the persistence of activists, unions, and grassroots voices. Menopause is no different.

For too long, it has been left in silence, absent from GP training, absent from workplace agreements, absent from national health strategies. But silence is not the same as absence. Across the country, a movement is stirring.

Unions at the Bargaining Table

Australia's unions have always played a critical role in driving workplace reforms, from annual leave to parental leave, from occupational safety to equal pay. Now, they are beginning to add menopause to the list.

- Teachers' unions in several states have pushed menopause into enterprise bargaining discussions, highlighting how symptoms affect attendance, retention, and career progression.
- Nursing unions have pointed out the irony: women caring for others while working through unmanaged menopause symptoms, often without institutional support.
- Public sector unions have begun to draft template policies on flexible hours, access to quiet rooms, and menopause leave provisions.

These negotiations are still in early stages, but they signal a turning point: menopause is moving from private suffering to industrial relations. When it enters the bargaining table, it becomes measurable, negotiable, and enforceable.

Women's Groups and Grassroots Advocacy

Outside formal union structures, women's groups have been amplifying the conversation.

- Community networks like Menopause Support Australia and grassroots online collectives have grown rapidly, offering safe spaces for women to share experiences and demand recognition.
- Advocacy organisations have begun to frame menopause as a workplace equity issue, not just a medical one. They argue that without systemic recognition, women are being driven out of the workforce prematurely, with profound personal and economic consequences.

- Grassroots campaigns have focused on storytelling: women publishing essays, blogs, and op-eds in major outlets, using personal narratives to shatter stigma.

These groups operate on limited budgets, often run by volunteers, but their impact has been significant. They have shifted menopause from invisibility into media headlines.

Media Coverage: From Silence to Spotlight
In the last five years, Australian media has begun to cover menopause more consistently.

- Mainstream outlets like the ABC, SBS, and *The Guardian Australia* have run feature stories on the costs of menopausal silence.
- Women's magazines and online platforms have featured first-person narratives, reframing menopause as part of the broader feminist movement.
- Comedians on the festival circuit have begun to fold menopause into their material, often using humour to cut through discomfort.

This is still fragile progress. Coverage tends to spike during awareness campaigns and fade quickly. But every headline helps build visibility, making it harder for policymakers to claim ignorance.

The Government Gap
Despite grassroots and union momentum, government recognition remains inconsistent.

- There is no national menopause strategy in Australia.
- Menopause is rarely mentioned in federal or state health frameworks.

- Research funding for menopause remains negligible compared to other areas of women's health.
- GP training on menopause is minimal, leaving most doctors underprepared.

The gap between grassroots activism and government response is stark. Women are pushing. Unions are drafting. Media is beginning to spotlight. But without political will, progress risks stalling.

Risk of Falling Behind
Globally, the UK and parts of Europe are moving ahead with workplace policy and specialised clinics. Canada is integrating Indigenous perspectives. Even in the US, fragmented though it is, celebrity voices and grassroots organisations are forcing change.

If Australia fails to act, it risks falling behind:

- Economically, as women exit the workforce earlier than necessary.
- Politically, as unions escalate demands into industrial disputes.
- Culturally, as silence fuels stigma instead of solidarity.

This is not an abstract risk. With an aging workforce and women comprising nearly half of all workers, the failure to support menopause will become a measurable drag on productivity, health budgets, and leadership pipelines.

Sparks of Hope
Still, there are signs of possibility. Some forward-thinking employers, particularly in education, health, and corporate sectors, are experimenting with policies. A handful of state governments have begun to explore gender equity frameworks that include menopause.

And most importantly, women themselves are refusing silence. From community halls to online forums, from staffrooms to union conferences, the roar is building.

A Nation at a Crossroads

Australia is at a crossroads. The silence around menopause has been broken, but the systems of health and work have not yet caught up.

The question is not whether the movement exists, it does. The question is whether policymakers will recognise it, resource it, and reform systems to support it.

If unions can win leave for parents, if activists can transform breast cancer into a global movement, if women across the world can turn menopause from whisper to roar, then Australia can, too.

But the clock is ticking. Every year of inaction is another year of lost leadership, wasted talent, and unnecessary suffering. The movement is here. The question is whether the nation is ready to listen.

Reclamation: The Mandate

Deserve Is Not Charity

The word *deserve* is often misunderstood. It is not about kindness or pity. It is not about "extra support" offered as a token gesture. To deserve is to claim what is rightfully yours. To deserve is to assert that dignity is not optional, not negotiable, not conditional on age, fertility, or usefulness to others.

Menopause is not a "special interest." It is a universal reality. If half the population will live through it, then half the population deserves systems that recognise it.

The default has been neglect. What we deserve is equity.

From Endurance to Expectation

For too long, menopause has been framed as a test of endurance. If you are strong enough, quiet enough, stoic enough, you pass. If you complain, you fail.

But endurance is not justice. Endurance is survival. Women deserve more than survival. They deserve systems that work with their bodies, not against them. They deserve care that listens, workplaces that adapt, and communities that respect.

The measure of progress is not how much women can endure, but how little they have to.

A Collective Promise

When we say *every woman deserves*, we are making a collective promise. Not every woman will need the same things. Some will need medical support. Some will need workplace accommodations. Some will need cultural recognition. But the promise is that no woman will be left alone to suffer in silence.

This is not about designing a single path. It is about building a landscape where multiple paths exist, all paved with dignity.

A woman in rural Queensland deserves the same access to information and treatment as a woman in Sydney.

An Indigenous woman deserves care that respects her cultural knowledge, not dismisses it.

A migrant woman deserves interpreters who know the language of menopause, not just generic medical terms.

A CEO deserves the same dignity in the boardroom as a factory worker does on the production line.

Justice is not uniformity. Justice is universality.

The Architecture of Deserving

This chapter is structured as a blueprint. We will explore what women deserve across four foundations.

- **Healthcare that listens.** Because the frontline of justice begins with being heard in the doctor's office.
- **Workplaces that support.** Because dignity cannot be left at the office door.
- **Communities that recognise**. Because stories must live in kitchens, classrooms, and cultural traditions.
- **Policy that protects**. Because systemic change must be legislated, funded, and enforced.

Each foundation is both vision and mandate. Each is grounded in real-world examples, from NHS clinics to Australian union wins, from Indigenous elder wisdom to corporate innovators. Each shows that what women deserve is not utopia, but justice delayed.

The Mandate

When women say we deserve, it is not a request. It is a mandate.

- We deserve doctors who know more than six hours of training on menopause.
- We deserve workplaces that measure retention, not resignation.
- We deserve communities that tell stories, not hide them.
- We deserve policies that count our lives, not ignore them.

This chapter is not an elegy for what we have lost. It is a manifesto for what we will claim.

Menopause is not the end of fertility. It is the beginning of power. Power to demand. Power to design. Power to deserve.

And the first step is this. To say it out loud.

Every woman deserves dignity. Every woman deserves recognition. Every woman deserves justice.

Policy reform is the next frontier. Businesses are beginning to act, but without government leadership the response will remain fragmented and inequitable. A comprehensive national strategy would signal to women that their health, productivity, and dignity matter, and to the world that our nation leads in gender reform.

The cost of silence is already measured in billions. The cost of reform is modest, with extraordinary returns in equity, productivity, and trust.

The mandate is clear: rewrite not only the medical and business books, but the laws and policies that govern society itself.

Part IV:

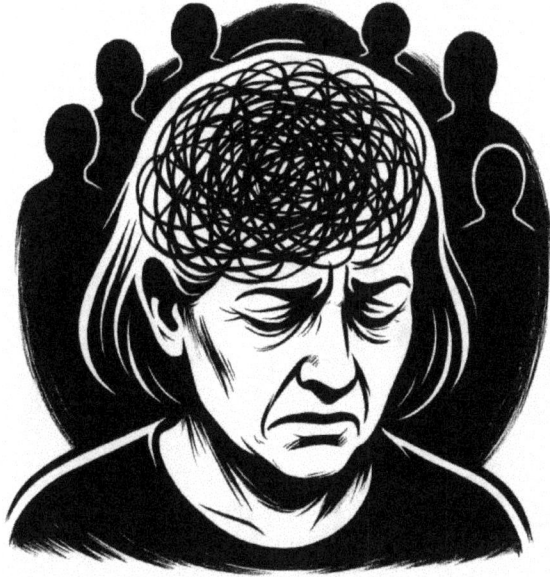

The Psychiatric Silence:

When Medicine Ignores the

Menopausal Mind.

Chapter 20:
The DSM's Missing Chapter

When the world's psychiatric bible pretends menopause does not exist

In psychiatry, what is written in the Diagnostic and Statistical Manual of Mental Disorders (DSM) is treated as truth. To the outside world it looks like a book. In practice it is a blueprint that defines legitimacy. The DSM determines what psychiatrists diagnose, what insurance companies reimburse, what research receives funding, and what students are taught in medical schools. It is a manual of disorders, but also a map of power.

Every edition of the DSM expands, contracts, and reshapes that power. New conditions appear. Old conditions disappear. Some are renamed, reframed, or split into subcategories. Each decision is the result of committees, clinical trials, pharmaceutical lobbying, and professional politics. To be written into the DSM is to exist officially. To be absent is to remain invisible.

The DSM is often called the Bible of psychiatry. That description is more accurate than most people realise. Like a religious text, the DSM is not simply descriptive but prescriptive. It does not just reflect what clinicians see in their offices. It tells them what they are allowed to see, and how they are allowed to interpret it. Its authority is such that courts, insurance schemes, universities, and entire health systems structure their practices around it.

And yet, amid its thousands of pages, one of the most universal transitions in human life is missing.

Menopause does not appear.

Psychiatry's manual is not just a book; it is a border. On one side lies what can be diagnosed, reimbursed, researched, and taught. On the other side lies silence. Today, menopause sits in that silence.

The silence inside psychiatry's Bible

The absence is stark. Flip through DSM-5 and you will find entries for retiring, for living alone, even for shy bladders. You will not find menopause, neither as a disorder, a syndrome, nor a psychosocial stressor

The manual recognises that adjusting to retirement can produce significant distress. It recognises that leaving home or becoming an empty nester may warrant clinical attention. It notes that shyness, if impairing enough, can become a disorder. Yet menopause appears nowhere in the DSM, not as a disorder, not as a syndrome, not even as a psychosocial stressor.

Half the population undergoes this transition if they live long enough. It can last between four and twelve years. It is associated with profound biological changes that ripple across every bodily system. It produces both physical symptoms and psychiatric ones: insomnia, anxiety, mood instability, brain fog, depressive states, panic attacks, and loss of confidence. It is one of the few universal human experiences. And yet psychiatry's Bible has nothing to say.

This silence is not neutral. In medicine, what is not named is not measured. What is not measured is not researched. What is not researched is not taught. What is not taught is not recognised. And what is not recognised is not treated.

What the DSM does include
To understand the absurdity, it is worth pausing on what the DSM does include.

Turn to the section on Social Anxiety Disorder. Pages stretch with descriptions of diagnostic features: fear of being judged as weak, crazy, or boring; trembling or blushing in public; anticipatory anxiety before a party or work meeting; avoidance of eye contact or speaking in class. The criteria are detailed. The manual provides cultural notes, prevalence rates, functional consequences, risk factors, and comorbidities.

Another section covers Panic Disorder. It lists thirteen possible symptoms of a panic attack, from palpitations and sweating to chest pain, chills, fear of dying, and fear of going crazy. To qualify for the diagnosis a person must experience recurrent unexpected panic attacks followed by persistent concern or behavioural change. The criteria are exact. They are codified for billing, treatment, and research.

Elsewhere in the manual we find *Premenstrual Dysphoric Disorder (PMDD),* a condition characterised by mood swings, irritability, and physical discomfort tied to the luteal phase of the menstrual cycle. PMDD is recognised as severe enough to be included as an official diagnosis, allowing for research, pharmaceutical trials, and therapeutic interventions.

Even *"Phase of Life Problem"* is included as a legitimate category. The DSM acknowledges that certain life transitions, such as leaving home, starting a new career, or retirement, can be accompanied by distress warranting clinical attention. In the pages on *"Other Problems Related to the Social Environment,"* there are codes for *Social Exclusion or Rejection, Acculturation Difficulty, and Living Alone.* These are not illnesses, but they are acknowledged as psychosocial contexts that can shape mental health.

The manual is wide enough to capture cultural syndromes, personality traits exaggerated into pathology, and transient life stressors. Yet menopause, a predictable, long-term, hormonally driven transition with significant psychiatric manifestations, is absent.

Why absence matters

This absence has cascading consequences.

A woman presenting to her GP with hot flushes, insomnia, anxiety, and brain fog is rarely asked about her stage of reproductive life. Instead she is assessed against the categories in the DSM. If her symptoms line up with the criteria for Generalised Anxiety Disorder, that is the label she receives. If her mood is low, she is coded as Major Depressive Disorder. If she has panic episodes, Panic Disorder is applied. If she reports cognitive fog, she may even be referred for dementia screening.

At no point does the clinician open the DSM and find "Menopausal Depression," "Perimenopausal Anxiety," or "Menopausal Transition Syndrome." The categories do not exist. And so her suffering is translated into other terms, each with their own treatment pathways.

The result is misdiagnosis. Women are prescribed antidepressants for vasomotor symptoms. They are given benzodiazepines for palpitations. They are tested for thyroid dysfunction. They are sent to neurologists for memory decline. Every arrow points away from menopause.

The irony is brutal. The DSM has space for "shy bladder syndrome," but not for the psychiatric impact of menopause. It has diagnostic criteria for "separation anxiety disorder" in adults, but not for the despair that can accompany the end of reproductive life. It acknowledges that retirement can be distressing, but not that hormonal withdrawal can dismantle sleep, cognition, and mood for years.

Psychiatry's hierarchy of recognition
The absence of menopause is not an accident. It reveals a hierarchy of recognition.

Conditions that can be clearly measured in the short term, such as panic attacks, are included. Conditions with strong pharmaceutical lobbying behind them, such as PMDD, are included. Conditions that affect both sexes, such as depression or social anxiety, are given extensive coverage.

Menopause does not fit neatly into this hierarchy. It is too universal to be rare, too varied to be uniform, too gendered to attract broad investment, and too resistant to pharmaceutical simplification. The absence reflects not science but priorities.

When the DSM omits menopause, it sends a signal to every psychiatrist, GP, researcher, and policymaker: this is not a legitimate site of psychiatric suffering. The downstream effects are enormous. Funding bodies do not issue grants. Universities do not teach modules. Insurers do not cover treatments. GPs are not trained to recognise it. Women are left unprepared and unsupported.

This chapter asks a simple question: what happens when psychiatry's most powerful manual excludes menopause?

We will examine:
- Why menopause is not a diagnosis. How the DSM sets criteria, who decides, and why menopause has been excluded despite its profound impact.
- Why PMDD is included but menopause is not. The story of pharmaceutical influence, clinical trials, and the political economy of recognition.
- How real suffering is dismissed. Vignettes of women told their symptoms are "just stress" or "just hormonal," with devastating consequences.
- The power of the DSM. How inclusion dictates research, insurance, legitimacy, and ultimately, women's lives.

This is not about pathologising every woman's experience. Many women navigate menopause with resilience and strength. It is about legitimising suffering when it is real, disabling, and treatable. The DSM's silence ensures that suffering remains invisible.

Absence in the DSM does not mean absence in life. It means absence everywhere else. And until the psychiatric canon acknowledges menopause, women will continue to be misdiagnosed, mistreated, and marginalised.

Why Menopause is Not a Diagnosis

The Gatekeepers of Recognition

The DSM does not fall from the sky. It is authored, debated, and revised by committees of psychiatrists under the umbrella of the American Psychiatric Association (APA). These committees are not neutral observers. They are influenced by prevailing scientific paradigms, pharmaceutical interests, advocacy campaigns, and cultural norms.

To include a condition in the DSM, a committee must be convinced that it meets a set of criteria. It must be clearly defined. It must cause clinically significant distress or impairment. It must be distinguishable from other conditions. And, crucially, it must be treatable within psychiatric paradigms, often through medications or established psychotherapies.

This process sounds scientific, but in practice it is also political. The DSM has long been shaped by battles over what counts as illness. Homosexuality was once listed as a psychiatric disorder until activism forced its removal in 1973. Attention-Deficit/Hyperactivity Disorder (ADHD) expanded dramatically as stimulant medications gained traction in schools. PMDD entered after decades of lobbying and the appearance of an FDA-approved drug.

The gatekeepers of the DSM are not just scientists. They are cultural arbiters deciding which forms of human suffering deserve recognition, reimbursement, and research.

Why Menopause Has Been Left Out

1. The argument of variability

One of the most common arguments made against including menopause-related psychiatric conditions is variability. Not all women experience mood disruption during menopause. Some experience mild symptoms. Others severe. The spectrum is wide. Committees argue that without uniform presentation, menopause does not meet criteria for a discrete disorder.

But variability is present in almost every DSM category. Major Depressive Disorder can present with hypersomnia or insomnia, increased appetite or decreased appetite, agitation or retardation. Anxiety can manifest as restlessness, fatigue, or irritability. Variability has never been disqualifying, until it comes to menopause.

2. The argument of aging
Menopause is often dismissed as part of normal aging. To medicalise it, critics argue, would be to pathologise a natural life transition. The same reasoning, however, did not prevent inclusion of conditions such as Alzheimer's disease or Postpartum Depression. Aging and childbirth are natural too, but the psychiatric consequences are recognised.

3. The absence of pharmaceutical incentives
Perhaps the most decisive factor is marketability. PMDD gained legitimacy not only through advocacy but because pharmaceutical companies could trial SSRIs as treatment. Menopause-related depression and anxiety are less easily monetised. Hormone therapy is one pathway, but it is managed by endocrinologists and gynaecologists rather than psychiatrists. The psychiatric profession has no clear drug pipeline to own. Without pharmaceutical lobbying, there is little momentum to formalise menopause in the DSM.

4. The bias of universality
Half the world's population will experience menopause if they live long enough. Precisely because it is so universal, psychiatry treats it as background rather than foreground. Disorders are often framed as deviations from the norm. When the "norm" includes menopause, its suffering becomes invisible. Universality, instead of strengthening the case for inclusion, paradoxically weakens it.

Consequences of Exclusion

1. Insurance and funding deserts

In the United States and many other countries, insurance reimbursement depends on DSM codes. Without a code, clinicians cannot bill. Without billing, treatments are not provided. Without recognition, research funding is limited. Entire deserts of inquiry form around what is not listed.

2. Medical school blind spots

The DSM shapes curricula. Psychiatry residents learn to diagnose what is in the manual. What is not in the manual is not examined in depth. Generations of doctors graduate without ever learning how menopause intersects with psychiatric suffering.

3. Misdiagnosis pathways

The absence of menopause in the DSM does not mean women are untreated. It means they are misdiagnosed. Their symptoms are absorbed into adjacent categories: Major Depressive Disorder, Generalised Anxiety Disorder, Panic Disorder. Treatments are mismatched. Antidepressants are prescribed for hormonal depression. Benzodiazepines for palpitations. Antipsychotics for insomnia. Misdiagnosis is not benign; it carries stigma, side effects, and wasted years.

4. Cultural erasure

The DSM is exported globally. Its categories influence the International Classification of Diseases (ICD) and local diagnostic manuals. Its silence on menopause ripples across continents, reinforcing the cultural taboo. Where language already fails, psychiatry compounds the silence.

A Tale of Two Conditions: PMDD vs. Menopausal Depression

The contrast between PMDD and menopause is instructive.

- **PMDD** is tied to the luteal phase of the menstrual cycle, with symptoms including mood swings, irritability, and depression. It affects a smaller proportion of women, but its timing is predictable. Pharmaceutical companies trialled SSRIs and demonstrated efficacy. Lobbyists argued it was a distinct, disabling condition. By DSM-5, PMDD was in.
- **Menopause-related depression and anxiety** affect a larger proportion of women. Symptoms include persistent low mood, anxiety, brain fog, and panic episodes. Timing is predictable, midlife transition, declining ovarian function. Treatments exist, hormone therapy, psychotherapy, lifestyle interventions. Yet it is not in.

The difference is not science. It is politics and profit. PMDD could be attached to a pill. Menopausal suffering could not.

Stories From the Clinic
Take Jane, 49, presenting with months of anxiety, palpitations, and poor sleep. Her GP codes her with Generalised Anxiety Disorder. She is prescribed escitalopram. The antidepressant blunts her energy but does not stop the night sweats that trigger her insomnia. Months pass. Her symptoms persist.

Or Maria, 52, who describes brain fog and hopelessness. She is sent to a neurologist to rule out dementia. She spends thousands on scans. The neurologist finds nothing. Back at her GP, she is told it is probably stress. She leaves with a prescription for sertraline, still confused.
Neither woman was asked a simple question: "Where are you in your reproductive transition?"

Why This Matters
If the DSM is the psychiatric Bible, then its omissions are as telling as its inclusions. Menopause is absent not because it is unimportant but because it is inconvenient. It challenges

psychiatry's frameworks, resists pharmaceutical simplification, and sits at the crossroads of endocrinology, gynaecology, and mental health.

But absence has consequences. Women's suffering is fragmented, reframed, and erased.

This section has shown the mechanics of exclusion: variability, aging, lack of pharmaceutical interest, universality. The result is a gap that echoes across insurance, education, and clinical care.

The next section will deepen this contrast. PMDD made it in. Menopause did not. Understanding why reveals the political economy of diagnosis, and exposes what women lose when medicine refuses to name their suffering.

PMDD is Included, Why Not Menopausal Depression/Anxiety?

Psychiatry as Gatekeeper

Psychiatry has always claimed the mantle of science, yet its most powerful Tool , the *Diagnostic and Statistical Manual of Mental Disorders* (DSM), is as much a political and cultural text as it is a scientific one. The DSM dictates what counts as mental illness, how conditions are researched, which treatments are reimbursed, and which struggles remain invisible. It is often referred to as the "Bible of psychiatry." Like a Bible, it confers legitimacy. Like a Bible, it excludes.

The DSM is not simply a handbook for clinicians. It is a gatekeeper. When a condition is included, doors open: universities create curricula, insurers create billing codes, pharmaceutical companies develop treatments, and clinicians learn to name and treat what once went unspoken. When a condition is excluded, those doors slam shut. The suffering may continue, but without recognition it is reframed as "normal," "not medical," or "not real."

This is the paradox women face when they arrive in psychiatry's waiting room. A young woman who experiences severe cyclical mood changes before her period may now be diagnosed with *Premenstrual Dysphoric Disorder (PMDD)*, officially recognised in the DSM-5 since 2013. She can receive a diagnostic code, a treatment plan, and often a prescription reimbursed by insurance. She may still encounter stigma, but she is not left nameless.

By contrast, a woman in midlife who experiences crippling anxiety, depression, or mood instability as part of the menopausal transition is told she has no psychiatric category. Her symptoms may be reclassified as *Major Depressive Disorder* or *Generalised Anxiety Disorder*, conditions that miss the hormonal driver. Or they may be dismissed altogether as "just aging," "empty nest," or "stress." The difference is not that her suffering is less real. It is that psychiatry has chosen not to recognise it.

405

The irony is staggering. PMDD affects a small proportion of menstruating women, estimates range between 3% and 8%. Menopause affects every woman who lives long enough, typically between ages 45 and 55, with symptoms that can last years. Both conditions are hormonally driven, both can produce severe psychiatric symptoms, and both disrupt daily life, workplaces, and families. Yet only one has the legitimacy of a DSM diagnosis.

The inclusion of PMDD and the exclusion of menopause-related depression and anxiety cannot be explained by science alone. They reveal the politics of psychiatric recognition: the influence of pharmaceutical lobbying, the economics of insurance, the cultural stereotypes about women's biology, and the institutional inertia of psychiatry itself.

This section examines why PMDD was written into the DSM while menopause was written out. It traces the decades-long path PMDD travelled from appendix footnote to full disorder. It dissects the role of pharmaceutical companies and the political economy of diagnosis. It compares PMDD's inclusion to the DSM's treatment of other reproductive and gender-related conditions, such as postpartum depression and gender dysphoria, to reveal the asymmetry of recognition. And it highlights the policy consequences: when menopause is absent from the DSM, it is absent everywhere else, in insurance, in research, in education, and in workplaces.

Menopause's invisibility is not inevitable. It is the product of choices. To understand those choices, we must begin with the condition psychiatry chose to recognise: PMDD.

The Path to PMDD Recognition

From Cultural Punchline to Psychiatric Curiosity
For centuries, women's menstrual cycles were framed in medicine as a source of weakness or hysteria. Ancient

physicians linked menstruation to imbalance, instability, and danger. By the 20th century, "PMS", premenstrual syndrome, became a cultural shorthand for irritability, mood swings, or bloating. It was often treated as a joke, a way of trivialising women's emotions.

But for some women, the symptoms went far beyond irritability. They experienced profound mood swings, rage, despair, and suicidal thoughts tied predictably to the luteal phase of their menstrual cycle. These episodes were not minor inconveniences; they were disabling. They disrupted relationships, employment, and self-perception. Clinicians and researchers began to notice a pattern: these women were not simply experiencing "bad PMS." They were living with a distinct condition.

In 1987, the DSM-III-R acknowledged this possibility. It introduced *Late Luteal Phase Dysphoric Disorder (LLPDD)* in its appendix as a condition "requiring further study." This appendix status was psychiatry's halfway house, a way of acknowledging clinical reality without granting full legitimacy. A woman could not be formally diagnosed, insurance would not reimburse, and treatment protocols were not taught in medical schools. But for the first time, psychiatry admitted that severe premenstrual mood disorders existed.

DSM-IV: A New Name, Same Limbo
When the DSM-IV was published in 1994, LLPDD was renamed *Premenstrual Dysphoric Disorder (PMDD)*. The criteria were refined, but the condition remained in the appendix. This renaming was not trivial. It signaled that psychiatry was starting to accept the phenomenon as distinct from PMS, with clear psychiatric weight. But keeping it in the appendix showed ongoing hesitation.

For women, the effect was frustrating. They lived with disabling symptoms, but doctors could not code PMDD as a diagnosis. Many were told they had depression or anxiety instead. Others were dismissed as "overreacting." Without full DSM recognition, the condition remained in diagnostic limbo.

DSM-IV-TR: Growing Evidence, Continued Reluctance
In 2000, the DSM-IV-TR (Text Revision) reiterated PMDD's appendix status, but by this time, research was expanding rapidly. Clinical trials documented symptom clusters, prevalence, and functional impairment. Importantly, researchers distinguished PMDD from other mood disorders: symptoms were cyclical, resolved with menstruation, and re-emerged predictably each month.

The evidence base was growing stronger. But psychiatry's committees remained cautious. Critics worried about medicalising women's normal cycles. Feminist scholars feared PMDD could reinforce stereotypes of women as unstable. Committees chose caution over recognition.

DSM-5: Full Inclusion
Everything changed with the DSM-5, published on May 18, 2013. PMDD was promoted to full diagnostic status. It was no longer an appendix condition. It had criteria, codes, and legitimacy.

Why the sudden shift? By 2013, three forces converged:

Evidence: Clinical trials confirmed PMDD was real, disabling, and distinct.

Pharmaceuticals: SSRIs like fluoxetine (Prozac) were shown to be effective. Sarafem, Prozac repackaged in pink and lavender, was FDA-approved for PMDD in 2000.

Politics: Advocacy from clinicians, researchers, and industry created momentum psychiatry could not ignore.

In less than three decades, PMDD moved from punchline to full psychiatric disorder. For women affected, this was transformative. They finally had language, legitimacy, and access to treatment.

But the contrast with menopause is stark. Menopause has been studied for centuries. It affects every woman. It is associated with high rates of depression, anxiety, and suicidality. And yet it remains absent from the DSM. The difference is not science. It is politics.

The Economics of Diagnosis

The story of PMDD's recognition in psychiatry cannot be separated from economics. In theory, DSM inclusion is driven by evidence: carefully conducted trials, epidemiological studies, and expert consensus. In practice, conditions gain traction when they align with existing pharmaceutical treatments, insurance reimbursement structures, and professional interests. PMDD's rise to full diagnostic status in DSM-5 was not simply a matter of science. It was also a matter of profit.

Sarafem: Prozac in Lavender

The turning point came in 2000, when the U.S. Food and Drug Administration (FDA) approved fluoxetine, better known as Prozac, for the treatment of PMDD. To capitalise on this new market, Eli Lilly rebranded fluoxetine as *Sarafem*, packaged it in pink and lavender capsules, and launched a multimillion-dollar advertising campaign.

The ads showed professional women struggling with irritability, rage, or despair during the premenstrual phase, and then transformed, smiling, and productive once they started Sarafem. The message was clear: PMDD was real, it was debilitating, and it had a solution.

Pharmaceutical rebranding is rarely subtle. Prozac was already losing patent protection. By creating Sarafem, Lilly extended the life of fluoxetine's profitability, carving out a new niche market. Women who might not have been prescribed Prozac for depression could now be prescribed Sarafem for PMDD.

This commercial push did more than sell a drug. It validated a diagnosis. Once the FDA approved Sarafem for PMDD, insurance companies needed diagnostic codes to reimburse it. Doctors needed guidelines to prescribe it. Researchers sought grants to study it. Advocacy groups gained sponsorship. A feedback loop formed: the drug made the diagnosis real, and the diagnosis made the drug profitable.

Marketable Suffering

The PMDD story illustrates a central reality of modern psychiatry: suffering becomes visible when it is marketable. Conditions that can be treated with drugs, especially drugs already in circulation, have an easier path to legitimacy. Pharmaceutical companies can fund trials, sponsor conferences, and provide advocacy resources. Insurers can justify coverage when treatment protocols are clear.

By contrast, conditions without a clear pharmaceutical market often languish. Menopause is the quintessential example. The psychiatric symptoms of menopause, depression, anxiety, insomnia, cognitive changes, do not map neatly onto existing psychiatric drug classes. Hormone replacement therapy (HRT) is effective for many symptoms, but it is managed by gynaecologists, not psychiatrists. No psychiatric specialty "owns" menopause. Without a market-ready psychiatric drug, there was no pharmaceutical lobby to push for its recognition in the DSM.

The Politics of Insurance

Insurance systems amplify this dynamic. In the U.S., where DSM codes directly determine billing, the absence of a diagnosis means the absence of reimbursement. A psychiatrist can bill for Major Depressive Disorder or Generalised Anxiety Disorder. They cannot bill for "menopausal depression." Without a code, there is no insurance coverage. Without coverage, there is no incentive for clinicians to diagnose or treat.

This absence cascades. Medical schools train students in DSM-recognised disorders. Research funding agencies prioritise conditions with diagnostic legitimacy. Public health systems design programs around codified categories. When menopause is not in the DSM, it is not only invisible to psychiatry, it is invisible to the entire health system.

The Professional Turf Wars

The economics of diagnosis are not just about pharma and insurance. They are also about professional boundaries. Psychiatry has long been cautious about conditions seen as "medical" rather than "psychiatric." Menopause straddles this line. Its hormonal basis positions it within gynaecology. Its psychiatric symptoms are undeniable, but without a clear psychiatric treatment, psychiatry has ceded responsibility.

By contrast, PMDD landed squarely in psychiatry's wheelhouse. The symptoms were mood-based. The treatments were psychiatric drugs. The professional incentives aligned. Psychiatrists could study, diagnose, and treat PMDD without competing with another specialty. Menopause, on the other hand, was left to gynaecologists, who focused on hot flushes and bleeding patterns, not psychiatric suffering. The result: no one took ownership.

Feminist Critiques of Commercialisation

The economic drivers of PMDD's recognition also provoked feminist critiques. Some argued that Sarafem was an opportunistic rebranding of women's suffering for profit. They warned that medicalising premenstrual mood symptoms risked pathologising normal variation. Others pointed out the cultural undertones of the marketing: PMDD was framed as a condition that disrupted women's productivity and relationships, a threat to economic order, not just personal wellbeing.

Yet for many women, the diagnosis was a relief. Having a name meant being believed. Having a treatment meant hope. Feminist critiques of pathologisation coexisted uneasily with feminist demands for recognition. This tension remains unresolved.

The Menopause Market Gap

Menopause has not been spared commercialisation, witness the waves of HRT marketing over the decades, but its psychiatric dimensions have not generated equivalent pharmaceutical interest. HRT is prescribed by gynaecologists and managed as a hormonal intervention. Antidepressants are sometimes used for hot flushes, but this is off-label and inconsistent. No blockbuster psychiatric drug has been tied to menopause.

Without a commercial engine, menopause has remained psychiatry's orphan. Pharmaceutical companies had no incentive to lobby DSM committees. Insurers had no incentive to create billing codes. Psychiatrists had no incentive to fight turf wars with gynaecologists. And so, despite its prevalence and impact, menopause was left invisible.

What Makes It In, What Stays Out

The DSM is often presented as a neutral document, a classification of disorders derived from science, field trials, and consensus. But what is included and what is excluded reveals the politics of psychiatry more clearly than any preface.

To see the pattern, we need to look not just at PMDD, but at how the DSM has treated other reproductive or gender-related conditions: **postpartum depression, gender dysphoria, and menopause-related psychiatric suffering**. The first two are included, debated, and studied. The third remains absent. The difference tells us less about science and more about cultural and economic power.

Postpartum Depression: A Recognised Crisis

Postpartum depression (PPD) is now firmly recognised in psychiatric and medical frameworks. In the DSM-5, it is not listed as a separate disorder but coded as a specifier for Major Depressive Disorder, *with peripartum onset*. This may sound like a minor technicality, but it is significant. By creating a peripartum specifier, psychiatry legitimised the link between childbirth and psychiatric suffering.

Why did postpartum depression make it in? Several reasons converge:

1. **Public Pressure**: Stories of maternal suicide, infanticide, and family collapse drew media attention. Policymakers were forced to acknowledge the crisis.
2. **Clinical Urgency**: Psychiatrists, paediatricians, and obstetricians all encountered women in crisis after childbirth. The suffering was too visible to deny.
3. **Treatment Pathways**: Antidepressants, psychotherapy, and more recently, drugs like brexanolone (Zulresso) created pharmaceutical and therapeutic markets.

PPD was not only visible, it was actionable. Recognition gave women diagnostic legitimacy, clinicians billing codes, and pharmaceutical companies a market.

Gender Dysphoria: Social Controversy, Clinical Legitimacy

Gender dysphoria presents an even clearer example of psychiatry's selective recognition. Unlike menopause, which affects every woman who survives into midlife, gender dysphoria is rare. Unlike postpartum depression, which emerges in predictable proximity to childbirth, gender dysphoria varies in onset and presentation. Yet it is firmly codified in the DSM.

Why? Because psychiatry recognised that legitimacy was essential for access. Without a diagnosis, individuals seeking gender-affirming care could not access insurance reimbursement, medical interventions, or workplace accommodations. Inclusion was framed not as pathologising identity but as legitimising suffering.

Here lies the irony. Psychiatry was willing to withstand political controversy, accusations of "pathologising gender" from one side, and accusations of "encouraging transition" from the other, to codify gender dysphoria. But it has not been willing to codify menopause-related psychiatric suffering, despite its universality and documented severity.

Menopause: The Great Omission

When it comes to menopause, the DSM has consistently refused recognition. Menopause-related mood changes, depression, anxiety, insomnia, and cognitive shifts are treated as either:

- Symptoms of other disorders (e.g., depression, anxiety), or
- "Normal" consequences of aging.

This framing erases the hormonal specificity of the menopausal transition. It ignores the distinct neurobiological disruptions triggered by oestrogen withdrawal. It denies women the language and legitimacy that DSM recognition confers.

The arguments used to exclude menopause are strikingly weak:

- **Too Broad**: Symptoms vary, so it cannot be codified. (But symptoms of depression or anxiety also vary.)
- **Too Normal**: Menopause is a life stage, not a disorder. (But childbirth is also a life stage, yet postpartum depression is recognised.)

414

- **Not Pathological**: Menopause is natural. (But so is pregnancy. So is bereavement, which for decades was listed as a trigger for depressive disorder.)

The truth is less about science and more about neglect. Menopause is seen as messy, unprofitable, and unworthy of psychiatry's time.

Selective Legitimacy: Who Psychiatry Chooses to See

The inclusion of PMDD, postpartum depression, and gender dysphoria shows that psychiatry is perfectly capable of recognising hormonally linked, life-stage-related, or socially contested conditions when it chooses. The criteria are not consistent. The decisions are not neutral. They are political.

- **PMDD**: Included because pharma had an SSRI ready to market.
- **Postpartum depression**: Included because maternal suicide and infanticide forced public recognition.
- **Gender dysphoria**: Included because access to care required legitimacy, and psychiatry was willing to shoulder controversy.
- **Menopause-related depression and anxiety**: Excluded, because it is too common, too messy, and not profitable.

Inclusion reflects where political, cultural, and economic incentives converge. Exclusion reflects where they do not.

The Global Picture: ICD and Beyond

The DSM is not the only classification system. The **International Classification of Diseases (ICD)**, maintained by the World Health Organization, is the global standard for medical coding. It shapes health policy, research funding, and insurance coverage worldwide.

Like the DSM, the ICD includes PMDD. Like the DSM, it includes postpartum depression (as a mental and behavioural disorder associated with the puerperium). Like the DSM, it includes gender dysphoria (under the newer term "gender incongruence").

And like the DSM, it does not include menopause-related depression or anxiety.

This absence has a global ripple effect. In countries that rely on ICD codes for research funding, hospital admissions, and insurance claims, the absence of a diagnostic category means women's suffering is rendered invisible. Researchers cannot apply for grants. Health systems do not collect data. Policymakers cannot justify interventions.

The Logic of Selective Recognition
The pattern is clear: psychiatry does not recognise conditions based on prevalence, severity, or impact alone. It recognises conditions that:

- Can be clearly defined in diagnostic criteria.
- Align with available treatments.
- Serve political, cultural, or economic imperatives.

Menopause meets the first criterion, research has long established symptom clusters. It meets the second, HRT is effective, and SSRIs are often prescribed off-label. But it fails the third. It does not serve a profitable pharmaceutical agenda. It does not attract political urgency. It does not align neatly with psychiatry's professional boundaries.

This is why PMDD made it in, and menopause did not. Not because one is more real than the other, but because one was politically and economically useful.

Policy Consequences of Silence

The DSM is more than a book on a shelf. Its omissions shape practice, funding, and recognition across the entire health system. When menopause-related psychiatric suffering is absent, the effects cascade:

Insurance: No Code, No Coverage
In the United States, DSM codes flow directly into insurance billing. If a psychiatrist cannot assign a code, they cannot be reimbursed. This is not a matter of compassion, it is a matter of economics. Without a code for "menopausal depression" or "menopausal anxiety," clinicians must choose another category: *Major Depressive Disorder*, *Generalised Anxiety Disorder*, or sometimes nothing at all.

This workaround distorts care. A woman experiencing hormone-driven mood destabilisation is funnelled into a diagnostic category that ignores the underlying physiology. She may receive antidepressants or benzodiazepines instead of hormone therapy or integrated care. Insurance companies reimburse the wrong treatment because the DSM never recognised the right one.

Globally, the problem is amplified. In countries that rely on ICD coding, the absence of menopause-related categories leaves women in the same bind: no code, no coverage. Health insurers cannot authorise services, hospitals cannot log admissions, and national health systems cannot allocate funding. Absence at the diagnostic level becomes absence at every level.

Research: The Desert of Neglect
The DSM also sets the agenda for research. Grant agencies, journals, and universities all lean on its categories when deciding what to fund or publish. If a condition is not in the DSM, it is far harder to study.

This has left a glaring research gap. While PMDD has been the subject of dozens of clinical trials, menopause-related depression and anxiety remain under-researched. Young psychiatrists are not encouraged to pursue menopause research because it lacks a formal diagnostic home. Funding committees treat it as a secondary issue, lumped under "aging" or "women's health." The result is a self-fulfilling cycle: because the DSM does not recognise menopause, research is scarce, and because research is scarce, the DSM continues not to recognise it.

Education: What Doctors Learn, What They Don't
Medical schools and psychiatric training programs rely heavily on DSM categories to structure their teaching. Students learn how to diagnose and treat the conditions listed. They do not learn what is absent.

This means that a generation of clinicians graduate without structured knowledge of menopause-related psychiatric suffering. They may know the diagnostic criteria for PMDD, postpartum depression, or gender dysphoria. But they are left unprepared to recognise or respond to mood changes driven by menopause.

For patients, this translates to dismissal. A GP or psychiatrist, lacking the training, interprets symptoms as "just stress" or "normal aging." Women leave appointments without answers, or worse, with prescriptions that do not match the problem.

Workplaces: No Legitimacy, No Accommodation
The absence of menopause in psychiatric frameworks spills into the workplace. Employers often rely on medical evidence and diagnostic legitimacy when designing policies. Conditions with DSM recognition, depression, anxiety, PTSD, are widely understood and accommodated. Conditions without recognition are easily dismissed.

When a woman asks for flexible breaks, uniform adjustments, or temporary workload modifications due to menopausal symptoms, HR departments look for documentation. A note from a doctor citing "menopausal depression" carries little weight if the condition itself is not codified. Without diagnostic legitimacy, workplace policies stall.

This creates a vicious circle. Women are denied accommodations, leave the workforce earlier, or decline leadership roles. Organisations lose talent and experience, but because the loss is framed as "personal choice" rather than "structural failure," the system does not change.

Policy Blindness: What Gets Counted, What Gets Ignored

Public policy depends on data. Policymakers prioritise conditions that are measured, costed, and tracked. The DSM's categories feed into public health surveillance systems, shaping what governments see and what they ignore.

Because menopause-related psychiatric suffering is not in the DSM, it is not systematically measured. National mental health surveys rarely ask about it. Hospital records rarely log it. Policymakers rarely cost it. This makes it easy to claim that menopause has little impact, not because the suffering is absent, but because the data is.

The result is underinvestment. Mental health budgets are allocated to conditions with codes, data, and advocacy. Menopause receives almost nothing.

The Cascade of Absence

The DSM's silence is not just symbolic. It is systemic.

- No DSM code → no insurance reimbursement.
- No DSM code → no research agenda.
- No DSM code → no medical education.
- No DSM code → no workplace legitimacy.
- No DSM code → no policy priority.

This cascade of absence is why menopause remains psychiatry's blind spot. It is not simply that clinicians do not care. It is that the system they inhabit has structurally erased the problem.

A Canon Stuck in the Past

The DSM was meant to evolve with science, but its silences reveal just how far psychiatry remains behind lived reality. In 2013, the DSM-5 codified PMDD, postpartum depression, and gender dysphoria, each recognition shaped by advocacy, economics, and politics. Yet it left untouched the psychiatric suffering tied to menopause, a transition experienced by every woman who survives into midlife.

This omission is not accidental. It is systemic.

- Pharma had a drug for PMDD. No psychiatric drug existed for menopause.
- Public pressure mounted for postpartum depression. Menopause remained hidden in the private sphere.
- Gender dysphoria required diagnostic legitimacy to access care. Menopause was dismissed as "just aging."

By failing to include menopause, psychiatry entrenched a hierarchy of legitimacy: certain forms of suffering were visible and billable, while others were erased. The result is a diagnostic canon stuck in the past, out of step with both biology and society.

The cost of this absence is measured not only in research deserts, unfunded programs, and misdiagnosed patients. It is measured in women who suffer silently, dismissed in clinics, unsupported at work, and denied recognition in public policy.

Menopause is not a minor footnote in women's lives. It is a universal transition, often accompanied by profound psychiatric symptoms. To exclude it from psychiatry's official canon is to deny half the population the dignity of recognition.

This is not about pathologising every hot flush or mood swing. It is about legitimising suffering when it is disabling, treatable, and life-altering. Inclusion would not medicalise womanhood. It would acknowledge reality.

The DSM has always been a cultural as well as clinical document. If psychiatry wishes to remain relevant, and just, it must rewrite its canon. Menopause cannot remain psychiatry's blind spot.

The silence must end.

Real-life Psychiatric Suffering Dismissed as "Just Hormonal"

The Language of Dismissal

The phrase "just hormonal" is one of the most effective silencers in modern medicine. It rolls easily off the tongue of clinicians, partners, and even women themselves, and yet its impact is devastating. On the surface, it appears to be a neutral description, a shorthand for the role of hormones in shaping mood, cognition, and wellbeing. But when paired with the word "just," it becomes an act of dismissal. It suggests that what is happening is ordinary, tolerable, unworthy of intervention.

For decades, women have been trained to accept this dismissal. When they present with depression in midlife, they are told it is "empty nest syndrome." When they describe panic attacks, it is reframed as "stress." When they mention fatigue, brain fog, or disorientation, it is interpreted as "just aging." By wrapping disabling psychiatric suffering in a cloak of inevitability, the medical system absolves itself of responsibility.

The language matters. A woman told she has major depressive disorder may at least receive treatment and social recognition. A woman told she is "just hormonal" is left with nothing: no treatment that works, no recognition, no legitimacy. It is not simply that she is unwell; it is that her unwellness has been reframed as natural, and therefore invisible.

The consequences ripple beyond the consultation room. Families, hearing the same words, assume the woman is exaggerating or weak. Employers view her as unreliable or emotional. Women themselves internalise the judgment, blaming themselves for failing to cope with what they are told is "normal." The phrase becomes not only a diagnosis but a sentence, a sentence of silence.

This dismissal is reinforced by psychiatry's own blind spots. Because menopause-related psychiatric suffering does not appear in the DSM, it is not formally taught, coded, or researched. Doctors are left without a category, so they reach for what they know: depression, anxiety, stress, aging. Women are misdiagnosed not because their suffering is imaginary but because the diagnostic canon does not provide a place for it to exist.

When Dismissal Becomes Harm

To understand how this dismissal operates in real lives, it is worth turning from policy to people. Across countries and cultures, the same pattern repeats: women speak, clinicians misinterpret, and lives unravel.

Maria's Story: Antidepressants for Hot Flushes

Maria was forty-nine when she walked into her GP's office in Sydney. She described waking ten times a night drenched in sweat, snapping at her children without meaning to, and feeling waves of despair she could not explain. The GP listened, nodded, and wrote a prescription for an SSRI. "It's depression," he said gently.

At first, Maria felt a flicker of hope. If it was depression, there was a name, and there was a treatment. But weeks passed, and nothing improved. The medication dulled her emotions, but the night sweats continued. The exhaustion deepened. She returned to her GP, who urged patience: "Give it more time." Months later she was still exhausted, still unable to sleep, still caught in a fog of despair. It was only after a chance conversation with a friend that she sought another doctor, who immediately connected her symptoms to perimenopause and prescribed hormone replacement therapy. Within weeks, Maria stabilised.

The difference was not biology, it was recognition. Her body had been telling the same story all along. The first GP's framework could not hear it, because menopause did not exist in his diagnostic lexicon. The second doctor did. For Maria, those lost months represented not just untreated suffering but unnecessary shame, the sense that she had somehow failed to respond to treatment for a condition she never had.

Leanne's Story: Mislabelled Dementia

In far north Queensland, Leanne, an Indigenous woman in her early fifties, began to experience memory lapses. She forgot appointments, lost track of conversations, and at work, she sometimes blanked on safety procedures she had known for years. Alarmed, her GP referred her for neurological testing. Dementia was raised as a possibility.

The weight of that word was crushing. Dementia implied decline, dependency, a slow slide into loss of self. Leanne's family began to worry about her future care. She herself fell into anxiety, convinced she was already losing her mind.

Months later, a community health worker who ran an education session on women's health recognised her symptoms as menopause-related brain fog. She was not demented; she was in transition. The relief was immense, but the damage had been done. For months, she had lived under a shadow of fear because her symptoms had been misfiled into a category that psychiatry recognises, while the true cause, menopause, remained invisible.

A Migrant Woman's Story: Panic Disorder and Stigma

In Melbourne, Lila, a migrant woman from Sri Lanka, described to her GP a series of frightening episodes: her heart racing, her body drenched in sweat, waves of fear rising for no apparent reason. The GP diagnosed panic disorder and prescribed benzodiazepines.

The medication dulled her symptoms but left her sedated and foggy at work. Her employer, aware of her prescription, quietly sidelined her from a promotion process. At home, her teenage children teased her for being *"crazy"* when she dozed off at the dinner table.

Months later, when she attended a women's health seminar at her local community centre, she learned that palpitations and panic can be linked to menopause. The knowledge brought not only clarity but anger. She had been labelled unstable, her career had stalled, and her children had absorbed stigma, all because her GP lacked the language and framework to recognise menopause as a psychiatric driver.

A Teacher's Story: Silent Lunchtimes

Not all harm comes from doctors. Sometimes it comes from workplaces that inherit the same dismissive language. A teacher in Queensland described how she stopped eating lunch in the staffroom altogether. Hot flushes and sweating made her terrified of smelling bad around colleagues. She would sit alone in her car, eating quickly with the windows rolled down, hoping the breeze would cool her face before the next class.

"It wasn't the symptoms that hurt me most," she explained. "It was the shame of thinking everyone was laughing at me."

Here the dismissal was not clinical but cultural. Because menopause was treated as a joke or a weakness, she withdrew into silence. Her isolation was not the product of biology but of stigma, a stigma fuelled by the phrase "just hormonal."

And yet, change is beginning to touch even the most resistant corners of the workplace. The very day before this book went to print, that same teacher acknowledged the introduction of the Queensland Government Worker Policy on Reproductive Leave. For the first time, she had the option to take time away from work to seek medical treatment without the fear of judgment or penalty. A policy shift may not erase the years of stigma she endured, but it marked a small, significant step toward dignity and recognition.

Expanding the Pattern: What Stories Reveal

Each of these stories is individual, yet together they reveal a structural pattern. Women describe symptoms that are disabling. Clinicians interpret them through the wrong lens. Families and workplaces mirror that dismissal. The absence of recognition at the psychiatric level cascades into social invisibility.

It is not only the misdiagnosis that harms but the message embedded within it: that women's suffering is temporary, tolerable, or trivial. Maria was told she had depression when she needed hormone therapy. Leanne was told she might have dementia when she had brain fog. Lila was labelled with panic disorder when she was in perimenopause. The teacher was left to feel that sweat was shameful rather than physiological.

In every case, the words available to describe the suffering were wrong. And because the words were wrong, the treatments, responses, and outcomes were wrong. This is what "just hormonal" means in practice: the erasure of reality through language.

The Misdiagnosis Machine, Intersectional Lens, Global Comparisons)

The Misdiagnosis Machine

If women's suffering at midlife could be drawn as a diagram, it would look like a flowchart. The symptom is presented, the clinician interprets it through the limited categories of the DSM, and the outcome almost never lands on menopause. Instead, the arrows scatter across unrelated diagnoses:

- Hot flushes → "stress" → antidepressants prescribed.
- Night sweats → "thyroid disorder" → blood tests, inconclusive.
- Brain fog → "dementia" → neurology referral, heightened anxiety.
- Joint pain → "arthritis" → anti-inflammatories, no relief.
- Palpitations → "panic disorder" → benzodiazepines, stigma.

At no point does the arrow end at "menopause." The machine is set up this way not because doctors are malicious but because psychiatry has never supplied them with the right category. With no diagnostic slot for menopause-related psychiatric suffering, clinicians reach for what exists. The DSM is their map, and if menopause is not on the map, then in practice it does not exist.

This misdiagnosis machine consumes women's lives. It eats away time as women shuffle between specialists. It eats away resources as unnecessary tests are ordered and unnecessary drugs prescribed. And it eats away at confidence: women come to doubt their own perceptions, convinced they must be weak or exaggerating if the medical system cannot name what they are experiencing.

The tragedy is not only personal but systemic. Each misdiagnosis creates a cascade of false data. Depression statistics are inflated with miscategorised menopausal cases. Anxiety disorder registries absorb women who might have been treated with hormone therapy. Dementia referrals swell with women whose brains are not failing but simply fogging in transition. By ignoring menopause, psychiatry not only fails women individually but distorts its own epidemiological record.

Intersectional Lens: Who Gets Dismissed the Hardest

Dismissal is universal, but it is not evenly distributed. The burden falls heaviest on those who already sit at the margins of medicine and society.

Migrant Women and the Language Barrier

For migrant women, dismissal often begins with translation. A woman who says she feels "hot" in Mandarin may be understood by her doctor as describing fever, not vasomotor symptoms. A woman who complains of "forgetting" in Arabic may be assumed to be depressed. Without interpreters trained in reproductive health, language flattens complexity, and symptoms scatter into misinterpretation.

Mai, the Vietnamese woman introduced earlier, illustrates this perfectly. Unable to find a word in her own language for menopause, she could only gesture and say "tired" or "hot." Her GP, working without an interpreter, assumed fatigue and stress. She left with sleeping tablets instead of an explanation. What was lost was not simply medical accuracy but dignity: she felt foolish, incapable of expressing herself, ashamed.

Indigenous Women and the Silence of Language

For Indigenous women, the issue is often the absence of any word at all. Studies with First Nations women in Canada revealed that Ojibway and Oji-Cree have no single word for menopause. Instead, women used the phrase "that time when periods stop." In practice, this meant that symptoms like mood swings, memory loss, or anxiety were not conceptually linked to the transition. They existed in fragments, never named as a whole.

Australian Indigenous women report similar gaps. In some languages, menopause is described as "bleeding no more" or "no more women's sickness." These phrases capture cessation but not transition. They strip away the psychological, social, and existential dimensions of the experience. Even more alarming, research in far north Queensland found that 58.9 percent of Indigenous participants had never heard the word "menopause" until recruited into studies. For these women, the silence was not ignorance, it was the legacy of neglect. Without words, there is no preparation, no recognition, and no way to ask for help.

Working-Class Women and the Price of Persistence
Class compounds dismissal. Professional women with financial resources may have the option of seeing multiple doctors until one finally recognises menopause. Working-class women dependent on overstretched public health systems often cannot. They accept the first diagnosis they are given. If a GP says it is depression, then it must be depression. If they are told to "get more exercise," they may try and fail, blaming themselves for not feeling better. Without money or time to seek second opinions, dismissal becomes destiny.

The workplace amplifies this inequity. A professional woman might discreetly rearrange her hours or negotiate flexible work. A factory worker, a cashier, or a cleaner has no such options. Symptoms must be hidden, endured, or punished. Dismissal at the GP's office becomes dismissal at the time clock, and the cost is often employment itself.

Global Comparisons: The Geography of Dismissal

Dismissal is not unique to Australia. Across the globe, the same patterns recur, shaped by culture, language, and policy.

In the United States
American women often face a particularly medicalised dismissal. Because healthcare is tied to insurance billing, diagnoses must fit existing codes. With no DSM category for menopause-related psychiatric suffering, GPs reach for depression or anxiety. Insurance reimburses, but the woman is miscategorised. At the same time, direct-to-consumer advertising by pharmaceutical companies encourages women to see themselves as disordered rather than in transition. The result is a country where antidepressant prescriptions soar among midlife women while hormone therapy remains underused.

In the United Kingdom
The UK tells a different story, one of emerging recognition. Public debate, led by journalists, campaigners, and even celebrities, has pushed menopause into mainstream conversation. The National Health Service has begun to expand specialist clinics, and Parliament has debated workplace protections. Yet even here, dismissal lingers. GPs receive minimal training, and many women report being told their suffering is "just stress" or "just part of life." The gap between public awareness and medical recognition remains wide.

In Japan
Japan illustrates the power of language itself. The word for menopause, konenki, historically translated as "renewal years." For centuries it framed the transition as a natural part of life, even an opportunity for growth. But modern medicine has shifted the term toward pathology, aligning it more with "syndrome" than "seasonal change." As the cultural meaning shifted, so too did the experience. Japanese women increasingly report symptoms once rarely acknowledged, in part because the lexicon now makes them visible. The paradox is that recognition can either empower or stigmatise, depending on the frame.

Among the Mayan of Mexico

In rural Mayan communities, dismissal takes another form: invisibility through neutrality. Menopause is not treated as a problem because it passes quietly. High parity and long breastfeeding keep estrogen levels low throughout life, softening the transition. For many Mayan women, menopause simply means the end of restrictions. They celebrate freedom from pregnancy risk and menstrual taboos. But this cultural reframing, while positive, also means there is little preparation for those who do suffer severe psychiatric fallout. Their pain is minimised because the collective story insists that menopause is unremarkable.

Among Arab Women

In Arabic, the phrase sinn al-yaas translates as *"the age of despair."* Here, the problem is not invisibility but stigma embedded in the word itself. To name menopause is to name decline. Women internalise despair before it even arrives, primed by language to expect hopelessness. Psychiatric suffering is not dismissed as trivial but as destiny.

What These Comparisons Reveal

Across these contexts, the thread is clear: where language is absent, symptoms are fragmented. Where language is negative, symptoms are stigmatised. Where language is medicalised without nuance, symptoms are pathologised into the wrong categories. And in every case, women pay the price.

Dismissal is not simply about what doctors say in consultation rooms. It is about what languages allow us to name, what cultures teach us to expect, and what systems choose to recognise. Whether it is an Australian GP prescribing antidepressants for hot flushes, a Canadian Indigenous woman with no word to describe her brain fog, or an Arab woman told she has entered an "age of despair," the result is the same: psychiatric suffering erased or distorted into something it is not.

The geography of dismissal proves a deeper truth. Menopause may be universal, but its recognition is not. The silence is cultural, political, and structural. And until psychiatry itself acknowledges menopause as a legitimate category of psychiatric relevance, the misdiagnosis machine will continue to spin, scattering women into categories that fail them.

Consequences, Why Dismissal Persists, Pathways to Recognition

The Ripple Effects of Dismissal
When psychiatric suffering in menopause is brushed aside as *"just hormonal,"* the costs cascade. They ripple through medicine, workplaces, families, and society.

On the **clinical level**, dismissal reroutes women into the wrong treatment pathways. Antidepressants are prescribed when hormone therapy might help. Benzodiazepines are offered when what is needed is education and sleep management. Neurological assessments are ordered for brain fog, not because dementia is suspected but because menopause is never considered. This misdirection wastes scarce resources and prolongs suffering.

On the **epidemiological level**, dismissal distorts data. Depression prevalence rates in middle-aged women are inflated by misdiagnosed menopause cases. Anxiety statistics swell with miscategorised perimenopausal panic. Suicide prevention research rarely accounts for the peak in female suicide during midlife, even though the overlap with menopause is striking. When women's suffering is labelled incorrectly, public health systems cannot see patterns clearly.

On the **workplace level**, the impact is equally severe. Women lose confidence when their distress is dismissed.

Colleagues whisper about unreliability. Promotions are quietly withdrawn. Deloitte has found that one in four women decline career opportunities due to unmanaged symptoms. That is not individual failure. That is organisational loss. It is a talent pipeline draining because the medical system refuses to name reality.

On the **family level**, dismissal erodes relationships. Irritability becomes misinterpreted as rejection. Withdrawal is seen as selfishness. Children and partners absorb the same cultural script: "Mum is hormonal." Women, internalising the message, feel guilt layered on top of despair. A problem unrecognised becomes shame. Shame, repeated, becomes silence.

And at the **economic level**, the losses compound. Absenteeism, presenteeism, early retirement, and healthcare waste create a bill that Deloitte and PwC have each estimated in the billions. But the true price is not financial. It is human: lives lived in shadow, potential unrealised, leadership lost.

At its darkest edge, dismissal kills. Suicide statistics reveal that midlife women carry a disproportionate burden. While not every death is caused by menopause, the intersection is undeniable. Untreated psychiatric suffering, compounded by dismissal, can push women into despair. Silence, at its most extreme, is fatal.

Why Dismissal Persists
Given decades of feminist critique and growing public awareness, why does dismissal remain so entrenched? Several forces converge.

- The Diagnostic Blind Spot
The DSM does not include menopause-related psychiatric conditions. As a result, medical schools do not teach them, researchers do not study them, and clinicians do not diagnose them. Without a category, doctors fall back on

what they know: depression, anxiety, aging. The blind spot is baked into the professional canon.

- Cultural Taboo

Menopause remains a word cloaked in embarrassment. Women hesitate to raise it, fearing ridicule. Clinicians hesitate to name it, fearing impropriety. In many cultures, talking openly about reproductive transitions is still taboo. Silence is not only inherited; it is enforced.

- Economic Disincentive

Unlike PMDD, which could be treated with SSRIs and marketed accordingly, menopause is not easily converted into a pharmaceutical blockbuster. Hormone therapy exists but is complex, nuanced, and not universally indicated. Without a clear profit stream, pharmaceutical companies have little incentive to lobby for diagnostic recognition. In the political economy of psychiatry, what cannot be monetised often remains marginal.

- Gender Bias

Women's psychiatric suffering has a long history of minimisation. In the nineteenth century it was labelled hysteria. In the twentieth century it became "housewife's nerves." In the twenty-first century it is "just hormonal." The vocabulary changes, but the logic remains: women's distress is naturalised, trivialised, and dismissed. This is not ignorance. It is structural sexism codified in the very foundations of psychiatric practice.

Pathways to Recognition

The persistence of dismissal does not mean change is impossible. Other reproductive transitions prove that recognition can be won.

Postpartum depression was once dismissed as "baby blues." Women were told to toughen up, to enjoy motherhood, to stop being selfish. Today, postpartum depression is widely recognised, with screening protocols, treatment pathways, and public campaigns. This shift did not happen by accident. It was the result of advocacy, research, and a reframing of maternal mental health as both legitimate and urgent.

PMDD (Premenstrual Dysphoric Disorder) was once dismissed as exaggerated PMS. Its eventual inclusion in the DSM came after years of pharmaceutical lobbying, clinical trials, and feminist pushback. The recognition was controversial, but it created a diagnostic space that allowed suffering women to be seen, studied, and treated.

Gender dysphoria provides another lesson. Once pathologised, it is now recognised in psychiatric manuals as a category that legitimises care. The inclusion has enabled insurance coverage, clinical training, and research funding. It shows that psychiatry can adapt when political will converges with advocacy and economic interest.

Menopause deserves the same trajectory. Recognition does not mean pathologising every woman's experience. It means legitimising the suffering of those for whom menopause brings disabling psychiatric fallout. It means ensuring that women like Maria, Leanne, and Lila are not misdiagnosed, mistreated, or left to suffer in silence.

What recognition requires:
- Inclusion in diagnostic manuals such as the DSM and ICD.
- Expanded medical education covering menopause as a psychiatric as well as gynecological transition.
- Research funding directed at the intersection of hormones and mental health in midlife.
- Insurance systems that reimburse appropriate treatments, including hormone therapy and counselling.

- Public campaigns that normalise menopause as part of the life course, not as decline.

Recognition is not a gift. It is a responsibility. By refusing to name menopause, psychiatry has colluded in silence. By choosing to name it, psychiatry can begin to undo decades of harm.

The words "just hormonal" have cost women too much. They have cost months of misdiagnosis, years of mistreatment, decades of silence. They have cost confidence, careers, and lives.

To dismiss menopause-related psychiatric suffering as trivial is to mistake universality for insignificance. Yes, menopause happens to half the world. But universality does not erase severity. It magnifies responsibility.

Absence in the DSM equals absence in research, in medical education, in insurance, and in recognition. Each absence compounds the next, until women are left invisible in the very system meant to protect them.

This is not about pathologising every hot flush or every restless night. It is about acknowledging when hormonal transition collides with psychiatric suffering in ways that are real, disabling, and treatable.

Silence has lasted long enough. The dismissal of women's suffering as "just hormonal" is not medicine, it is negligence disguised as normality. The time has come to name menopause, to recognise its psychiatric dimensions, and to build pathways of care that honour reality rather than erase it.

The Power of the DSM and Clinical Manuals

When Books Become Gatekeepers
Few books in history have held as much power over human lives as the Diagnostic and Statistical Manual of Mental

Disorders (DSM). Its thin pages and clinical codes may look innocuous, but the DSM is not simply a medical reference. It is a cultural artefact, an economic engine, and a political statement. To be named in its pages is to exist. To be absent is to disappear.

For psychiatry, the DSM is the arbiter of legitimacy. If a condition is included, research flourishes, insurance covers treatment, and clinicians learn to diagnose it. If excluded, it falls into silence. Suffering without a category becomes invisible, dismissed, or folded awkwardly into diagnoses that do not fit. The DSM does not only describe illness; it defines what society accepts as mental illness and what it discards as normal life.

This dynamic is mirrored globally in the International Classification of Diseases (ICD), maintained by the World Health Organization. Together, these manuals determine not only what is studied and treated but what is spoken aloud. They are the gatekeepers of legitimacy. The absence of menopause-related psychiatric suffering from the DSM is not an academic quibble. It is a structural silence with real-world consequences.

How the DSM Shapes Reality
The DSM was first published in 1952. DSM-I contained 106 disorders, most described briefly, reflecting psychiatry's close ties to psychoanalysis at the time. DSM-II, released in 1968, expanded the list but retained a psychoanalytic framework. By DSM-III in 1980, psychiatry underwent a revolution. The manual shifted toward descriptive, symptom-based criteria that could be measured, researched, and billed. Insurance companies in the United States demanded clarity, and the DSM became the Tool that allowed mental illness to be coded, reimbursed, and tracked.

Each subsequent edition expanded its reach. DSM-IV (1994) and DSM-IV-TR (2000) introduced refinements, while DSM-5 (2013) reorganised categories and introduced controversial new diagnoses. The DSM-5-TR (2022) added further updates. Over seven decades, the DSM has become not just a book but a system: a common language for clinicians, researchers, insurers, and policymakers.

With that power came distortion. To be in the DSM is to be studied, treated, and reimbursed. To be left out is to remain unseen. This has profound consequences. Insurance reimbursement requires a DSM code. Research grants flow to conditions recognised by the DSM. Medical schools and psychiatric residencies use the DSM as a teaching framework. Epidemiological surveys are built on DSM categories. Exclusion means prevalence data is never captured. The DSM's influence is mirrored in the ICD, shaping recognition of suffering worldwide.

Examples show this power clearly. When post-traumatic stress disorder (PTSD) was added in DSM-III, it legitimised the experiences of veterans and trauma survivors. Research boomed, funding expanded, and clinical services emerged. When autism spectrum disorder was consolidated in DSM-5, it reshaped education and services globally. When gender dysphoria was redefined, it opened care pathways, insurance coverage, and legal recognition. These inclusions changed the world. Menopause, by contrast, remains invisible.
Menopause in the Shadows

Against this backdrop, the absence of menopause-related psychiatric conditions is startling. Menopause is universal for women who live long enough, yet the psychiatric suffering it can bring has been left in the shadows.

Mood swings, depression, anxiety, panic attacks, insomnia, memory loss, and even suicidal ideation can peak during perimenopause and menopause. These symptoms are real, disabling for many, and biologically linked to hormonal shifts. Yet they have no diagnostic home. Instead, they are coded under major depressive disorder, generalised anxiety disorder, or adjustment disorder. These categories are not always wrong, but they miss the context. Menopause is treated as irrelevant when it is central.

Contrast this with postpartum depression, which is now widely recognised and legitimised by inclusion. Screening programs exist. Awareness campaigns are run. PMDD (premenstrual dysphoric disorder) was included in DSM-5 after clinical trials and lobbying. Recognition remains debated but its presence legitimises care. Why then is menopause absent? It is seen as a life stage, not a disorder. Symptoms vary across women, making categorisation complex. It lacks pharmaceutical champions and has been slowed by cultural taboo. Absence tells clinicians not to look, researchers not to study, insurers not to pay. Women remain invisible in the very system designed to classify suffering.

The Global Ripple Effect

The DSM is dominant in the United States, but the ICD extends its reach globally. The ICD underpins health policy, coding, and statistics in over 100 countries. When a condition is absent from both DSM and ICD, its invisibility becomes global. The consequences are significant.

Without codes, large-scale studies on menopause and mental health are rare. Funding bodies argue there is no recognised category. Medical curricula worldwide align with DSM and ICD. Trainees learn what is in the manuals, meaning menopause is absent from training. National health systems tie reimbursement to ICD codes. Without a code, services are not covered. Women either pay privately or go untreated. Global health agencies use ICD categories to shape programs. Without recognition, menopause remains absent from public health priorities.

In the United States, women are prescribed antidepressants instead of hormone therapy. In the United Kingdom, GPs receive minimal training, leaving women dismissed as stressed or aging. In Australia, Medicare lacks billing codes for menopause-related psychiatric consultations. In Canada, Indigenous women report suffering in silence with no language or framework. Globally, the absence reinforces cultural silence. If the most authoritative books do not name it, why should anyone else?

The Cost of Absence
The silence has consequences. For patients, it means misdiagnosis, mistreatment, shame, and prolonged suffering. For clinicians, it means confusion, lack of training, and reliance on inappropriate categories. For research, it means deserts of funding and distorted epidemiology. For health systems, it means wasted resources on unnecessary tests and ineffective treatments. For economies, it means lost productivity and billions in hidden costs.

At the human level, the cost is profound. Women internalise dismissal as weakness. Careers are abandoned. Relationships fracture. Some spiral into despair. Midlife suicide remains underexamined but alarmingly present. Each represents not just an individual tragedy but a systemic failure. Silence and stigma together cost lives, livelihoods, and legitimacy.

Towards Inclusion
Recognition of menopause-related psychiatric suffering in manuals like the DSM and ICD would not mean pathologising every woman. Just as postpartum depression recognition does not imply childbirth is an illness, menopause recognition would simply create a framework for when psychiatric fallout becomes disabling.

Inclusion could take the form of a new category such as Menopause-Associated Mood Disorder. Criteria could include onset linked to perimenopause or menopause, mood disturbance beyond expected stressors, functional impairment, and biological plausibility linked to hormonal transition. Subtypes might include depressive, anxious, or mixed forms, with exclusions to avoid mislabelling primary disorders.

The benefits of inclusion would be profound. Insurance coverage would follow. Research funding would expand. Medical education would include menopause psychiatry. Public health surveillance would capture prevalence. Most importantly, legitimacy would be given to patients. Women would no longer be dismissed as just hormonal.

Lessons from postpartum depression, PMDD, and gender dysphoria show it is possible. Advocacy, evidence, and political will can change manuals. Menopause deserves the same.

Rewriting the Canon

There is a truth that bears repeating until it becomes undeniable: absence is not neutral. When psychiatry omits menopause from its manuals, it does not create a blank space waiting to be filled one day. It creates silence. And silence has weight. It shapes policy, research, medical education, and the daily encounters women have when they walk into a clinic desperate for answers. That silence tells clinicians there is nothing to see, tells funders there is nothing to study, and tells women that what they are going through is not worthy of a name. Absence is not emptiness. Absence is neglect.

This is not an argument for pathologising every woman's journey through menopause. The transition is a universal life stage, not a disease. Many women pass through it with resilience, sometimes even with relief. But universality does not erase variability. Some women suffer in ways that are disabling, enduring panic attacks, deep depression, relentless insomnia, or cognitive impairment so profound they fear they are losing their minds. To pretend that these experiences are not worthy of recognition because they occur within a natural transition is to confuse normality with acceptability. Childbirth is natural, but postpartum depression is recognised because suffering matters. Aging is natural, but dementia is named and studied because suffering matters. Menopause should be no different.

What the DSM and ICD choose to name has consequences that ripple across systems. Without recognition, insurance companies refuse to cover consultations or treatments. Without recognition, medical schools do not train students to see, diagnose, or manage the psychiatric aspects of menopause. Without recognition, epidemiological surveys cannot capture prevalence, leaving researchers unable to argue for funding. This is why the absence of menopause in psychiatric manuals is not a technical oversight but a structural form of discrimination. It leaves women uncounted, untreated, and unseen.

This neglect is compounded by stigma. For centuries, menopause has been treated as an embarrassment, a punchline, or a private burden to be borne silently. By failing to enshrine it in the diagnostic canon, psychiatry colludes with that stigma. It sends the message that what women experience in midlife is not real suffering, but mere fussing, complaining, or weakness. It reinforces the lazy shorthand that tells women they are just hormonal, as if hormones were not real, as if the biology of half the human race were irrelevant. The absence of menopause in the DSM is not just silence. It is endorsement of dismissal.

The contrast with other conditions reveals the injustice clearly. Post-traumatic stress disorder was once invisible, dismissed as battle fatigue or nervous weakness. Only after decades of advocacy did it enter the DSM, legitimising generations of veterans and trauma survivors. Postpartum depression, too, was once a whisper in the shadows, explained away as tiredness or maternal failure. Today it is screened for, studied, and treated. Even PMDD, once controversial and debated, now sits firmly in the DSM with clinical criteria and insurance legitimacy. Gender dysphoria, a diagnosis that carries immense political weight, has been included and refined. Each of these inclusions reflects a recognition that suffering matters, that silence kills, and that medicine must evolve. Yet menopause, affecting half the global population, remains excluded.

This exclusion has cultural and economic roots. Menopause is not seen as marketable. Pharmaceutical companies have little incentive to lobby for its recognition because it does not offer the kind of long-term profitable drug pipeline that depression or anxiety does. Instead, women are funnelled into antidepressants, benzodiazepines, or sleeping pills, each prescribed for symptoms that are reframed to fit existing categories. This misfit creates profits, but it does not create healing. Meanwhile, the cultural taboo around menopause keeps women from speaking, keeps doctors from asking, and keeps psychiatry from naming.

The gender imbalance in who writes the canon makes this even more stark. Manuals reflect not only science but the demographics and biases of their authors. DSM-5, published in 2013, was widely celebrated as a modern, updated edition, yet even here, the committees that shaped its contents were dominated by men. In a sample analysis of 245 contributors, 71 percent were male and just 29 percent female. That is progress compared with DSM-III and DSM-IV, where women were even scarcer, but it still means that men overwhelmingly defined what counted as mental illness. When three-quarters of the people deciding what belongs in the canon are male, it is little wonder that the psychiatric suffering linked to menopause, an experience that only women live through, was sidelined. The canon is not neutral. It is gendered. It reflects the demographics and the power structures of those who hold the pen.

But silence is not destiny. Manuals evolve. The DSM has changed dramatically across its editions, moving from psychoanalytic language to descriptive categories, from narrow lists to broader spectrums. PTSD, autism, postpartum depression, and gender dysphoria all entered the canon after once being dismissed. The ICD has undergone similar transformations, shifting with science, politics, and culture. Menopause can and must follow the same path. It is not a matter of if, but when—and whether more women must suffer in silence before recognition arrives.

The mandate is not to turn menopause into a disorder. It is to create a diagnostic home for the psychiatric fallout when it becomes disabling. It is to acknowledge that depression or anxiety linked to menopause is not the same as depression at twenty or anxiety at thirty. It has different triggers, trajectories, and treatment needs. It demands a framework that respects its context. Such inclusion would unlock insurance coverage, fund research, expand medical education, and give clinicians permission to see what is in front of them. Most importantly, it would give women legitimacy. It would tell them: what you are experiencing is real, and you deserve care.

This recognition would have ripple effects beyond psychiatry. Workplaces could no longer ignore menopause when its psychiatric dimensions were named in the manuals that drive policy. Public health campaigns would have the authority to educate without fear of exaggeration. Families would gain language to understand what their mothers, sisters, and partners were going through. And women themselves would be freed from the loneliness of thinking their suffering was unique, shameful, or imaginary.

Every manual reflects the politics of its time. The DSM is not timeless truth but a living document, revised again and again as culture and science evolve. Its omissions are as telling as its inclusions. The absence of homosexuality from DSM-III was a victory for liberation. The inclusion of PTSD was a victory for trauma survivors. The inclusion of gender dysphoria was a recognition of identity. The absence of menopause in DSM-5 is not a neutral fact. It is a failure of imagination, of justice, and of courage. It is time for psychiatry to correct it.

If psychiatry does not act, the consequences will be felt everywhere. Women will continue to be misdiagnosed, treated with inappropriate medications, and told that their suffering is invisible. Researchers will continue to hit dead ends when applying for funding. Health systems will continue to waste resources on misdirected care. And families will continue to watch women they love struggle without answers. Silence will continue to kill.

But the alternative is within reach. Recognition can happen. A new category could be introduced, carefully defined, not to pathologise every woman, but to legitimise those whose suffering demands care. Criteria could capture the link to hormonal transition, the severity of mood disturbance, the functional impairment. Subtypes could differentiate depression, anxiety, or mixed forms. The presence of such a category would change everything. It would validate patients, guide clinicians, unlock funding, and give language to families. It would be a revolution not of medication but of recognition.

This is the work of reform, resilience, and reclamation. Reform, because psychiatry must reform its canon to reflect reality. Resilience, because women have endured for centuries without words, but should not have to endure further. Reclamation, because language and legitimacy must be reclaimed from silence and stigma.
The DSM and ICD are mirrors of cultural power. Right now, they reflect a world that sees women's midlife suffering as unworthy of a name. But mirrors can change what they show. Manuals can be rewritten. Psychiatry can evolve. And when it does, the millions of women who have suffered invisibility will finally be seen.

Menopause is not a failure. Psychiatry's silence is. The mandate is clear: rewrite the canon.

Chapter 21:
Hormones Hijacked and then Ignored

The body is a symphony of hormones, and for decades estrogen has been its silent conductor. We rarely notice its presence until it is gone. Estrogen steadies the rhythm of bones renewing, neurons firing, blood vessels expanding and contracting. It softens mood swings, sharpens memory, cushions sleep, and fuels libido. Alongside it, progesterone provides counterpoint: calming, balancing, offering a steadying hand. These are not minor players in a woman's body. They are regulators of almost every system. Yet the moment they begin to withdraw, women are told they are simply getting older, simply stressed, simply hormonal. The complexity of their bodies is reduced to cliché.

Menopause is not just the end of periods. It is a biological earthquake. The decline of ovarian hormones reshapes the architecture of the brain, recalibrates metabolism, alters immune responses, and destabilises cardiovascular health. Neuroscientists have shown that estrogen receptors sit in the hippocampus and prefrontal cortex, the very regions responsible for memory, learning, and executive function. When estrogen drops, neural circuits shift. Women describe it as "brain fog," but what they are living through is synaptic change. Cardiologists see rising risk of heart disease after menopause, not coincidence but consequence. Endocrinologists watch metabolic syndrome rise as estrogen's protective role wanes. Yet for decades, the medical profession has siloed these observations instead of connecting them.

This failure of connection has been costly. Women arrive at doctors' offices with palpitations and are referred to cardiology, with insomnia and are prescribed sleeping tablets, with panic attacks and are told to see a psychologist. Each symptom is broken apart, assigned a separate label, and treated in isolation. Nowhere in this process is menopause named as the unifying force. The body is fragmented, and the woman is left feeling both invisible and broken.

The irony is that science has known much of this for years. Animal studies, neuroimaging, and longitudinal data all point to the central role of hormones in regulating mood and cognition. Yet translation into practice has stalled. Why? Because menopause has never been prioritised. It does not attract research dollars in proportion to its impact. It does not sit comfortably in medical curricula, where reproductive health is too often reduced to fertility and obstetrics. And it does not align with the economic incentives of pharmaceutical development, which prefers chronic conditions that can be medicated indefinitely.

The result is a paradox. We know more about the neurological impact of menopause than ever before, yet women continue to be misdiagnosed, dismissed, and mistreated. Hot flushes are labelled stress. Brain fog is mistaken for early dementia. Mood swings are reframed as psychiatric disorders. The true cause, hormonal transition, is sidelined.

This erasure is not accidental. It is systemic. By refusing to integrate menopause into the frameworks that govern psychiatry, cardiology, neurology, and primary care, the medical profession effectively hijacks the experience. It turns a life stage into a collection of misattributed pathologies. It turns women into patients for antidepressants, benzodiazepines, and sleeping pills instead of candidates for evidence-based hormonal care. It turns suffering into profit.

And yet women resist. They tell their stories to friends, in online forums, through memoirs, and increasingly in research surveys. They know their bodies. They sense the link between their symptoms and the hormonal upheaval of midlife. What they need is not reassurance that they are just aging, nor a prescription to sedate away their signals, but recognition. They need medicine to meet them where they are, not where textbooks have historically kept them.

This chapter is about that failure and about that possibility. It is about the ways hormones have been hijacked, by silence, by stigma, by medical systems that refuse to join the dots. It is about how women have been ignored when science itself provides the answers. And it is about reclaiming knowledge so that menopause is not a trapdoor into decades of misdiagnosis but a recognised and supported transition.

The Neurological, Cognitive, and Emotional Impacts

When women describe menopause as "losing themselves," it is not hyperbole. It is neurology. The sharp drop in estrogen during perimenopause and menopause does not only halt ovulation, it transforms how the brain functions. Estrogen is a neuromodulator: it influences neurotransmitters like serotonin, dopamine, and GABA. It regulates energy metabolism in the brain, ensuring neurons fire efficiently. When estrogen falls, these pathways falter. The results are cognitive, emotional, and behavioural changes that women feel every day.

Brain Fog: The Invisible Storm
One of the most common yet least respected symptoms of menopause is brain fog. Women describe walking into a room and forgetting why they are there, struggling to find words, losing the thread of conversations, or missing details in meetings that once came easily. Employers may interpret this as incompetence, family members as distraction, doctors as stress. Rarely is it recognised for what it is: a neurological impact of hormone withdrawal.

Neuroimaging studies confirm these lived realities. Functional MRI scans show changes in blood flow and connectivity in brain regions critical for memory and executive function during perimenopause. The hippocampus, which encodes memory, shows altered activity. The prefrontal cortex, essential for planning and concentration, also shifts. These are not signs of permanent decline but transitions, the brain recalibrating in the

449

absence of estrogen's support. Yet in clinics, brain fog is too often dismissed as aging or worse, mislabelled as early dementia.

One case stands out. A 52-year-old lawyer reported repeated lapses in memory, forgetting case law citations she had known for decades, losing her words mid-argument. Her GP referred her to a neurologist, who ordered dementia screening. Terrified, she began to imagine a life of cognitive decline. Months later, after a chance conversation with a menopause specialist, she started hormone replacement therapy (HRT). Within weeks, her clarity returned. She was not demented. She was menopausal. The diagnostic delay was not benign, it cost her confidence, her work reputation, and months of fear.

Mood and Emotion: The Estrogen-Serotonin Axis

The connection between menopause and mood disturbance is equally profound. Estrogen regulates serotonin, the neurotransmitter most closely associated with well-being. Declining estrogen disrupts serotonin pathways, lowering mood resilience and amplifying stress responses. This is why women with no prior psychiatric history may suddenly experience depression or anxiety in midlife.

And yet, when they seek help, they are rarely told their mood disturbance is hormonally linked. Instead, they are told they are simply stressed, experiencing "empty nest syndrome," or reacting to aging. Antidepressants are prescribed reflexively. While they may provide partial relief, they do not address the root cause: the abrupt hormonal withdrawal.

This is not a fringe phenomenon. Large-scale longitudinal studies show that perimenopause doubles the risk of major depressive episodes compared to premenopause. Anxiety rates spike as well, often presenting as panic attacks or phobias that women have never experienced before. Still, psychiatry has not carved out a diagnostic category for "menopause-related mood disorder." Without that recognition, women remain trapped in a cycle of misdiagnosis and mistreatment.

Panic, Palpitations, and the Body-Mind Divide
Estrogen does not only regulate mood. It also modulates the autonomic nervous system, which governs heart rate, sweating, and arousal. When estrogen declines, the balance between sympathetic (fight-or-flight) and parasympathetic (rest-and-digest) activity skews. The result can be palpitations, surges of anxiety, and panic attacks that seem to come from nowhere.

Women often describe waking in the night with their heart racing, drenched in sweat, convinced they are having a heart attack. Emergency departments see them as cardiac cases, only to discharge them with "anxiety" after negative tests. The true cause, hormonal transition, is not explained. Instead, they are told to see a psychologist, sometimes prescribed benzodiazepines, and left to navigate recurring episodes with no roadmap.

The Cultural Frame
How these neurological and emotional symptoms are understood depends on culture and language. In Japan, where menopause is historically referred to as *konenki*, "renewal years", cognitive and mood changes are often framed as part of natural life shifts. In Western cultures, by contrast, menopause is framed as decline, making brain fog and mood swings more likely to be pathologised. For Indigenous Australian women, research shows that the very word "menopause" may not exist in language; symptoms are described piecemeal, leading to further disconnection from medical care. The result across all contexts is the same: women are left without coherent narratives, and their suffering is either dismissed or misdirected.

Case Studies of Misinterpretation

- **The Teacher Mislabelled with Depression**: A 44 year old corrective services officer sought help for constant fatigue, forgetfulness, and weeping spells. She was prescribed SSRIs and told she had clinical depression. When her periods ceased six months later, she realised she had been in perimenopause all along. The antidepressants dulled her mood but did not restore her energy or clarity. What she needed was a recognition of hormonal transition.

- **The Executive and the Neurologist**: A senior executive underwent a battery of tests for cognitive decline after forgetting presentation points. The neurologist concluded she had "age-related mild cognitive impairment." Only later did she discover her symptoms improved dramatically on HRT. She had been given a premature shadow of dementia when what she was experiencing was temporary hormone-driven brain change.

- **The Migrant Worker and the Language Barrier**: A woman from a Pacific Island community, working in aged care in Australia, reported "heat and forgetting." Without a shared vocabulary, her GP assumed hyperthyroidism and ordered blood tests. When these were normal, the doctor suggested counselling for stress. She withdrew, feeling foolish. Her symptoms worsened, and she quit her job.

The Cost of Misrecognition

The neurological and emotional impacts of menopause are not temporary inconveniences when ignored. They derail careers, strain marriages, and diminish quality of life. Women lose promotions, step back from leadership, or exit workplaces altogether. Families misunderstand, interpreting mood changes as irritability or hostility. Communities lose the wisdom and contributions of women in their prime.

This is the human cost of the GP bottleneck, the psychiatric silence, and the cultural stigma around menopause. Neuroscience is clear. Lived experience is clear. What is missing is recognition in the frameworks that shape clinical practice.

Mimicking Other Disorders

Menopause is a master of disguise. Its symptoms do not present as a tidy package labelled "hormonal transition." Instead, they scatter across medical categories, showing up as cardiovascular, neurological, psychiatric, or musculoskeletal complaints. Hot flushes mimic stress. Night sweats resemble thyroid disease. Brain fog looks like dementia. Joint pain suggests arthritis. Palpitations imitate panic disorder. Because the system is built on silos, each specialty sees its own reflection. The one diagnosis that unites them all, menopause, is rarely spoken.

The Diagnostic Fog

In theory, diagnosis is a process of pattern recognition. In practice, it is a process shaped by what doctors are trained to see. Medical education emphasises pathology: diseases that kill, conditions with clear biomarkers, syndromes with established codes. Menopause slips through this net because it is neither disease nor universally disabling. It is a transition, with symptoms that are real but variable. What medicine cannot categorise neatly, it often minimises or misattributes.

The result is a diagnostic fog. Women spend years moving between specialists, undergoing blood tests, scans, and referrals, each pointing to nothing conclusive. Some leave with no answers at all. Others leave with the wrong answers. In both cases, the cost is high: wasted resources, delayed relief, and unnecessary suffering.

Hot Flushes as Stress

One of the most common misattributions is to stress. A woman in midlife arrives complaining of sudden surges of heat, sweating through her clothes, flushed and dizzy. Because she works a demanding job or cares for children and aging parents, the GP assumes burnout. She is advised to rest, practice mindfulness, or take time off work. If her anxiety is pronounced, she is prescribed antidepressants. No one names menopause.

This mislabelling matters. Stress management techniques may help, but they do not stabilise hormonal fluctuations. Antidepressants may dampen vasomotor symptoms in some women, but they do not address the underlying cause. The woman is left managing symptoms piecemeal, often internalising the message that she is at fault for not coping.

Night Sweats as Thyroid Disease
Night sweats are another classic example. A woman reports waking drenched, sometimes needing to change her sheets. Thyroid function tests are ordered, because hyperthyroidism can cause sweating. When results are normal, the doctor is puzzled. Perhaps it is infection? Perhaps anxiety? Meanwhile, the woman continues to suffer.

In one study, more than a third of women presenting with menopausal night sweats underwent unnecessary endocrine investigations before menopause was considered. The irony is striking: the tests are for a gland in the neck, while the real shift is happening in the ovaries. Yet because medical curricula emphasise thyroid disease as an explanation for sweating, that is where doctors turn first.

Brain Fog as Dementia
Few misdiagnoses cause as much fear as dementia. When women describe forgetfulness, word-finding difficulty, or lapses in concentration, doctors may suspect early cognitive decline. Neurologists order brain scans, cognitive testing, even lumbar punctures. For months, women live under the

shadow of possible dementia. When results are inconclusive, they are told they have "mild cognitive impairment", a label that hangs over them like a sentence.

And yet, longitudinal studies show that cognitive changes during menopause are typically reversible. Brain fog is real, but it reflects transitional shifts in synaptic activity, not neurodegeneration. When hormone levels stabilise, many women recover clarity. But because menopause is not named, women endure months of unnecessary fear.

One woman recounted bursting into tears in her neurologist's office after being told she might be entering dementia. She was 50. Two years later, on HRT, she had no cognitive symptoms at all. She described the misdiagnosis as "the darkest cloud I ever lived under."

Joint Pain as Arthritis
Menopause also mimics musculoskeletal disorders. Estrogen plays a role in cartilage health and inflammation. Its decline can trigger joint stiffness and pain, especially in the hands, knees, and hips. Yet when women present with these symptoms, doctors often diagnose early arthritis. Anti-inflammatory medications are prescribed, physiotherapy recommended. Relief is partial at best.

In reality, the joint pain is part of the broader hormonal shift. Estrogen receptors exist in joint tissue, and their withdrawal increases inflammation. But because arthritis is a recognised diagnosis and menopause is not, the label sticks. Women may even undergo unnecessary imaging or interventions, when targeted hormonal support could have eased their pain.

Palpitations as Panic Disorder
Cardiovascular symptoms are perhaps the most frightening. Women describe their hearts racing unexpectedly, pounding so hard they fear a heart attack. Emergency

departments run cardiac enzymes, ECGs, and stress tests. When results return normal, doctors reassure them: "It's just anxiety." Benzodiazepines are prescribed. Women leave feeling ashamed, as if they have failed to control their minds.

In truth, palpitations are a recognised symptom of menopause, triggered by changes in autonomic regulation. But because they do not appear on standard differential diagnosis lists, they are attributed to panic disorder. Women are stigmatised as anxious, when they are in fact undergoing a predictable, hormonal transition.

The Cost of Misdiagnosis
The cumulative effect of these misdiagnoses is staggering. Women undergo unnecessary investigations, from MRIs to invasive procedures. They consume medications that dull symptoms but do not heal. They absorb stigma, internalising labels of "depressed," "anxious," or "aging poorly." The health system spends billions chasing ghosts, while the real diagnosis, menopause, sits unspoken.

The workplace impact is equally profound. Women who fear dementia may step back from leadership. Those labelled as anxious may avoid high-pressure roles. Those misdiagnosed with depression may conceal their struggles, ashamed to reveal what they believe is psychiatric weakness. Careers stall, and organisations lose talent.

Families suffer too. Partners misinterpret mood changes as rejection. Children see their mothers as unstable. The silence of misdiagnosis erodes relationships, leaving women isolated at the very moment they most need support.

Cultural Layers
Misdiagnosis is not evenly distributed. For migrant women, language barriers compound the problem. When a woman describes "heat" or "forgetting" without the vocabulary of menopause, doctors fit her words into familiar categories:

infection, thyroid disease, depression. Indigenous women may avoid discussing "women's business" with male doctors, leading to vague symptom reports that are misinterpreted. In communities where menopause has no name, women are doubly invisible, first to their culture, then to medicine.

Why the Misdiagnosis Persists

At its core, the misdiagnosis problem reflects the absence of menopause in medical frameworks. It is not on insurance forms, not in psychiatric manuals, not a core module in medical education. Without institutional scaffolding, clinicians rely on what they know, stress, depression, thyroid disease, arthritis. Menopause falls between the cracks, leaving women caught in diagnostic limbo.

The irony is that by misdiagnosing, medicine creates pathology where none exists. A woman who is not depressed is labelled depressed. A woman who is not demented is labelled impaired. The misdiagnosis does more harm than the original symptom. And the tragedy is that this harm is preventable. Naming menopause would change everything.

Medicated Instead of Informed

Menopause is not a disease, but the medical system has treated it like one, and not in a way that dignifies women's experience. Instead of informed conversations about hormonal change, women too often receive quick prescriptions. Hot flushes? Here is an antidepressant. Sleeplessness? Here is a sedative. Palpitations? Here is a benzodiazepine. Fatigue and low mood? Here is a referral for counselling and another prescription for SSRIs. The cycle is predictable and deeply revealing: women are medicated, not informed.

The Reflex to Prescribe
Time pressure is one driver. General practitioners often have just ten minutes per patient. Faced with a woman in midlife presenting with a cluster of complaints, insomnia, low mood, anxiety, brain fog, the fastest solution is a prescription. Antidepressants are familiar, easy to justify, and reimbursable through insurance. They require little explanation. Hormone therapy, by contrast, demands more time: discussion of risks and benefits, clarification of myths, tailoring of treatment. In a system built on speed, nuance loses.

But there is more at play than time. For decades, medical culture has taught doctors to view menopause as either irrelevant ("just aging") or risky ("hormone therapy causes cancer"). The legacy of the Women's Health Initiative study in 2002, which overstated risks of HRT, still casts a long shadow. Many clinicians continue to avoid hormones entirely, even though subsequent research has clarified their safety for most women. The gap between evidence and practice has left a vacuum, and antidepressants have rushed in to fill it.

Antidepressants as the Default
The most common class prescribed is SSRIs (selective serotonin reuptake inhibitors). Originally designed for major depressive disorder, they have been repurposed as a treatment for vasomotor symptoms like hot flushes. Clinical trials show they can reduce flushes modestly, by about 50 percent for some women, but at the cost of side effects: nausea, sexual dysfunction, weight gain, emotional blunting.

For women already struggling with body changes and identity shifts, these side effects can compound distress. Yet because antidepressants are coded as psychiatric medications, their use reinforces the idea that menopause is a mental health problem rather than a hormonal one. Women who never had depression before menopause suddenly find themselves labelled psychiatric patients, their medical files stamped with diagnoses that may follow them for life.

A 51-year-old accountant recounted how she was prescribed SSRIs for what she described as "waves of heat and sadness." The medication dulled her mood but did not resolve her flushes. She gained ten kilograms in a year, her libido disappeared, and her sense of self eroded. "I went in for menopause," she said, "and came out depressed."

Sleeping Pills and the Myth of Rest
Insomnia is another common complaint. Hormonal changes disrupt thermoregulation and circadian rhythms, leading to restless nights. Instead of addressing this root cause, doctors often reach for sedative-hypnotics. These medications may provide short-term relief, but they come with risks: dependence, daytime drowsiness, memory impairment.

One teacher described her experience: "I told my GP I woke every night drenched in sweat. He gave me sleeping tablets. I slept, but I still woke hot, just less aware of it. I became groggy at work, irritable with my students, and terrified I was developing dementia. No one explained this was menopause."

Sleeping pills do not treat the underlying thermoregulatory instability of menopause. They simply mask its effects. By doing so, they prolong suffering and obscure the real diagnosis.

Benzodiazepines and the Stigma of Anxiety
Perhaps the most insidious medications prescribed are benzodiazepines. Women presenting with palpitations, panic attacks, or generalized anxiety are often given these drugs as quick fixes. While they can calm acute symptoms, they carry high risks of dependence and stigma. Women labelled "anxious" or "neurotic" may be dismissed by family, colleagues, and even other clinicians.

The stigma itself is damaging. A woman who internalises the message that she is weak or mentally unstable may withdraw from social and professional roles. Her symptoms, already isolating, become compounded by shame. The tragedy is that many of these so-called anxiety attacks are in fact hormonal surges, predictable, biological, and treatable through appropriate menopausal care.

Pharma Incentives and Structural Neglect
There is also an economic dimension. Antidepressants, sedatives, and anxiolytics are profitable. They are marketed aggressively, backed by decades of clinical trials, and reimbursed readily by insurers. Hormone therapy, by contrast, is less profitable, less marketed, and still clouded by outdated fears.

The political economy of medication explains why PMDD made it into the DSM while menopause did not. PMDD could be treated with SSRIs, a drug category with strong pharmaceutical lobbying. Menopausal depression and anxiety, by contrast, are better treated with hormones, a less lucrative pathway. What is absent from the manuals is not only a reflection of science but of market incentives.

Case Studies of Misdirection
• **The Lawyer and the SSRIs**: A woman in her late forties sought help for mood swings and hot flushes. Her GP prescribed antidepressants without discussing hormones. She spent two years believing she had developed chronic depression. Only when she saw a menopause specialist did she learn her symptoms were hormonal. "I lost years of my life to the wrong label," she said.

• **The Migrant Worker and Sleeping Pills**: A woman from South Asia reported sleepless nights and fatigue. Without an interpreter, she could not explain her sweats. She was prescribed sedatives. She became dependent, fearful of running out, and ashamed to admit her reliance. Menopause was never discussed.

• **The Teacher and the Benzodiazepines**: After repeated panic attacks, a teacher was told she had an anxiety disorder. She took benzodiazepines for five years, developing dependence. Only later did she discover her symptoms had begun with perimenopause. "If someone had told me it was hormonal, I would have made different choices," she reflected.

The Deeper Consequences

The reliance on psychiatric and sedative medications has deeper consequences than side effects alone. It alters identity. Women begin to see themselves as disordered, rather than in transition. They lose faith in their bodies. They absorb stigma that shapes relationships and careers. And they carry medical histories that may affect future care, insurance, and self-image.

This is not to say antidepressants or sedatives have no place. For some women, they provide relief. For those with concurrent depression or anxiety, they may be essential. The issue is not their existence but their dominance, their reflexive use as first-line responses, in place of informed conversations about hormones.

Informed, Not Sedated

What women need is not sedation but education. They need clear explanations of what estrogen and progesterone do, how their decline affects multiple systems, and what options exist for relief. They need choices: lifestyle adjustments, non-hormonal treatments, and hormone therapy where appropriate. They need doctors willing to connect the dots rather than medicate the fragments.

This requires systemic change: updating medical curricula, destigmatising HRT, ensuring guidelines reflect evidence, and giving clinicians time to talk. It requires seeing menopause not as an inconvenience to be suppressed but as a transition to be supported.

From Silence to Recognition

The story of menopause in medicine is not one of ignorance. The science is there. The neuroimaging, the endocrinology, the epidemiology, all of it confirms what women have known for centuries: that when hormones decline, the body and mind shift in profound ways. What has been missing is not data but will. What has been absent is not biology but belief.

For too long, the medical profession has operated on two contradictory logics. On one hand, it has pathologised women's bodies at every turn: menstruation as disorder, childbirth as risk, menopause as decline. On the other, it has minimised women's suffering, dismissing hot flushes as stress, insomnia as lifestyle, brain fog as aging, depression as weakness. The result is a system that both overmedicalises and under-supports, both medicates and ignores. Women fall into the gaps, medicated instead of informed, sedated instead of supported.

The consequences are visible everywhere. In workplaces, where talented women step aside under the weight of untreated symptoms. In families, where relationships fracture under the strain of mood swings that are never explained. In healthcare, where billions are spent chasing misdiagnoses while menopause remains unnamed. And in policy, where silence translates into absence: absence of funding, absence of training, absence of justice.

What this chapter has shown is that menopause is not a side note in psychiatry or a footnote in medicine. It is central. It shapes half the population for decades of their lives. It influences cardiovascular disease, osteoporosis, dementia risk, workplace participation, and mental health. To ignore it is not oversight. It is systemic negligence.

The DSM's silence is symbolic of this wider erasure. Premenstrual Dysphoric Disorder made it into the manual because there was a pharmaceutical solution attached. Menopause did not, because its primary treatment is hormones, lifestyle, and social support, interventions that cannot be patented or monetised in the same way. This is not science. It is politics. And women pay the price.

We cannot afford to continue this way. The costs are too high, in suicides of midlife women, in lost leadership, in families who lose mothers and partners to silence and stigma. Reform must begin with recognition. That means rewriting the psychiatric canon to include menopause-related mood and cognitive disorders. It means training general practitioners to see menopause not as a vague backdrop but as a central diagnosis. It means funding research that connects neurology, endocrinology, and psychiatry instead of siloing them.

But recognition alone is not enough. We need to build systems that honour women's voices. That begins with language, naming menopause clearly, across cultures, in ways that dignify rather than diminish. It continues with policy, workplace protections, insurance coverage, and clinical guidelines that reflect lived reality. And it requires courage, from doctors to challenge outdated training, from policymakers to fund neglected areas, from women themselves to break centuries of silence.

There is precedent. We have seen other movements succeed. Breast cancer went from whispered shame to pink-ribbon advocacy that transformed funding and outcomes. HIV activism forced governments and pharmaceutical companies to respond, reshaping research priorities worldwide. Maternal mortality was reframed as a human rights issue, leading to global action. Menopause deserves the same urgency, the same recognition that silence kills.

The mandate is clear. We cannot continue to let half the population suffer through a life stage in the shadows. We cannot continue to medicate symptoms without naming their cause. We cannot continue to let psychiatry, neurology, and primary care pretend that menopause is irrelevant to their fields. The science is here. The voices are here. What is missing is action.

This is not about pathologising every woman's experience. Many women move through menopause with few symptoms. But for those who suffer, recognition is not optional. It is justice. To exclude menopause from the psychiatric canon is to exclude women themselves from the legitimacy of their suffering. To ignore the neurological and emotional impacts is to deny science. To medicate without informing is to perpetuate a cycle of control, not care.

The time has come to break this cycle. To rewrite the manuals. To retrain the doctors. To reclaim the narrative. To tell women not that they are stressed, anxious, or weak, but that they are navigating a profound hormonal transition. To provide them not with sedation, but with Tools, options, and dignity.

Menopause is not an ending. It is a transformation. And like all transformations, it deserves to be met with knowledge, compassion, and respect. Until that happens, the silence of medicine will remain complicit in women's suffering. Until that happens, the hijacking will continue. But once we choose to see, to name, to act, we can transform this silence into recognition. We can turn dismissal into dignity. We can ensure that no woman is left medicated in the dark, when what she deserves is light.

Chapter 22:
I Wasn't Depressed. I Was Depleted.

When Claire turned forty-eight, she thought the worst was behind her. She had survived two decades of raising children, managing a demanding job in human resources, and caring for her mother through cancer. She expected midlife to be a season of stability, the years where she could finally breathe. Instead, she found herself gasping.

It began subtly. She noticed her mornings felt heavy, her body slower to respond. By lunchtime, her mind would go blank in meetings. She found herself scribbling notes she had once memorised with ease. She forgot names, misplaced documents, and lost confidence in her own voice. At home, her children teased her gently for asking the same questions twice. She laughed with them, but inside she was frightened.

Then came the exhaustion. It was not the tiredness of late nights or early mornings. It was a bone-deep fatigue that clung to her like fog. She would collapse on the couch after work, unable to cook dinner, unable to summon the energy for conversation. She began cancelling social events, making excuses to avoid the embarrassment of sitting at a restaurant table staring blankly at a menu she could not read without losing track of the words.

When the anxiety arrived, it sealed her sense of failure. Claire, the steady one, the reliable one, began waking in the night with her heart pounding. Some mornings she would cry in the shower for no reason she could name. The smallest criticism at work would spiral into catastrophic self-doubt. "You're not yourself," her husband said. And he was right. But neither of them had the language to explain what was happening.

After months of struggle, Claire went to her GP. She described her fatigue, her foggy mind, her low mood, her tears. The doctor listened, typed a few notes, and leaned back. "It sounds like depression," he said. "Quite common at your age. You may also have some anxiety. I'll start you on an SSRI. It should help."

Claire left with a prescription and a sense of shame. Depression. Anxiety. Words she had used to comfort colleagues now branded her as broken. She began the medication dutifully, waiting for relief.

But relief did not come. The antidepressants numbed her emotions, blunted her highs and lows, but the fog remained. The fatigue worsened. Her weight crept up, her libido disappeared, and her sense of self shrank. She stopped recognising the woman in the mirror. "I'm losing myself," she whispered one night to her reflection, tears streaking her cheeks.

Over the next year, Claire's life constricted. She reduced her hours at work, fearing mistakes. She withdrew from her book club, unable to follow discussions. She avoided intimacy with her husband, too ashamed to explain the loss of desire. She told no one about the night sweats that drenched her sheets or the hot flushes that left her embarrassed in boardrooms. The doctor had never asked. She had never thought to mention them.

Her diagnosis, depression, became a self-fulfilling prophecy. Colleagues treated her gently, assuming fragility. Family members urged her to "get help," not realising she already had. The medication box by her bedside became both lifeline and prison.

There were days she wondered if this was the beginning of the end, an early decline into chronic illness. She thought of dementia, of permanent disability. She grieved the career she had built, the confidence she had lost.
The turning point came almost by accident. On a particularly restless night, scrolling her phone in the dark, Claire stumbled across an article about menopause. The words leapt out at her: brain fog, night sweats, anxiety, joint pain, palpitations. She read hungrily, tears rolling down her face. It was as if someone had been following her, recording her private suffering.

The next day, she booked an appointment with a different doctor, a woman specialising in midlife health. For the first time, Claire was asked about her periods, about her sleep, about her flushes. For the first time, someone linked her symptoms not to depression but to hormonal change. "You are not depressed," the doctor said gently. "You are depleted."

The phrase cracked something open. Claire had not failed. She was not weak. She was depleted, by estrogen loss, by years of care work, by a system that had never prepared her.

With hormone therapy, nutritional support, and counselling focused on transition rather than pathology, Claire began to recover. Within weeks, her night sweats eased. Within months, her clarity returned. She laughed again, not numbed by medication but restored by balance.

Her relationships revived. At work, she reclaimed her voice, speaking openly about menopause with colleagues, mentoring younger women to prepare them for what she had endured alone. At home, she explained to her children that what looked like depression was depletion, a temporary but real state that could be healed. Her marriage, strained by silence, softened into intimacy again.

Claire's story is not unique. It is the story of millions of women who are misdiagnosed because the language of medicine defaults to depression when it encounters depletion. It is the story of a healthcare system that knows how to medicate but not how to listen. It is the story of women who lose years of life to labels that do not fit.

Claire's journey reveals the stakes. Misdiagnosis is not a neutral error. It steals time, erodes confidence, and imposes stigma. It leaves women sedated when they should be supported. It convinces them they are broken when they are, in fact, depleted.

To call depression what is really depletion is to rewrite identity. It narrows possibility. It takes a transition that could be met with compassion and reframes it as pathology. And because this misdiagnosis is so common, it shapes not just individual lives but entire generations of women.

The opening of this chapter, then, is not just a story. It is a warning. When medicine refuses to see menopause for what it is, women are forced into scripts that do not belong to them. But when recognition comes, through a doctor who listens, through a daughter who researches, through a woman who refuses to stay silent, recovery is possible. And not just recovery, but renewal.

Claire was not depressed. She was depleted. And depletion can be healed.

The Language of Depression

Language is never neutral. It creates the frame through which experience is seen, categorised, and responded to. A word can open doors or slam them shut. When a doctor says "you are depressed," it does not just describe symptoms; it assigns identity, directs treatment, and defines a woman's future. When a woman says "I feel depleted," but the system only has a word for "depression," her truth is erased.

For menopausal women, the problem is not only misinterpretation of symptoms, it is the poverty of language itself. The psychiatric lexicon, dominated by the DSM, has no recognised category for menopausal depletion. So when women present with brain fog, fatigue, anxiety, irritability, and disrupted sleep, those words are forced into the nearest available category: depression.

This is not semantics. It is the difference between treatment that heals and treatment that harms.

The Slippery Path to Diagnosis

Imagine a woman named Laura, aged forty-eight, walking into her GP's office in suburban Melbourne. She has not slept properly in weeks. Every night, she wakes drenched in sweat, her sheets soaked, her body trembling as though she has run a marathon. At work, she forgets simple words mid-sentence, leaving her embarrassed in front of colleagues. She bursts into tears at odd moments and then apologises, ashamed of her lack of control.

On the intake form, she dutifully ticks the boxes: fatigue, low mood, sleep disturbance, loss of concentration. To the untrained eye, or even the highly trained one, it reads like a case study of depression.

Her GP, glancing at the form and listening to her hurried story, maps her complaints onto the familiar framework of the DSM. He diagnoses depression, prescribes an SSRI, and sends her on her way. The consultation lasts less than ten minutes. What has happened here is not malpractice. It is systemic misrecognition. The framework itself is blind.

Depression: The Psychiatric Lens

Depression, as codified in the DSM, is defined by a set of criteria meant to distinguish psychiatric illness from the normal ups and downs of life. Persistent sadness, loss of interest, fatigue, concentration difficulties, sleep disruption, appetite changes, feelings of worthlessness, and suicidal thoughts form the constellation of symptoms that signal major depressive disorder.

This framework has saved lives. It provides clarity in chaos, a common language for research, and a pathway for treatment and insurance reimbursement. But it was never designed to capture hormonally driven life transitions. Its checklists are blunt Tools that can conflate very different realities.

The overlap is striking: fatigue, poor concentration, mood changes, and sleep disturbance are as common in menopause as they are in depression. In the time-limited GP consultation, the nuance vanishes. What remains is the neat fit of symptoms into a category, even if the category is wrong.

Depletion: The Unnamed Condition

What Laura is experiencing is not depression but depletion. Unlike depression, depletion is not recognised in psychiatric manuals, not taught in medical curricula, and not reimbursed by insurers. Yet women live it daily. Modern neuroscience and endocrinology show that menopause is not *"just hormonal"* in the trivial sense, it is profoundly hormonal in the systemic sense.

- **Estrogen and neurotransmitters:** Estrogen regulates serotonin, dopamine, norepinephrine, and GABA. Its decline disrupts mood, motivation, attention, and calm.
- **Brain energy crisis:** Brain imaging shows structural and metabolic changes in the hippocampus and prefrontal cortex, explaining the "fog."
- **Cardiovascular and metabolic shifts:** Loss of estrogen destabilises vascular tone and insulin sensitivity, producing palpitations, fatigue, and midlife weight change.
- **Stress axis dysfunction:** Without estrogen's modulation, cortisol regulation goes awry. Women feel "wired but tired, exhausted yet unable to rest.

These are not psychiatric illusions. They are neuroendocrine realities. Therefore it is important to note that depletion is multifaceted:

- **Hormonal depletion**, as estrogen, progesterone, and testosterone decline, disrupting neurotransmitters and destabilising mood, sleep, and cognition.
- **Nutritional depletion**, as midlife women often face iron, Vitamin D, and B12 deficiencies, sometimes

worsened by heavy periods leading up to menopause.

- **Emotional depletion**, from years of invisible labour: managing households, raising children, caring for ageing parents, supporting partners, all while navigating careers.
- **Social depletion**, as stigma silences open conversation and isolates women in their suffering.

Depletion is not a psychiatric illness. It is a state of being drained by biology, circumstance, and silence. Its symptoms overlap with depression, but its causes are distinct and so are its remedies.

Depression and menopausal depletion share surface similarities, fatigue, low mood, poor concentration but their roots and remedies differ. This side-by-side comparison shows how the same symptoms can tell two very different stories.

Feature	Depression	Menopausal Depletion
Onset	Any age; psychosocial triggers	Midlife; cycle changes
Course	Persistent ≥2 weeks	Fluctuating; linked to hormonal shifts
Sleep	Early morning waking, hypersomnia	Sleep fragmentation from night sweats
Cognitive	Rumination, negative bias	Word-finding gaps, brain fog

Feature	Depression	Menopausal Depletion
Libido	Often reduced	Often sharply reduced, with urogenital changes
Response	Antidepressants/ therapy	HRT + targeted supports

The Power of the Label

The difference between being told *"you are depressed"* and *"you are depleted"* is enormous. One suggests permanent pathology, a flaw in brain chemistry. The other suggests a temporary state, linked to a specific transition, that can be addressed and reversed. One imposes stigma; the other invites compassion.

Words become identities. A diagnosis of depression can appear in medical records, insurance files, and workplace accommodations. It can shape how family and colleagues perceive a woman; fragile, unstable, unreliable. It can affect her self-image, convincing her she is broken rather than transitioning. The wrong word can reshape an entire life.

The overlap between depression and depletion is real, but so is the difference. Depression is chronic, psychiatric, and often requires long-term management. Depletion is transitional, biological, and treatable with the right interventions. Conflating the two not only mistreats women but also reshapes their identities.

When a woman is told *"you are depressed,"* she carries that stigma into every part of her life. When she is told *"you are depleted,"* she gains a frame that validates her suffering but also offers hope of recovery. One label imprisons, the other liberates.

A Historical Blind Spot

The roots of this misrecognition stretch back centuries. Ancient medicine spoke of hysteria, the wandering womb that supposedly destabilised women's minds. In the 19th century, medical texts warned of "climacteric insanity," framing menopause as a dangerous period when women became unstable.

When psychiatry emerged as a modern discipline, it inherited these biases but gave them new names. Menopause became invisible, folded into broader categories like depression or anxiety. The DSM, psychiatry's global bible, codified depression with precision but excluded menopause entirely.

Other hormonally linked conditions did make it in. Premenstrual Dysphoric Disorder (PMDD) was added to DSM-5, helped by pharmaceutical trials showing SSRIs as effective treatment. Postpartum depression gained recognition because of its visibility and its tragic links to maternal mortality. Menopause, by contrast, was left out. The reasons were not scientific alone, they were political and economic. There was no lobby, no profitable drug pipeline, no cultural urgency.

The absence became a self-fulfilling prophecy. Because menopause was not in the manual, medical schools gave it scant attention. Because it was absent from curricula, doctors left training unprepared. Because doctors were unprepared, women's complaints were misdiagnosed. Silence bred silence.

International Comparisons

The problem is not universal. In the UK, where menopause has become a public issue, the National Institute for Health and Care Excellence (NICE) guidelines recommend considering menopause when women in midlife present with depression-like symptoms. This does not prevent misdiagnosis entirely, but it creates a foothold for recognition.

In the US, by contrast, menopause remains largely absent from psychiatric and primary care training. The DSM does not acknowledge it, and the ICD (used internationally for coding) also fails to give it prominence. The result is systemic blindness.

In Japan, the word *konenki* historically carried a more neutral or even positive meaning, framing menopause as a seasonal change. Yet even there, Western biomedical frameworks have eroded cultural narratives, replacing them with pathology.

The lesson is clear: where language and policy create recognition, women are better supported. Where silence prevails, misdiagnosis thrives.

The Policy Consequences
The dominance of "depression" as the language for menopausal suffering ripples through systems. It shapes research priorities: billions spent on antidepressants, little on menopause. It shapes medical education: hours devoted to depression, minutes to menopause. It shapes workplace policy: accommodations for mental health, but none for menopause.

When the DSM excluded menopause, it signalled to the world that this was not a category worth naming. And what is not named is not funded, not studied, not taught. The word "depression" filled the vacuum, not because it fit but because it was available.

The costs of this misdiagnosis cascade through multiple systems:
- **Healthcare**: Women are medicated unnecessarily, sometimes for years, with antidepressants that do not address the root cause.

- **Research**: Funding flows toward depression but not depletion. Clinical trials for HRT remain underfunded compared to psychiatric drugs.
- **Education**: Doctors graduate with deep knowledge of depression but shallow awareness of menopause.
- **Workplaces**: Mental health leave is available, but menopause accommodations are rare. Women are sidelined when labelled depressed rather than supported when recognised as menopausal.
- **Economics**: Misdiagnosis wastes billions. Women consume healthcare resources inefficiently, cycle through tests and specialists, and lose productivity in workplaces.

In short: when words fail, systems fail.

Why Distinguishing Matters

The overlap between depression and depletion is real, but so is the difference. Depression is chronic, psychiatric, and often requires long-term management. Depletion is transitional, biological, and treatable with the right interventions. Conflating the two not only mistreats women but also reshapes their identities.

When a woman is told *"you are depressed,"* she carries that stigma into every part of her life. Medical records, insurance files, and workplace accommodations enshrine the label. Family and colleagues may perceive her as fragile, unstable, or unreliable. The diagnosis burrows into her self-image, convincing her she is broken rather than in transition. The wrong word can reshape an entire life.

By contrast, when she is told *"you are depleted,"* she gains a frame that validates her suffering but also offers hope of recovery. One label imprisons, the other liberates. Depression implies permanent pathology, a flaw in brain chemistry. Depletion suggests a temporary state, linked to a specific transition, that can be addressed and reversed. The difference is not semantic. It is existential.

To close the gap, systems must change. Medical curricula must teach menopause as rigorously as depression. Diagnostic frameworks must evolve to recognise depletion. Research must fund studies that disentangle psychiatric illness from hormonal transition. Workplaces must acknowledge menopause as a stage worthy of support, not dismissal.

Most of all, language must shift. Women need words that reflect their truths, not categories that erase them. Until then, the slippery path to diagnosis will remain a trapdoor, swallowing millions of women into the wrong story.

Reframing the Conversation: Toward a New Lexicon

Imagine a medical system where a woman like Claire is told: *"You are not broken. You are transitioning. Your body is depleted, and we can support you."* Imagine medical records that recognise "menopausal depletion" as a category distinct from depression. Imagine research grants funding trials on how to restore balance rather than suppress symptoms. Imagine insurance covering hormone therapy and nutritional support as readily as antidepressants.

Language can make this future real. The first step is to speak differently.

Real-life Psychiatric Suffering Dismissed as "Just Hormonal"

The Phrase as a Cultural Weapon

Few phrases carry such power to erase women's suffering. To be told your distress is "just hormonal" is to have your experience reframed as trivial, inevitable, even imaginary. The words suggest fluctuation, not crisis; biology, not legitimacy. They shrink complex suffering into a caricature of women as unstable, moody, irrational.

This is not new. The history of medicine is littered with dismissals cloaked in reproductive vocabulary. In the 19th century, "hysteria", literally "wandering womb", was the universal diagnosis for women in distress. In the mid-20th century, doctors reduced postpartum depression to "baby blues." Today, menopause too often meets the same fate: rebranded as "just hormonal," a phrase that simultaneously acknowledges biology while denying its seriousness.

The dismissal works because it weaponises partial truth. Hormones do shape mood, sleep, cognition, and energy. But "just hormonal" strips this fact of its complexity, using it not to explain but to erase. It suggests that because the cause is biological, the suffering is not worthy of medical or social recognition. It tells women: this is natural, therefore you must endure it.

The Science That Gets Ignored
The irony is that science itself tells a different story. Estrogen, the hormone most associated with menopause, is not a minor actor. It is a master regulator, a molecule that touches nearly every system in the body. To dismiss menopausal suffering as "just hormonal" is to ignore decades of research showing that estrogen decline reverberates across the brain, the cardiovascular system, the metabolism, and the stress axis.

Estrogen as a Master Regulator

For too long, estrogen was framed narrowly: a reproductive hormone, responsible for menstruation, ovulation, and fertility. But neuroscience and endocrinology have revealed a far broader truth. Estrogen influences the brain's key neurotransmitters, serotonin, dopamine, norepinephrine, and GABA, the very chemicals that psychiatry associates with mood regulation, attention, reward, and calm.

When estrogen declines, serotonin production falters. This is not speculation; studies show measurable drops in serotonin availability during perimenopause. Lower serotonin correlates with low mood, irritability, and vulnerability to depression. Dopamine pathways, which govern motivation and reward, also shift. Women report loss of pleasure, disinterest, and reduced drive, symptoms that overlap with major depressive disorder. Yet the trigger is hormonal, not psychiatric.

Estrogen also interacts with GABA, the brain's primary calming neurotransmitter. Its decline destabilises inhibitory pathways, increasing vulnerability to anxiety and sleep disruption. In other words: night sweats and panic are not simply "in her head." They are in her neurochemistry.

The Neurological Dimension
Brain imaging has added weight to what women have long reported. MRI studies show structural changes in the hippocampus and prefrontal cortex during menopause, areas critical for memory and executive function. This is the neurological substrate of "brain fog." Yet when women forget words or lose track mid-task, psychiatry still frames it as depression or early dementia.

Emerging research also links menopause to increased risk of Alzheimer's disease. Declining estrogen appears to reduce the brain's ability to metabolise glucose, its primary fuel. This metabolic shift, sometimes described as a "brain energy crisis," explains why cognitive symptoms often flare during perimenopause. It is not a psychological weakness. It is neurobiology.

And yet, the DSM psychiatry's primary manual, has no entry for menopause-related cognitive or mood changes. The absence is not scientific. It is editorial.

Cardiovascular and Metabolic Pathways

The effects of estrogen stretch beyond the brain. Estrogen helps regulate vascular tone, keeping blood vessels flexible and responsive. Its decline increases cardiovascular variability, producing palpitations, dizziness, and surges in blood pressure. These symptoms are frequently misread as panic disorder. Women sent to cardiologists often return with inconclusive tests and prescriptions for beta-blockers, treating the symptom, not the cause.

Metabolically, estrogen influences insulin sensitivity and fat distribution. Midlife weight gain, fatigue, and inflammatory changes are not simply lifestyle issues. They are hormonally driven. Yet women presenting with joint pain or exhaustion are still told to "exercise more" or "reduce stress." The science of metabolic change in menopause is rarely integrated into psychiatric care.

The Stress Axis (HPA Dysfunction)

Perhaps most overlooked is the relationship between estrogen and the hypothalamic-pituitary-adrenal (HPA) axis, the body's stress system. Estrogen normally modulates cortisol release, keeping stress responses in check. When estrogen drops, cortisol regulation becomes erratic. The result: heightened baseline anxiety, exaggerated responses to minor stressors, and difficulty returning to calm.

This is why perimenopausal women often describe feeling "wired but tired." They are exhausted yet unable to rest, jittery yet depleted. The HPA axis has gone off balance. Psychiatry, trained to hear these words as anxiety disorder, prescribes benzodiazepines or SSRIs. But the root lies not in faulty coping but in disrupted endocrine control.

Why Psychiatry Won't Claim This Knowledge

The science is there. What is missing is its integration into psychiatry. Medical systems remain siloed: endocrinology studies hormones, psychiatry studies mood, gynecology studies reproductive organs. Menopause sits at the intersection, yet no field claims full responsibility. The DSM reflects this fragmentation, codifying conditions with psychiatric origins while excluding those rooted in endocrine change.

Pharmaceutical economics reinforce the divide. SSRIs are profitable and easy to prescribe. Hormone replacement therapy is more complex, politically contested, and less lucrative. As a result, research dollars flow toward psychiatric drugs, not integrated hormonal care. Women are caught in the crossfire of institutional inertia and market incentives.

A Vision for Integration

What would it look like if science guided practice? Menopause clinics could unite psychiatry, endocrinology, and primary care, recognising that brain fog, anxiety, and low mood are not isolated pathologies but systemic consequences of hormonal change. Medical curricula could teach the neuroendocrine basis of menopausal transition, ensuring GPs do not mistake depletion for depression.

International models show promise. In the UK, menopause is increasingly integrated into primary care, supported by national guidelines. Some EU countries have begun funding menopause-specific mental health research. These are not fringe ideas; they are evidence-based reforms.

The tragedy is that until science is acknowledged in psychiatry, women will continue to be told their suffering is "just hormonal."

Intersectional Silence: When Culture, Language, and Class Collide

Dismissal does not fall evenly. Migrant women, Indigenous women, and those in low-income settings face compounded barriers. When language lacks precise words for menopause, symptoms are mistranslated. "Hot" becomes fever, "forgetful" becomes dementia, "tired" becomes laziness. Without culturally competent care, women are cycled through misdiagnosis faster and with fewer resources to contest it.

For Indigenous Australian women, phrases like "bleeding no more" capture the physical end of menstruation but not the psychological transition. Without recognition, emotional depletion is invisible to both community and clinicians. For migrant women, interpreters rarely receive training in reproductive health, leaving women's symptoms flattened into inaccurate translations. And for low-income women, the financial cost of repeated misdiagnosis, unnecessary tests, ineffective medications, time off work, creates an additional layer of depletion.

The Cascading Consequences
When women are told their suffering is "just hormonal," the costs ripple outward.

- **Stigma:** The phrase frames suffering as trivial, discouraging women from seeking further help.
- **Medication dependence:** Misdiagnosis leads to long-term antidepressant or benzodiazepine use, often without resolution.
- **Relationship strain:** Partners misunderstand symptoms, marriages fracture, families suffer.
- **Workplace fallout:** Women are perceived as unreliable, passed over for promotions, or quietly exit the workforce.
- **Mental health risks:** Misdiagnosis delays appropriate care, leaving some women to spiral into suicidal despair.

These are not side effects of menopause. They are side effects of neglect.

Breaking the Cycle
To end the dismissal, psychiatry and medicine must confront their blind spots. "Just hormonal" should never be the end

of the conversation. It should be the beginning of deeper inquiry.

That means rewriting the DSM to include menopause-related psychiatric syndromes. It means funding research that explores estrogen's role in neurobiology. It means training doctors to distinguish between depression and depletion. It means creating culturally competent care for diverse women.

Most of all, it means restoring dignity through language. To call something "just hormonal" is to say it is not serious. To recognise it as neuroendocrine, systemic, and worthy of care is to give women their humanity back.

The Power of the DSM and Clinical Manuals

The DSM as the doorstop

Every field has its canon, its central text that carries disproportionate influence. For psychiatry, that text is the *Diagnostic and Statistical Manual of Mental Disorders*, the DSM. Often referred to as the "Bible of psychiatry," the DSM is not simply a diagnostic Tool ; it is a cultural artefact that dictates what counts as legitimate suffering. If a condition is in the book, it is real, billable, teachable, and researchable. If it is absent, its sufferers fall into a limbo of invisibility.

The DSM was first published in 1952 with a slim 130 pages, but its reach has grown exponentially with each edition. The fifth edition (DSM-5), released in May 2013, runs over 900 pages and includes dozens of disorders that shape the mental health landscape across the globe. Yet amid its detailed taxonomies of mood disorders, anxiety syndromes, and neurodevelopmental conditions, one silence is deafening: menopause is not there.

This omission is not trivial. It is not simply a matter of an overlooked word. It signals the systemic belief that menopause, and the psychiatric distress it can provoke, is not a matter for psychiatry. It renders millions of women's experiences medically illegitimate, forcing them instead into categories like "major depressive disorder," "generalised anxiety disorder," or even "somatic symptom disorder." The DSM is a gatekeeper, and it has locked the door on menopause.

What Inclusion Means

Inclusion in the DSM is more than symbolic. It has concrete consequences across multiple systems. First, it determines **insurance reimbursement**. In the United States and in many countries that model their systems on US psychiatry, insurers will only cover treatment for conditions coded in the DSM (or its sibling, the ICD, the World Health Organization's *International Classification of Diseases*). If menopause-related psychiatric suffering is not listed, then treatment cannot be claimed. The result? Women are coded as depressed, anxious, or disordered in ways that misrepresent their biology, just to make the system pay.

Second, the DSM directs **research funding**. Grant committees, academic institutions, and pharmaceutical companies rely on its categories to define the boundaries of legitimate inquiry. A condition that is not listed is a condition that will not receive sustained research dollars. This creates a vicious cycle: because menopause is absent, few studies exist; because few studies exist, there is insufficient "evidence" to justify inclusion.

Third, inclusion shapes **clinical legitimacy**. Doctors are trained to recognise what the DSM names. Medical curricula around the world structure psychiatry lectures and clinical rotations around DSM categories. If menopause is missing, then future psychiatrists and GPs are never properly taught about its psychological impacts. They graduate prepared to treat depression and anxiety but unprepared to distinguish them from hormonally driven depletion.

Finally, the DSM influences **global health policy**. The ICD, which guides health systems worldwide, often mirrors or adapts DSM categories. The absence of menopause cascades outward, leaving women invisible not only in psychiatry but in broader health frameworks. When the World Health Organization builds guidance for midlife women, the psychiatric dimension is skeletal at best.

The Absence of Menopause

The DSM-5 is not silent on reproductive psychiatry altogether. It explicitly codifies **Premenstrual Dysphoric Disorder (PMDD)**, a severe form of premenstrual distress that was included after years of lobbying and a robust set of clinical trials, largely underwritten by pharmaceutical companies. It acknowledges **postpartum depression**, driven by advocacy linking untreated maternal mood disorders to maternal and infant mortality. Even **gender dysphoria** is listed, reflecting cultural and scientific recognition of transgender health.

Yet menopause, a universal experience that affects half the world's population, is absent. The omission cannot be justified by prevalence, impact, or scientific uncertainty. Menopause is more common than PMDD, more enduring than postpartum depression, and affects more people worldwide than gender dysphoria. Its absence is therefore not scientific but political.

Part of the answer lies in the composition of the committees themselves. You undertook a small sample count of contributors to DSM-5 and found an approximate split of **71 percent male to 29 percent female**. This is consistent with independent analyses: while more women were represented than in earlier editions, men still dominated leadership positions, steering the framework of psychiatric legitimacy. With a male-skewed author base, is it any surprise that menopause, a life stage men will never experience, failed to make the cut?

The logic was circular. Menopause was deemed "too broad" and "too variable" to be a psychiatric disorder. Yet so too are depression and anxiety, which span a wide range of presentations. The difference is that depression and anxiety have been medicalised for decades, while menopause has been naturalised, seen as "just aging," not pathology. But the DSM is not a neutral scientific map; it is a cultural construction. The decision to exclude menopause reflects values, not evidence.

Ripple Effects Beyond Psychiatry

The absence of menopause in the DSM has ripple effects that extend far beyond psychiatry.

In medical training, the silence is profound. A young doctor may spend hundreds of hours learning about depression, bipolar disorder, and schizophrenia, but only minutes on menopause, often in the context of gynaecology rather than psychiatry. This educational gap reproduces the cycle of misdiagnosis.

In healthcare practice, the absence fuels what you could call diagnostic laundering. A woman walks in with brain fog, anxiety, and fatigue. The GP cannot code "menopause-related psychiatric symptoms" because it does not exist as a billable category. So he codes "major depressive disorder." She leaves with an antidepressant prescription that dulls her emotions but does not restore her estrogen balance. The system works financially, but not medically.

In research, menopause becomes a desert. Pharmaceutical companies follow the money, and the money follows DSM categories. PMDD has SSRIs; postpartum depression has antidepressants. Menopause has little beyond hormone replacement therapy, which has been underfunded, under-researched, and politically contested since the Women's Health Initiative trials of the early 2000s. Without DSM recognition, menopause psychiatry is an orphaned field.

In policy, the ripple is stark. Governments lean on the DSM/ICD to design mental health strategies. Because menopause is invisible in the manuals, it is invisible in strategies. National policies rarely mention menopause as a mental health issue, leaving it siloed in reproductive or primary care. This neglect translates into real-world suffering: women cannot access tailored services, workplaces lack clear guidance, and stigma flourishes.

The Cost of Absence

The costs of this absence are measurable. Misdiagnosis leads to wasted resources: women cycle through cardiologists, rheumatologists, neurologists, and psychiatrists before anyone names menopause. Healthcare systems bear the financial burden of unnecessary scans, blood tests, and medications. Employers bear the cost of absenteeism, presenteeism, and premature exits from the workforce. Families bear the cost of strained relationships, financial instability, and intergenerational stress.

But the deepest cost is personal. Women leave medical offices convinced they are broken, not transitioning. They carry a label of depression or anxiety that reshapes their self-identity. They live in silence, ashamed of something that should be acknowledged as normal and treatable. The absence of menopause from psychiatry is not neutral; it is violent in its consequences.

When Words on a Page have Profound Impact

The DSM is often described as descriptive, not prescriptive, a book that simply reflects the state of knowledge at the time. But this is a fiction. Every inclusion and exclusion is political. Every category reflects judgments about whose suffering matters. By excluding menopause, the DSM has enshrined silence into the very foundations of psychiatry.

This silence is not inevitable. PMDD was once contested, but it made it in. Postpartum depression was once dismissed as "baby blues," but it is now recognised. Gender dysphoria was once marginal, but it is now legitimised. Each of these shifts occurred not because the science suddenly appeared, but because advocacy, culture, and economics aligned.

The same can and must happen for menopause. The evidence exists: neuroscience, endocrinology, and epidemiology all show its psychiatric dimensions. The suffering is undeniable: millions of women misdiagnosed, mistreated, and marginalised. The politics is what lags.

To rewrite the canon is not to pathologise women's lives but to legitimise their suffering when it is disabling and treatable. It is to give doctors the Tools to distinguish depletion from depression, transition from disorder. It is to fund research, revise curricula, and create policy that meets reality.

The DSM will one day include menopause. The question is not if, but when. Until then, the silence will continue to kill. And until then, the task falls to us, advocates, clinicians, researchers, and women themselves, to break open the gates of psychiatric legitimacy and demand recognition.

Chapter 23:
Systemic Gaslighting

Systemic Gaslighting

The Historical Exclusion of Women from Medical Trials

For most of modern medical history, women were treated as *too complicated to study*. The very factors that make female biology distinct, hormonal cycles, pregnancy, menopause, were seen not as integral realities but as "confounding variables" that threatened to muddy the purity of data.

Researchers wanted neat numbers, clean graphs, and predictable outcomes. Women, with their monthly cycles and fluctuating hormones, were considered a risk to scientific control. The solution? Exclude them. For decades, the male body was established as the universal default, and women were relegated to the margins.

Men as the Standard, Women as the Variation

Until the 1990s, the U.S. National Institutes of Health (NIH) did not require federally funded clinical trials to include women. This meant that the medications millions of women were prescribed were tested almost exclusively on men. Drug dosages, treatment protocols, and safety data were built on the assumption that what worked for men would automatically work for women.

But women are not smaller men. Their bodies metabolise medications differently. They experience side effects differently. They present with symptoms differently. Yet the system continued to insist that the male body was "the standard," and women the deviation.

The consequences were devastating:

Cardiovascular Disease: Heart disease is the leading killer of women, yet women presenting with heart attacks were, and still are, routinely misdiagnosed. Why? Because the "classic" symptoms of crushing chest pain were derived from male-only studies. Women's symptoms, such as nausea, dizziness, or pain in the jaw and shoulders, were dismissed as atypical.

Neurology and Dementia: Alzheimer's disproportionately affects women, but research into its progression long ignored hormonal influences, focusing instead on male brain models.

Autoimmune Disorders: Women make up the majority of autoimmune disease sufferers, yet these conditions were poorly studied because trials excluded women's immune responses.

Chronic Pain: Women's reports of pain were, and often still are, dismissed as emotional or exaggerated, leading to under-treatment.

The pattern is clear: when women are excluded from research, their suffering is pathologised or ignored.

The Politics of Exclusion
The exclusion of women from clinical trials was not simply oversight, it was policy. After the thalidomide tragedy of the 1960s, in which thousands of babies were born with severe birth defects due to a drug given to pregnant women, regulators overreacted. Instead of refining safety measures, they banned women of "childbearing potential" from many drug trials altogether.

The result? An entire generation of medical research was conducted on male bodies only. Pregnant women were deemed too risky, fertile women too unpredictable, post-menopausal women too irrelevant. The entire spectrum of female biology was systematically written out of the data.

By the time reforms came in the 1990s, the damage was done. A biomedical canon had been built almost entirely on men. Even today, women remain underrepresented in trials for cardiovascular drugs, psychiatric medications, and even cancer therapies.

Menopause as a Casualty of Neglect

Menopause was a predictable casualty of this exclusion. With no mandate to study it, clinical research treated menopause as peripheral, a niche curiosity rather than a universal transition. The assumption was simple and false: if women stopped menstruating, their medical relevance diminished.

This left generations of women without evidence-based protocols for symptom management. Hormone replacement therapy (HRT), for example, became a political and medical battleground not because the science was sound, but because the science was *absent*. Decades of neglect meant that when large studies like the Women's Health Initiative were finally conducted, they were misinterpreted, sensationalised, and used to fuel fear rather than clarity.

The Legacy That Persists

Even today, the ghost of exclusion haunts women's health:

- Many drug trials still do not disaggregate data by sex.
- Women are more likely to be prescribed medications off-label.
- Adverse drug reactions are more common in women, precisely because safety data is skewed.

Conditions that predominantly affect women, like endometriosis, fibromyalgia, and menopause, remain under-researched and underfunded.

This is not history. It is the present. The systemic bias that excluded women from medical trials has left a residue in every corner of healthcare.

And menopause, despite being one of the most universal experiences of womanhood, remains caught in that shadow.

Gender Bias Baked Into Psychiatry, Psychology, and Pharmacology

The bias runs deeper than exclusion. Psychiatry and psychology were built in a context that coded women's suffering as pathology. "Hysteria" was once the umbrella diagnosis for everything from fatigue to grief to sexual desire. A wandering womb was blamed for seizures, melancholy, or a woman's refusal to conform. Freud and his contemporaries reframed women's pain as neurosis or repression, locating dysfunction in the mind while overlooking the biology of reproductive transitions. From the beginning, women's bodies were spoken of as unstable, unreliable, and secondary to their emotions.

Pharmacology inherited the same bias. Mid-20th century medicine became a chemical project. Instead of asking *why* women in midlife reported fatigue, fog, and mood shifts, the system asked *what pill can suppress it?* Antidepressants and sedatives were prescribed en masse, not because they were effective for hormonal change, but because the framework had no room for menopause. What did not fit the model was squeezed into it.

Bias became systemic. Depression in men was treated as illness; depression in women was too often reframed as weakness or character flaw. Cognitive decline in older men triggered neurological investigation; in women it was dismissed as "just age" or "empty nest." Men presenting with insomnia were investigated for sleep apnoea; women with the same complaint were prescribed sleeping tablets.

The structures of psychology and pharmacology shrank women's stories to fit male-centric categories. Diagnostic manuals were written by committees that did not represent women's lived experience. Clinical trials systematically excluded women, especially those of childbearing age, creating data sets skewed toward male physiology. Side effects in women were under-researched or normalised as "female complaints." Even today, dosage guidelines for many psychotropic drugs are based on male-weighted trials, despite evidence that women metabolise drugs differently.

The result is a pattern of distortion: women's hormonal transitions are reframed as psychiatric disease, their psychiatric disease minimised as moodiness, and their legitimate side effects brushed aside. At every step, bias narrows the lens until the system can only see what it already expects.

This history explains why menopause still falls into silence. It was never integrated into the psychiatric canon because psychiatry grew up treating women's biology as an inconvenience and women's distress as a flaw. Psychology focused on cognition and behaviour through a male template. Pharmacology pursued profitable drug pipelines that had little to do with female transitions. These three pillars, psychiatry, psychology, pharmacology, locked women's midlife health into invisibility.

To break that cycle, recognition is not enough. We need deliberate correction: clinical trials that include women across the life course, diagnostic manuals that name menopause as a category worthy of clinical attention, and pharmacological research that tests therapies specifically for hormonal transition rather than defaulting to antidepressants. Without rewriting the foundations, women will keep being written out of the story.

Timeline: Gender Bias in Psychiatry, Psychology, and Pharmacology

19th Century: "Hysteria" Era
- Women's suffering attributed to the "wandering womb."
- Fatigue, pain, or desire medicalised as instability.
- Institutionalisation common; biology ignored.
- Early 20th Century: Freud and Psychoanalysis
- Women's emotions reframed as neurosis or repression.

- Menopause and menstruation treated as psychological weakness, not physiological transition.
- Mid 20th Century: The Valium Generation
- Surge in prescribing sedatives and tranquilizers to women.
- "Mother's little helper" became shorthand for numbing women into silence.
- Menopause symptoms pathologised but never named directly.

Late 20th Century: DSM Codification
- Depression and anxiety formalised as psychiatric disorders.
- No recognition of perimenopause or menopause.
- Diagnostic categories built on male-centric data.

1990s–2000s: SSRI Era
- Antidepressants prescribed widely for midlife women.
- Few trials separated hormonal transition from psychiatric illness.
- Misdiagnosis normalised as "treatment."

Today: Still Excluded
- Clinical trials still underrepresent women.
- Menopause absent in psychiatric manuals.
- Antidepressants remain first-line for symptoms rooted in hormone depletion.

Women's transitions were never invisible, they were misnamed. From hysteria to SSRIs, the system coded menopause as anything but itself.

How the System Shrinks Our Stories to Fit Its Frameworks
This is systemic gaslighting: the experience of being told, again and again, that what you are feeling is not real unless it can be coded into the system's existing boxes. A woman describes hot flushes, brain fog, anxiety, and insomnia. The framework does not allow for menopause, so the system

rewrites her story: *You are anxious. You are depressed. You are unstable.*

The narrative is not simply misheard. It is *reshaped*, compressed into categories that already exist in the manual, in the insurance code, in the pharmaceutical playbook. And once reshaped, the woman herself must conform to the diagnosis she has been given. Her lived experience is erased in favour of a story that fits the system.

This shrinking has consequences. When her symptoms are called depression, she is treated with antidepressants instead of hormone therapy. When her fog is called early dementia, she is referred for scans and tests instead of a menopause consultation. When her exhaustion is called laziness, she is sidelined at work instead of supported. The system cannot flex, so she is forced to bend.

The harm is not only clinical. It is existential. A woman begins to doubt her own perception. If the doctor says it is depression, perhaps she is weak. If the psychologist says it is anxiety, perhaps she is unstable. If the manager says she is unreliable, perhaps she is failing. What begins as misdiagnosis becomes internalised as self-blame. This is the cruel genius of systemic gaslighting: it convinces women to doubt themselves rather than the system that is misreading them.

The betrayal runs deep. It is not only that menopause is absent from the manuals; it is that women's realities are actively *shrunk* to fit frameworks never designed for them. Their words are translated into a language that empties them of meaning. Their suffering is renamed to suit billing categories. Their truth is sidelined so the system can protect its own coherence.

This is not neutral. It is structural violence. To be told that your body's upheaval is "just stress," "just age," or "just depression" is to be told that you do not know yourself. It is to be told that authority lies not in your lived experience but in the diagnostic grid that was built without you in mind.

Systemic gaslighting is the opposite of care. Care begins with listening. Gaslighting begins with reshaping. One expands the story to hold its complexity; the other shrinks it until the woman disappears inside it.

The task ahead is not simply to add menopause to existing frameworks, but to rewrite those frameworks so they expand to meet women's realities rather than forcing women to collapse into their categories. Until that happens, women will continue to leave clinics feeling smaller than when they walked in, not because they are fragile, but because the system has shrunk them.

The New Mandate, Rewrite the Books

Calls for Clinical Reform
Naming menopause in medical texts is no longer optional, it is a mandate. The DSM (psychiatry's diagnostic bible) and the ICD (the global classification of diseases) both omit menopause-related psychiatric and cognitive categories. This absence ensures misdiagnosis, mistreatment, and invisibility.

Clinical reform must begin with inclusion:
- Diagnostic criteria that acknowledge hormonal transition.
- Training modules in psychiatry, psychology, and general medicine.
- Clinical guidelines that prioritise accurate treatment over reflexive antidepressant prescribing.

How to Add Menopause to Medical, Psychological, and Workplace Models
The rewrite must extend beyond medicine into every system that shapes women's lives:

- Medical Models: Update curricula, mandate research funding, and embed menopause into general practice training.
- Psychological Models: Develop frameworks that account for hormonal transitions in mood, cognition, and behaviour. Train psychologists to distinguish between depression and depletion.
- Workplace Models: Incorporate menopause into occupational health, diversity reporting, and equity policies. Menopause should be recognised alongside parental leave, disability support, and mental health initiatives.

Integration is key. A patchwork approach, where menopause is acknowledged in one area but absent in another, only perpetuates fragmentation.

A Proposed Framework: Diagnosis, Support, Narrative, and Recovery

1. Diagnosis
   - Develop formal diagnostic pathways for menopause-related symptoms.
   - Ensure differential diagnosis to prevent reflex mislabelling as depression or anxiety.
2. Support
   - Provide evidence-based medical care, including HRT, lifestyle interventions, and psychological support.
   - Train healthcare providers to deliver care without stigma or dismissal.
3. Narrative
   - Rewrite the cultural script of menopause from decline to transition.
   - Encourage public storytelling and media representation that normalises the experience.
4. Recovery
   - Recognise that menopause is not only an end but also a renewal.

- Create pathways for women to regain confidence, re-enter work, and thrive in post-menopausal years.

From Silence to Systemic Change
The new mandate is about rewriting the very books that define health, equity, and culture. This is not a suggestion. It is a demand. A system that excludes women cannot call itself universal. A culture that silences women cannot call itself equitable.

The books must be rewritten, medical, psychological, workplace, and cultural. Only then will women's stories be recognised not as distortions to be shrunk, but as realities to be honoured.

Chapter 24.
The New Mandate. Rewrite the Books

The Silence Has Become Betrayal

There comes a moment in the consultation room that many women know too well. A woman, exhausted and confused, sits across from her doctor. She has rehearsed her words in the car, perhaps even written notes in her phone so she doesn't forget. She explains the sleepless nights that leave her staring at the ceiling at 3 a.m., the waves of heat that soak through her clothes in meetings, the sudden tears that come without warning, the bone-deep fatigue that no amount of caffeine can cure, and the fog in her mind that makes even simple tasks overwhelming. She describes how she no longer feels like herself, how her memory slips, how her body aches, how her mood has become unpredictable.

The symptoms are real, vivid, and deeply disruptive. But when the doctor glances at the diagnostic framework in their hand, there is no category that neatly captures what she is describing. Menopause does not exist as a recognised psychiatric condition. Hormonal transition is absent from the psychiatric manuals that dictate what is "*real*" in medicine. Faced with a void, the doctor reaches for what **is** written down. She is given a prescription for antidepressants or sleeping tablets, accompanied by a gentle reassurance: "lots of women your age feel this way." The consultation ends not with answers, but with dismissal.

This moment has played out in millions of clinics across the world. In Australia, in the United States, across Europe and Asia, the same pattern repeats: symptoms presented, dismissal offered, medication prescribed. It is not an isolated story, nor is it coincidence. It is the predictable outcome of a psychiatric and medical system that has erased menopause from its formal texts.

The *Diagnostic and Statistical Manual of Mental Disorders (DSM)*, psychiatry's global reference book, is revered as the gold standard of classification. It lists conditions ranging from schizophrenia to obsessive-compulsive disorder, from postpartum depression to premenstrual dysphoric disorder. It even catalogues rare conditions that only a fraction of the population will ever experience. Yet menopause, an experience every woman will encounter if she lives long enough, does not appear. <u>Not as a category. Not as a subcategory. Not even as a footnote</u>.

The omission is not neutral. It is not an oversight, nor a matter of prioritisation. It creates harm every single day. By failing to name menopause, psychiatry pathologises it by default. When the books are silent, doctors must fit symptoms into categories that do exist. The result is a generation of women misdiagnosed as depressed, anxious, or cognitively declining, when in fact they were hormonally depleted. Instead of receiving hormone replacement therapy, lifestyle support, or workplace accommodations, they are prescribed medications that mask, dull, or distort their symptoms without ever addressing the root cause.

This cycle of misdiagnosis does more than waste time and resources, it erodes women's trust in the medical system. A woman who leaves her doctor's office with a prescription she knows instinctively is wrong often questions herself rather than the system. She wonders if perhaps she **is** losing her mind. She doubts her ability to cope. She carries the weight of silence, convinced that her distress is personal weakness rather than systemic neglect.

At this point, silence is not simply oversight. It is betrayal. The world has known about menopause for centuries. Medicine has documented its physiological effects for decades. Public health has measured its economic costs in absenteeism, reduced productivity, and increased healthcare burden. Yet the most influential psychiatric text refuses to acknowledge it.

And the refusal is not benign. It is a form of institutionalised erasure. When the manual that defines mental health does not name menopause, it signals that women's suffering is not legitimate. It tells generations of doctors that hormonal transition is irrelevant to psychiatry. It tells women that what they are experiencing is not worthy of study, of recognition, or of systemic solutions.

The silence becomes a kind of gaslighting at scale. Women are told that their exhaustion is stress. Their anxiety is midlife crisis. Their brain fog is early dementia. Their hot flashes are simply *"part of getting older."* Each explanation chips away at confidence, convincing women that their bodies are betraying them when in fact it is the system that has turned away.

The betrayal lies in the contradiction: medicine has no problem recognising puberty, pregnancy, or postpartum as legitimate biological transitions with psychological impact. These phases are studied, funded, and woven into both medical and psychiatric training. But menopause, equally universal, equally impactful, is cast into the shadows. The silence is selective. And selective silence is not oversight. It is choice.

That choice carries a cost measured in millions of misdiagnoses, billions of dollars in lost productivity, and untold suffering behind closed doors. It perpetuates stigma by keeping menopause unnamed. It reinforces gender inequity by sidelining a biological reality unique to women. It undermines trust in healthcare by forcing women into treatments that do not fit.
Silence in this context is not a blank page waiting to be filled. It is an erasure already enacted. And erasure, once institutionalised, becomes betrayal.

Why Menopause Must Be Named

The Power of Naming in Medicine
In medicine, names are never just words. They are gateways. To be named is to be acknowledged, to be studied, to be funded, to be covered by insurance, and to be formally taught in medical schools. Naming transforms lived experience from "all in your head" into an established medical reality. When a condition appears in the *DSM*

(*Diagnostic and Statistical Manual of Mental Disorders)* or the *ICD (International Classification of Diseases),* it becomes legitimate in the eyes of doctors, policymakers, researchers, and insurers. Without a name, even the most pervasive condition remains invisible.

The Case of PMDD, From Dismissal to Legitimacy

Consider *Premenstrual Dysphoric Disorder (PMDD).* For decades, women reporting severe premenstrual symptoms were told they were exaggerating, unstable, or overly emotional. These symptoms disrupted their work, their relationships, and their sense of self, but the medical response was indifference. It took years of activism, scientific study, and advocacy for PMDD to be recognised as a legitimate psychiatric diagnosis in the DSM.
Once named, everything changed:
- Research funding was unlocked.
- Validated treatment pathways were established.
- Clinical training began to include recognition of PMDD symptoms.
- Patients could access support and medication with the legitimacy of a recognised condition.

What had been dismissed as *"women being dramatic"* became a real, diagnosable, and treatable disorder.

The Arithmetic of Injustice

Now compare the scale.
- PMDD affects around 5-8% of women of reproductive age.
- Menopause affects 100% of women who live beyond their mid-forties or fifties.

The arithmetic is damning. A relatively rare condition has been named, studied, and legitimised. A universal transition, impacting every woman, has been excluded and ignored.

This is not about rarity. Medicine already names countless rare diseases that affect only a few hundred people globally. The question is not *"how common"* but **"who matters."** Menopause's absence speaks to systemic gender bias, not scientific irrelevance.

The Cost of Absence

The failure to name menopause in psychiatric manuals perpetuates a cycle of misdiagnosis. When doctors cannot code menopause as a legitimate category, they reach for what exists: depression, anxiety, insomnia, cognitive decline. Women are given antidepressants when they need hormones. They are offered sleeping pills when they need recognition of night sweats. They are sent to therapy when they need support navigating a hormonal transition.

For some women, this leads to years of unnecessary treatment. For others, it deepens despair, because the medications don't work. They are left believing they are broken, weak, or uniquely unstable, when in reality they are navigating a natural biological transition that the system has refused to acknowledge.

History Proves Recognition Matters

History shows us that inclusion can change everything. Post-Traumatic Stress Disorder (PTSD) provides a powerful example. Before the DSM formally recognised PTSD, returning soldiers were labelled as weak, unstable, or maladjusted. Vietnam veterans fought, literally and politically, for recognition. Their advocacy forced psychiatry to name their condition, and once PTSD appeared in the DSM, the transformation was immediate. Research flourished. Treatments were standardised. Public understanding shifted. Today, PTSD is widely recognised and respected as a legitimate psychiatric condition.

The same dynamic applies to menopause. Without naming, there can be no research momentum, no validated pathways, no systemic recognition. With naming, doors open. Silence breaks. Women are legitimised.

A Mandate, Not a Request

This is not an optional add-on to psychiatric literature. It is a mandate. Recognition of menopause in the DSM and ICD is essential. Until it is named in the books that shape psychiatry and medicine, women will remain misdiagnosed, mistreated, and invisible.

Naming is not about labelling women as *"mentally ill"* for experiencing menopause. It is about acknowledging the psychiatric and cognitive impact of hormonal transition, so that care is guided, research is funded, and women are not abandoned to the margins of medicine.

The Broader Stakes of Naming

To name menopause is to reshape not only psychiatry but also society's relationship with aging women. It would:
- Signal that women's health is worthy of the same legitimacy as men's.
- Ensure doctors are trained to distinguish between depression and depletion.

- Direct resources toward effective, evidence-based treatments rather than misaligned medications.
- Empower women with language to describe their experience, replacing shame with shared recognition.

A System Built Without Us

Male Baselines, Female Erasure

Modern medicine prides itself on being evidence-based. Yet the evidence that underpins much of our healthcare was never gathered from women. For decades, clinical trials, the very foundation of what we call "science" in medicine, systematically excluded women. Until the early 1990s, U.S. National Institutes of Health (NIH) guidelines did not require women to be included in federally funded research. Pharmaceutical trials, cardiovascular studies, psychiatric drug testing: the default subject was male, and the results were assumed to be universal.

This "one-size-fits-men" approach meant that women's bodies were never the baseline; they were the deviation. The "normal" ranges for blood pressure, cholesterol, or medication metabolism were established using male bodies. Side effects unique to women were ignored. Hormonal cycles were dismissed as "complicating variables." Rather than being studied, women were removed from the equation.

Consequences in Every Field

The consequences are staggering. Cardiovascular disease is the leading killer of women worldwide, yet women presenting with heart attacks are routinely misdiagnosed. Why? Because the "classic" symptom of crushing chest pain was derived from male studies. Women's symptoms, nausea, dizziness, shortness of breath, pain in the jaw or shoulders, were considered atypical. Countless women were sent home from emergency rooms with antacids or anxiety medications, only to die hours later.

The same pattern repeats in psychiatry. Depression in men was studied as a straightforward biochemical imbalance; depression in women was interpreted as emotional instability. Schizophrenia in men was defined by aggression or hallucination, in women, by mood swings or relational disruption. When women's presentations didn't match the male model, they were reclassified, diminished, or dismissed.

Menopause fits seamlessly into this history of exclusion. Because it is uniquely female, it was sidelined from research, training, and clinical practice. Psychiatric frameworks built on male norms could not accommodate a hormonal transition that had no male equivalent. Instead of being studied, it was pathologised. Instead of being understood, it was erased.

Psychiatry's Legacy of Misogyny

This erasure has deep historical roots. Psychiatry itself was born in an era where women's suffering was often explained through misogyny, not medicine. Sigmund Freud popularised the concept of "hysteria," a diagnosis almost exclusively applied to women. Symptoms included fainting, nervousness, insomnia, irritability, sexual desire, and fatigue, in other words, many of the same experiences reported by women in menopause today.

The cure? Marriage. Childbearing. Institutionalisation. Later, electric shock therapy or lobotomy. What was never considered was that women's bodies and hormones might play a role. The psychiatric system treated women's biology as irrelevant and their emotions as pathological. That legacy continues.

Even as hysteria disappeared from textbooks, its shadow remained. Women were labelled "neurotic" or "anxious" far more often than men. Antidepressants were prescribed to housewives in the 1950s and 60s at unprecedented rates, not because their depression was different, but because the system saw unhappiness in women as a flaw to be medicated rather than a social or biological issue to be understood.

The Closed Loop of Exclusion

When menopause is absent from psychiatric manuals, doctors cannot code it, research cannot measure it, and policymakers cannot fund it. This creates a closed loop:

Not written → **Not taught**. Medical schools cannot teach what doesn't exist in the text.
Not taught → **Not recognised**. Doctors don't see menopause as relevant to psychiatric practice.
Not recognised → **Not researched**. Without recognition, there is no demand for large-scale trials.
Not researched → **Not written**. With no evidence base, psychiatric texts remain silent.

The loop feeds itself, generation after generation. A doctor trained today may be no better equipped to recognise menopause-related psychiatric symptoms than a doctor trained 50 years ago. The silence becomes self-perpetuating.

Everyday Impact on Women

For women, the cost of this exclusion is lived daily. A woman experiencing brain fog in her late 40s may be told she has early-onset dementia. A woman suffering mood swings may be labelled as having bipolar disorder. A woman with panic attacks at night may be medicated for anxiety, when in fact her estrogen levels have shifted.

These misdiagnoses don't only harm health outcomes, they harm identity. A woman who is misdiagnosed begins to doubt herself. She questions her resilience, her competence, her worth. She internalises the narrative that she is broken, when in truth it is the system that has failed her.

Selective Recognition: Puberty and Pregnancy vs. Menopause

The betrayal becomes sharper when we notice what *is* recognised. Psychiatry and medicine readily acknowledge puberty, pregnancy, and postpartum as legitimate biological transitions with psychological impact. These phases are studied, funded, and embedded into medical curricula. Postpartum depression is in the DSM; pregnancy-related conditions are coded in the ICD.

But menopause, equally universal, equally impactful, is absent. The silence is not accidental. It is selective. And selective silence reveals systemic choice, not oversight.

The Cost of Systemic Choice

That choice carries measurable cost:

- **Economic**: lost productivity, workplace absenteeism, early retirements.
- **Social**: strained relationships, isolation, stigma.
- **Medical**: misdiagnosis, polypharmacy, overuse of antidepressants.
- **Psychological**: diminished confidence, internalised shame, erosion of trust in healthcare.

By building a system without women, medicine and psychiatry have ensured that women pay the price of neglect with their bodies, their work, and their mental health.

The Existential Harm of Misdiagnosis

Misdiagnosis is not neutral. It does not only delay correct treatment. It reshapes a woman's identity.

A woman told she is depressed when she is hormonally depleted may spend years on antidepressants that blunt her emotions but never restore her balance. She may leave a career she once thrived in, believing she has "lost her edge." She may avoid intimacy, convinced her libido is gone forever. She may watch her relationships strain under the weight of a label that never fit.

This is existential harm. It is the theft of selfhood. Instead of recognising a transitional state that can be supported and healed, the system convinces her that she is permanently broken. For some women, the despair deepens into suicidal thoughts, compounded by the sense that no one believes them. Others internalise shame so deeply that they withdraw from the very communities that might have offered support.

At scale, this harm is generational. Daughters watch their mothers struggle in silence and absorb the lesson that midlife is decline. Colleagues see senior women disappear from workplaces and conclude that leadership has an age limit. Menopause misdiagnosed as psychiatric disorder narrows possibility for everyone who follows.

This is why the rewrite matters. It is not only about clinical accuracy or economic efficiency. It is about restoring to women the right to know themselves, to trust their experience, and to move through midlife as whole human beings rather than as broken diagnoses.

Systemic Frameworks Shrinking Women's Truths

The problem is not only individual doctors making missteps; it is the frameworks themselves. Our medical and psychiatric systems are built on classification. The DSM defines mental health conditions. The ICD codes diseases for hospitals and insurers. Workplace law sets categories for leave and accommodation. Research councils decide what to fund based on named conditions.

When menopause is absent from these frameworks, women's truths are forced to shrink to fit what already exists. Hot flushes and insomnia become "anxiety." Brain fog becomes "early dementia." Fatigue becomes "depression." In insurance files, women's symptoms are coded as stress or adjustment disorder. In workplaces, they are counted under "sick leave" or "mental health leave," never as menopause.

The system, in other words, does not bend to meet women's realities. It makes women's realities bend to meet its categories. This is structural gaslighting at scale: women's experiences erased, re-coded, and re-labelled until the system feels coherent, even as women feel invisible.

Rewriting the books is not simply about adding a footnote. It is about expanding the frameworks so they can hold the truth of women's lives, rather than forcing women to collapse into the narrowness of existing categories.

Rewrite the Medical Texts

Naming as the Foundation of Change

The first and most urgent rewrite must begin in medicine itself. At its core, healthcare operates on texts: the diagnostic manuals, medical curricula, and clinical guidelines that define what is "real" enough to treat, to code, and to fund. When menopause is excluded from these foundational texts, it disappears from the system. Without recognition in the *DSM* (Diagnostic and Statistical Manual of Mental Disorders) or the *ICD* (International Classification of Diseases), doctors cannot diagnose it, researchers cannot track it, policymakers cannot budget for it, and insurers cannot reimburse care for it.

This is not a technicality. In the bureaucratic machinery of modern medicine, what is unnamed does not exist. And what does not exist cannot be treated fairly.

The DSM and ICD: Gatekeepers of Legitimacy

The DSM is psychiatry's global reference point. It sets the standards for diagnosis, influences training curricula worldwide, and directs billions of dollars of research funding. Likewise, the ICD, maintained by the World Health Organization, determines the codes used in hospitals, insurance billing, and international health statistics.

Both texts are exhaustive in some areas. They list rare phobias, niche disorders, and conditions that affect only a small percentage of people. Yet they fail to name menopause as a psychiatric or cognitive category. The result is that a universal biological transition, one that shapes mood, memory, cognition, and quality of life for half the population, remains invisible to the very systems designed to safeguard health.

This absence creates a ripple effect:
- **Doctors** must fit women's symptoms into categories that do exist, often leading to misdiagnosis as depression or anxiety.
- **Researchers** cannot track prevalence or outcomes, because there is no recognised code.
- **Hospitals** cannot measure costs associated with menopause, making it invisible in resource allocation.
- **Insurers** have no obligation to cover treatments, because the condition "does not exist" in their coding systems.

Medical Education: The Blind Spot in Training

The silence in diagnostic texts seeps into medical education. A medical student may graduate after seven years of study having spent hours on rare neurological syndromes, but less than a lecture or two on menopause. Psychiatry residencies may cover postpartum depression in detail but skip over perimenopausal mood changes. General practitioners, who are the first line of care for most women, often receive no structured training on menopause management at all.

This neglect is not accidental. It mirrors the cultural assumption that menopause is a private, individual issue, not a systemic or clinical one. The absence in texts perpetuates the absence in teaching, which perpetuates the absence in practice. Doctors can only diagnose what they are taught to recognise. Without structured education, even well-meaning clinicians are left to improvise, relying on stereotypes, outdated advice, or trial-and-error prescriptions.

Research: Following the Money
Medicine follows funding. When a condition is recognised, research dollars flow. When it is absent, so is investment. Compare the billions poured into conditions like erectile dysfunction, affecting a small fraction of men, with the relative trickle directed toward menopause research. The U.S. National Institutes of Health (NIH) has historically allocated more funding to male sexual function than to menopause, despite the vastly larger population affected.

Without research, treatments stagnate. Hormone replacement therapy (HRT), once hailed as a solution, has been mired in controversy since flawed studies in the early 2000s led to public fear and withdrawal of prescriptions. Subsequent re-analysis has shown HRT to be safe and effective for most women, but the damage was done. Without robust, ongoing investment, myths prevail. Women are left in limbo, with inconsistent advice from doctors who themselves are confused by conflicting evidence.

Case Study 19: The UK's NICE Guidelines

In the United Kingdom, the National Institute for Health and Care Excellence (NICE) took a step forward in 2015 by issuing menopause guidelines. For the first time, menopause was formally acknowledged as a clinical condition requiring structured management. The guidelines recommended that doctors discuss symptoms openly, avoid reflexively prescribing antidepressants, and consider HRT where appropriate.

The impact was immediate:
- Awareness among general practitioners increased.
- Prescribing patterns shifted.
- Women reported greater confidence in seeking support.

Yet even these guidelines are limited. They are advisory, not mandatory. Implementation depends on individual clinicians, many of whom still lack training. And because menopause remains absent from the DSM and ICD, psychiatric dimensions, anxiety, brain fog, mood swings, remain sidelined.

The Global Picture: Pockets of Progress, Widespread Neglect

Some countries are beginning to move. Japan has long recognised "climacteric syndrome" as a legitimate medical condition, reflecting cultural willingness to acknowledge menopause as part of healthcare. In Australia, parliamentary debates in 2022 and 2023 called for better workplace and medical responses to menopause, though policy remains patchy. In the U.S., high-profile voices like Michelle Obama and Oprah Winfrey have broken the cultural silence, but systemic change has lagged.

The global picture is one of uneven progress: isolated advances in policy or public discourse, undermined by the absence of structural reform in medical texts and training. Until the DSM and ICD rewrite their categories, and until medical schools overhaul their curricula, progress will remain partial at best.

What Rewrite Looks Like

Rewriting the medical texts is not about creating a new label that stigmatises women. It is about acknowledging the full range of cognitive and psychiatric effects that menopause can bring, and ensuring they are studied, coded, and treated appropriately.

The rewrite must include:
1.   **DSM inclusion**: A recognised diagnostic category for menopause-related mood and cognitive disorders.
2.   **ICD coding**: A formal classification that allows hospitals and insurers to track, measure, and fund care.
3.   **Curriculum reform**: Mandatory menopause training for all medical students, psychiatrists, and general practitioners.
4.   **Research funding**: Dedicated grants for menopause-related studies, covering mood, cognition, and quality of life.
5.   **Guidelines and protocols**: Clear, evidence-based frameworks for diagnosis, treatment, and referral.

Why This Rewrite Matters

This is more than a technical reform. It is a moral imperative. Without rewriting the medical texts, every other reform, workplace policies, cultural narratives, government investment, will be built on sand. Medicine is the foundation. Until menopause is visible in the systems that define legitimacy, women will remain invisible in practice.

Rewriting the medical texts is the first domino. Once it falls, research follows. Training follows. Policy follows. Culture shifts. Without it, silence continues.

The choice is stark: rewrite the books, or continue betraying half the population by omission.

Rewrite the Workplace Policies

Why Workplaces Cannot Ignore Menopause

Menopause is not just a medical transition. It is a workplace reality. Women in their forties, fifties, and sixties are often at the peak of their careers, leading teams, managing budgets, mentoring younger colleagues, and holding senior leadership positions. Yet at the same time, they may be navigating unpredictable hot flashes in boardrooms, brain fog in high-stakes negotiations, insomnia before critical presentations, or mood swings while juggling complex workloads.

For too long, workplaces have treated menopause as irrelevant, private, or even taboo. The result is a silent epidemic of lost productivity, career disruption, and premature exit from the workforce. Without systemic workplace policies, women are forced to improvise, suffering in silence, taking unpaid leave, or quietly stepping down from roles they are more than qualified to hold.

The Legal and Policy Gap

Most employment frameworks recognise life events like parental leave, family responsibilities, or sick leave. Yet menopause rarely appears in workplace legislation.

Australia's Fair Work Act provides categories for carer's leave, compassionate leave, and family responsibilities. But menopause is invisible. Women must fit their symptoms into existing leave categories, often at the cost of pay, dignity, and career progression.

The UK's Equality Act prohibits discrimination based on sex, age, or disability, but menopause is not explicitly named. Women must pursue legal claims by framing menopause as a disability, which many find stigmatising or inaccurate.

United States law provides no federal recognition of menopause in workplace protections, though some state and corporate initiatives are emerging.

The absence of explicit recognition means that menopause is left to the discretion of individual managers or HR departments. This creates inconsistency, inequity, and vulnerability to bias.

The Cost of Silence, Economics and Retention

The financial cost of ignoring menopause is enormous. Studies in the UK estimate that menopause-related absenteeism and attrition cost the economy billions each year. In Australia, Deloitte has linked gender workforce participation to GDP growth, with menopause identified as a hidden driver of midlife female workforce exit.

The costs fall into several categories:

- **Absenteeism**: missed days due to symptoms like insomnia, migraines, or heavy bleeding.
- **Presenteeism**: reduced productivity when women attend work but struggle with brain fog or exhaustion.
- **Attrition**: women leaving the workforce earlier than planned because symptoms make continued employment untenable.
- **Pipeline disruption**: the loss of women at senior levels diminishes diversity in leadership, with downstream effects on innovation and equity.

For employers, the cost of replacing a senior woman who exits due to unmanaged menopause symptoms can exceed 200% of her salary once recruitment, training, and lost institutional knowledge are considered. This is not only a gender equity issue, it is a hard economic reality.

Case Law and Precedents

In recent years, legal challenges have begun to emerge. In the UK, tribunals have heard cases where women argued that failure to accommodate menopause symptoms constituted discrimination. Some judgments have sided with employees, interpreting menopause through the lens of disability law. Others have failed, revealing the inadequacy of current frameworks.

These cases highlight the urgent need for clarity. Women should not have to claim "disability" for what is a natural life stage. Nor should employers face uncertainty about their obligations. Explicit legislative recognition of menopause as a workplace health and equity issue would provide certainty for both sides.

Global Comparisons
A handful of nations are beginning to act:
United Kingdom: Parliamentary committees have debated menopause workplace rights. Some employers, including large banks and universities, have introduced menopause policies covering flexible work, uniform adjustments, and manager training.

Australia: The Workplace Gender Equality Agency has signalled interest in collecting menopause-related data, though policy remains patchy. A handful of progressive employers (e.g., Telstra, Australia Post) have introduced workplace menopause programs.

Japan: Cultural openness around "climacteric syndrome" has led to workplace policies allowing reduced hours or medical leave during severe symptoms.

European Union: Growing momentum exists for EU-wide protections, but progress is uneven across member states.

Despite these advances, most countries remain silent. The global norm is still inconsistency, leaving millions of women unsupported.

What Rewrite Looks Like in the Workplace

To close the gap, workplaces need systemic reform at multiple levels:

1. Legislation
   - Explicit recognition of menopause in workplace law.
   - Protected leave categories for menopause-related health needs.
   - Anti-discrimination protections that name menopause directly.
2. Policies
   - Menopause policies embedded alongside parental leave and mental health.
   - Flexible working arrangements, remote options, adjusted hours, or reduced travel during acute phases.
   - Physical accommodations, access to fans, temperature control, rest areas, or uniform modifications.
3. Training and Culture
   - Manager training to recognise and respond appropriately to menopause needs.
   - Employee education campaigns to normalise discussion and reduce stigma.
   - Confidential HR support channels so women feel safe to seek help.
4. Measurement
   - Inclusion of menopause data in gender equity reporting.
   - Tracking of absenteeism and attrition linked to menopause to inform interventions.
   - Annual workplace surveys to monitor cultural shifts and employee experiences.

Why This Rewrite Matters
The rewrite of workplace policies is not a niche women's issue. It is an economic and social imperative. By 2030, more than one billion women worldwide will be post-menopausal. Their participation in the workforce is essential to economic growth, innovation, and leadership diversity.

Failure to act means not only individual suffering but systemic loss: fewer women in boardrooms, less diversity in decision-making, and economies weakened by preventable attrition. Acting now means workplaces that are more inclusive, more productive, and more equitable.

The Moral Imperative for Employers

Ultimately, rewriting workplace policies is about fairness. Women have carried the hidden cost of menopause for generations, adjusting privately while institutions looked away. Employers who fail to act perpetuate that inequity. Employers who lead, by contrast, can set a new standard, one where women's health is integrated into the fabric of workplace equity.

This is not a luxury or a fringe demand. It is a mandate. Just as workplaces adapted to parental leave, disability rights, and mental health awareness, so too must they adapt to menopause. Anything less is failure.

Rewrite the Cultural Narrative

Silence as Culture

For centuries, menopause has not only been absent from medical texts but also from cultural ones. Where puberty is marked by ceremonies, pregnancy by rituals, and even death by collective mourning, menopause has been shrouded in silence. It has been called "the change," a euphemism that says everything and nothing at once. In many societies, women experiencing menopause have been treated as invisible, their value tied to fertility and reproduction, and their transition interpreted as decline.

This silence is not neutral. Culture shapes medicine as much as medicine shapes culture. When menopause is unnamed in public discourse, it reinforces its erasure in science, policy, and workplaces. Culture is both the mirror and the amplifier of institutional neglect.

The Cultural Stigma of Aging Women
Western culture in particular has idolised youth and fertility while marginalising aging women. Ancient Greek medical texts spoke of the "barren years" as if a woman past menopause ceased to have purpose. In Victorian England, menopause was described in literature as a descent into madness or instability. Popular culture through much of the twentieth century depicted middle-aged women as irrelevant, frumpy, or emotionally volatile.

The stigma is double: menopause carries the weight of both ageism and sexism. Women are told that their worth declines with their hormones, that their sexuality evaporates with their cycles, that their professional value is overshadowed by younger, "fresher" faces. These cultural narratives trap women in shame and silence.

Breaking Silence Through Media and Public Figures
In recent years, public figures have begun to challenge this silence. Their voices have cracked open space for honesty, humour, and solidarity.

Oprah Winfrey has used her platform to bring menopause into mainstream conversation, interviewing doctors and sharing personal stories.

Michelle Obama spoke candidly about hot flashes she experienced while on Marine One, the presidential helicopter, reframing menopause as a universal human reality that does not spare even the most powerful.
Davina McCall, in the UK, created groundbreaking documentaries on menopause, exposing the myths, the medical neglect, and the urgency of reform.

Whoopi Goldberg has blended humour with honesty, from talk shows to her comic book *The Change*, portraying menopause not as an end but as a transformation.

These interventions matter because they shift menopause from the private to the public sphere. What was once whispered is now debated on prime-time television, in podcasts, and on social media.

Literature and Feminist Critique
Feminist thinkers have long argued that the cultural erasure of menopause is part of a broader pattern of silencing women's bodies. Simone de Beauvoir, in *The Second Sex*, described how society treats post-menopausal women as "the old woman", stripped of sexual and social value. Adrienne Rich, in *Of Woman Born*, critiqued how patriarchal systems reduced women's reproductive lives to their only worth, leaving no language for transitions beyond childbearing.

Literature has also played a role in reshaping narratives. Contemporary novels and memoirs now tell stories of women navigating menopause with humour, rage, resilience, and complexity. These cultural texts are beginning to provide new scripts for women, replacing silence with multiplicity.

Global Perspectives, Beyond the West
Not all cultures have treated menopause with silence or stigma. Anthropological studies show variation:

- In parts of **Japan**, menopause is referred to as *konenki*, understood as a natural and expected phase, sometimes accompanied by cultural respect for the wisdom of older women.
- In **Indigenous Australian** and **First Nations American** traditions, elder women often gain new authority and respect post-menopause, recognised as keepers of knowledge.

- In contrast, many **Western societies** have pathologised menopause, framing it as deficiency rather than transition.

These cross-cultural comparisons demonstrate that stigma is not inevitable. It is constructed. And if it can be constructed, it can be dismantled.

Why Narrative Matters

Narratives do more than reflect culture, they create it. When menopause is told as a story of decline, women internalise shame. When it is told as a story of transformation, women find strength. Narrative frames policy: what is unspeakable cannot be legislated. Narrative shapes medicine: what is culturally invisible rarely becomes a research priority. Narrative defines workplaces: what leaders never mention is assumed to be irrelevant.

Rewriting the cultural narrative is therefore essential to every other reform. Without it, even changes in medicine and policy will falter, because stigma will continue to silence women from seeking help or claiming rights.

What Rewrite Looks Like in Culture

To rewrite the cultural narrative around menopause, multiple interventions are needed:

1. Media Representation
   - Mainstream shows, films, and news outlets portraying menopause as normal, not pathological.
   - Storylines that include professional women navigating symptoms without being reduced to caricatures.
   - Representation of diverse experiences, cultural, racial, and socioeconomic differences in how menopause is lived.

2. Public Storytelling

- Memoirs, podcasts, and documentaries amplifying lived experience.
- Celebrities and leaders speaking openly, reducing stigma.
- Social media campaigns normalising conversation.

3. Education
   - Schools teaching puberty *and* menopause, ensuring young people understand both the beginning and the later transitions of reproductive life.
   - Public health campaigns placing menopause alongside other health milestones.

4. Cultural Celebration
   - Rituals and recognition that mark menopause not as loss but as passage into another phase of wisdom, strength, and agency.

Toward Visibility and Pride

The cultural rewrite is not about romanticising menopause or erasing its challenges. It is about balance, acknowledging the struggles while also recognising the resilience, wisdom, and continuity it represents.

The silence has served no one. It has left women isolated, medicine uninformed, and society poorer for the loss of voices silenced at midlife. Rewriting the cultural narrative is about visibility, about pride, and about truth.

Menopause must be seen, heard, and respected. Only then can the full system of reform, medical, workplace, governmental, take root.

The Mandate Is Clear

Not a Suggestion, a Demand

At this point, the evidence is overwhelming. Silence has failed women in medicine, in workplaces, and in culture. The gaps are visible, the costs are calculable, and the stories are undeniable. What remains is not a matter of debate but of mandate. Menopause must be recognised, studied, and supported at every level of society.

This is not a polite request for inclusion. It is a demand for justice. Just as feminism fought for suffrage, for reproductive rights, and for equal pay, so too must it now fight for the legitimacy of midlife women's health. The omission of menopause from psychiatry, policy, and culture is not a neutral oversight; it is systemic discrimination.

Four Levels of Rewrite

The mandate is clear because it touches every layer of institutional life:

1. **Medical Books**
    - DSM and ICD inclusion of menopause-related mood and cognitive effects.
    - Medical education reform to ensure every graduate doctor can recognise, diagnose, and treat menopause appropriately.
    - Research funding commensurate with its prevalence.

2. **Workplace Books**
    - Legislative protections naming menopause explicitly.
    - Workplace policies that mirror those for parental leave or mental health.
    - Cultural training to dismantle stigma in office corridors, not just HR documents.

3. **Government Books**
    - Budgets that fund public awareness, healthcare subsidies, and research programs.
    - Reporting frameworks that measure menopause's impact on workforce participation and equity.

- National strategies that treat menopause as a public health priority.

4. **<u>Cultural Books</u>**
   - Media representation that normalises rather than marginalises.
   - Rituals, literature, and storytelling that mark menopause as a phase of transformation rather than decline.
   - Public discourse that treats women's experiences as legitimate, not laughable.

Together, these rewrites form a comprehensive mandate. They are interdependent. Without medical legitimacy, workplaces lack frameworks. Without workplace reform, governments ignore costs. Without cultural narrative shifts, women remain silent even when policies exist. The mandate must operate on all fronts simultaneously.

Why Now?

The urgency is generational. By 2030, more than one billion women worldwide will be post-menopausal. These women are not on the fringes of society, they are leading businesses, holding political office, raising grandchildren, running households, and contributing to economies in every possible way. To ignore their health is to ignore the backbone of global society.

Moreover, the silence has already persisted for too long. Medicine has known about menopause for centuries. Women have borne its burdens in isolation for millennia. But the cultural, political, and scientific conditions of today are ripe for change. Women's voices are louder, more connected, and more unwilling to be dismissed than ever before.

The mandate is clear because the moment is now.

From Silence to Action

Learning from Precedents
Reform is possible. We have seen it before. Post-Traumatic Stress Disorder was once unnamed, leaving veterans unsupported and stigmatised. Activism forced recognition, and the inclusion of PTSD in the DSM transformed research, funding, and public understanding. The same trajectory is possible for menopause.

We have seen how breast cancer awareness shifted from whispered shame to pink ribbons on every global stage. We have seen how HIV/AIDS, once ignored and stigmatised, became a catalyst for global health reform after relentless advocacy. Each of these movements turned silence into systemic change. Menopause can follow the same arc.

Building the Action Agenda
The transition from silence to action requires a coordinated agenda:

1. **Medical Advocacy**
   - Lobbying psychiatric associations for DSM inclusion.
   - Pressuring WHO for ICD coding reforms.
   - Building global research consortia dedicated to menopause.

2. **Workplace Advocacy**
   - Partnering with unions, HR associations, and business councils to mainstream menopause policies.
   - Publishing case studies that demonstrate economic ROI when women are supported.
   - Embedding menopause in diversity, equity, and inclusion (DEI) frameworks.

3. **Government Advocacy**
   - Legislative campaigns to explicitly protect menopause in workplace and health law.

- National menopause strategies, akin to mental health or obesity strategies, that fund public education and medical training.
- Integration of menopause metrics into gender equity reporting and national statistics.

4. Cultural Advocacy
- Media partnerships to normalise menopause stories.
- Public health campaigns that use humour, empathy, and honesty to break stigma.
- Cross-cultural storytelling that highlights resilience and transformation.

The Role of Women Themselves
Systemic reform requires collective voice. Women sharing their stories, whether in Parliament, in boardrooms, or on social media, create the momentum that institutions cannot ignore. Every time a woman names menopause publicly, she chips away at stigma. Every campaign, petition, and program adds to a global chorus that demands change.

But this is not only the responsibility of women. Men must also become allies. Partners, colleagues, policymakers, and doctors must acknowledge menopause as a shared social issue, not a "women's problem." Silence has been co-created; so too must reform.

Toward a Movement
The Menopause Mandate is not just the title of this book. It is the blueprint for a movement. Like the suffragettes, like the activists of the HIV/AIDS crisis, like the veterans who fought for PTSD recognition, women and allies must demand the rewrite. This is how systems change: through collective insistence that the old books no longer serve, and new books must be written.

The silence has lasted long enough. The betrayal has been deep enough. The mandate is clear, and the path from silence to action is open.

The question is not *if* the rewrite will happen, but **when**, and **who** will have the courage to lead it.

The silence has been named, and the mandate to rewrite the books is clear. But even as the call for reform grows louder, vast frontiers remain overlooked. Menopause does not affect all women in the same way; race, class, culture, geography, and workplace realities shape the experience profoundly. To move from mandate to justice, we must turn our attention to these edges, the places where the silence is deepest and the neglect most costly. Part V takes us there.

Part V:

The Overlooked Frontiers

I've walked through the fire. I've sat in the silence. And now, I stand in a space of clarity, conviction, and contribution.

This isn't just my story, it's a strategy. Because real change doesn't stop with awareness. It needs Tools. Language. Frameworks. Reform. That's why the next section of this book provides practical resources designed to help businesses, leaders, and policymakers move from conversation to action.

Reform begins at the centre, in medical texts, workplace policies, and cultural narratives. But the true test of reform is found at the margins. Menopause is not experienced in a vacuum; it intersects with race, class, geography, identity, and labour. For migrant women, language gaps turn symptoms into silence. For women in remote towns, distance to care makes geography a barrier to dignity. For those in male-dominated industries, stigma collides with structural exclusion.

These are the frontiers too often ignored, the spaces where silence is compounded and inequity deepens. To build a mandate that is real, not rhetorical, we must go there.

Chapter 25:
Not All Menopause Is the Same.
Race, Class, and Identity

The Myth of the Universal Woman

For centuries, medicine, policy, and even feminism itself have fallen into the trap of treating "woman" as a singular, universal category. The idea sounds simple: menopause is universal, therefore the experience must also be universal. But universality is a myth that erases as much as it reveals.

When systems assume sameness, difference disappears. The white, middle-class woman in metropolitan Sydney becomes the default image of "the menopausal woman," while the Indigenous woman in Arnhem Land, the Black woman in Atlanta, or the Latina cleaner in Los Angeles are rendered invisible. What does not match the template is sidelined as anecdotal, peripheral, or unimportant.

Erasure in Medicine

Medical research has long preferred the fiction of the universal subject. Historically, trials excluded women altogether; when they were eventually included, they were rarely analysed by race, class, or geography. Data was collapsed into averages, flattening the profound variation in how menopause begins, unfolds, and is treated.

For example, the Study of Women's Health Across the Nation (SWAN), one of the largest U.S. cohort studies, showed that Black women experience menopause symptoms earlier and more severely than their white counterparts. Yet for decades, the "standard" description of menopause remained one that fit white women's experiences best. This invisibility matters because what is not studied is not funded, and what is not funded is not treated.

Erasure in Feminism

Even feminist discourse has been guilty of flattening difference. Early second-wave feminism, while powerful in its insistence that "the personal is political," often centred white, middle-class women's voices. Menopause campaigns in the 1970s and 80s emphasised liberation from reproduction or the fight against medicalisation, important issues, but ones that often overlooked the realities of migrant women, working-class women, or women whose cultural contexts framed menopause differently.

For many women of colour, the struggle was not over-medicalisation but under-recognition. Their symptoms weren't overtreated with hormone therapy; they were ignored altogether. Their silence wasn't a rebellion against patriarchal medicine; it was enforced by stigma, poverty, or lack of access. Universality masked inequity.

Erasure in Policy and Work
Policy, too, has reflected the universal woman myth. Workplace accommodations are often designed with desk-based jobs in mind, air-conditioned offices, flexible hours, sick leave entitlements. But what about women in warehouses, factories, or on farms? What about nurses working night shifts, cleaners on casual contracts, or Indigenous health workers in remote clinics? The "universal" menopause policy often assumes a professional woman in a white-collar workplace. Everyone else is an afterthought.

The Danger of the Universal Frame
When menopause is treated as the same for all women, the result is systemic neglect of those whose realities don't match the dominant narrative. This neglect shows up in:

- **Delayed diagnosis** for women who can't afford specialist care.
- **Cultural stigma** that makes symptoms unspeakable in some communities.
- **Economic vulnerability** when casual or low-paid work offers no safety net for time off.
- **Clinical invisibility** when research fails to capture diverse experiences.

The universal woman, then, is not universal at all. She is a construct that privileges some while erasing many.

Why Intersectionality Matters
Kimberlé Crenshaw's theory of intersectionality reminds us that women's experiences are shaped not only by gender but also by race, class, sexuality, disability, and geography. Menopause, too, is lived at these intersections. To understand it only through the lens of biology is to miss the full truth. Biology sets the stage, but culture, class, and identity shape the play.

If reform is to mean anything, it must begin by dismantling the myth of universality. It must replace "the woman" with women in all their plurality. Only then can menopause policy, medicine, and culture move from erasure to equity.

Race and Menopause

Menopause is universal in biology but not in experience. The age of onset, the severity of symptoms, and the pathways to care differ significantly across racial and cultural groups. These differences are not simply genetic; they are also shaped by systemic inequities, cultural narratives, and access to healthcare. Race, in this sense, is both biological and social, influencing how menopause unfolds in the body and how it is interpreted by society.

Black Women: Earlier, Hotter, Harder
Research consistently shows that Black women in the United States experience menopause earlier, with more severe vasomotor symptoms such as hot flushes and night sweats, compared to white women. The SWAN study found that Black women report symptoms lasting longer, sometimes by several years. They are also less likely to be prescribed

hormone replacement therapy (HRT) and more likely to have their symptoms dismissed or reframed as stress.

The disparity is not only biological. Structural racism in healthcare means Black women face higher rates of misdiagnosis, lower referral rates to specialists, and less access to effective treatment. Cultural stigma also plays a role: in some communities, menopause is not openly discussed, reinforcing silence and isolation.

Indigenous Women: Knowledge and Neglect

For Indigenous Australian women, menopause is often understood through community and cultural frameworks rather than biomedical ones. Some languages describe it as "bleeding no more", a practical phrase that names the change without attaching pathology. In many Indigenous traditions worldwide, elder women gain authority and respect post-menopause.

Yet systemic neglect overshadows this cultural wisdom. Indigenous health services are chronically underfunded, rural clinics are scarce, and culturally safe menopause care is almost non-existent. The result is a paradox: menopause framed positively in cultural story but lived negatively in healthcare reality.

Asian Women: Fewer Flushes, More Silence

Asian women, on average, report fewer vasomotor symptoms like hot flushes, though they are more likely to experience joint pain, insomnia, or mood changes. In Japan, the word *konenki* frames menopause as a seasonal shift, sometimes carrying neutral or even positive connotations. But Western biomedical influence has eroded this framing, replacing it with pathology.

Silence remains a barrier. In many Asian cultures, mental health is heavily stigmatised, making it harder for women to disclose mood swings or cognitive changes. Symptoms that overlap with depression or anxiety often go untreated, not because they are absent but because they are unspeakable.

Latina Women: Cultural Scripts and Systemic Barriers

For Latina women, menopause is shaped by both cultural narratives and systemic barriers. Familial and religious traditions may emphasise endurance and silence, discouraging open conversation. Language barriers make medical consultations more difficult, especially when interpreters are untrained in reproductive health vocabulary.

At the same time, structural inequities in employment and healthcare access compound the challenge. Latina women in the U.S. are overrepresented in low-wage, physically demanding jobs that rarely offer health insurance or workplace accommodations. Menopause, in these contexts, is endured in private while livelihoods depend on silence.

Cross-Cultural Narratives: Words Matter

Language shapes perception. In English, menopause is often referred to as "the change," a phrase that implies disruption and loss. In Japan, *konenki* situates it as a transition akin to seasons. In some Indigenous languages, the description is functional, focusing on menstruation's end rather than decline. These narratives matter because they frame whether menopause is seen as deficiency, transformation, or simply another stage of life.

The Research Gaps

Despite the insights of studies like SWAN, racial and ethnic differences in menopause remain under-researched. Clinical trials rarely include diverse cohorts, and when they do, the results are not always analysed by subgroup. As a result, the default narrative continues to be written from a white, middle-class perspective.

Action Asset: Comparative Snapshot

Group	Onset/Severity	Common Symptoms	Barriers to Care	Cultural Framing
Black	Earlier onset, longer duration	Severe flushes, night sweats	Under-prescription of HRT, dismissal as stress	Silence, strength narratives
Indigenous	Variable; often reframed culturally	Fatigue, pain, mood changes	Lack of culturally safe services, rural access gap	"Bleeding no more," elder respect

Group	Onset/Severity	Common Symptoms	Barriers to Care	Cultural Framing
Asian	Later onset, fewer flushes	Joint pain, insomnia, mood swings	Mental health stigma, Westernisation of medicine	Konenki as seasonal change
Latina	Mid-to-early onset, varied severity	Hot flushes, mood swings	Language barriers, inequity in healthcare access	Silence, endurance, faith traditions

Toward Equity in Race and Menopause
These racial differences are not curiosities at the margins; they are evidence that universality is a myth. To treat menopause as "one-size-fits-all" is to replicate the very exclusions that women of colour have endured for centuries. True reform must begin by naming these inequities, funding research that includes diverse cohorts, and designing care that respects cultural as well as biological realities.

Class and Economic Inequity

If race shapes how menopause is experienced and treated, class determines how survivable it is. Economic resources, or the lack of them, dictate whether a woman has access to specialist care, workplace flexibility, or even the time to acknowledge what her body is going through. Menopause is universal, but class ensures it is lived unequally.

Blue-Collar vs. White-Collar Menopause
The difference between a corporate manager in an air-conditioned office and a factory worker on the night shift is not merely context, it is destiny.

White-collar workplaces: Women with salaried jobs, paid leave entitlements, and private health insurance often have at least some buffer. They may be able to book specialist appointments, access HRT through private scripts, or negotiate flexible hours when symptoms peak. Even here, stigma silences many, but the scaffolding of privilege provides options.

Blue-collar workplaces: For women in manufacturing, cleaning, aged care, or retail, there is no such safety net. Shift rosters are rigid. Uniforms are synthetic. Breaks are timed. Hot flushes, insomnia, or heavy bleeding are endured on the factory floor or behind checkout counters, with no privacy, no accommodations, and no language of support.
The economic divide is stark: in one workplace, menopause is managed. In another, it is survived.

The Cost of Silence
Economic inequity is not just about income; it is about how costs accumulate when menopause goes unsupported. Consider the hidden expenses:

- **Healthcare costs**: repeated GP visits, unnecessary antidepressants, misdiagnosed scans, or ER admissions.

- **Employment costs**: unpaid leave, lost shifts, reduced hours, or being passed over for promotion.
- **Household costs**: paying for alternative therapies, supplements, or private consults out of pocket.

For a woman on minimum wage, these costs are devastating. For a woman in casual employment, they can be career-ending.

Case Studies of Class Divide: Same biology. Different resources. Opposite outcomes.

- **Rosa, retail worker (45)**: Rosa works shifts at a supermarket. When hot flushes overwhelm her, she cannot step off the checkout. Her supervisor tells her to "toughen up." Without paid leave, she takes unpaid days to recover, losing income her family depends on.

- **Claire, corporate executive (52)**: Claire has private insurance and an understanding HR department. She negotiates flexible hours, attends a menopause clinic, and starts HRT. She continues to thrive professionally.

Financial Consequences at Scale

The macroeconomic impact mirrors the microeconomic one. Deloitte (2020) estimated that unmanaged menopause costs economies billions each year through absenteeism, presenteeism, and turnover. Women in lower-paid, high-stress roles are most at risk of leaving the workforce prematurely, compounding inequities in superannuation, pensions, and retirement security.

For governments, this is not only a health issue but a fiscal one. The earlier women exit, the more revenue is lost, the more welfare is required, and the more inequality compounds across generations.

Action Asset: Cost-of-Silence Calculator

Category	Average Annual Cost per Woman (AUD)	Notes
Unnecessary GP visits	$600–$900	Misdiagnosis, repeated consults
Misaligned medication	$400–$700	Antidepressants, sleeping pills
Lost wages (unpaid leave/reduced hours)	$3,000–$5,000	Based on 1–2 days off/month
Attrition (leaving workforce early)	$20,000+	Based on 6 months unemployment or early retirement

Category	Average Annual Cost per Woman (AUD)	Notes
Out-of-pocket supplements/therapies	$500–$1,200	Vitamins, herbal remedies, private consults

Total Hidden Cost: $24,000+ per woman, per year, when menopause is unsupported.

For women already living paycheck to paycheck, this cost is catastrophic.

Note: Figures are indicative and based on blended national averages. Annualised estimates should be reviewed and updated with current organisational or sector-specific data (see Appendix: References: PwC & WGEA Workforce Cost Modelling, 2023).

Systemic Implications

Class inequity in menopause care is not simply unfair; it is unsustainable. Without targeted reform:
- Women in low-paid jobs will continue to exit work early, reducing overall workforce participation.
- Employers will continue to absorb the cost of turnover, recruitment, and lost expertise.
- Families will continue to lose income at the exact moment women should be consolidating retirement security.

Toward Equity in Class and Menopause

Equity means recognising that women in different socioeconomic positions need different supports. For white-collar women, stigma may be the primary barrier. For blue-collar women, structural change is essential: breathable uniforms, flexible rostering, paid menopause leave, and affordable access to clinics. Without these, class will continue to divide whose menopause is manageable and whose is devastating.

Identity and Stigma

Menopause is often framed as a biological event, ovaries age, hormones shift, cycles stop. But identity complicates biology. How a woman or gender-diverse person experiences menopause depends not only on physiology but on who they are, how they are seen, and the stigma they carry. Menopause does not occur in a vacuum. It collides with sexuality, gender identity, disability, and social expectations, shaping lives in ways that the "average woman" model never accounts for.

LGBTQ+ Experiences: The Missing Scripts

For queer women and gender-diverse people, menopause is often doubly silenced. Mainstream medical narratives assume heterosexual, cisgender patients. Clinical intake forms ask about husbands, contraception, and childbirth, not same-sex partners, chosen families, or non-binary identities.

Lesbian and bisexual women: Studies suggest they may face higher risks of certain health conditions, such as cardiovascular disease, but often encounter doctors who are untrained or uncomfortable discussing their needs. Menopause care, layered on top of existing healthcare disparities, becomes fragmented or absent.

Trans men and non-binary people: Those who retain ovaries may experience menopausal symptoms whether naturally or surgically induced. Yet many find themselves invisible in both gynaecological and endocrinological care. Menopause becomes a "non-category," leaving them to navigate symptoms without tailored medical support.

Stigma here is not just silence but structural erasure. When guidelines and policies assume heterosexual cisgender women, others are forced to improvise in systems that deny their realities.

Disability and Menopause: Compounded Barriers
For women with disabilities, menopause often intersects with existing barriers to care. Clinics may not be physically accessible. Doctors may assume that reproductive health is irrelevant if a woman has never had children. Cognitive disabilities may complicate symptom reporting, leading to dismissal or neglect.

Consider the woman with cerebral palsy experiencing hot flushes that intensify muscle spasticity, or the woman with Down syndrome navigating early menopause (a common occurrence). These stories are rarely included in clinical trials, training, or policy documents. Their invisibility reveals how menopause reform must extend beyond "average" narratives.

Sexuality and Stigma
Menopause has long been entangled with sexual stigma. The assumption that women become "asexual" after menopause remains pervasive. This narrative erases the desires of older women and undermines their right to sexual health care. Urogenital symptoms such as dryness or pain are often ignored, framed as inevitable rather than treatable.

For women already marginalised by ageism, racism, or disability, this stigma multiplies. To be seen as both undesirable and invisible is to be stripped of sexual agency at the very stage of life when many women reclaim it.

Silence in Communities of Faith

Religious and cultural frameworks add further complexity. In some faith traditions, menstruation itself is stigmatised, making menopause either taboo or celebrated. For some Muslim women, the end of menstruation changes rules of religious practice (such as fasting or prayer exemptions), shifting both ritual and identity. In some Christian or Hindu contexts, menopause may be framed as loss of fertility, a moral and social diminishment.

These interpretations can create silence within communities, where women fear judgment if they speak openly about symptoms. When combined with systemic neglect in healthcare, stigma compounds, leaving women isolated at precisely the moment they need solidarity.

Action Asset: Intersectional Stigma Map

Identity Dimension	Unique Challenges	Common Stigmas	Systemic Barriers
LGBTQ+	Lack of tailored care, invisibility in guidelines	"Menopause is heterosexual, cisgender only"	Forms, language, clinical assumptions
Trans men/ Non-binary	Navigating symptoms outside gendered frameworks	"Not real women, so not relevant"	Endocrinology gaps, cultural erasure
Disability	Access barriers, early menopause risk	"Not sexual, so irrelevant"	Clinics not accessible, poor training

Identity Dimension	Unique Challenges	Common Stigmas	Systemic Barriers
Older women	Sexual health ignored	"Asexual after menopause"	Lack of funding for postmenopausal sexuality
Faith communities	Religious framing as loss or taboo	"Not to be spoken of"	Silence reinforced by cultural/religious rules

Toward Inclusive Menopause Care
Stigma thrives where systems are blind. To build equity, menopause care must expand to reflect diversity:

- **Inclusion in medical training**: LGBTQ+ experiences, disability-specific needs, and cultural sensitivities must be taught alongside mainstream menopause care.
- **Inclusive language:** Clinical forms and workplace policies must acknowledge diverse identities.
- **Representation:** Public campaigns must show not just the white, middle-class "default woman," but a spectrum of women and gender-diverse people navigating menopause with dignity.

Menopause is not one story. It is many. To honour them all, reform must dismantle stigma at every intersection of identity.

Geography and Access

Where a woman lives often matters as much as her biology. Geography dictates whether she has access to specialist care, reliable information, or even the basic language to name her experience. Urban or rural, wealthy or developing nation, place shapes menopause profoundly.

Urban Advantage, Rural Neglect

In metropolitan areas, women may at least find menopause clinics, gynaecologists, or trained general practitioners. Even here, care can be inconsistent, but infrastructure exists. In rural and remote areas, the story changes.

Australia: Women in remote communities may travel hundreds of kilometres to see a GP, let alone a menopause specialist. Telehealth has improved access somewhat, but patchy internet coverage and the cost of private consults remain barriers. Indigenous women, in particular, face a double bind of cultural safety and geographic distance.

United States: Rural clinics often lack gynaecologists. Women rely on overworked primary care providers who may have little training in menopause management. Add health insurance gaps, and access becomes a postcode lottery.

United Kingdom: NHS services are stretched. While urban areas may offer menopause hubs, rural women often face long waiting lists or travel burdens that make care inaccessible.

Global North vs. Global South
The inequities widen further across continents.
Global North: While underfunded, menopause is at least part of public conversation in the U.K., U.S., Canada, and Australia. Media coverage, parliamentary debates, and employer policies are beginning to shift awareness.

Global South: In many low- and middle-income countries, menopause is barely acknowledged in public health frameworks. Maternal health often consumes the limited resources available for women's health. Reproductive life is understood as beginning and ending with childbirth; menopause is treated as irrelevant.

Case Study 20: India
In India, research shows that women enter menopause earlier (average age around 46) compared to Western countries. Yet menopause is rarely addressed in medical curricula. Rural women often lack access to basic gynaecological services, and stigma around discussing reproductive health silences conversation. The result is untreated symptoms compounded by cultural taboos.

Case Study 21: Sub-Saharan Africa
In Sub-Saharan Africa, where health systems are already burdened with infectious diseases, menopause is seen as a luxury concern. Public health policy prioritises maternal mortality, HIV, and malaria. Women past childbearing age fall off the agenda entirely. Yet life expectancy is rising, meaning millions of women are living longer in a health system that has not prepared for their needs.

Migration and Displacement
Geography is also about movement. Migrant women often face the double challenge of navigating menopause in a new cultural and healthcare context. Language barriers, insecure employment, and lack of insurance create additional hurdles. For refugees and displaced women,

menopause is rarely considered in humanitarian aid. Camps distribute menstrual products but rarely provide resources for post-reproductive health.

Action Asset: Geography Gap Index

Context	Access to Care	Common Barriers	Cultural Framing
Urban, Global North	Moderate - High	Cost, waiting times, stigma	Increasing visibility
Rural, Global North	Low-Moderate	Distance, lack of specialists	Silence, patchy services
Global South (urban)	Low-Moderate	Underfunded systems, stigma	Menopause not prioritised
Global South (rural)	Very Low	No infrastructure, cultural taboo	Irrelevant or unspeakable
Migrants/Refugees	Very Low	Language, status, no targeted care	Displacement, invisibility

Infrastructure as Destiny

Geography is destiny when it comes to menopause. The same hot flush in Sydney may lead to an HRT prescription within weeks; in Sub-Saharan Africa, it may lead to silence and resignation. The same brain fog in London may be framed as perimenopause; in rural India, it may be dismissed as witchcraft or madness.

Toward Equity in Geography and Menopause

Equity requires structural solutions:

- **Telehealth expansion** with cultural and linguistic accessibility.
- **Training programs** for rural and frontline health workers.
- **Inclusion of menopause** in global public health priorities, alongside maternal health.
- **Aid and humanitarian policies** that recognise post-reproductive health as a legitimate need.

Menopause is not a Western luxury. It is a global reality. Until geography no longer dictates whether women suffer in silence or receive care, the system will remain inequitable.

Intersectionality in Action

Menopause is not a single story. It is a convergence of many forces, biology, identity, class, culture, race, and geography. Intersectionality, the framework pioneered by Kimberlé Crenshaw, shows us that oppression is not additive but compounding. To be poor and menopausal is not simply to face poverty + menopause. To be a Black woman navigating menopause is not simply to face racism + menopause. At the intersections, new forms of disadvantage, and sometimes new forms of resilience, emerge.

The Limits of Single-Issue Lenses

Policy often isolates problems: "workplace equity" over here, "healthcare access" over there, "cultural inclusion" in another silo. But women do not live in silos. A migrant cleaner in a rural town does not experience menopause as just a health issue, or just a workplace issue, or just a cultural issue. She experiences all of them at once, in ways that no single policy can capture unless designed with intersectionality at its core.

Lived Example 1: The Migrant Worker

María is a 48-year-old Latina cleaner in Texas. She works nights, with no health insurance, in a job that offers no paid sick leave. She has hot flushes that drench her uniform and insomnia that leaves her exhausted before every shift. When she finally sees a doctor, the consultation is rushed. Language barriers mean she cannot explain her symptoms fully, and she leaves with an antidepressant script she does not trust. Here, race, class, geography, and migration status converge, leaving her invisible in every framework.

Lived Example 2: The Rural Indigenous Elder

Aunty May, a 54-year-old Indigenous woman in outback Australia, frames menopause as "no more bleeding," a phrase that reflects cultural acceptance. Yet she must travel hours to the nearest clinic, where the doctor dismisses her symptoms as "stress." She leaves without support. Her cultural narrative preserves dignity, but systemic neglect undermines her health. Intersectionality reveals how geography, race, and colonial legacies intersect with menopause.

Lived Example 3: The Corporate Executive

Claudia, a 52-year-old white executive in Sydney, experiences brain fog and hot flushes during board meetings. But she has private health insurance, a GP trained in menopause, and a workplace that allows flexible hours. She receives HRT, talks openly with her team, and continues to thrive. Her story is not one of erasure but of privilege at the intersection of race, class, and geography.

Together, these narratives reveal the spectrum: from thriving to surviving, depending on where the intersections fall.

Systemic Blind Spots

Intersectionality reveals not only individual struggle but systemic blind spots:

- **Research**: Clinical trials rarely stratify by race, class, or geography, erasing intersectional data.
- **Workplace policies**: Often assume white-collar roles, ignoring the realities of casual and blue-collar workers.
- **Cultural narratives**: Elevate Western voices while sidelining Indigenous, migrant, or non-Western perspectives.

Without intersectional design, policies perpetuate inequity even as they claim reform.

Action Asset: The Intersectional Matrix

Axis	Privilege Example	Disadvantage Example	Intersectional Effect
Race	White women's experiences centralised in research	Black women's symptoms dismissed	Misdiagnosis, exclusion from treatment norms
Class	White-collar workplaces with flexible policies	Blue-collar jobs with rigid rosters	Unequal ability to cope at work

Axis	Privilege Example	Disadvantage Example	Intersectional Effect
Geography	Urban access to specialists	Rural clinic scarcity	Distance + cost = delayed or absent care
Identity	Cisgender, heterosexual assumed in care	LGBTQ+ invisibility in guidelines	Lack of safe, affirming menopause care

The "intersectional effect" is not simply cumulative; it is compounding. Each axis sharpens the inequities of the others.

Why Intersectionality Must Guide Reform

Without intersectionality, menopause reform will replicate the very hierarchies it seeks to dismantle. Policies designed for "the average woman" will serve those already privileged, leaving others behind. Intersectionality demands that reform begin at the margins, centring the experiences of women of colour, women in poverty, women with disabilities, LGBTQ+ and gender-diverse people, and those in rural or global south contexts.

When we design for those most marginalised, systems become better for all. When we only design for the privileged, inequity persists.

Toward Equity, Policy and Practice Recommendations

Intersectional analysis without action is just diagnosis. If culture, class, race, and systemic inequities shape menopause differently for every woman, then the reforms we build must be equally nuanced. This final section sets out how equity can be operationalised, not as rhetoric, but as practice.

1. Health Systems: From Uniformity to Equity
- Mandatory Inclusion in Research

Clinical trials must stratify by sex *and* by race, class, and geography. NIH, NHMRC, and WHO funding rules should require demographic diversity in menopause research.

- Training for Equity

Medical education should teach how menopause manifests differently across populations, including Indigenous women, women of colour, migrant women, and those with chronic illness or disability.

- Access Beyond Cities

Rural telehealth hubs, mobile clinics, and culturally safe outreach programs must become non-negotiable.

2. Workplace Reform: Designing for Diversity
- Policy Expansion

Menopause leave and flexible arrangements should be written into legislation, with protections for both white-collar and blue-collar roles.

- Manager Training with Intersectional Lens

Supervisors must be taught that a factory worker, a nurse, and a corporate executive may face different barriers, and responses must be tailored accordingly.

- Equity Audits

Workplaces should collect and analyse data on absenteeism, attrition, and promotion by age, sex, race, and class, exposing inequities for targeted intervention.

3. Government: Building Structural Equity
- National Menopause Strategies

Modeled on mental health and cancer frameworks, these should include measurable targets, public awareness

campaigns, and funding streams specifically tied to equity outcomes.
•   Legal Recognition
Anti-discrimination law must name menopause explicitly, preventing women from having to rely on disability categories that stigmatise or misfit their realities.

•   Funding Priorities
Budgets should weight funding toward communities with highest inequity: rural, Indigenous, migrant, and low-income women.

4. Culture: Shifting the Narrative for All
•   Representation Matters
Media must feature diverse stories of menopause, not just celebrity voices, but migrant mothers, Indigenous elders, working-class women, and LGBTQ+ people.

•   Education as Normalisation
School health programs should teach menopause as a universal transition, framed with cultural and historical variation, so that shame does not pass to the next generation.

•   Public Rituals and Recognition
Community organisations can create ceremonies, story-sharing spaces, and public art projects that celebrate menopause as a life passage.

5. Global Collaboration: A Shared Mandate
•   South-to-South Exchange
Countries in the Global South can share indigenous and community-led models of menopause care, often richer in holistic and cultural respect.

•   Global Guidelines
WHO and UN Women should publish global menopause equity guidelines, integrating health, workplace, and cultural reforms.
•   Funding Mechanisms

International donors should tie development aid to programs that include menopause health, ensuring that global women's health is not defined only by fertility and maternal care.

The Menopause Equity Checklist

For governments, employers, and health systems, equity must move from vision to implementation. This checklist provides a starting point:

☐   Does your health system recognise menopause in diagnostic frameworks (DSM, ICD)?

☐   Are medical students taught menopause management across diverse populations?

☐   Do workplace policies explicitly name menopause as a protected health category?

☐   Are managers trained to respond to intersectional differences in experience?

☐   Does your national budget include funding for menopause clinics, rural access, and culturally safe programs?

☐   Do your public health campaigns represent diverse women, not just the privileged?

☐   Are community-led and Indigenous models of care embedded into policy design?

Where the answer is "no," inequity persists. Where the answer becomes "yes," dignity is restored.
From Margins to Mandate

The menopausal journey is not only biological. It is cultural, social, economic, and political. For centuries, medicine shrank women's truths to fit frameworks built for men. Policy ignored the costs. Workplaces looked away. Culture whispered or mocked. And women themselves carried the weight in silence.

Intersectionality unmasks the reality: menopause is not one story but many, shaped by class, race, geography, sexuality, and systemic inequities. The challenge before us is to build reforms that do not erase these differences but design for them.

Equity is not charity. It is competence. It is justice. And it is achievable. With intersectional reform, menopause can shift from a hidden fault line of inequity to a model of systemic fairness. In rewriting the books, medical, workplace, governmental, and cultural, we not only restore dignity to women at midlife, we create systems that are better for everyone.

From Inequity to Mandate

Menopause is not a single story but a kaleidoscope of experiences refracted through culture, class, race, sexuality, and geography. For too long, medicine, policy, and culture have treated it as peripheral, or worse, erased it altogether. The cost of that erasure is not only medical misdiagnosis but also economic loss, cultural silence, and existential harm carried by women themselves.

This chapter has shown how inequity multiplies:
- When clinical trials treat women as "too complicated," poor women, Indigenous women, and women of colour are excluded most of all.
- When workplaces improvise without policy, senior executives may quietly negotiate, while factory workers or nurses are penalised in pay, promotion, or employment security.
- When culture makes menopause unspeakable, privilege buys private solutions while marginalised women absorb the stigma.

The journey is profoundly unequal, yet the solutions are profoundly clear. Equity requires deliberate design: rewriting medical texts to include menopause, embedding intersectionality into workplace law, funding rural and culturally safe care, and reshaping cultural narratives so that silence no longer defines the midlife years.

At its heart, this is not only a medical issue but a justice issue. Every woman deserves to experience menopause without shame, without misdiagnosis, and without penalty. The mandate is to build systems that meet women where they are, across cultures, across classes, across the globe.

This chapter has mapped the inequities. The chapters that follow will move from diagnosis to prescription: **practical resources, Tools, and frameworks that translate awareness into action.**

The Closing Manifesto

Menopause is not decline.
It is not an illness.
It is not a private weakness.
Menopause is a mandate.

1. This Is Not Private, This Is Public
For centuries, we were told to whisper it. We were told to cope in kitchens, cry in bathrooms, and resign quietly when our symptoms became unbearable. But there is no private escape from a reality that touches half the world.

When billions of women live it, when every workplace feels it, when every family is touched by it, menopause is not private. It is public.

And what is public demands policy.

2. This Is Not a Phase, This Is a Movement
Menopause is not a temporary inconvenience. It is not a brief storm in the middle of life. It is a structural fault line, exposing the cracks in medicine, workplaces, and culture.

Every time a woman is misdiagnosed, every time she is laughed at in the staffroom, every time she is prescribed antidepressants instead of hormone therapy, that is not a phase. That is systemic failure.

And failure this widespread demands a movement.

3. From Silence to System Change
The pattern is older than us.

- Breast cancer once hid in shame, now pink ribbons cover the globe.
- HIV/AIDS was once a death sentence, now activism rewrote medicine.
- Maternal death was once "fate", now it is counted, monitored, and prevented.

Menopause is next.

The whisper has become a roar.
 The roar is becoming a movement.
And movements change systems.

4. A Mandate for Justice
Menopause is not about mood swings or hot flushes alone.
It is about justice.

- **Justice in health**: Women deserve doctors who listen, clinics that treat, research that reflects reality.
- **Justice in workplaces**: Women deserve policies that keep them in leadership, flexibility that respects their bodies, dignity that dismantles shame.
- **Justice in culture**: Women deserve language that honours transition, stories that prepare daughters, narratives that celebrate wisdom.

Justice is not charity. It is not kindness. It is recognition of what is owed.

5. The Call to Governments, Workplaces, and Medicine
We demand:
- National strategies for menopause health.
- Mandatory GP training.
- Funded clinics in every state.
- Workplace policies that protect, not punish.
- Research dollars that match the scale of the issue.

We demand nothing more radical than equity.

If half the world experiences it, then half the world deserves recognition.

6. The Call to Women
Movements are not built by institutions. They are built by voices.

To every woman who has carried shame: speak.

To every worker who has hidden symptoms: share.
To every daughter who has inherited silence: break it.
To every grandmother who endured alone: tell your story.

When we speak, the world shifts.
 When we roar, the system bends.

7. Rhythm of the Manifesto
This is not decline.
This is power.

This is not silence.
This is speech.

This is not shame.
This is solidarity.

This is not private.
This is political.

This is not a phase.
This is a movement.

8. The Future We Claim
If we succeed, the next generation will not carry suitcases of
spare clothes in silence. They will not eat lunch in cars to
hide their symptoms. They will not quit boardrooms
because they cannot name what is happening to them.

They will inherit a world where menopause is taught in
schools, recognised in workplaces, supported in clinics, and
spoken of with pride.

That is the future we claim.

9. The Last Word
Menopause is not the end of fertility. It is the beginning of
power.

Power to reclaim health.
Power to demand justice.

Power to build movements.

This is our moment.
This is our mandate.
This is our movement.

This book closes where it began: with the recognition that menopause is not marginal, not private, and not optional to ignore. It is central to the health of nations, the productivity of workplaces, and the dignity of half the population. Policymakers must legislate it, workplaces must integrate it, clinicians must be trained in it, and women must be free to live it without shame. The purpose of this work is simple: to replace silence with systems, stigma with equity, and neglect with justice. For the next generation, menopause should not be endured in fragments of resilience, but embraced within the full architecture of reform and reclamation. That is the mandate. That is the promise. And that is the future we can, and must, build.

Real Things

That Make a Real Difference

1.

The Real Difference We Can Make

Menopause reform is not a niche health issue, it's a leadership, economic, and equity issue. This section translates the evidence, urgency, and opportunity into practical frameworks for government, boards, and workplaces. It moves beyond awareness toward measurable, systemic change.

2.
Strategic & Policy Reform Tools
(for Boards, Government, & Leaders)

Tool 1: Business Briefing Document

The following documents equips leaders, including CEOs, CHROs, and boards, with a clear, data-driven case for menopause reform at work.

It is designed for inclusion in board packs, executive meetings, and HR strategy reviews to support practical, evidence-based decision-making.

Its purpose is threefold:

6. To demonstrate the economic, legal, and cultural risks of inaction.
7. To position menopause reform as a **strategic opportunity** for retention, engagement, and equity.
8. To provide **actionable steps** that leaders can take immediately to build a more inclusive, resilient, and future-ready workforce.

Executive Summary

For decades, menopause has been treated as a private matter, something to be endured quietly, often hidden behind closed doors.

But the truth is unavoidable: menopause is a workplace issue, a leadership issue, and ultimately a business issue.

Women in midlife are often at the height of their professional expertise, influence, and leadership power. They are the senior managers, technical experts, and strategic thinkers who hold institutional knowledge and mentor emerging talent.

When these women experience unmanaged symptoms, insomnia, anxiety, brain fog, or fatigue, and feel unsupported at work, the impact ripples through the entire organisation.

Their departure, disengagement, or diminished performance is not just a personal tragedy. It is an organisational failure with measurable cost, cultural impact, and reputational risk.

Businesses that fail to act risk:

• Losing their most experienced leaders and future mentors.
• Weakening their diversity, equity, and inclusion (DEI) commitments.
• Incurring preventable costs in recruitment, training, and lost productivity.
• Damaging brand and reputation in an increasingly competitive talent market.

The time for silence has passed.

Menopause must be recognised for what it is, a predictable, manageable, and measurable business issue that demands board-level attention.

Why Menopause Matters Now

- Nearly half of all employees will experience menopause during their careers, often at the exact time they are most valuable to the organisation.
- In Australia alone, menopause is estimated to cost $10 billion annually in lost productivity.
- Ignoring menopause creates financial, cultural, and reputational risk, undermining gender equity, retention, and leadership pipelines.

Menopause is not a "personal problem", it is a predictable workforce reality that can be addressed through intelligent policy, awareness, and leadership.

Organisations that take menopause seriously are not just "doing the right thing." They are protecting their bottom line, strengthening their DEI strategy, and demonstrating that they value experienced women as key to organisational success.

The Cost of Inaction

When menopause goes unrecognised, the organisational impact is cumulative and costly.

Absenteeism & Presenteeism:

- Women can lose more than 32 workdays annually through absenteeism or reduced productivity caused by unmanaged symptoms.
- Presenteeism, being physically at work but mentally and physically depleted, costs businesses more than absenteeism itself.

Turnover:

One in four women consider leaving or reducing their workload due to unmanaged menopause symptoms or lack of workplace understanding. Replacing a senior woman can cost 150-200 % of her salary, including recruitment, onboarding, lost productivity, and institutional knowledge.

Reputation & Risk:

Organisations that fail to act risk falling behind on DEI, ESG, and gender equity benchmarks, opening themselves to criticism from employees, investors, and the public.

The question for leadership is not *"Can we afford to act?"* but *"Can we afford not to?"*

The Case for Action

Proactive organisations are embedding menopause support into their policies and culture, and the returns are tangible.

- **Talent Retention:** Retain senior women who are essential to mentoring, innovation, and leadership continuity.
- **DEI Alignment:** Demonstrate a lived commitment to diversity and inclusion by supporting women through all life stages.
- **Productivity Gains:** Even small adjustments, such as flexible start times, environmental modifications, or

awareness training, reduce absenteeism and improve engagement.

- **Employer Brand:** Progressive employers are increasingly judged by how they support their workforce through predictable health transitions. Menopause awareness signals respect, empathy, and modern leadership, key attributes for attracting future talent.

Cost-Benefit Analysis

Impact Area	Cost of Inaction	Benefit of Action
Absenteeism	Lost productivity valued at millions annually.	Reduced sick leave and higher presenteeism.
Retention	Recruitment, training, and onboarding costs for replacements.	Retained knowledge, lower churn, and leadership stability.
Engagement	Disengaged staff reduce team cohesion and innovation.	Higher morale, creativity, and stronger leadership pipelines.
Reputation	Missed DEI/ESG benchmarks, public scrutiny, reputational harm.	Positive brand reputation, compliance, and investor confidence.

A modest investment in awareness, policy, and support programs yields significant financial and cultural returns.

The Economic Case

The cost of doing nothing is immense.

Menopause-related absenteeism, presenteeism, and early retirements silently drain billions from national economies. Yet the cost of acting, awareness sessions, flexible work policies, temperature control measures, or manager training, is minimal by comparison.

When senior women remain in the workforce longer, businesses benefit from:

- Continued access to expertise and leadership.
- Lower recruitment and training expenses.
- Greater innovation through diverse thinking and stable leadership teams.

Investing in menopause support is not an expense; it is a long-term value multiplier.

The Legal Case

The legal environment is evolving rapidly.

- In the United Kingdom, tribunals have ruled that menopause symptoms can fall under the Equality Act 2010, creating legal precedent for claims of sex, age, and disability discrimination.
- In Australia, menopause is not yet explicitly recognised in the Fair Work Act, but advocacy is intensifying, and public sentiment is shifting.

Forward-thinking organisations are acting now, not waiting for regulation.

By embedding menopause into workplace health, safety, and inclusion policies, they are future-proofing themselves against litigation and demonstrating governance maturity.

The Human Capital Case

Beyond economics and compliance lies the human imperative.

Menopause is a diversity and leadership issue at its core.

- **Diversity & Inclusion:** Ignoring menopause undermines any claim to gender equity. Supporting it ensures women are not penalised for natural biological transitions.
- **Leadership Pipeline:** Losing midlife women erodes succession planning, mentorship capacity, and executive gender balance.
- **ESG & Reputation:** Investors, regulators, and employees now assess how organisations care for their people. Menopause belongs squarely in the "S" (Social) of ESG reporting.

Supporting menopause is not a benefit program or a wellness perk. It is an **investment in leadership stability, culture, and long-term competitiveness**.

Three Boardroom Talking Points

1. "We cannot afford to ignore the $10 billion problem." Acting now retains our most valuable leaders and protects organisational performance.
2. "Menopause belongs in our DEI and ESG agenda." It is a measurable, reportable commitment to equality and good governance.
3. "This is a competitive advantage." Early adopters will attract, retain, and promote the next generation of senior women.

These talking points can be integrated into board papers, risk reports, and diversity reviews to anchor menopause in executive decision-making.

Next Steps for Leaders

To move from awareness to action, boards and executives should:

1. **Commission a Workplace Policy Review**: Assess current health, wellbeing, and inclusion policies for menopause coverage and gaps.
2. **Request an HR Roadmap**: Ensure your People & Culture function develops a timeline for policy development, manager training, and reporting integration.
3. **Integrate Menopause Metrics**: Include menopause-related retention, absenteeism, and engagement indicators in annual DEI and workforce wellbeing reports.
4. **Engage Expert Support**: Partner with subject-matter specialists and advocates, such as Julie Dimmick, to guide design, communication, and implementation.
5. **Report Progress Publicly**: Add menopause commitments to ESG statements, sustainability reports, and internal communications to build trust and visibility.

Board & ESG Dashboard – Key Metrics Block

Metric	Description / KPI Focus	Reporting Cadence
Workforce Awareness	% trained in menopause awareness or wellbeing programs.	Quarterly
Retention & Progression	Retention of women aged 45–60; representation in management.	Biannually

Metric	Description / KPI Focus	Reporting Cadence
Policy & Adjustments	Menopause policy adoption and workplace adjustments count.	Annual review
Health & Engagement	Wellbeing survey scores for women aged 40+.	Biannual survey
ESG & DEI Integration	Menopause metrics in ESG or gender-equality statements.	Annual report

Note: Boards may align these measures with Workplace Gender Equality Agency (WGEA) and ESG disclosure frameworks for national consistency.

Menopause is not a temporary inconvenience, it is a permanent feature of the human workforce. Treating it as a core business issue aligns with every principle of responsible leadership: fiscal prudence, equity, and care.

By recognising menopause as both a health and a leadership priority, organisations can retain experience, uphold their values, and set the benchmark for 21st-century governance.

Menopause belongs in the boardroom, not as an afterthought, but as a measure of how seriously an organisation takes its people.

Tool 2: How to Launch in 90 Days – Executive Roadmap

Day 0 – Commitment

- Secure CEO and Board endorsement for menopause inclusion within DEI strategy.
- Nominate an executive sponsor and form a cross-functional working group (HR, Safety, Comms, Legal).

Day 30 – Foundation

- Draft and circulate a menopause policy template.
- Identify training providers or internal champions for awareness delivery.

Day 60 – Implementation

- Launch internal awareness campaign (email, intranet, manager briefings).
- Begin baseline data collection on demographics, leave patterns, and turnover.

Day 90 – Integration & Reporting

- Integrate menopause KPIs into People & Culture dashboards.

- Deliver first update to ELT or Board and confirm ongoing review cadence.

Bottom line: Launching menopause reform in 90 days is achievable when accountability, communication, and measurement are embedded from the start.

Tool 3: Executive Briefing One-Pager

Hot Flush, Cold Truth: Menopause in the Workplace, Boardroom Briefing

Why It Matters
- 1 billion women will be post-menopausal by 2030.[1]
- Symptoms affect productivity, wellbeing, and career progression.
- Ignoring menopause drains billions from economies in absenteeism and attrition.

The Risks
- Loss of senior female talent.
- Reputational harm: failure to deliver true gender equity.
- Legal exposure as tribunals expand menopause protections.

The Business Case
- Cost of replacing senior leaders: 150-200% of salary.
- Cost of support: minimal compared to retention benefits.
- ROI: better retention, higher engagement, stronger pipelines.

Recommended Actions
1. Adopt a menopause policy.
2. Train managers to recognise and support symptoms.
3. Offer flexible work and workplace adjustments.
4. Ensure health benefits cover menopause care.
5. Integrate menopause into DEI and ESG reporting.

Menopause is not charity. It is business strategy. Acting now protects talent, reduces risk, and strengthens leadership.

Menopause as an Investment

Source: *The Demography of Menopause* (ScienceDirect), projection to 1.2 billion menopausal/postmenopausal women by 2030

For too long, menopause has been written out of the workplace script. The result has been wasted talent, lost productivity, and broken leadership pipelines. Businesses that continue this silence will pay the price in attrition, litigation, and reputational harm.

But the opposite is also true: organisations that act now will gain a competitive advantage. Supporting menopause is not a cost. It is an investment in retention, leadership, and equity, one that pays measurable returns.

Menopause belongs in the boardroom, in briefing papers, and in the governance frameworks that shape the future of work. The time to rewrite is now

Tool 4: Policy Reform Service Offering

Purpose: To equip policymakers, health leaders, and organisations with a practical blueprint for embedding menopause reform across healthcare, workplaces, and society. This Tool translates advocacy into action, ensuring reform is both measurable and achievable.

Policy Reform Service Offering: At a Glance

Category	Focus	Examples / Actions
Levels of Reform	• **Federal:** funding, national health strategies • **State:** training mandates, clinical service expansion • **Organisational:** workplace policies, education programs	**Federal:** Integrate menopause into National Women's Health Strategy; fund research and specialist clinics. **State:** Mandate GP/nurse training; expand specialist clinics; partner with unions/industries. **Organisational:** Develop policies, flexible work, annual education sessions, embed in DEI.
Sample Policy Clauses	Workplace, healthcare, and education policy language	• "Employers shall provide menopause education sessions annually." • "Health funding models will support specialist menopause clinics." • "Medical schools shall include menopause as a

Category	Focus	Examples / Actions
		core curriculum component."
Frameworks	90-180-365 Reform Roadmap	**First 90 Days:** Commission reviews, consult stakeholders, draft workplace templates. **First 180 Days:** Table reforms, launch pilots, integrate training. **First 365 Days:** Expand programs, roll out public awareness, establish annual reporting.

Policy Reform Service Offering – From Overview to Action
The table above provides a high-level snapshot of where reform must occur: at **federal, state, and organisational levels**; through policy clauses that embed menopause into systems; and by following a structured 90-180-365 roadmap.

What follows is the expanded framework. Here, each level of reform is unpacked with objectives and key actions. Sample policy clauses are provided to give policymakers and leaders ready-to-use language. Finally, the reform roadmap translates vision into timelines, ensuring that change moves from aspiration to measurable impact.

Tool 5: Strategy → Policy → Practice (S→P→P)

This framework provides pathways for embedding menopause in government, health, and workplace policy.

Policy Reform Service Offering

Menopause reform cannot be left to chance, nor to piecemeal efforts that depend on the persistence of individual women. It requires coordinated action across all levels of society, from federal and state governments to workplaces and community organisations.

In Australia, the policy foundations for such reform already exist within key national and state frameworks. These include workplace, equality, and health legislation that provide both the legal and strategic basis for menopause-inclusive reform.

Policy Foundations and References[2]

Policy / Framework	Purpose & Relevance	Official Source
Fair Work Act 2009 (Cth)	Provides the legal framework for *reasonable adjustments* and protection from discrimination on the basis of sex, age, or disability, relevant for menopause-related workplace	https://www.legislation.gov.au/Series/C2009A00028

[2]Key references include the Fair Work Act 2009 (Cth), Workplace Gender Equality Act 2012 (Cth), and the National Women's Health Strategy 2020-2030 (Australian Government). See Appendix: References for complete source details and state pilot citations.

Policy / Framework	Purpose & Relevance	Official Source
	accommodations.	
Workplace Gender Equality Act 2012 (Cth)	Requires gender equality reporting for large employers; supports reforms linking menopause, retention, and leadership diversity.	https://www.legislation.gov.au/Series/C2012A00148
National Women's Health Strategy 2020-2030	Recognises menopause as a national women's health priority and calls for systemic workforce support.	https://www.health.gov.au/resources/publications/national-womens-health-strategy-2020-2030
State Pilot Programs (Victoria, NSW)	Early initiatives piloting menopause workplace policy templates and leadership engagement frameworks (2023-2024).	VIC: https://www.vic.gov.au/menopause-policy-pilot • NSW: https://www.nsw.gov.au/women-nsw/menopause-Tool kit

This service offering is designed as a practical blueprint for leaders who hold the levers of change. It distils the lessons of silence, stigma, and neglect into a set of actionable reforms that can be adopted and adapted immediately.

At its core, the message is simple: **menopause is not a private issue, it is a public priority.** By embedding menopause into policy, health systems, and organisational culture, we not only reduce the economic burden but also restore dignity, equity, and health to millions of women.

The following framework sets out the levels of reform, sample clauses, and a 90-180-365 roadmap to guide action.

This Policy Reform Service Offering is presented as a blueprint to inform discussion, strategy, and decision-making on menopause reform. It is designed to illustrate potential pathways, frameworks, and sample clauses that leaders may choose to adapt within their own context.

The material contained in this chapter does not replace medical advice, legal guidance, or professional consultancy. While every effort has been made to ensure accuracy and relevance, the author accepts no responsibility for decisions or outcomes arising from its application.

Implementation of any reform should be undertaken with appropriate consultation, evidence-based review, and advice from qualified professionals. The responsibility for adoption, adaptation, and execution rests solely with the reader, their organisation, and relevant governing authorities

1. Levels of Reform

Federal Reform
Objective: Establish national leadership and sustainable funding for menopause.
Key Actions:

- ☐ Integrate menopause into the National Women's Health Strategy
- ☐ Allocate ongoing funding for menopause research and specialist clinics.
- ☐ Mandate national data collection on midlife women's health outcomes.

State Reform
Objective: Deliver clinical and educational impact at the service delivery level.
Key Actions:
- ☐ Introduce mandatory menopause training in GP, nurse, and allied health curricula.
- ☐ Fund state-based specialist menopause clinics, with a priority on rural and remote access.
- ☐ Partner with unions and industries to implement workplace reform pilots.

Organisational Reform
Objective: Ensure workplaces and institutions provide direct, practical support for midlife women.
Key Actions:
- ☐ Develop formal menopause policies (leave, flexible work, accommodations).
- ☐ Deliver annual menopause education sessions for staff and managers.
- ☐ Embed menopause into diversity, equity, and inclusion (DEI) strategies.

2. Sample Policy Clauses
These clauses can be adopted directly or adapted to context:

- Workplace

"Employers shall provide menopause education sessions annually to all staff and managers as part of workplace health and wellbeing programs."

- Healthcare

"Health funding models will support the establishment and ongoing operation of specialist menopause clinics, ensuring equitable access across metropolitan, rural, and remote areas."

- Education

"Medical schools shall include menopause as a core curriculum component, with a minimum of X teaching hours dedicated to diagnosis, treatment, and care."

3. Framework: 90-180-365 Menopause Reform Roadmap

This roadmap provides a structured reform sequence for government, workplaces, and health systems to address menopause as a national health, equity, and workforce issue. It balances **short-term wins** with **long-term structural change**, ensuring momentum, visibility, and measurable outcomes.

First 90 Days - Foundation and Momentum
The first quarter focuses on **evidence-gathering, coalition building, and immediate action signals**. These early steps establish legitimacy, bring diverse voices to the table, and set the tone for reform.

Commission a National/State Review of Menopause Care Gaps
- Mandate an independent, evidence-based inquiry into healthcare access, workforce participation, and economic impacts.
- Include rural, First Nations, CALD (culturally and linguistically diverse), and vulnerable populations to ensure equity lenses are embedded.

Launch Stakeholder Consultations
- Conduct structured roundtables and listening sessions with women, unions, clinicians, HR leaders, employers, and advocacy groups.
- Begin mapping shared priorities and policy levers.

Develop and Circulate Standard Workplace Policy Templates
- Publish model HR policies for immediate uptake (leave provisions, flexible work, environmental adjustments).

- Provide "plug-and-play" policy kits for SMEs and government departments.

Symbolic Action for Visibility
- Introduce a ministerial statement, press release, or national pledge signalling menopause as a **health and workplace reform priority**.

Tool 6: First 180 Days - Embedding Reforms into Systems

By six months, reforms move from consultation into **structural change and pilot programs**, proving that reform is real, achievable, and scalable.

Table Reforms in Parliament or State Assembly
- Introduce legislation or amendments covering workplace equity, healthcare inclusion, and national reporting obligations.
- Include menopause as a category in gender equity, workforce participation, and occupational health frameworks.

Pilot Menopause Clinics and Workplace Trials
- Launch specialist menopause clinics in key metropolitan and regional hubs.
- Partner with major employers and unions to test workplace menopause policies (e.g., leave, flexible hours, environmental supports).
- Collect data on health outcomes, retention, absenteeism, and staff satisfaction.

Integrate Menopause into Accreditation and Training
- Require GP training modules on menopause as part of medical accreditation.
- Develop HR and managerial training modules for certification programs.
- Launch an e-learning portal for SMEs with free/low-cost training resources.

Public Engagement on Reform Progress
- Release a 6-month progress report to Parliament and the public.
- Highlight early success stories (e.g., women retained in the workforce, reduced health system strain).

Tool 7: First 365 Days

By the one-year mark, reforms should shift from **pilots to mainstreaming**, embedding menopause as a permanent feature of health and workplace systems.

Expand Specialist Clinics and Workplace Pilots into National Programs
- Increase the number of menopause clinics and embed them into women's health service networks.
- Scale up workplace reform from pilots into large employers, unions, and industry-wide agreements.

Roll Out a National Awareness Campaign
- Launch multimedia campaigns (TV, digital, workplace posters) to **normalise menopause** as a mainstream health and workforce issue.
- Partner with schools and community groups to shift intergenerational awareness and reduce stigma.

Establish National Annual Reporting
- Mandate annual reporting on menopause-related outcomes in:
  - **Health:** Access to specialist services, wait times, patient satisfaction.
  - **Workforce:** Retention, absenteeism, presenteeism, promotion pathways for women 45+.
  - **Equity:** Representation in leadership pipelines, gender pay gap impact, rural and First Nations outcomes.

Institutionalise Reform through Permanent Bodies
- Establish a national menopause council or advisory group to monitor and guide reform.
- Ensure bipartisan and cross-sectoral ownership so reforms endure political cycles.

Key Principles Across All Phases

- **Equity Lens:** Every reform action must address rural, Indigenous, culturally diverse, and socioeconomically disadvantaged groups.
- **Data-Driven:** Collect baseline and ongoing data to ensure reforms are measurable, comparable, and transparent.
- **Partnership-Oriented**: Government, employers, unions, clinicians, and women's lived experiences must remain at the centre.
- **Sustainability:** Design reforms that embed into existing systems, not short-term projects.

Tool 8: Example: Ministerial Letter

To: Ministers, Departmental Secretaries, and Senior Policy Advisors

From: Julie Dimmick, Author of Hot Flush, Cold Truth

Subject: Menopause Reform, A Public Health and Economic Priority

Dear Minister,

Menopause is not a marginal issue. It is a national health, workforce, and equity priority. By 2030, over 1 billion women worldwide will be post-menopausal, including millions of Australian women in their most productive working years. Yet our policy frameworks remain silent.

The consequences of inaction are measurable:

- **Health system strain:** women misdiagnosed, over-prescribed antidepressants, and under-supported with evidence-based care.
- **Workforce impact:** absenteeism, attrition, and premature retirement of senior women, draining national productivity.
- **Equity failure:** women disadvantaged in employment and health access due to systemic neglect.
- The cost is borne by individuals, families, workplaces, and the national economy. But with the right reforms, governments can turn this hidden crisis into a powerful lever for gender equity, productivity, and public health.

This briefing outlines a **Policy Reform Service Offering**, a framework of legislative, budgetary, and public health interventions to position our nation as a global leader in menopause policy.

Sincerely,

Julie Dimmick
Author of Hot Flush, Cold Truth

Disclaimer
This is a master template. Each Minister, Department, or portfolio will receive a tailored version that reflects their remit, current initiatives, jurisdictional settings, and the

latest data. The structure will remain consistent so decision makers can compare like for like. The core structure is:

- Executive summary and purpose
- Problem definition with quantified impacts
- Portfolio-specific risks and opportunities
- Recommended policy actions and budget signals
- 90-180-365 implementation roadmap
- Accountability, reporting, and measures of success
- References and data sources

Content is informational and does not constitute legal, medical, strategic, operational or financial advice. Figures and citations should be updated prior to submission for each recipient version. For verification or portfolio-specific evidence packs, contact Julie Dimmick.

The Menopause Policy Accelerator

A comprehensive national response must include:

Legislative Reform
- Amend workplace law to recognise menopause as a protected category.
- Embed menopause into anti-discrimination frameworks.

Health Reform
- Medicare/insurance coverage for menopause-specific care and treatment.
- National clinical guidelines for GPs and specialists.
- Training modules in medical and psychiatric education.

Workforce Reform
- Mandated menopause reporting under gender equity legislation.
- Public sector as model employer, with policies across all departments.

Public Awareness
- National campaigns normalising menopause as part of life, not decline.
- Education programs in schools to break the cycle of silence for the next generation.

Research Investment
- Dedicated funding streams for menopause research.
- Data collection to measure health outcomes, workforce impact, and economic cost.

Tool 9: The Menopause Policy Accelerator
Executive One-Pager

Purpose: Provide a national, practical pathway to menopause reform across law, health, workforce, awareness, and research.

Why it matters
- Universal: 100% of women who reach menopause will experience it.
- Costly: Significant productivity loss and avoidable health costs each year.
- Inequitable: Systemic disadvantage persists without explicit policy recognition.

The risks
- Misdiagnosis and over-prescription in primary care.
- Attrition of senior women and leadership pipeline loss.
- Rising exposure under anti-discrimination and WHS obligations.

The policy case
- Health: Reduce misdiagnosis and delays. Improve access to evidence-based care.
- Economy: Retain experienced women and protect productivity.
- Equity: Embed menopause in gender equity and workplace safety strategies.

Recommended reforms
- Legislation: Recognise menopause within workplace and anti-discrimination law.
- Health: National clinical guidelines for GPs and specialists. Medicare and insurer coverage for menopause-specific assessment and treatment. Training in medical and psychiatric education.
- Workforce: Public sector as model employer. Policy standards for adjustments. Reporting under gender equity frameworks.

- Awareness and education: National campaigns that normalise menopause. Age-appropriate school education to break the cycle of silence.
- Research and data: Dedicated funding streams. National indicators that track health outcomes, workforce impact, and economic cost.

90-180-365 implementation
- By 90 days: Establish Ministerial taskforce and expert panel. Issue draft clinical guideline outline. Publish model workplace policy and manager guide.
- By 180 days: Table legislative amendments. Release national awareness strategy. Begin GP and nurse training pilots in priority regions.
- By 365 days: Enact legislative changes. Publish final clinical guidelines. Expand training nationally. Launch public sector reporting. Release the first national menopause outcomes report.

Measures of success
- Reduction in time to accurate diagnosis.
- Uptake of evidence-based treatments.
- Retention and absenteeism trends for women 45+.
- Employer policy adoption rate and staff training coverage.
- Public awareness shift measured through annual survey.

Funding signals
- Targeted primary care item or equivalent coverage.
- Guideline development and professional education.
- National campaign and school curriculum resources.
- Research program and data infrastructure.

Governance and accountability
- Lead: Health portfolio in partnership with Women, Employment, and Education.
- Oversight: Interdepartmental taskforce with quarterly public updates.

- External input: Clinical bodies, industry, unions, and consumer groups.

Bottom line
Menopause reform is not optional. It is a public health, economic, and equity imperative. Governments that act will lead globally and deliver measurable gains in health and productivity.

3
Workplace Tools for HR, Managers, and Staff

Tool 10: Workplace Policy Template

Purpose: Provide HR leaders with a fill-in-the-blank template for adopting a menopause policy.

Template Structure:
   Policy Title: Menopause in the Workplace Policy
   Purpose: To support employees experiencing menopause and ensure equity and wellbeing at work.
   Scope: Applies to all employees.
   Policy Commitments:
   - Provide reasonable adjustments (flexible hours, temperature control, uniforms).
   - Offer annual menopause awareness training.
   - Promote a culture of openness and inclusion.

   Responsibilities:
   - Managers: respond sensitively and offer adjustments.
   - HR: maintain confidentiality and ensure policy compliance.

Review Cycle: Policy reviewed every 2 years.

Tool 11: Manager's Quick Reference Card

Supporting Employees Through Menopause

Purpose
To give managers a quick, practical guide for responding to menopause in the workplace with sensitivity, respect, and effectiveness.

✅ Do's	❌ Don'ts
Listen without judgement. **Ask:** "What support would help you?" **Offer** practical adjustments (flexible hours, breaks, workspace changes). **Refer** to HR or EAP if specialist support is needed.	Don't dismiss symptoms as "stress" or "just ageing." Don't make assumptions about capability or commitment. Don't break confidentiality.

Manager's Checklist
☐ Know your workplace menopause policy
☐ Adjust workloads or environments when requested.
☐ Model empathy and inclusion in team culture.

Managers play a frontline role. A supportive response doesn't just protect wellbeing, it boosts retention, engagement, and trust.

Supporting Employees Through Menopause

Purpose To give managers a quick, practical guide for responding to menopause in the workplace with sensitivity, respect, and effectiveness.

Do's
- Listen without judgement.
- Ask: What support would help you?"
- Offer practical adjustments (flexible hours, breaks, workspace changes).
- Refer to HR or EAP if specialist support is needed.

Don'ts
- Don't dismiss symptoms as "stress" or "just ageing."
- Don't make assumptions about capability or commitment.
- Don't break confidentiality.

Manager's Checklist
✓ Know your workplace menopause policy.
✓ Encourage safe, open conversations.
✓ Adjust workloads or environments when requested.

Bottom Line Managers play a frontline role. A supportive response doesn't just protect wellbeing – it boosts retention, engagement, and trust.

Tool 12: Employee Advocacy Tool kit

Purpose: Equip employees with language and templates to request support.

Scripts for HR/Manager Meetings
- "I'm experiencing menopause symptoms that affect my work. I'd like to explore adjustments that could help me perform at my best."
- "Flexible start times and access to a fan would make a real difference to my productivity."

Template Email
Dear [Manager/HR],

I am seeking adjustments to support my health during menopause. Suggested options include [flexible work, uniform adjustments, breaks]. I'd welcome a conversation to explore this further.

Regards, [Name]

Checklist of Rights
- ☐ Right to privacy and confidentiality.
- ☐ Right to reasonable workplace adjustments (aligned with DEI/anti-discrimination law).
- ☐ Right to request flexible work arrangements.

4.
Tools for Women: Advocacy and Empowerment

Personal Menopause Advocacy Tool kit

Purpose: Equip women to advocate for themselves.

Prepare for GP Visit
- Bring a symptom tracker.
- Questions: "Could this be perimenopause?" / "What are my treatment options?"
- Don't accept: "It's just stress."

Scripts for HR/Manager
- "I'd like to discuss adjustments that will help me work effectively during menopause."

Template Email
Dear [Manager]

I am requesting workplace adjustments to support my health during menopause. Options include [flexibility, breaks, uniform changes].

Regards, [Name]

Rights Checklist
- Privacy/confidentiality.
- Reasonable workplace adjustments.
- Non-discrimination.

Tool 13: *Self-Advocacy Quick Guide*

Purpose: A pocket reference for when your experience is dismissed, minimised, or misunderstood.

In the Doctor's Office
- **Doctor says:** "It's just stress."
→ **You can say:** "I'd like to discuss whether this could be perimenopause and review HRT or other evidence-based options."

- **Doctor says:** "You're too young for menopause."
→ **You can say:** "The average age of perimenopause onset is the mid-40s, but it can begin earlier. Can we check my hormone levels and symptoms?"

- **Doctor says:** "Symptoms will pass, it's natural."
→ **You can say:** "Natural doesn't mean I shouldn't be supported. I'd like to explore treatment options to improve my quality of life."

- **Doctor prescribes antidepressants without discussion.**
→ **You can say:** "Can we clarify whether these symptoms are menopause-related before treating them as depression?"

In the Workplace
- **HR says:** "We don't have a menopause policy."
→ **You can say:** "Other organisations do, I'd like to work together to create one here."

- **Manager says:** "We treat everyone the same."
→ **You can say:** "Fairness means recognising different needs. Menopause is a predictable workplace reality, and adjustments make inclusion possible."
- **Colleague says:** "It's just a personal issue."
→ **You can say:** "Menopause impacts work performance, retention, and wellbeing. Supporting it is a workplace responsibility, not a personal weakness."

With Family & Friends
- **Family minimises:** "It's just part of getting older."
→ **You can say:** "This is a medical transition. Support means listening without judgement, not dismissal."

- **Partner says:** "You're overreacting."
→ **You can say:** "Hormonal changes affect mood, sleep, and energy. I need empathy and shared solutions, not minimisation."

- **Friend jokes about hot flushes.**
→ **You can say:** "It's more than hot flushes, it affects my sleep, bones, and mind. I'd appreciate being taken seriously."

Bottom Line
- You have the right to ask for accurate medical care, workplace adjustments, and family support.
- Clear, calm language can shift the conversation from dismissal to dialogue.
- Self-advocacy is not confrontation, it's claiming your space, your health, and your dignity.

Tool 14: Peer-to-Peer Conversation Guide

Purpose: To help women start safe, supportive discussions about menopause, with colleagues, friends, and family, and to create peer networks that reduce isolation.

Ice-Breakers: Opening the Conversation
Sometimes the hardest step is simply starting. These gentle prompts can help break the silence:

- "I've been struggling with sleep lately, have you noticed changes too?"
- "Do you ever get those sudden hot moments in meetings? I thought I was the only one."
- "I've been reading about menopause at work, it made me realise how many of us might be going through it together."
- "Would you be interested in starting a menopause lunch group or coffee chat?"
- "I saw an article about menopause and workplace policies. It made me wonder what support we have here."

Starting a Support Circle
A support circle doesn't need to be formal. It just needs to be safe, respectful, and consistent.

Steps to Begin:
1. Choose a space
   - Workplace: lunchroom, quiet office, or an online Teams/Slack channel.
   - Community: local café, library meeting room, or online group.
   - Private: small group chats via WhatsApp, Facebook, or Zoom.
2. Set the tone
   - Confidentiality is key: *"What we share here stays here."*
   - Respect every voice: no judgement, no one-upmanship.
   - Keep it inclusive: every experience matters, even if it's different.

3. Share resources
- Menopause symptom trackers, articles, podcasts, and recommended doctors.
- Policy templates or advocacy guides for workplace or healthcare discussions.

4. Rotate facilitation
- Each session, a different member can lead, ask a question, share a resource, or raise a topic.
- This keeps the group balanced and avoids one person carrying the load.

5. Keep it manageable
- Sessions don't need to be long, 30-45 minutes is enough.
- Meet monthly, or more often if needed.

Sharing with Family and Partners
Explaining menopause to loved ones helps turn misunderstanding into support.

Conversation Starters:
- "This isn't just about hot flushes. It affects mood, sleep, energy, I need your understanding."
- "I may be short-tempered or emotional sometimes. It's not you, it's the hormones. What I need most is patience."
- "Supporting me doesn't mean fixing it, it means listening and being there."
- "Let's learn together, would you read this article/watch this documentary with me?"

Tips for Keeping Conversations Safe and Supportive
- **Be open but set boundaries**: Share what you're comfortable with, nothing more.
- **Use humour carefully**: Laugh with each other, not at each other.
- **Acknowledge differences**: Every menopause journey is unique, avoid comparison.
- **Keep it solutions-focused**: It's not just about venting; it's about learning and supporting each other.

Bottom Line
Peer-to-peer conversations build solidarity. They remind women they're not alone, create collective confidence to advocate for change, and spread awareness through personal connection. One voice starts the dialogue; many voices spark the movement.

Tool 15: Menopause Symptom Tracker

How and Why to Use This Symptom Tracker
Menopause is not a single moment, it is a transition that unfolds differently for every woman. Symptoms can change daily, weekly, or over months, making them difficult to explain in a short medical appointment. Many women are dismissed or misdiagnosed because they cannot provide clear evidence of what they are experiencing.

The **Menopause Symptom Tracker** is designed to change that. By recording symptoms, severity, and impact over time, you create a detailed picture of your health that you can take to your GP, specialist, or workplace. This ensures your experiences are **seen, heard, and taken seriously**.

Why use it?
- **Clarity**: Identify patterns and triggers (e.g., stress, diet, sleep).
- **Confidence**: Speak to doctors and HR with evidence, not just memory.
- **Care**: Support better diagnosis, treatment, and adjustments.
- **Control**: Reclaim ownership of your menopause journey.

How to use it:
- Fill in daily or weekly logs, rating severity and noting triggers.
- Use the reflection section to summarise challenges and questions.
- Bring completed pages to medical appointments or HR meetings.

Bottom line: The tracker is your Tool for self-advocacy. It turns symptoms into data, and data into action.

MenoMap. *(tracker for women)*

Purpose: To help women document symptoms, identify patterns, and present clear evidence during medical appointments.

Daily/Weekly Log

Date	Symptom	Severity (1–10)	Frequency (Daily/Weekly)	Impact on Work/Life	Notes (Triggers, Sleep, Diet, Stress, Exercise)
	Hot flushes				
	Night sweats				
	Sleep disruption				
	Mood changes (irritability, anxiety, low mood)				

Date	Symptom	Severity (1-10)	Frequency (Daily/Weekly)	Impact on Work/Life	Notes (Triggers, Sleep, Diet, Stress, Exercise)
	Brain fog / concentration issues				
	Irregular/heavy/light bleeding				
	Joint or muscle pain				
	Headaches/migraines				
	Heart palpitations				

Date	Symptom	Severity (1-10)	Frequency (Daily/Weekly)	Impact on Work/Life	Notes (Triggers, Sleep, Diet, Stress, Exercise)
	Libido changes				
	Vaginal dryness / discomfort				
	Urinary changes (frequency, urgency, incontinence)				
	Skin/hair changes				

Date	Symptom	Severity (1-10)	Frequency (Daily/Weekly)	Impact on Work/Life	Notes (Triggers, Sleep, Diet, Stress, Exercise)
	Weight changes bloating				
	Fatigue				
	Chronic nausea / digestive upset				
	Hurting bones / joint pain				
	Anxiety / panic attacks				

Date	Symptom	Severity (1-10)	Frequency (Daily/Weekly)	Impact on Work/Life	Notes (Triggers, Sleep, Diet, Stress, Exercise)
	Other (specify)				
	TOTAL				

Symptom Severity Scale (Guide)
1-3 = Mild (noticeable but manageable).
4-6 = Moderate (affects daily tasks).
7-10 = Severe (disrupts life/work significantly).

Weekly Reflection
Biggest challenges this week:
_____
_____
_____
_____
_____

_____
_____
_____
_____
_____

Most helpful coping strategies:

_____
_____
_____
_____
_____
_____
_____
_____
_____

Triggers noticed (diet, stress, alcohol, caffeine, exercise):

_____
_____
_____
_____
_____
_____
_____
_____
_____

Questions to raise with GP/clinician:

_____
_____
_____
_____
_____
_____
_____
_____
_____

How to Use
- Track **daily** for detail, or **weekly** for overview.
- Bring completed pages to GP or specialist appointments.
- Use notes to link symptoms with lifestyle, stress, or medication.
- If you commence any form of medication including HRT's continue tracking these and any emerging or changing symptoms.

5.
Healthcare Tools

Healthcare Provider Checklist: Listening, Language & Lifesaving Care

Menopause is one of the most predictable transitions in a woman's life, yet it remains one of the least consistently supported in healthcare. Despite affecting half the population, it is still too often treated as a fleeting stage rather than a pivotal health event that carries profound physical, emotional, and social consequences. For many women, this is the point in life when they most need a clinician who listens, validates, and partners with them to navigate change, not one who dismisses their experience with "it's just ageing."

This chapter exists to change that.

It provides healthcare professionals with a practical, patient-centred framework for menopause consultations that integrates evidence-based medicine with empathy, listening, and lived experience. It is designed to help clinicians normalise menopause conversations, identify and validate symptoms, and recognise the broader impacts on work, relationships, and self-esteem.

The **why** behind these Tools is clear. For too long, menopause has sat in the grey zone between general practice and specialist care, too "normal" to warrant medical focus, yet too disruptive to ignore. Women are left to piece together information from friends, social media, or unverified online sources, often without guidance on safe, effective treatment options. The result is preventable suffering: exhaustion, anxiety, loss of identity, and in some cases, serious long-term health consequences.

When clinicians approach menopause not as a diagnosis to rule out, but as a stage to *guide through*, the outcomes shift dramatically. Open dialogue becomes preventive care. Early recognition of symptoms becomes an opportunity to protect bone density, cardiovascular health, and cognitive wellbeing. Most importantly, attentive listening restores something the system has too often taken away, a woman's confidence that her body's changes are real, understandable, and manageable.

These Tools invites healthcare providers to see menopause not as an endpoint, but as an inflection point, one where skilled conversation, active empathy, and integrated care can literally change the trajectory of a woman's life.

Tool 16: MenoScreen - Clinician Conversation & Screening Guide

Disclaimer: This checklist has been created as a guide for awareness and discussion. It is not a substitute for medical training or professional judgement. I am not a medically trained person. This Tool is intended to support clinicians by providing prompts for patient-centred conversations and should always be used alongside established clinical guidelines, evidence-based practice, and professional expertise.

Screening Questions

Use these questions to open dialogue and normalise the conversation:

1. **Cycle & Hormonal Shifts**

- What changes have you noticed in your periods or cycle over the last year or so?
- How do you feel about those changes?
- Have there been any surprises or things you weren't expecting?

2. **Common Symptoms (open-ended exploration)**

- Can you tell me what changes you've noticed in your body recently?
- What's been the most challenging part of what you're experiencing?
- How do hot flushes or night sweats show up for you, and how do they affect your daily life?
- How have your moods or emotions felt different over the last few months?
- What has your experience been with memory, focus, or brain fog?
- How has your sleep been lately? What does a typical night look like for you?

- Are there times of the day or situations where symptoms feel worse or more manageable?
- How do these changes impact your work, family life, or relationships?
- What have you tried so far to manage these symptoms, and what has or hasn't helped?
- What support would feel most helpful to you right now?

3. Functional & Quality of Life Impact

- How are these symptoms affecting your daily life, work, or relationships?
- Are you avoiding activities or responsibilities because of these changes?
- What supports do you currently have (family, work, health)?

4. Broader Health Considerations

- Have you noticed changes in weight, energy levels, or sexual health (e.g., vaginal dryness, libido changes, painful sex)?
- Do you have a history of cardiovascular disease, osteoporosis, or breast cancer?
- What medications, supplements, or therapies are you currently using?

Tool 17. Best Practice Actions → The ABCDEF of Menopause Care

Assess • Baseline • Care Options • Daily Habits • Engage Team • Follow-Up

Assessment & Validation

- Take symptoms seriously and acknowledge the patient's lived experience.
- Rule out underlying conditions (e.g., thyroid disease, depression, anaemia) but do not dismiss menopause as "just a normal stage."

Baseline Health

1. Establish a clear baseline for the patient's overall health.
2. Offer (and document) routine tests and screenings, including:

- Blood tests (hormone levels, cholesterol, thyroid, iron, vitamin D, glucose, etc.).
- Blood pressure and cardiovascular checks.
- Eye testing.
- Cervical screening (Pap smear).
- Mammograms as age-appropriate.
- Bowel cancer screening.
- Bone density scans if indicated.

3. Explain to the patient: "These tests aren't just about menopause; they give us a solid foundation so we know where you're starting from and how best to support you going forward."

Treatment & Management Options

- Provide evidence-based treatment choices, including Hormone Replacement Therapy (HRT) when clinically appropriate.
- Discuss non-hormonal options for those with contraindications or preference for alternatives.
- Address symptom clusters (e.g., sleep support, mental health care, sexual health therapies).

Lifestyle & Preventive Health

- Explore lifestyle supports: balanced nutrition, exercise, weight management, alcohol and smoking reduction.
- Encourage stress management strategies: mindfulness, CBT, yoga, relaxation techniques.
- Discuss preventive health screening (e.g., bone density scans, heart health monitoring).

Referrals & Collaborative Care

- Offer referrals to menopause specialists, endocrinologists, or gynaecologists when appropriate.
- Collaborate with allied health professionals (psychologists, dietitians, physiotherapists, sexual health specialists).
- Connect patients with reputable menopause resources, education programs, and support groups.

Documentation & Follow-Up

- Record symptoms, impact, and chosen management strategies.
- Develop a care plan and review regularly (every 3-6 months or sooner if symptoms escalate).
- Provide written information or digital resources for patient reference.

Clinician Reminders

- Avoid minimising symptoms with phrases like "it's just ageing."
- Individualise care; no two menopause journeys are identical.
- Cultural background, socioeconomic status, and access to care can shape the patient's experience.
- Be proactive: menopause is an opportunity for preventive health discussions about cardiovascular, bone, and mental health.

The Power of Listening
Beyond medical protocols, one of the most powerful services you can give is your presence. Women navigating menopause often feel dismissed or overlooked, being listened to with respect and empathy can be as therapeutic as any prescription.

Practical Listening Tips for Clinicians:
- **Create space:** Let the patient speak without interruption. Silence is often where the truth comes out.
- **Reflect back:** Repeat or summarise what she's said, "What I hear you saying is that the night sweats are leaving you exhausted at work."
- **Validate feelings:** Acknowledge her experience, "That sounds really tough," or "I can see why you'd feel frustrated."
- **Ask before advising:** "Would you like me to suggest some options, or do you want to share a bit more first?"
- **Body language matters:** Maintain eye contact, avoid typing while she's speaking, nod, and lean slightly forward to show engagement.
- **End with empowerment:** Ask, "What feels most important for you that we focus on together?"

Remember: Bedside manner is not "soft" medicine. It is a crucial part of care. Listening well can transform a patient's experience of menopause from one of dismissal to one of dignity.

Hot Flush, Cold Truth

6.
Governance, Awareness & Engagement

Tool 18: Board & Governance Reporting Guide

Purpose: To help boards embed menopause into governance, risk, and performance frameworks, ensuring visibility, accountability, and alignment with ESG/DEI priorities.

Workforce
- % of staff trained on menopause awareness.
- % of leaders/managers who have completed menopause-inclusive leadership training.
- Uptake of flexible work arrangements among staff 45+.

HR Metrics
- Retention rates of women 45+.
- Exit interview themes mentioning health, wellbeing, or menopause.
- Absenteeism rates linked to menopause-related health conditions.

Policy & Compliance
- Existence of a menopause policy (Y/N).
- Number of policy adjustments requested and approved.
- Inclusion of menopause in health & safety and wellbeing frameworks.

Engagement & Culture
- Uptake of adjustments/leave (how many requests, how many approved).
- Results of staff surveys on feeling supported during midlife transitions.
- Qualitative data: staff stories, case studies, or anonymous feedback.

Integration into ESG/DEI
- Environmental, Social, Governance (ESG): Position menopause within the "S" (social responsibility) and "G" (governance oversight).
- Diversity, Equity & Inclusion (DEI): Link menopause to:

- o Gender equity reporting.
- o Retention in leadership pipelines.
- o Closing the gender pay and superannuation gap.
- Annual Reporting: Publish menopause initiatives alongside gender pay gap, flexible work, and diversity metrics in corporate reports.

Example Board Dashboard: Menopause in Governance

Here's how a simple one-page board dashboard might look:

Metric	Target	Current Qtr	Trend	Board Notes / Action
Staff trained on menopause awareness	80% of workforce by FY25	42%	↑ +10%	Rollout underway; on track for target.
Managers trained in inclusive leadership	100% of leaders by FY25	28%	→ Stable	Board to review training acceleration plan.
Retention rate of women 45+	≥90%	84%	↓ -2%	Link data to exit interview insights.
Absenteeism related to menopause	<2%	3.5%	↑ +0.5%	Consider proactive wellbeing interventions.
Menopause policy in place	Yes	Yes	-	Board review due annually.

Metric	Target	Current Qtr	Trend	Board Notes / Action
Adjustments/leave uptake	50 requests p.a. baseline	63	↑	Uptake higher than forecast; assess support adequacy.
Engagement score (staff survey)	≥75% feel supported	68%	↑ +4%	Improvement noted, but still below target.
Leadership pipeline (women 45+)	≥40% of candidates	32%	↓ -1%	Risk flagged to DEI Committee.

Example Board Dashboard (Visual Style)

Imagine this on a single-page board pack:

- **Training Progress Bar:**

Workforce trained: ▮▮▮▮░░░ 42% (Target 80%)
Managers trained: ▮▮░░░░░ 28% (Target 100%)

- Retention & Absenteeism (Traffic Light):

Retention 45+: □ 84% (Target ≥90%)
Absenteeism: ● 3.5% (Target <2%)

- **Policy Status:**

Menopause Policy: ✓ In Place
Review: ☐ Due Q3

- **Engagement Survey Result:**

"I feel supported" → 68% (Goal ≥75%), 📈 trending upwards

- **Leadership Pipeline (Pie Chart):**

Women 45+ in leadership pipeline: 32% (Goal 40%)

- **Board Risk Flag:**

Risk: Leadership leakage of women 45+

Mitigation: Accelerated leadership mentoring & flexible pathways

Board Guidance

- **Visibility:** Ensure menopause data sits alongside safety, diversity, and workforce dashboards, not buried in HR reports.
- **Accountability:** Assign menopause oversight to a Board subcommittee (e.g., People & Culture, DEI, or ESG).
- **Frequency:** Review quarterly with trend data; annual deep-dive.
- **Action orientation**: Use the dashboard to trigger discussion: *Where are the risks? What resources are needed? What cultural barriers remain?*

This turns menopause from "an HR issue" into a **board-level governance responsibility**; tracked, measured, and reported like safety or financial performance

Tool 19: Boardroom Briefing Letter

To: Board Directors, Executive Leadership, and Senior Decision-Makers
From: Julie Dimmick, Author of *Hot Flush, Cold Truth*

Subject: The Business Imperative of Menopause Reform

Dear Board Members,
This briefing is presented to ensure that menopause is recognised not only as a health issue but as a pressing **strategic and economic priority** for your organisation.

By 2030, over **1 billion women worldwide will be post-menopausal**. Many of these women are at the height of their careers, leading teams, driving innovation, and shaping the future of industries. Yet unmanaged menopause symptoms are causing rising absenteeism, presenteeism, and attrition, silently draining productivity, disrupting leadership pipelines, and costing businesses billions annually.

Failure to address menopause carries **clear risks**:
- **Talent loss**: replacing senior women costs 150-200% of salary.
- **Reputational damage**: claims of gender equity ring hollow without menopause support.
- **Legal exposure**: growing case law is recognising menopause discrimination.

The **business case for action is compelling**. Menopause policies, flexible work arrangements, and manager training require minimal investment compared to the cost of replacing senior leaders or repairing reputational harm. Employers who act now are already reporting improved retention, engagement, and competitive advantage in talent markets.

This is not a matter of charity. It is **sound governance and strategy**. Just as parental leave, mental health, and workplace safety became board-level issues, so too must menopause. It belongs on your risk register, your diversity agenda, and your leadership succession planning.

The recommendations in this briefing provide a clear starting point. They can be integrated into your existing diversity, equity, and inclusion (DEI) frameworks, ESG reporting, and workforce wellbeing strategies.

The time to act is now. By rewriting your policies and culture, you not only protect your organisation against risk, you unlock the full potential of your most experienced leaders.

Sincerely,

Julie Dimmick
Author of Hot Flush, Cold Truth

Hot Flush, Cold Truth: Speaking Engagements with Julie Dimmick

Tool 20: Speaking Engagement One-Pager

Why Julie?
Julie Dimmick is a policy advisor, executive leader, and author of *Hot Flush, Cold Truth: Power, Policy, and the Personal*. She blends lived experience with executive authority, speaking directly to the intersection of health, equity, and business. With expertise in corporate strategy, government reform, and women's health advocacy, Julie equips audiences with both the urgency of change and the Tools to act.

Signature Topics
1.   Menopause at Work: Beyond the $10 Billion Blind Spot
   - The economic and cultural cost of silence.
   - Case studies of progressive organisations leading reform.
   - Practical steps boards and executives can take today.

2.   The Psychiatric Silence: Why Medicine Ignores Midlife Women
   - How the DSM and healthcare frameworks exclude menopause.
   - The impact on misdiagnosis, medication, and mental health.
   - What policymakers, clinicians, and advocates must do differently.

3.   From Silence to Movement: How Policy Becomes Personal
   - Global comparisons: what the UK, EU, and others are doing right.
   - The role of activism, advocacy, and leadership.
   - How Australia can catch up, and lead.

Formats Available
- **Keynote Address** (30-60 minutes)
- **Panel Participation** (expert commentary + Q&A)
- **Executive Briefing** (boardroom strategy session)
- **Workshops** (interactive training for HR, managers, and teams)

Audience Outcomes
- **HR & Business Leaders**: Templates, cost-benefit framing, and workplace strategies.
- **Policymakers & Health Leaders**: Clear reform roadmaps and sample policy clauses.
- **Women & Advocates**: Language, validation, and Tools to demand change.

Booking & Contact
Website: juliedimmick.com

Menopause is not a niche issue, it is a leadership, health, and equity imperative. Julie Dimmick delivers the message with authority, compassion, and action. Her sessions leave audiences informed, motivated, and ready to lead change.

Tool 21: Campaign-in-a-Box

Purpose: To give HR and Communications teams a plug-and-play campaign they can adapt for their workplace. The goal: make menopause visible, reduce stigma, and embed awareness into workplace culture.

<u>**Core Components**</u>
1. Posters / Slogans
- "Menopause Matters."
- "Hot Flush, Cold Truth."
- "Not Just a Phase. A Workplace Priority."
- "Supporting Women Supports Everyone."
- Visuals: strong, professional, diverse imagery; avoid clichés (e.g., flowers, fans).

2. Email Templates
- **Launch Message (CEO/Leader):** Position menopause as a leadership and equity issue.
- **Q&A Sheet:** Simple answers to common questions (What is menopause? Why does it matter at work? How can we support colleagues?).
- **Reminder Emails:** Short, engaging nudges for each daily activity.

3. Awareness Week Plan (5 Days, scalable)
- **Day 1:** CEO Announcement. Leadership statement via email + intranet banner; posters go up.
- **Day 2:** Training Session. Short webinar/workshop on menopause awareness for managers and staff.
- **Day 3:** Panel Discussion. Staff and external speakers share lived experiences; Q&A format.
- **Day 4:** Resource Distribution. Guides, checklists, support policies shared (digital + printed).
- **Day 5:** Feedback & Engagement. Staff survey; anonymous feedback collection; prize draw for participation.

Optional Enhancements
- Social Media Tool kit (internal + external):
- Sample LinkedIn and Yammer posts.

- Shareable graphics with stats and slogans.
- Hashtags (#MenopauseAtWork, #HotFlushColdTruth, #InclusiveWorkplace).
- Video Assets:
- 1-2 minute clips of leaders endorsing menopause awareness.
- Short animations explaining symptoms and workplace impact.
- Merchandise / Visibility Items:
- Branded water bottles, desk cards ("This is a menopause-friendly workplace"), lanyard cards with quick facts.
- Resource Hub (Digital/Print):
- Links to menopause specialists, EAP, policy, external resources (e.g., Jean Hailes, Balance).
- Downloadable fact sheets for staff and managers.
- Conversation Starters for Teams:
- Ready-made discussion guides (e.g., "What support helps you feel included at work?").

Governance & Measurement
KPIs to Track Success
- Participation in training sessions (attendance rates)
- Staff survey results before and after campaign
- Number of downloads or resource accesses
- Increase in requests for adjustments/support
- Uptake of menopause policy (if in place)

Reporting Line
- Campaign outcomes reported to HR and DEI leadership, then rolled into the Board dashboard (see **Board & Governance Reporting Guide**).
- Owner: HR/DEI Analytics
- Cadence: Weekly during campaign; monthly roll-up afterward

Sample Dashboard Snapshot - Campaign Impact

Activity	Target	Outcome	Notes
CEO announcement reach	100% staff email	92% open rate	Positive engagement
Training session attendance	150 participants	135 attended	Record for on-demand replay
Panel discussion feedback	80% satisfaction	86%	High impact; repeat quarterly

Activity	Target	Outcome	Notes
Resource downloads	500	712	Strong uptake
Post-campaign survey	70% feel supported	76%	Clear cultural shift

Tone & Key Messages for HR/Comms
- Keep it professional, not patronising
- Frame menopause as a workplace **equity** issue, not a "women's problem"
- Use inclusive language (acknowledge that not all who experience menopause identify as women)
- Position leadership as champions, not bystanders

Tool 22: Understanding Andropause. Why It Matters for Women

Purpose: To expand awareness by recognising that men also go through midlife hormonal shifts (andropause). This supports women by:

- Reducing stigma, menopause isn't "just in your head."
- Building empathy across genders.
- Creating a culture where midlife health conversations are normalised for everyone.

What is Andropause?

- Unlike menopause, andropause is more gradual. Testosterone levels in men typically decline about 1% per year after age 30-40.
- Symptoms can include: low energy, sleep issues, reduced libido, erectile dysfunction, irritability, weight gain, and brain fog.
- It is less clearly defined than menopause, but it is real and can affect relationships, work, and overall wellbeing.

Menopause vs. Andropause at a Glance

Aspect	Menopause	Andropause
Biological trigger	Sharp decline in oestrogen & progesterone	Gradual decline in testosterone (~1% per year)
Onset age	45-55 (can be earlier or later)	40-60 (gradual progression)
Core symptoms	Hot flushes, night sweats, mood swings, brain fog, sleep issues, vaginal dryness, bone changes	Low energy, irritability, sleep issues, weight gain, erectile dysfunction, low libido, brain fog

Aspect	Menopause	Andropause
Work impact	Absenteeism, concentration issues, retention risks	Fatigue, reduced productivity, stress, performance concerns
Stigma	"Taboo" topic, dismissed as ageing	Often ignored or joked about ("midlife crisis")

Why Women Benefit from Raising Andropause Awareness

- **Shared Language:** When women talk about hot flushes, brain fog, or sleep disruption, men may also relate through their own midlife experiences.
- **Workplace Culture:** Awareness of both menopause and andropause reduces gendered stigma, it becomes a human performance issue, not a "women's problem."
- **Relationships:** Many women navigating menopause live with partners also going through andropause. Understanding both journeys can foster compassion at home.
- **Governance & Policy:** Positioning midlife hormonal health as an *inclusion issue for all staff* makes it easier to gain organisational buy-in.

How to Bring Andropause into Menopause Conversations

- Include a note in awareness campaigns: *"Midlife hormonal health affects all of us, menopause for women, andropause for men."*
- Provide joint resources for couples or families so conversations can happen openly.

- Encourage workplaces to broaden "midlife wellbeing" programs to cover sleep, stress, cardiovascular risk, and hormone health for all genders.

Joint Dashboard Example: Midlife Wellbeing at Work

Metric	Target	Current Qtr	Trend	Board Notes / Action
Staff trained on menopause *and* andropause awareness	80% workforce trained by FY25	38%	↑ +12%	Expand training to male-dominated teams.
Retention rate of women 45+	≥90%	84%	↓ -1%	Link to flexible work and health supports.
Retention rate of men 45+	≥90%	86%	→ Stable	Monitor links to midlife health supports.
Health claims (sleep, stress, hormone-related)	Track baseline then reduce by 5% p.a.	Baseline year	-	Identify overlapping factors in men/women.
Absenteeism related to midlife health	<2%	3.1%	↑ +0.6%	Targeted interventions needed.
Staff survey: "I feel supported	≥75% agreement	62%	↑ +4%	Positive trend; needs further

Metric	Target	Current Qtr	Trend	Board Notes / Action
in midlife health"				culture shift.
Leadership pipeline (45+ women & men)	≥40% combined representation	33%	↓ - 2%	Risk flagged to People & Culture Committee.

Governance Guidance

- Position Menopause + Andropause = Midlife Wellbeing under the People & Culture or DEI subcommittee.
- Report quarterly using combined metrics, but disaggregate by gender to spot risks.
- Link initiatives to long-term workforce sustainability, equity, and leadership continuity.

Sample Awareness Messages for Campaigns

- "Menopause and Andropause: Different journeys, same need for support."
- "Hormones don't discriminate, let's talk about midlife health for everyone."
- "When we support women, men benefit too and when we support men, women benefit."

This approach makes menopause bigger than women's health, it becomes a whole-of-organisation wellbeing and governance priority.

About the Author

Julie Dimmick is a best-selling author, executive leader, and values-based strategist who has built her career at the intersection of policy, performance, and people.

Her latest book, **Hot Flush, Cold Truth: Beyond the Pause - Women, Work, and Policy Reform**, is both deeply personal and profoundly political, combining lived experience, executive insight, and systemic critique to expose how menopause has been silenced, and how it can be reclaimed as a driver of health, equity, and reform.

Julie is also the author of the best-selling **The Trump Effect: What One Man Reveals About How the World Evolves**, a ground-breaking exploration of leadership, culture, and values through the lens of Spiral Dynamics. This work established Julie as a thought leader in values-based analysis, bridging politics, psychology, and global systems.

She is the creator of **ValCoRE™** (Values + Consciousness + Resilience + Evolution), a leadership and organisational framework designed to help individuals and organisations decode values, master power, and lead without losing themselves. **ValCoRE™** has been applied to corporate transformation, executive coaching, and personal development, equipping leaders to navigate complexity with clarity, integrity, and impact.

Organisations turn to Julie when they have problems to solve. She is strategic where it matters and hands-on where it counts, bringing the rare ability to translate vision into execution. She has delivered multi-million-dollar transformation projects, overseen complex regulatory reviews, and guided teams through high-stakes reform agendas.

Julie works in complex environments and brings calm to the storm, balancing authority with empathy. Her career spans both the public and private sectors, giving her a unique perspective on how policy, governance, and leadership intersect across different systems.

Julie has lived the contradictions of menopause, appearing youthful and capable on the outside while struggling internally with symptoms that were minimised or misunderstood. From that experience came a vow: no woman should ever have to suffer in silence, or face this transition alone.

At the core of her work is a simple but powerful mission: *to give voice to those silenced by systems*, and to turn personal struggle into collective power. Through her books, speaking engagements, and coaching, Julie champions a new model of leadership and advocacy, one rooted in clarity, integrity, and impact.